THE RHETORIC OF SINCERITY

Cultural Memory
in
the
Present

Mieke Bal and Hent de Vries, Editors

THE RHETORIC OF SINCERITY

EDITED BY
Ernst van Alphen,
Mieke Bal,
AND Carel Smith

STANFORD UNIVERSITY PRESS

STANFORD, CALIFORNIA

Stanford University Press
Stanford, California
© 2009 by the Board of Trustees of the Leland Stanford Junior University.
All rights reserved.

Printed in the United States of America on acid-free, archival-quality paper.

Library of Congress Cataloging-in-Publication Data
The rhetoric of sincerity / edited by Ernst van Alphen, Mieke Bal, and Carel Smith.
    p. cm. — (Cultural memory in the present)
  Includes bibliographical references and index.
  ISBN 978-0-8047-5827-7 (cloth : alk. paper)
  1. Sincerity in literature.   2. Sincerity—Political aspects.   3. Sincerity--Social
aspects.   I. Alphen, Ernst van. II. Bal, Mieke, 1946–   III. Smith, C. E. (Carel E.)
IV. Series.
  PN56.S57R44 2009
  809'.93353—dc22

                         2008026105

Typeset by Bruce Lundquist in 11/13.5 Adobe Garamond

Contents

Contributors

LESLIE A. ADELSON, Professor of German Studies and Graduate Field Member of Comparative Literature; Jewish Studies; and Feminist, Gender, and Sexuality Studies; currently chairs the Department of German Studies at Cornell University in Ithaca, New York. She has most recently published *The Turkish Turn in Contemporary German Literature: Toward a New Critical Grammar of Migration* (Palgrave Macmillan, 2005). Other publications include *Making Bodies, Making History: Feminism and German Identity* (University of Nebraska Press, 1993), and the English-language edition of Zafer Senocak's *Atlas of a Tropical Germany* (University of Nebraska Press, 2000).

ERNST VAN ALPHEN is Professor of Literary Studies at Leiden University, the Netherlands. His publications include *Francis Bacon and Loss of Self* (Harvard University Press, 1994), *Caught by History: Holocaust Effects in Contemporary Art, Literature, and Theory* (Stanford University Press, 1997), *Armando: Shaping Memory* (NAi Publishers, 2000), and *Art in Mind: How Contemporary Images Shape Thought* (University of Chicago Press, 2005).

MICHAEL BACHMANN studied German Philology, Theatre Studies, and Political Science in Mainz and Paris. He is currently writing his Ph.D. thesis on authorizing strategies in Holocaust representation, and he teaches at the Department of Theatre Studies at Mainz University. He is also a member of the IPP (International Postgraduate Programme) *Performance and Media Studies* at Mainz.

MIEKE BAL, cultural critic and theorist, holds the position of Royal Dutch Academy of Sciences Professor. She is also based at the University of Amsterdam, where she was a founding Director of the Amsterdam

School for Cultural Analysis, Theory, and Interpretation (ASCA). She is also a documentary maker and video artist. Her books include *Travelling Concepts in the Humanities: A Rough Guide* (University of Toronto Press, 2002), *Louise Bourgeois' Spider: The Architecture of Art-Writing* (University of Chicago Press, 2001), and *Quoting Caravaggio: Contemporary Art, Preposterous History* (University of Chicago Press, 1999). *A Mieke Bal Reader* appeared in 2006 (University of Chicago Press).

JILL BENNETT is Director of the Centre for Contemporary Art and Politics at the University of New South Wales (Sydney). Her most recent book is *Empathic Vision: Affect, Trauma and Contemporary Art* (Stanford University Press, 2005). She is also a curator.

KATHERINE BERGERON is Professor of Musicology at Brown University. In her scholarship she has specialized in the vocal repertories of turn-of-the-century France. Her book, *Decadent Enchantments* (University of California Press, 1998), is a study of the nineteenth-century revival of plainchant by French Benedictine monks. She recently completed *Voice Lessons*, a history of the French *mélodie* in the years around 1900.

MAAIKE BLEEKER is Professor of Theatre and Performance Studies at Utrecht University and works as a dramaturge with various theatre directors, choreographers, and visual artists. She publishes on contemporary theatre and performance. She co-edited two volumes, *Body Check* (Rodopi, 2002) and *Theater Topics 1: Multicultureel Drama?* (Amsterdam University Press, 2005). Her book *The Locus of Looking* is in press.

CESARE CASARINO is Associate Professor of Cultural Studies and Comparative Literature at the University of Minnesota. He is the author of *Modernity at Sea: Melville, Marx, Conrad in Crisis*, as well as of numerous articles on literature, film, and philosophy.

REINDERT DHONDT studied Romance Languages and Literatures and Modern History at the University of Leuven and at Paris-IV-Sorbonne. Since 2005 he has been a member of the research unit Literary Relations and Post/national Identities at K.U. Leuven. His research deals with the concept of "New World Baroque" in recent Latin American literature.

YASCO HORSMAN is Assistant Professor of Comparative Literature at the University of Leiden. In 2004 he graduated from Yale University with a dissertation on the themes of judgment and forgiveness in the writings of Arendt, Brecht, and Delbo. He is currently preparing his dissertation for publication.

FRANS-WILLEM KORSTEN is Assistant Professor of Literary Studies at Leiden University. He is the author of *Lessen in Literatuur* (Vantilt, 2002) and *Vondel Belicht: Voorstellingen van Soevereiniteit* (Verloren, 2006).

DAVID MCNEILL is Deputy Director of the University of New South Wales Centre for Contemporary Art and Politics. He has published and curated exhibitions on contemporary Asian, African, and Australian art, the impact of globalization on the production and consumption of art, and the relationships between art and nationalism.

CAREL SMITH teaches at Leiden University in the Faculty of Law. His main topics of interest are legal interpretation and the institutional theory of law. His most recent book is *Regels van rechtsvinding* (*Rules of Legal Adjudication*, Boom Juridische Uitgevers, 2005). He is co-organizer of a series of discussions at the Ministry of Justice in The Hague.

JANE TAYLOR holds the Skye Chair of Dramatic Art at the University of the Witwatersrand in Johannesburg, South Africa. She is writing on the "performance of sincerity" for *Yours Sincerely,* a book on performance, authenticity, and evidence. She has published widely in the field of contemporary South African cultural politics. Among many plays and curatorial projects, she wrote *Ubu and the Truth Commission* for artist/director William Kentridge and the Handspring Puppet Company (1996).

HENT DE VRIES is Professor of Humanities and Philosophy in the Humanities Center and the Department of Philosophy at Johns Hopkins University, and Professor of Philosophy at the University of Amsterdam. Among his books are *Philosophy and the Turn to Religion* (Johns Hopkins University Press, 1999), *Religion and Violence: Philosophical Perspectives from Kant to Derrida* (Johns Hopkins University Press, 2002), and *Minimal Theologies: Critiques of Secular Reason in Theodor W. Adorno and Emmanuel Levinas* (Johns Hopkins University Press, 2005). With Mieke Bal, he edits the book series *Cultural Memory in the Present,* published by Stanford University Press. He is also the editor of *Political Theologies* (Fordham University Press, 2006).

ALISON YOUNG is Professor of Criminology at the University of Melbourne, Australia. She is an editor of the *Australian and New Zealand Journal of Criminology*, *Feminist Theory*, the *Griffith Law Review*, and *Law and Critique*. Her most recent book is *Judging the Image* (Routledge, 2006). New research projects include a study of cinematic and literary representations of crime and an examination of graffiti writers' narratives of cultural belonging.

THE RHETORIC OF SINCERITY

Introduction

Ernst van Alphen and Mieke Bal

In times of intercultural tensions and conflicts, sincerity matters. Traditionally, sincerity concerns a natural enactment of authenticity anchored in, and yielding, truth. Such enactment is easily misunderstood in intercultural situations. Moreover, sincerity is considered fundamentally corporeal rather than textual. Within such logic, truth is enacted through the body and imagined as an integrated semiotic field. Beyond the truth that is stated, this field includes the unwittingly emitted signs of the body.

This traditional view is based on the common sense defense of sincerity. While easily disavowed by semiotically aware cultural critics, this view is not so easily, or facilely, dismissed. Like the Lacanian disavowal and simultaneous recognition of ideology ("I know very well but all the same . . ."), this view persists because it means too much to be sold cheaply. Such a defense might run, crudely, "Look, whatever you might tell us about historical origins and rhetorical articulations, isn't sincerity something that we need and must *always* have needed?" Think of "sincerity" as, for instance, an issue of love, or of truth telling between any two persons in many kinds of meaningful relations where one party has reason to care whether the words of the other party are honest in their account of sentiment, desire, or disposition. This issue engages a binary opposition of the starkest kind. Either the lover or friend is sincere and relational bliss follows; or he or she is outright lying, thus entailing a plot of insincerity and deception off which many a novel feeds.

In the larger public-cultural field, one can also think of all of the denunciations of "postmodern irony" that have marked public discourse (at least in the West) over the past two decades, denunciations that tend to valorize the authentic and the sincere over political intelligence and rhetorical sophistication. This conception of the postmodern is so easily disqualified precisely because it dared challenge the above-mentioned traditional view of sincerity by undermining the binary, hence absolute, conception of truth that sustained it. These two examples suggest right away that sincerity is firmly lodged both in personal relations and in public and political tensions. For this reason, it is necessary to bring the concept of sincerity to closer scrutiny today, at a cultural moment when tensions, explicitly or implicitly cast in terms of either *sincerity* or *rhetoric*, often play themselves out in cross- or intercultural confrontations.

Such a formulation makes clear that the issue of sincerity cannot be appropriated as the exclusive domain of any intellectual field or academic discipline. Indeed, it has always been a rather under-illuminated yet present issue in many disciplines. Sincerity plays a major role in law, the arts (in literature, but just as much in the visual and performing arts), and religion. This is not surprising when we look at the historical background of the concept. *Sincerity* enters the English language in the sixteenth century, during an epoch in which the theater emerges as the dominant idiom of secular representation, and at a time of major religious changes. As much as we may like to disavow the analogy, the present historical moment has much in common with that historical era. This is clear when we realize that now as then, religious and cultural conflicts take place at the same time that representational idioms and media undergo major transformations. To honor this historical analogy and learn from it, this book focuses mainly on the present, while the historical origin of the term *sincerity* is discussed in order to better understand its present manifestations and ramifications.

One element that the two moments of sincerity's introduction in the sixteenth century and its questioning today (in this book) share is intercultural contact and subsequent tensions. Therefore, this book is concerned with the ways in which the performance of sincerity is culturally specific. Another common feature between the two eras is the major developments in media culture. As the printed book gained access to public culture and theater became a primary cultural mode of expression, sincerity became entangled in medial forms that complicated, already at the beginning, the integrated semiotic field where body and mind were believed to be one. Today, sincerity is equally enacted in various ways in different media and disciplines. We now foreground that acting aspect by invoking the term *performance*—a "doing" instead of a "being." Both law and the arts study such enactments. This book's assumption, that sincerity consists of a performance, implies a special focus on the theatricality of sincerity: its bodily, linguistic, and social performances, and the success, or felicitousness, of such performances. Central to our discussion, therefore, is the notion of "acts of sincerity." What do acts of sincerity in speech or enactment do, produce, or fail to do and produce? This invocation calls for an examination of the ways in which we need to bracket or transfigure "sincerity" rather than simply dismissing it.

This raises the question of what it is that is performed in such acts. In a traditional sense, sincerity indicates the performance of an inner state on one's outer surface so that others can witness it. But the very distinction between inner self and outer manifestation implies a split that assaults the traditional integration that marks sincerity. This idea of expression entails the possibility of a dialogue between the inner self and its external representation. The idea of this expression (including the potential dialogue it entails) is the starting point of Chapter 1. With this conception, sincerity is tightly bound up with an equally traditional view of subjectivity. In order for sincerity to come to the surface and, indeed, enter the social realm, a specific notion of subjectivity is necessary. This notion assumes that we, as individuals, have an "inner self" responsible for our conduct, performances, and speeches—in effect, all the ways in which we manifest ourselves for others.

This notion of subjectivity—bound up, in turn, with a dichotomy of mind and body—has been severely deconstructed in past decades. Yet sincerity, both as producer and as effect of this notion of subjectivity, has not been thought through in relation to such critiques. Though many no longer believe in the traditional notion of subjectivity, sincerity, it appears, has been more difficult to relinquish, and thus remains unreflectively present in many social discourses. Given the two examples of love and postmodern irony mentioned above, this reluctance to engage sincerity in a general critique of subjectivity points to an attachment we will take seriously, even if we do not cling to it. This book attempts to supply such critical reflections on sincerity, especially in its relation to subjectivity. The first part of this book, "Sincerity as Subjectivity Effect," deals with the complex and often buried relations between subjectivity and sincerity. Here, historical beginnings are confronted with contemporary practices, particularly in literature, the arts, law, and philosophy—areas in which these conventions are still influential.

In the first place, the analysis concerns the way the bond between subjectivity and sincerity, however naturalized it has become, is not natural. This becomes apparent in the second part, "Declining Sincerity," when subjects actually decline to participate in the culture of sincerity. Such subjects refuse, or ignore, the pressure to endorse a form of subjectivity that relies on, and consists of, a distinction between mind and body, inner and outer, personal and social. As a result, they demonstrate that there is no inner self that manifests itself bodily through performance, and as a consequence, the inner self cannot be witnessed. Not coincidentally, such subjects often belong to what has been construed as "subalternity." This occurrence of a refusal of the dominant form of subjectivity goes to show that the standard concept of subjectivity is not a given, but is instead constantly negotiated and construed—and therefore able to be declined.

But *declining*—a verb chosen for its connotations of polite negotiation—is not a facile cancellation, for such a cancellation can be no more than wishful thinking. Sincerity, in that negotiation, is the sting of subjectivity, the Achilles heel where subjectivity as we know it can be undermined. This happens when the mechanisms that produce the effects of sincerity no longer function.

This second part of the book is devoted to reflections and case studies on examples of cultural productions that encompass such subjectivity-threatening acts of declining sincerity. In the wake of such acts, alternative kinds of subjectivity emerge. A glimpse of such possibilities, as well as their difficulties in coming to full articulation, will be given in discussions of cinematic, artistic, literary, and philosophical texts.

We can now notice these alternative subjectivities through the way in which they decline sincerity, because what we call here "traditional subjectivity" is no longer generally considered valid. Does the weakened status of this notion of subjectivity entail a wholesale rejection of sincerity as an issue of social, cultural, and political interaction? Should we decline sincerity because it is rooted in an inner-outer split in which we no longer believe? Such a rejection would be problematic given the ongoing, crucial political and cultural function of speech acts that have been associated with sincerity (such as vows or oaths) or its absence (such as deceit, lying, hypocrisy, or political maneuvering). That rejection is the wrong conclusion, encouraged by a vulgarized and misunderstood "postmodern irony" that this book does not endorse. A different analysis and evaluation of such speech acts—the idea that performance overrules expression—must not be mistaken for a naïve dismissal of all such acts as "just" play. The undeniable presence and persistence of these acts co-exist, instead, with a transformed conception of subjectivity, a transformed idea of what we believe today to be sincere behavior or expression. This suggests that sincerity can be reframed outside of its bond with subjectivity. The current importance and widespread presence of the media make such reframing necessary.

For this reason, the third part of the book, "Sincerity as Media Effect," proposes somewhat polemically to consider sincerity as framed by media, so as to become a media effect instead of a subjectivity effect. If the notion of sincerity has a future, it lies in this framework. Hence the title of the volume, which stipulates that sincerity is best understood and analyzed as an issue of rhetoric. The third part, therefore, recasts the issues discussed in the first and second parts. Sincerity cannot be dismissed because, while not an integrated consequence and qualification of subjectivity, it is an indispensable *affective* (hence, social) process between subjects. Affect is understood here as intensities that are circulated among subjects. Media play a major role in such circulations and transmissions. As Jill Bennett argues, mass media function as "vectors" for the "migration of affect." Sincerity becomes a primary stake in such circulations through media, so it can be said to become a "media effect."

To counter the possible misunderstanding of a categorical "newness" of contemporary media, we use the term *rhetoric* to point to such effects. For, with hindsight, the subjectivity-bound notion of sincerity has always been a rhetorical one as well. This rhetorical nature of the notion puts any attempt to stage sincerity as the "outing" of the inner self always already under erasure. This erasure, or bracketing—but not wholesale rejection—of the notion of sincerity is the common thread that runs through all the essays in this volume.

*

Each of the following chapters discusses an aspect or argument surrounding sincerity that contributes to the overall "sincerity complex" we are constructing in this book. In the first chapter, Jane Taylor locates a history of the semiotics of sincerity. She identifies and locates the emergence in the sixteenth century of particular rhetorical and performative apparatuses of sincerity, designed to render visible the ideological and productive effects of sincerity. This purpose of the performance of sincerity reverses the standard idea of sincerity because the claim of the latter is precisely that it is a mode of self-expression generally held to be nondiscursive, transparent, and outside of ideology: in other words, spontaneous. Taylor argues that sincerity emerges in sixteenth-century England as a result of the complex negotiations in the shifting terrain among religious devotion, Roman Catholic authority, royal prerogative, and Protestant ambitions. Before the schism there was little room for such spiritual connoisseurship, as faith largely consisted in compliance with a set of givens, rather than in individual interpretation. However, the instrument of investigative terror, the heresy trial, with its specific nexus of power, anxiety, and authenticity, made a conception of sincerity necessary.

Essentially, Taylor proposes that sincerity arises in order to resolve the problem of the paradox of the forced confession. A scrutiny of these confessions throughout the sixteenth century reveals that there is an evolving dialectic between external performance and internal convictions. Therefore sincerity is necessarily a problem of performance. Problematically, though, performance is characterized as insincere because it provides an instrument that makes it possible to represent an inner state on the surface, and thus to falsify it. An inner universe is weighed against external significance. Taylor develops her argument on the basis of, among other artifacts, Shakespeare's *Titus Andronicus* and *Hamlet* and Caravaggio's paintings *The Martyrdom of St. Matthew* and the first version of *The Conversion of St. Paul*. In all cases conversion and sincerity result in a crisis of representation, particularly if the body is interpreted as carrying absolute meanings for the condition of the inner being. The problem is ultimately one of figuring in the body those states of consciousness that are incorporeal. This raises problems of logic with the configuration of racial identity. Within this semiotics the figure of the "converted Jew" creates a special problem because Jews, at the time, were considered "black." Thus, the rhetoric of sincerity is at odds with the rhetoric of race; only through a "transparent" skin can we see the inner self. The two rhetorics make contradictory appeals to an identity that is located either within, or on, the surface, that is, the skin. Thus, from the beginning, both sincerity and race are undermined.

So far, the discussion has been concerned with the performance of what people say. But regardless of content, sincerity plays its part in "pure" performance, for example, in the sounds produced by voices. Katherine Bergeron offers a case study of lyrical sincerity in the culture of late-nineteenth-century France, where lyric was defined as "natural." Her case is the legendary actress Sarah Bernhardt. Jules Renard once described the voice of Sarah Bernhardt as a sound so sincere and pure that "you don't even notice it," a sound, he said, "like the song of the trees, or an instrument's monotone noise." The description hardly squares with our contemporary views of the great actress, known today more for melodrama than for monotone. And yet Renard's key images—of naturalness and discretion—suggest another set of values at work, values that shed light not only on Bernhardt, but also on a whole expressive culture that emerged in France after 1870.

Bergeron's chapter reflects on that culture, on a time when the republican embrace of rural France made naturalness a virtue and sincerity a democratic duty. If painters took to the hills, looking for a truer vision *en plein air*, poets and musicians took to the same air in search of a purer lyric accent. Verlaine called this "accent music," and listening to Bernhardt's diction, we begin to understand why. The example of her voice, captured on record by Pathé in 1903, serves as a launching point for a meditation on the material conditions for lyric sincerity, conditions that also yielded a form of modern melody whose most salient trait is a performance one does not even notice.

At the time of the beginning of sincerity, the notion had implications for state politics as well as for individual identity. Considering three plays by the seventeenth-century Dutch playwright Joost van den Vondel, the third chapter, by Frans-Willem Korsten, argues against expectations from the traditional view that hypocrisy can be a useful skill for ambitious politicians, that it is even inevitable for people who operate in complex organizations. Korsten argues that hypocrisy is structurally and functionally built into any system of political representation. In this context he explores sincerity as a necessary qualification in a political system, a qualification that works on the basis of relationships. He considers sincerity as a passion that lifts the individual's care of self to a collective level. This leads to a consideration of what happens when someone who speaks in public is immediately seen politically, as the representative of a certain group, in a society that consists of several groups-in-relation. In this respect, hypocrisy is a double-edged sword. Whereas hypocrisy is functional in systems of political representation, its inscription onto systems of relations is destructive. As a result, hypocrisy leads to a society of suspicion. Vondel's plays suggest what is required to avoid such a society.

Sincerity is particularly relevant for a consideration of legal practice, up to today. We tend to think that sincerity is primarily a question of the defendant's credibility. But all agents involved are bound by at least the appearance of sincerity. The judge, in particular, is bound to this norm. In his contribution, Carel Smith looks at the role of the judge and considers how the expectation of sincerity is in tension with the status of rules. He deals with the question of what legitimates the judge's verdict when deciding, for example, a case of negligence, discrimination, or robbery. Legal adjudication is conceived as a rule-governed activity: the establishment of a rule of obligation is the result of a complex interplay of standards of adjudication, the final ruling being the inference from a rule of obligation and the facts of the case. To justify the decision in a hard case is to vindicate the interpretation. In short, decision follows interpretation. But legal practice does not confirm this doctrine. Often, the decisive argument to interpret a rule one way rather than another is directed by the fairness of the ruling that would result. The principle "decision follows interpretation" should, therefore, be converted into "interpretation follows decision." This reversal entails a different status for sincerity.

Indeed, this view of legal adjudication is severely contested, for it seems to be at variance with the sincere belief of judges that their judgments are based on law-based reasons. Their interpretations are not jus-tifications in retrospect, but the verdicts' very reasons. According to the majority of legal agents, to hold the principle "interpretation follows deci-sion," then, is to charge the caste of judges with being insincere, and to consider the legitimization of their rulings as "merely rhetorical."

This first part ends with an exploration by Hent de Vries of what it means to "live" a theory, or more precisely, to live one's theory and to do so seriously and thereby sincerely. With this he does not mean the reduc-tion of life to theory, of living theoretically—which would mean, follow-ing ordinary usage, living hypothetically, and hence not really living at all. Rather, he aims to establish a connection between the rhetoric of sincerity and what may turn out to be a specifically modern—though also classi-cally tragic—problem of sincerity. To this effect he addresses the question of whether living theory, or living one's theory, requires a certain accep-tance of truth, truthfulness, trust, and trustworthiness: indeed, of accept-ing seriousness and sincerity.

In this sense of "living theory" as living one's theory rather than merely having one, or of a theory sustaining itself only to the extent that it is lived and alive, Stanley Cavell's work is an indispensable guide. Cavell draws attention to an absence in even the most sophisticated readings of J. L. Austin's *How to Do Things with Words*, such as those by Derrida and Shoshana Felman. He is referring to a line from Euripides' *Hippolytus* of crucial importance to speech act theory. Austin translates this line as: "my tongue swore to, but my heart did not" (1975, 612). Thus, the last chapter of this part returns to the beginning: Taylor's analysis of conversion and confession, the transformation of the inner self as manifested outward.

In the second part of the book, that old bond is not so much rejected as it is bracketed. Rejection presupposes awareness as a conscious act. With the word *bracketed* we seek to do justice to something below the threshold of recognition. This part is devoted to subjects who simply do not engage with the kind of subjectivity that demands sincerity and the concomitant implications of a division between inner and outer being. What happens when sincerity is no longer the manifestation of an interior state on a per-son's body because that distinction itself is not recognized? This reverses the situation. Now, the (formerly) outward manifestation is the only basis for interaction with personhood, and it must be dealt with in the ostensive absence of anything else to fall back on. From the perspective of those who decline sincerity, this is not an issue: they only act, indifferent to attempts to peek beneath their "surface." This discussion begins with an essay in which Cesare Casarino considers the indifference to sincerity in the context of the articulation of the modern sexual subject—a subject whose very interpellation depends on producing a hidden truth so as to be able to confess it.

Casarino analyzes an emblematic moment of a 1964 documentary on the sexual mores of Italians, *Love Meetings*, by Pier Paolo Pasolini. The interviewer, who asks his questions from within the modern sexual subjectivity just described, receives a politically sophisticated answer from a child, an answer that undermines the modern technology of power that Foucault calls "the deployment of sexuality." The author alleges the case of Foucault's assessment of *Love Meetings*. The philosopher's review constitutes at once a highly perceptive and a crucially symptomatic account of Pasolini's intellectual project. Foucault's assessment of *Love Meetings* ought to be read as an attempt to turn Pasolini into the privileged precursor of Foucault's final project. Pasolini's critique of the "deployment of sexuality" needs to be read as integral to Pasolini's ambivalent engagement with Gramsci and, in particular, with Gramsci's articulation of "The Southern Question."

The "Southerner," here, articulates a subjectivity that goes against the grain of that modern sexual subjectivity. Not coincidentally, the interviewees, being both Southern and children, happen to be "subaltern" subjects. Considering the relations between subalternity and an act of declining sincerity even where sincerity is most expected—when disclosing something about their sexuality—this chapter shows glimpses of an alternative subjectivity. These glimpses become visible in some of the ways in which Pasolini's project at once uncannily anticipates as well as significantly diverges from Foucault's own articulation of the modern sexual subject.

But one does not need to be a subaltern to decline modern subjectivity—although it certainly seems to help. Similarly, one doesn't need to stand in a court of law to challenge from within the alleged sincerity of the legal process. In the second chapter of this part, Yasco Horsman discusses the paradoxes of confession through an analysis of J. M. Coetzee's acclaimed novel *Disgrace* (1999). Upon its publication, *Disgrace* was widely read as a response to the proceedings of South Africa's Truth and Reconciliation Commission. As is well known, during these proceedings applicants were granted amnesty for crimes committed during the apartheid years in return for a full disclosure of past deeds. The TRC became a ritual in which a common "humanity" was established through scenes of repentance and forgiveness. The first part of *Disgrace* can be read as both an allegory of this ritual and as a criticism of a structural problem inherent in the scene of confession. In this scene, an issue pertaining to speech act theory comes up. As an admission of guilt, a confession depends on the utterance of certain well-known formulae in order to be recognized as an act of confession. Yet in order for this performance to be successful it needs to be perceived as serious, heartfelt, and hence sincere. As John Lurie, the central character of *Disgrace*, points out, this implies that a confession exceeds the strictly legal function and enters a different domain, that of psychology or religion.

The chapter begins with a consideration of the paradoxes of confession as dramatized by the novel. It then offers an interpretation of part two of the novel, which depicts Lurie's disgrace resulting from his refusal to participate in a confession ritual. Part two of the novel consists of a series of loosely connected events that never quite culminate in a moment of closure. The dejected subjectivity of the character can be read as a consequence of Lurie's refusal of a "rhetoric of sincerity" that would have grounded his words. He refuses sincerity because he considers it merely a rhetoric. By refusing that rhetoric, he also loses his modern subjectivity; he becomes "like a dog." Due to his refusal he becomes a kind of "honorary" subaltern subject.

The next chapter in this second part discusses how the workplace also yields its forms of declining subjectivity: labor relations produce their own "refusniks." David McNeill argues that in the post-fordist labor landscape of the developed world, the requirements for constant demonstrations of sincerity augment more traditional forms of surveillance within disciplinary regimes. Accordingly it is no longer enough to work efficiently and productively. In addition, or even instead, it has become obligatory to participate eagerly and believe in the policies and ambitions of the employer, and by extension, the state. As labor becomes more precarious, new protocols have developed through which enthusiasm and loyalty can, and must, be performed. Sincerity, here, is understood as the congruence of avowal and actual feeling. Thus it serves as a means for the assessment of these performances. These performances colonize the totality of both the domestic sphere and of civil society itself.

McNeill proposes the concept of "a-sincerity" as a means of understanding the ways in which these strategies organize acquiescence and aid the expansion of contemporary capitalist social relations. He investigates aesthetic strategies that create spaces outside the structures of identification offered by the state and other institutions. This concept of a-sincerity casts its shadow over all other cases discussed here, and especially that of migratory labor and the untenable subjectivity it entails. This will be analyzed in the final chapter of this part.

Leslie Adelson discusses why the notion of (in)sincerity cannot be applied to qualify migratory subjects. In her much-debated book *Globalization and Its Discontents*, Saskia Sassen rightly characterizes migrant laborers late in the twentieth century as "emblematic subjects" of a global economy dating back to the 1970s. The emblematic labor of literary configurations of migration in the same period is perhaps far more difficult to discern. While much scholarship on the literatures of migration continues to presuppose an authentic migrant self who either suffers indignities or celebrates hybridity sincerely, this presentation offers interpretive alternatives for evaluating the rhetorical conceit and social deixis of personhood in transnational literatures of migration.

Not meant to be a person at all, the cipher of the illegal migrant laborer in Aras Ören's emblematic novella of 1981, *Bitte nix Polizei* (*Please No Police*), invites contemplation of the changing hieroglyphic of ethnicity in our time. While this presentation shares certain precepts with Rey Chow's account of "ethnicity as alienated labor," Turks in Germany are not "protestant ethnics" as Chow defines the term. Adelson correspondingly reads the desire for "personhood" in *Bitte nix Polizei* through an altogether different form of commodification, one that cannot be grasped by any rhetoric of sincerity at all. Beyond the indifference toward sincerity because of its confining implications for personhood, the practical impossibility of sincerity here casts aside the subject of normative subjectivity.

But such casting aside of the notion of sincerity altogether is not quite possible, for we still need to be able to address forms of deceit that can only be defined in opposition to it. In order to retain a useful analytical concept of sincerity it is necessary to theorize it without ties to such forms of subjectivity. To consider the manifestations of insincerity that we come across daily, we turn to mass media. For it is there that we can see how a traditional notion of subjectivity, far from just surviving its critique, is created every time anew by means of rhetoric. Clearly, holding on to such a notion of subjectivity serves a purpose. Hence, for an effective political critique of (in)sincerity without falling back on this traditional notion, we must consider sincerity no longer as a subjectivity effect but as a media effect.

This, at least, is the consequence of the thesis of Jill Bennett's essay, which investigates sincerity as an aesthetic practice that is used by modern media in the global-political context. In recent times, global politics have been driven by a "precautionary principle." Military action and anti-terrorist legislation are justified in terms of an imagined catastrophe; hence politicians seek license to act on what they think *may* happen if they don't act, rather than on evidence of what *will* happen. In this context the performance of sincere belief has acquired a special currency. Where there is no evidence of the presence of an imminent terrorist attack, the basis for offensive action rests solely on the perception of a threat. To this end, the population must feel the presence of danger and experience fear, and politicians must manifest strength of conviction; as in classicist literature where "le vrai" was considered less important than "le vraisemblable," *believing* is what counts, even if it is acknowledged that one may be wrong to believe.

Many analysts, such as documentary filmmaker Michael Moore, have commented on the ways in which a global culture of fear has been actively engendered by media and government operations since September 11, highlighting the way that sensation and affect—in particular, the negative affects of fear and anxiety—have become central to politics. Chapter 10 investigates sincerity—conceived of as the congruence of belief, feeling, and expression—in this global-political context, guided by media. The nature of the affect is here no longer a qualification of the subject, but an effect transmitted by the media: hence, a "media effect."

Bennett's essay focuses on aesthetic practices that challenge the manner in which the contagion of fear, combined with the performance of belief, has come to stand for a "realist" assessment of danger.

One of the critics of this disingenuous form of realism, Jacques Derrida, has also been a subject—in many senses of this now-charged word!—of films. The next chapter in this part takes a look at Derrida's appearances on film in order to trace, through the concept of "spectralité," an alternative form of sincerity. Michael Bachmann treats spectrality on an iconic and discursive level, while it is also inscribed into the films' media-specific systems of belief. Derrida has published several texts dealing with this spectral logic in which something supposedly sincere—testimony or confession, for instance—is necessarily haunted by the possibility of fiction. Bachmann argues that in these films, Derrida on film—poised between his image and its other—is staged, and stages himself, as a ghost. He thus authorizes his philosophical discourse in the form of a "spectral" sincerity that seeks to escape conventional binaries such as truth and fiction. In Derrida's own "projection" of thoughts, sincerity relates to their *mise en scène* rather than to their actual "truth."

Alison Young, in the following chapter, traces the difficulties of achieving sincerity where truth is not in question but its "graspability" is, namely in the wake of trauma. Young examines the extent to which sincerity and insincerity are implicated in each other by considering different genres and their varying reputations for sincerity. Ultimately she discusses the expectations and affects of sincerity and insincerity with reference to two distinct genres: the report of a governmental commission of inquiry and a short documentary film. Both texts concern the traumatic events of September 11. The issue of sincere genres or representations raises additional problems when the representations concern traumatic events, for it is often said that survivors of trauma lack the ability to resolve their experiences through representation. They relive the traumatic event without mediation.

The two texts, a report and a documentary, attempt to work through the suffering caused by the events. Both genres appear to confirm sincerity, but both texts are also paradoxical. Their paradoxes are, however, of a different nature, because their affective sincerity effects derive from very different post-traumatic symptoms. Young concludes that both texts are, and are not, sincere. The sincerity effect turns out to be conditional upon the sincere, that is, implicated in it. In the limit-case of texts occasioned by the legacy of trauma, we have reached the aporia of sincerity.

But as with rhetoric, considering sincerity a media effect does not make it any less culturally powerful; hence, far from being dismissed, it must be taken extremely seriously. In the next chapter, Maaike Bleeker does just that, in proposing a literal sense of theatricality and performance to come to grips with sincerity as a media effect with political ramifications. She argues for the potential of theatricality for the analysis of sincerity as a performance of authenticity and truth. Instead of equating theatricality with mimetic inauthenticity (as the Oxford English Dictionary does), and therefore in opposition to what is true and authentic, she proposes to understand theatricality in terms of a destabilization of the clear-cut distinction between true and false. Theatricality is not a matter of spectacle, exaggeration, or make-believe, but instead denotes those moments in which we become aware of how we are implicated within what appears to us as true or false. Theatricality points to the relationship between the performance of authenticity and a culturally and historically specific point of view. This makes theatricality an ambiguous pointer since it relocates truth and authenticity, at least partly, in the eye of the beholder.

The final chapter shifts this discussion to a smaller scale in order to make this view of sincerity available for more detailed cultural analyses. It proposes a "sincerity genre." Reindert Dhondt focuses on the desire of "tout dire" (Sade) as a literary conviction that paradoxically seems to undermine veracity in the autobiographical works of the Cuban writer Reinaldo Arenas (1943–1990) and the French author and photographer Hervé Guibert (1955–1991). At the end of their lives, both authors committed to paper their own private lives and those of their intimate circle, in a desperate attempt to write against time and death—the time of death. Like Michel de Montaigne, who defined his *Essais* as a project to describe himself "totally naked" (*tout nu*), Arenas and Guibert seem to reject all artificial masquerade in order to provide a truthful and adequate self-portraiture. Nevertheless they cannot refrain from providing a fictional and fictitious *veritas* because their writing is mannered, bent, and at times even baroque or grotesque. Although the two authors assert the right to say *everything* according to the truth in order to conclude an "autobiographical pact" with their readers, they probe the limits of sincerity not only by a stylistic extravagance, but also by an excessive disclosure of their personal past.

*

Together, the essays in this volume offer a double vision. First, they propose a cultural-historical analysis of the notion of sincerity. They explain why the concept emerges in Western culture with specific meanings and ramifications. But such an analysis is also a *démasqué* of the notion. At the same time, this analysis does not turn the concept of sincerity into a museum piece: it remains in use. Sincerity has an incredible resilience, which necessitates two further steps. On the one hand, it is necessary to bracket, or even actively refuse, sincerity where it would otherwise continue to exert its oppressive potential. On the other hand, the state of the world in which the opposite of sincerity continues to function—thanks to the rhetoric of sincerity—requires a new theorization of the concept. Within this new theorization the issue of sincerity is no longer one of "being" sincere but of "doing" sincerity. The way in which one deploys media can be sincere, or not. This openness shifts the status of the concept; it goes some way toward protecting it against a dualistic perspective of rights and wrongs, thereby facilitating a more complex and productive critical analysis.

PART I

SINCERITY AS SUBJECTIVITY EFFECT

"Why do you tear me from Myself?"

TORTURE, TRUTH, AND THE ARTS
OF THE COUNTER-REFORMATION

Jane Taylor

For some time now I have been asking myself, "What is sincerity and how is it performed?" The very idea of the "performance of sincerity" seems a contradiction, because sincerity cannot stage itself. It is something of an intangible precisely in that its affects and its effects must remain beyond calculation, must exceed rational description and instrumental reason. Sincerity cannot be deployed. Whenever "sincerity" names itself, it ceases to exist. It is a value that is vouched for through an exchange of social consensus in which it cannot itself trade.

In this essay, I am attempting to understand representations of personhood from the perspective of sincerity during the political, economic, and philosophical upheavals that characterize urbanization and modernization during the European Reformation. Yet this is in the first instance a theoretical rather than an historical project. How does a continuous selfhood persist across a context of rupture? My habit is to expect the arts to interpret such complex events.

So to begin I will turn to one of the most compelling scenes from that most gruesome Renaissance play, *Titus Andronicus*, an early work by Shakespeare. In the middle of the drama, the Moor Aaron is captured and threatened with death, and he is asked whether he renounces his past deeds of rapine, murder, and plunder. Aaron resists the consolation of remorse. There is some perverse grandeur in his will to integrity. He is not cowed into asserting a new self with which to revile his old self. Lucius, Titus's son, continues with the questioning: "Art thou not sorry for these heinous deeds?" Aaron's defiant answer is:

> Ay, that I had not done a thousand more.
> Even now I curse the day—and yet I think
> Few come within the compass of my curse—
> Wherein I did not some notorious ill,
> As kill a man, or else devise his death;
> Ravish a maid, or plot the way to do it;
> Accuse some innocent and forswear myself;
> Set deadly enmity between two friends;
> Make poor men's cattle break their necks;
> Set fire on barns and haystacks in the night,
> And bid the owners quench them with their tears.
> Oft have I digged up dead men from their graves
> And set them upright at their dear friends' door,
> Even when their sorrows almost was forgot,
> And on their skins, as on the bark of trees,
> Have with my knife carved in Roman letters
> 'Let not your sorrow die though I am dead.'

(Titus Andronicus 5.1: 124–140)

Aaron's confession becomes an outrage because he uses it as an opportunity to iterate (and thus reiterate) the actions for which he is condemned. His is no compliant political subjectivity.

Rereading this scene recently, I was struck by a set of striking resonances with an episode from our present: the initial phase of international engagement in Iraq. You might recollect the press statements made by Saddam Hussein's Minister of Information, Mohammad Saeed al-Sahaf, who subsequently became the Iraqi Foreign Minister. The press seemed to revel in his statements, which generally vilified the coalition of the willing and declared how soundly they were being thrashed within the precinct of Baghdad, their livers roasting over the fires of the faithful. These statements were interpreted by the Western media as reckless and flagrant lies, as models of scandalous folly. In the spirit of this triumphalist chau-

vinism, a website even sprang up, "We Love the Iraqi Information Minister," which was a forum dedicated to lampooning al-Sahaf's statements
and general demeanor.

The awful owning up of actions that we witness in Aaron's ambiguous "confession" is curiously exhilarating. Aaron's speech suggests that
the renunciation of the self is perhaps more humiliating than the naming
of vile deeds. This is a logic that will emerge as part of the shift from a
Roman to a Romantic conception of sincerity, such as will come to be figured through the writing of Rousseau.

It struck me that what we may have been watching was a performance that arose from a distinct tradition with a logic and mode of representation that differs from those presumed to be normal within the idioms
of post-Protestant Western television. Whatever else the statements may
have been undertaking, I began to suspect that al-Sahaf's statements were
discursive, not so much truth claims as boasts. And here I do not wish to
understate their real political meanings in the contexts of current global
conflict as well as the media war. The point is, boasts of this sort are neither "true" nor "untrue." Rather, they do a different kind of work. Boasting traditions have been much diminished in the West largely due to a
shift described as technological: the emergence of print and the massifica-
tion of literacy.

Traces of such boasts, however, do remain in heroic epics such as
Beowulf, or in fishing stories and second-hand car-dealerships.[1] Moreover,
within my particular context, they are the substance of a vibrant oral tradition referred to by scholars as "praise poetry," in which idiom the "praises"
of a dignitary or visitor are hailed aloud as a kind of moral armature before
public events. Warriors, too, traditionally sing their own praises, boasting of previous victories in battle, recounting a famous moment, or mag-
nifying aspects of personal potency. Women also sing praises and are
praised, though these are often covert and context-defined events. Several
scholars have undertaken remarkable research in these fields.[2] However,
in part because of the uneven ideological structures of core and periph-
ery in disciplines and debates, such knowledges generally stay enclaved
off within regional studies, where they inform and thicken ethnographic
description.

Walter Ong's now classic work has documented the moment in
which similar research entered metropolitan debate, with his account of

the impact of Milman Parry's early-twentieth-century work on Homer (1982). Parry drew on evidence from *The Iliad* and *The Odyssey* to suggest that substantial differences were evident between oral and written modes of thought and expression. I would suggest that this theoretical insight has enormous implications within the new global discursive regime.

I am increasingly persuaded that there are conventions of performance and reception that have become so habitual and naturalized within our cultural spheres that much of what is transacted between us has been effectively rendered invisible. This is the insight I have been considering in order to locate a semiotics of sincerity. My purpose is to show that by identifying and locating the historical emergence of a particular rhetorical and performative apparatus of "sincerity," one can render the ideological and productive effects of sincerity visible. This is because sincerity's claim is precisely that it is a mode of self-expression generally held to be nondiscursive, transparent, and outside of ideology. I have sought to determine what is being masked by that set of assumptions.

Beginnings

One may as well invoke a scene of origins. It is 1532. John Frith, of serious purpose, is in flight for his life, making his way from England, the homeland turned enemy, to Antwerp and his family who await him. His ultimate destination will be Germany, where his brilliant friend William Tyndale continues the work of printing the Bible in English. As Frith approaches the Essex coast, he is arrested on a warrant issued by Sir Thomas More, Chancellor to Henry VIII. Over the succeeding months in the Tower, More challenges Frith on several fundamentals. Frith has disputed the supremacy of the Pope; he has rejected the notion of purgatory on the grounds that there is no scriptural basis for the idea; and, perhaps most heretically of all, he has used radically materialist arguments to deny transubstantiation.

More is precisely the wrong sort of opponent for Frith. The Chancellor has taken up the task of defending theological orthodoxy against both the secular absolutist appetites of the English king and Lutheranism. As a result, More ironically ends up constituting all by himself a kind of threshold between the theocratic Middle Ages and emergent Protestantism in all of its variety. Yet he is, it seems, in the most complex of ways a sincere man. So too is Frith. It is thus not wholly remarkable that one of the first written records of the word *sincere* in English arises in an exchange between these two individuals. Compellingly, in this instance, neither More nor Frith uses the term to characterize himself. Rather, in Frith's text, *An Answer to Thomas More*, the word occurs in his brief sketch of the medieval scholar, John Wycliffe. "Master Wickliffe," Frith's text indicates, was "noted . . . to be a man . . . of a very sincere life."[3] Several points are worth attention here. One is that "sincere" as used does not refer to the condition of Wycliffe's inner being. Rather, it describes Wycliffe *as evidenced* through a life witnessed by others.

Why did Wycliffe provide a touchstone in the dispute between the two scholars? Two full centuries earlier he had been associated with the hand-written first translation of the Bible into English; he had also denied the Eucharist its literal status as body and blood of Christ. In 1532 John Frith's offenses were similar. Perhaps the conjunction of these theological disputes is inevitable. In pre-modern semiotics, the word participates in a necessary mystical conjunction with the thing that it names in the world. Similarly, by analogy, transubstantiation relies on a logic of magical similitude, whereby like substances (blood and wine) are literal equivalents rather than metaphors of one another. Thus, just as the totemic link between the body and the bread is broken through the renunciation of transubstantiation, so in similar terms there has been a severing of the allegedly natural bond between a word and the thing that it represents. The translation of sacred text into multiple, destabilizing vernacular versions, which furthermore are made available for individual interpretation, threatens to overthrow the world. A new representational order is coming into being, one that will allow for paper money to stand for gold, and that will distribute the production of value across a system, where integers are reconceived in relational rather than in essential terms. As has been noted by Foucault, signification is being invented. Symbolic conflicts can have profoundly material effects. Within the coming decade, Frith would be executed for betraying Rome, while More would be executed for serving her.

My second etymological example I cite for very particular purposes. The text to which I refer here is published at the close of the decade following the executions of Frith and More. Catherine Parr's text from 1548,

Lamentacions of a Synner, is not cited in the Oxford English Dictionary's etymological history, even though the word "sincere" occurs six times in Parr's text. The omission is striking given, on one hand, Parr's formidable legacy within the history of women writers, and on the other hand, the familiar trope of woman's discursive position as the exemplum of *insincerity*, which in itself should make Parr's reiterations of the term worth attention. Nonetheless, the gender biases of the archive result in a failure to recognize Parr's place in an etymology on the discourses of sincerity.

Parr was Henry VIII's sixth consort and queen of England, and she is acknowledged to have been the first known Englishwoman to publish a work of prose in the sixteenth century. She engaged in various intellectual and cultural projects. As an energetic advocate of the dissemination of religious texts in the vernacular, she was a sponsor of the translation of Erasmus's *Paraphrases* into English. During the dangerous last years of Henry's reign, Stephen Gardiner, bishop of Winchester, plotted to destroy her, and he attempted to implicate her through the trial for heresy of one Anne Askew, who was brutally tortured in 1546. Askew was assaulted so violently that she had to be seated when they finally burned her to death. But she died without implicating Catherine. Parr's *Lamentacions of a Synner* is a prose narrative documenting a spiritual journey, and it was published after her husband the king's death.[4]

Parr's own insistent protestations of sincerity might suggest that the astute woman was interrogating her own motives. She had, after all, lived out her life within that security which Henry's protection had guaranteed her. Her enemies, such as Gardiner, were offended by her Lutheran principles, and they sought repeatedly to associate her with Askew, accusing her of hoarding prohibited books in attempts to alienate her from the king, whose self-styled Protestantism was of a decidedly more pragmatic and opportunistic sort (Hiscock 2002, 179). At one point a Bill of Articles, which outlined her heterodox beliefs, was drawn up against her, largely on the evidence of her extensive heretical library. The lucky Parr saw the document and strategically submitted herself to Henry, throwing herself upon his mercy.[5] Parr's case suggests that political acumen is not necessarily incompatible with piety. Clearly this astute woman recognized the need to position herself in relation to the favor of the king while perhaps at the same time courting God himself, the one absolute authority whose power surpassed even her late husband's.

What I am suggesting here is that "sincerity" emerges by the complex negotiation in the shifting terrain between religious devotion, Roman authority, royal prerogative, and Protestant ambitions.[6] Before schism there was little room for such spiritual connoisseurship, as faith largely consisted of compliance with a set of givens, rather than individual interpretation. The instrument of investigative terror, the heresy trial—with its specific nexus of power, anxiety, and authenticity—made a conception of sincerity necessary. The introduction of the Inquisition under Gregory IX in the thirteenth century licensed the use of torture, and thus by the sixteenth century the main instrument of investigation had shifted from the somewhat arbitrary "trial by ordeal" to the violent extraction of confession. Given this history, we may propose that sincerity essentially arises in order to resolve the problem of the forced confession.[7] A notion of "evidence" such as we now commonly understand it, as something objective and extra-human, was yet to be invented. The truth of the self was generally associated with conscience, the terrain within, that which is unseen. How could such a truth be tested?

This is in part the philosophical burden carried by *Hamlet*. I would suggest that we witness the Danish prince in the moment of a shift in existing regimes of truth-claims and forensic practice. The scientific procedures that are to emerge over the next three hundred years are not yet available and Shakespeare has to invent an instrument of forensic testing that will have significant impact on succeeding generations of writers and philosophers. Perhaps inevitably, the technology that he deploys arises from what is the dominant arena of secular culture in the English sixteenth century, Shakespeare's own discipline of stage-craft.

What is revealed by a scrutiny of these confessions throughout this period is that there is an evolving dialectic between external performance and internal convictions. Sincerity is necessarily a problem of performance. Problematically though, performance is characterized as insincere, because it provides an instrument that makes it possible to represent an inner state upon the surface. During the Renaissance the inherited classical anxieties about truth and representation are pondered over as questions about performance. Actors and playwrights begin to discourse upon their art. The origins of a critical language are evident in the language through which acting is being professionalized in order to distinguish it from dissembling. One of the first tracts to imagine the actor as professional is Thomas Heywood's *An Apology for Actors* (1612). Here the term "personate" is used to capture the idea of the performer inhabiting the person of the character he is playing. "Personate" has been identified by historians as a new usage, and presumably a fresh conception of acting (Targoff 1997, 51). In this period acting treatises generally explore the dialogue between the inner self and its external representation, an issue that reaches its most sophisticated articulation by the eighteenth century in Diderot's *The Paradox of the Actor* (1773).

The terms within which Hamlet seeks to verify the truth of his dead father's claims about Claudius's betrayal rest upon an argument about self, sincerity, and performance. The forensic instrument that Hamlet uses is derived from acting theory, and Hamlet's strategy is to test Claudius's inner condition and measure it against his external behavior. The episode makes manifest what will become a lingering preoccupation for modernity: the desire that the body be an unambiguous signifier of truth.

During the much-cited "Mousetrap" episode, Hamlet instigates a troupe of traveling players to recreate the events of his father's death in front of the prime suspect, Claudius, whom Hamlet suspects of that murder. The scene introduces us to one of the models of performance suggested by the play. When Hamlet is coaching his performers before they go on stage, he marvels at the authority with which these actors can assume the features and expressions of grief, giving a completely persuasive deception. Their acting is too close to dissembling for the Danish prince, and it appears to make a mockery of his own performance of authentic grief at the death of his father:

> Is it not monstrous that this player here
> But in a fiction, in a dream of passion,
> Could force his soul so to his whole conceit
> That from her working all his visage waned,
> Tears in his eyes, distraction in's aspect,
> A broken voice, and his whole function suiting
> With forms to his conceit? And all for nothing.
> For Hecuba!
> What's Hecuba to him, or he to Hecuba,
> That he should weep for her?

(2.2: 528–536)

Hamlet had earlier asserted, with regard to his own "true" feelings, "I have that within which passes show" (1.2). This is the invention of a moral economy. An inner universe is weighed against external signification in a nuanced calculus through which the natural balance will come to define both exemplary Englishness and sincerity.[8]

So here we have it again, that anxiety about a split between the outer and the inner self. The "rhetoric of sincerity" that was emerging across a diffuse but defining terrain is testing and producing modern subjectivity in contradictory ways. On one hand, the sincere self is a solitary creature, inward looking, self-reflexive. Yet on the other hand, sincerity can be called upon to stage itself in relation to an external authority. The individual subject acquires a vast semiotics of gesture and expressive style, from materials as diverse as the confessional broadsheet to play texts and portraits, sermons, letters, and conduct books. These performance technologies somehow both arise from, yet also produce, an inner world. In other words, this is a fundamentally dialectical production of being for which there is an unresolved contest over internal versus external authority. An apparatus for conjuring up a performance of sincerity is learned through the disciplines of the larger cultural context, yet in such a way as to be wholly naturalized to the individual subject. The persuasive arts of sincerity take their authority largely from this. So when Catherine Parr attests to her own sincerity, she draws on strategies and codes that inhabit and manage her, rather than those that she manages; in the end she is impelled by inner voices.

Sincerity is precipitated by the Reformation and the Counter-Reformation, through which the old metaphysics was surrendered under violent contest between Catholic and Protestant precepts. One archive of the ideological trauma of the era resides in the records of the torture and execution of countless pious men and women. Another is evident within the symbolic arena. New works of art seek to break with the iconographies of medieval representational practice, even while some have sedimented within them tropes pointing back to archaic and magical modes of thought. In other words, they deploy both pre- and post-Reformation pictorial logic. A new order of rhetoric is coming into being, and there are traces of both residual and emergent forms of representation. At times the figures in and of this rhetoric seem over-determined because of the contradictory work they do.

There is evidence to suggest that the emerging representational realism in the period is at times co-present with archaic elements of magical similitude, with realism and typology co-present within a single scene. In making my case I will consider the representational problem raised by that irreducible contradiction for the era, the figure of the converted Jew.

A Figure of (In)Sincerity

My own situation as a South African who has in the past decade observed the acts of self-renunciation precipitated by the Truth and Reconciliation Commission (the hearings into apartheid-era human rights abuses in that country) is no doubt central to my interest in the theoretical terrain of the sincere conversion. At the same time I have been considering analogous contemporary cases, such as recent war crimes tribunals and the destabilization prompted by redefinitions of modern geopolitical identities. One of the most nuanced and complex meditations on conversion from recent history arises in the testimony of Adriano Sofri, the Italian political journalist who was imprisoned on dubious grounds for his alleged participation in the political execution of a policeman.

The so-called "Slaughter Commission" that resurrected this case was a judicial enquiry into left-wing activities in Italy between the 1960s and 1980s. Under questioning, Sofri characterizes his experience of dislocation at trying to integrate the several facets of his being.

I had to overcome a resistance to fighting an old battleground I had abandoned a long time ago. I couldn't defend myself as I am today, with my more rounded thoughts . . . my good manners and my old books. I had to defend the person I was then, sharp-tongued, vituperative, constantly on the move. I was faced with the alternative of confounding time and identifying absolutely with the person I was, or denouncing that person and losing my relationship to my own past. (Jones 2003, xii)

The burden described here is of a self who must both renounce and contradictorily retain a prior set of behaviors in order to be integrated across a temporal and epistemic break.

Conversion narratives identify distinct selves within the individual across an arc of time, and they are structured in such a way as to resolve the tensions between sameness and difference. Throughout the early modern period, conversion provokes considerable theological, political, and theoretical debate, particularly in relation to the upheavals prompted by the Reformation and the Counter-Reformation. The vexing question for religious authority turned on how to test the sincerity of any such alleged conversion, which in turn resulted in the policing of theological boundaries for safeguarding against heresy, as believers began to straddle the terrain between "inside" and "outside" the fold. The imperative to establish and defend orthodoxies became overbearing.

Particularly vehement was the theological conflict over the multiple personhood of the Trinitarian God. Unitarianism, which regarded the three-in-one Godhead as unscriptural, was especially suspect, and many were put to death for confronting the Reformed Church's orthodoxies in this matter. The brilliant intellectual Servetus, who was the first person to discover and describe the pulmonary circulation of the blood, happened also to be a Unitarian and was executed with Calvin's sanction. Yet, while there was an effective proscription on engaging with the question of multiplicity and personhood in relation to the Godhead, the problem of identity remained a pivotal enquiry within the secular domain. Hence, a split emerged as theology and philosophy diverged, and the all-important enquiry into personhood was thus effectively divided into two disarticulated problems in the early modern era. On the one hand, theological orthodoxy defended the Trinity with a lethal vehemence, while on the other hand philosophy produced the discourses and technologies integral to the production of the unitary self of modernity.

By the end of the seventeenth century, John Locke would engage in a dangerous dispute with Edward Stillingfleet, Bishop of Worcester, on the question of identity. The archive of letters provoked by that heated encounter suggests the volatility of the conflict whenever religious dogmas on personhood engaged too closely with philosophy's various "essays concerning human understanding." This is how Locke had staged the problem of identity: "Person . . . is a Forensick Term appropriating Actions and their Merit; and so belongs only to intelligent Agents capable of a Law, and Happiness and Misery. This personality extends it *self* beyond present Existence to what is past, only by consciousness, whereby it becomes concerned and accountable, owns and imputes to it *self* past Actions, just upon the same ground, and for the same reason, that it does the present" (Locke 1990, 340). In effect, Locke is asserting that "the Person" as an integrated unique integer is a necessary legal fiction, through which actions can be attached to persons in a narrative of accountability, and I suppose, of authorship, authority, and authenticity.[9] Consciousness is the site of identity, but such consciousness itself has no evident site. Thus Locke's famous case of a man who might be recognized as the same *man* when mad as when sane, yet would not be the same *person*.

Nonetheless one realm in which the theological and the philosophical continue to address one another is through the metaphoric language of the visual arts. I would suggest that the Baroque captivation with images of metamorphosis provides one sustained metaphoric experiment in personhood. Similarly, the trope of conversion allows for the perilous terrain about identity across difference to be traversed via another means. More particularly, "conversion" establishes a device for exploring the multiplicity of the self through an emerging "rhetoric of sincerity."

As Sofri's case demonstrates, conversion poses the exemplary problem for any notion of the continuous subject, because it constitutes an absolute rupture between past and present selves. More specifically, throughout the Reformation era, conversion was regarded with skepticism, because in numerous cases the professions of a new faith arose out of political expediency and fear of physical torture. This is not to imply that there are no sincere conversions. Rather, I am examining conversion and sincerity as a challenge for representation, particularly if the body is interpreted as carrying absolute meanings for the condition of the inner being. The history of painting provides a particularly compelling point of access to the discourses on conversion and its alibi, sincerity.

I will ground my discussion by turning to two paintings generally attributed to Caravaggio on the same theme, the "conversion of St. Paul."[10] The first (Figure 1.1) is now usually identified as a first version that was rejected upon its completion, although there is some suggestion that it is possibly a particularly skilled copy of a Caravaggio (Morassi 1952, 118–119).[11] In this essay I am not setting out to examine whether this "conversion" scene belongs to Caravaggio's oeuvre. Rather, I am analyzing how the painting grapples with a representational problem that is evident across a range of Caravaggio's works. I will formulate that representational problem in the question, "What language is appropriate for the staging of 'sincerity'?" This is, at the same time, a dilemma for philosophy, law, the church, the theater (including the emerging idiom of opera), and the plastic arts.[12]

It is a dilemma that in some ways precipitates modernity's preoccupation with that covert being who has taken up residence within the household of the self. The horror, for authority, is that there is no way of knowing or proving the disposition of this being, regardless of external constraints or interventions. If Caravaggio's *The Martyrdom of St. Matthew* and the first version of the *Conversion of St. Paul* are considered alongside one another, the *Conversion* seems to be drawing on formal resolutions that Caravaggio arrived at for his *Martyrdom of St. Matthew* (Figure 1.2).

FIGURE 1.1. Caravaggio (Michelangelo Merisi da) (1573–1610), *The Conversion of Saint Paul.* Coll. Odescalchi Balbi di Piovera, Rome, Italy. © Scala / Art Resource, New York. Reproduced by permission.

FIGURE 1.2. Caravaggio (Michelangelo Merisi da) (1573–1610), *The Martyrdom of Saint Matthew*. San Luigi dei Francesi, Rome, Italy. © Scala / Art Resource, New York. Reproduced by permission.

It is, after all, documented that the *St. Matthew* had an enormous public impact, and the innovative intensity with which the artist used heterodox methods to rethink orthodox themes brought Caravaggio considerable attention and celebrity. It is thus likely that Caravaggio would have remained in a conversation with this work when he received the commission to paint one of the founding scenes of Christian mythology, the moment of St. Paul's radical conversion from persecutor of the early Church to Christian evangelist. As described in the Book of Acts, that event is, at once, both dramatic and spiritual.

Let us briefly consider the dialogue between the two paintings first in formal terms, and then second in relation to their ideological purposes. In both of these paintings, chiaroscuro effects emphasize a diagonal muscular arm that reaches down toward the right. This arm within a secular plane is crossed by a substantial dramatic oblique of metaphysical action from the upper right to bottom left corners. Human and divine forces are in some way manifestly at odds. In both these works, a sacred presence reaches into the action "as if" from heaven, but actually from much the same plane as the upper horizon of earthly action. In other words, the distinction between secular and sacred realms is propositional, discursive rather than absolute. In the *Conversion*, the muscular rump of the horse functions in the same way as the pillow of cloud in the *Martyrdom*, preventing the divine figures from tumbling into the realm of human drama. A feathery plume in the upper left corner in both paintings provides a counter-weight to this vignette of aerial activity. These repetitions between the two works suggest not only that a unity of imagination is at work, but also that the scene of redemption figured in the *Conversion* is at one level a scene of violence as well. I will return to this point later.

The motif of conversion has provided Caravaggio with the thematic material of several of his most significant works. A number of his canvasses deal with related material, such as the *Conversion of Mary Magdalen* and the tactile *Incredulity of St. Thomas* (Figure 1.3), in which the saint probes the fact of the risen Christ, his index finger moving between outer plane and inner substance. While in a narrow sense this work is not a conversion scene, it does make the case that Caravaggio is exploring the problem of manifest truth. The *Martyrdom of St. Matthew* overtly deals with what is in some terms the antithesis of conversion—that is, spiritual fidelity in defiance of a threat to the self. But twentieth-century excursions in site-specific art have made us all alert to the significance of context. Therefore, it matters that the chapel for which the painting was commissioned had very specific contemporary associations with the politics of conversion. The Contarelli Chapel, in the Basilica of San Luigi dei Francesi in Rome, had been dedicated to St. Matthew by the French Cardinal Matthieu Contrei some twenty years earlier. An ambitious decorative program for the chapel was begun but delayed, probably due to the intervening years of violent religious war in France.[13]

FIGURE 1.3. Caravaggio (Michelangelo Merisi da) (1573–1610), (copy after), *The Incredulity of Saint Thomas*. Uffizi, Florence, Italy. © Scala / Art Resource, New York. Reproduced by permission.

In 1593, the Huguenot claimant to the French throne, Henri de Navarre, had for the second time abjured the Protestant faith within which he had been raised, and for the second time converted to Catholicism. Navarre's second conversion has been interpreted as largely driven by political and pragmatic imperatives. It is in some ways a shadow repetition of a traumatic conversion to Catholicism that he had undergone as a young man after the slaughter of thousands of Huguenots at the St. Bartholomew's Night massacre. The horror of that event had prompted the young man to renounce his Reformed religion, probably a complex combination of conviction and fear as well as a desire to contain further bloodshed. This conversion did not hold, however. He reverted to his Huguenot beliefs until 1593, when he again converted to Catholicism. (It may of course be possible to characterize this turn back to Protestantism as a second conversion, according to which account Henri would convert three times, not twice). Henri's "double conversion" prompted frequent incredulity in certain Catholic sectors, and the question of his insincerity has become a trope within records of the period, which speculate that his enactment arose from political expediency in order to unite France under his throne. Nevertheless, the conversion was claimed as a significant religious victory for the Counter-Reformation. In October 1600, Henri married Marie de Medici, consolidating his relationship with the Church of Rome. It was in the years leading up to that marriage that Caravaggio was commissioned to paint three works depicting key episodes in the life of St. Matthew, the namesake of the French Cardinal Matthieu Contrei.[14]

   This is the immediate context of *The Martyrdom of St. Matthew*, and I suggest that the conjunction of these factors gives rise to a kind of "political unconscious" that has implications for Caravaggio's "Conversion" paintings commissioned just after this period. It is within this charged ideological setting that Caravaggio learns the arts of history painting and of church patronage. The contemporary discourses around authenticity, performance, and sincerity with which his patrons were engaged must have been common currency. This set of ideological disputes is neither identical to nor distinct from Caravaggio's own aesthetic and representational experiments, through which the artist is attempting to solve the problem of figuring *in the body* those states of consciousness that are noncorporeal. Michael Fried's influential study, *Absorption and Theatricality*, considers the distinctively French eighteenth century and Diderot's call for a dynamic dialectic between reflection and performance (1). I am suggesting that Caravaggio's artistic experiment in the Baroque era is struggling to find a visual rhetoric that engages with related concerns, but in an earlier moment, during a period of trans-cultural crisis between specific Protestant and Catholic currents within broad theological contests of schism and its differential conceptions of performance and of reverie. I would suggest that the historical factors informing artistic activity in the Baroque era are expressive of the volatility generated between regional and universal ambitions. They will have meaning for the figuring of self-reflexive habits and sincerity for succeeding generations. The Contarelli Chapel in the French Cathedral in Rome thus bears a trace of this ideological re-invention of French piety, while it is also the context within which Caravaggio is inventing a lexicon through which to consider the self and its performances. Hence, while the commissions for the chapel are determined by the conditions of the local context, they have ramifications for the universal church as it then defined itself.[15]

Such a context would surely have informed the theological climate when Caravaggio was commissioned to paint two works for the Cesari Chapel in the Santa Maria del Popolo. The two works were to be a *Conversion of St. Paul*, alongside a *Crucifixion of St. Peter*. Before I turn to consider the *Conversion of St. Paul*, it is worth reminding ourselves of the Biblical account that lies behind the painting. Saul of Tarsus was a Jewish Talmudic scholar involved in the early persecution of Christians, many of whom had at that stage converted from Judaism. The Book of Acts gives a vivid account:

> And Saul, yet breathing out threatenings against the disciples of the Lord, went unto the high priest, and desired of him letters to Damascus to the synagogues, that if he found any of this way, whether they were men or women, he might bring them bound unto Jerusalem. And as he journeyed, he came near Damascus: and suddenly there shined round him a light from heaven: and he fell to the earth, and heard a voice saying unto him, Saul, Saul, why persecutest thou me? And he said, who art thou, Lord? And the Lord said, I am Jesus whom thou persecutest. . . .
>
> And Saul arose from the earth; and when his eyes were opened, he saw no man: but they led him by the hand, and brought him unto Damascus.
>
> And he was there three days without sight, and neither did eat nor drink. (Acts 9: 1–5; 8–9)

It is only some chapters later in the Book of Acts that we are informed parenthetically that Saul is also called "Paul," and from this point on it is as Paul that the text names him, as if conversion takes some while to stick.

Through the process of the reinvention of the self, Paul redirects his mission to address a primarily gentile community, contradictorily confirming the necessary link between his faith and his ethnicity at the same moment that he undermines it. He asserts that his religion is for both Jew and non-Jew, a discursive gesture that nonetheless confirms ethnicity as the primary signifier of identity. This is not without significance for early modern discourses on race and nation. In considering these implications, I will turn to a comparative examination of the two conversion paintings. The earlier treatment (let's call it "version 1") is formally much more diffuse in its focus than "version 2," and has been characterized as Mannerist in its handling of the theme (Figures 1.1 and 1.4).[16]

While Saul wears a proto-Roman costume, the figure is at the same time conspicuously Jewish, cast within a set of iconographic conventions. He has the red hair and beard associated with the exemplary figure of betrayal, Judas. His groom, too, has the long beard, hooked nose, and lidded eyes of the stereotype. There are several noteworthy details in the scene. Saul's skirt made of leather strips is caught in tangled curls around his groin, and the handling of shadow and folds suggests an anxious figuring of circumcision. Circumcision is testimony to an identity located within the logic of the body, and as such it is a marker of Jewish particularism. Contradictorily,

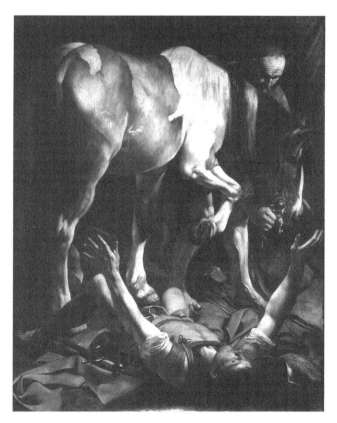

FIGURE 1.4. Caravaggio (Michelangelo Merisi da) (1573–1610), *The Conversion of Saint Paul*. Santa Maria del Popolo, Rome, Italy. © Scala / Art Resource, New York. Reproduced by permission.

though, this is a particularism that is evidenced *both* through the cultural trace (circumcision, beard) and the biological trace (red hair, lidded eyes).

It is remarkable how ambiguous Caravaggio's rendering of the body is here, because the complex attention to the man's musculature, his nipples, and the fleshy color palette suggest the naked torso. At the same time, however, there are traces of short, capped sleeves on the figure, and the handling of this detail on the right arm in particular gives the uncanny impression of a body that is flayed (Figure 1.4). This suggests the much-favored Renaissance iconography of Marsyas, who when skinned alive was heard to cry, "Why do you tear me from myself?" (Wind 1968, 171). Michelangelo's *Last Judgment* (Figure 1.5) bears an image on this subject that on one hand refers to the Platonic mysteries of Bacchus, while it has been interpreted both as a self-portrait of the artist and an avatar of St. Bartholomew holding up his own flayed skin (Wind 1968, 171).

According to legend, St. Bartholomew was flayed for having converted the king of Armenia, again linking the trope of conversion to the emblem of the flayed man.[17] In Michelangelo's treatment, the slurried facial features that remain as a last trace of identity on the shucked skin bear no resemblance to the image of the saint from whose hand the human pelt hangs. The transfiguration has left Bartholomew not as a Vesalian flayed man, but rather, he is already resident in his resurrected body as both Socratic figure and as saint in an idealized emblem of transcendence and self-knowledge.

The ambiguity over outer and inner selves in Caravaggio's handling may be in part conventional, a representation of body armor. Nonetheless I would suggest that in this very singular handling of the figure, a surplus of meanings is generated. The confusion over whether Saul is clad or naked suggests a disquiet about the substance of his conversion. Sincerity arises at an intangible point of intersection between inner conviction and external representation. A similar ambiguity is evident in the figure of "The Prophet" by Marlene Dumas (on the cover of this volume). In an act of expressive candor, the prophet disrobes, baring himself to us; however, in fact what he reveals is another garment, a simple white caftan that carries the signification of nakedness.

Saul's ambiguous body provides a metaphoric iconography through which to explore true versus false faith, but it is at the same time integral to emerging discourses about personhood.[18] For the gentile, conversion is

FIGURE 1.5. Michelangelo Buonarroti (1475–1564), Saint Bartholomew (a detail from *The Last Judgment*). Sistine Chapel, Vatican Palace, Vatican State. © Scala / Art Resource, New York. Reproduced by permission.

a matter of conscience, and the realigning of oneself as either Catholic or Protestant would not in the first instance be evident upon the body. The Jew discursively bears a somatic set of representations that always exceeds and supersedes whatever inner state he may inhabit. The converso Jew is thus necessarily constituted as a deceiver.

Thus in the early modern period the trope of conversion buttresses emerging discourses on racial and national identity. In 1611, the King James Bible asserts a communion of faith that transcends ethnicity. Paul's letter to the Romans attempts to insist that "he is not a Jew, which is one outwardly; neither is that circumcision, which is outward in the flesh: But he is a Jew, which is one inwardly; and circumcision is that of the heart, in the spirit" (Romans 2:28–29). This is why it is striking that Saul is not renamed "Paul" until some chapters after the event of the conversion. It is as if the rhetoric of sincerity is at odds with the rhetoric of race, in their contradictory appeals to an identity that is located alternately within, or on, the surface.

If we reconsider the biblical account of Paul's conversion, we note that he was blinded for three days and had to be led by the hand to a place of shelter, where for those three days he neither ate nor drank. Let us imagine: during these days the shocked man is living in a state of sensory deprivation and thrown in upon himself with little sensory stimulus. He loses all external markers of identity, and he must assume that this is now the permanent condition of his being. This is when Paul reinvents himself, producing a new universalist discourse that determines that his faith is for both Jew and non-Jew.

At this point it is instructive to turn to version 2 of "The Conversion of St. Paul," the work that is unambiguously identified as Caravaggio's canvas (Figure 1.4). The differences between the two paintings are striking. Here, Paul is no longer the figure of the Jew. His red hair and long beard have been replaced by a clean chin and short dark curls. He has become effectively a Roman youth. The contradictions are very suggestive. Does the second painting imply that the work of conversion has so utterly transformed Saul that he is effectively no longer a Jew, or does it rather suggest that all who are in Christ are non-Jewish? Alternatively, is it telling us that the Baroque church was uneasy at having so conspicuously Jewish a patriarch figured as the author of Christian orthodoxies? Perhaps that last explanation might account for the putative rejection of the first version of the commission that stages Paul as Saul. Whatever these two paintings do tell us, they indicate that the conflation of race and religious discourses in this era generates contradictions that cannot be easily resolved within the ever more naturalistic representational practices of the early modern era. As we know, value will increasingly be marked upon the skin as the incidence of intercultural contact is accelerated.[19]

Commentators have identified the European engagement with Hebrew scholarship at the end of the sixteenth century as evidence of a profound shift from policies of expulsion to an inducement to conversion,

partly because Reuchlin's vast Hebrew concordance published in 1556 had
begun theoretically to resituate the Jewish community in relation to Christian eschatology. The conversion of the Jews was somehow necessary to
God's eternal plan. Nonetheless this situated the Jewish community in an
all but intolerable position, as inevitably their motives for conversion were
seen as suspect. The Conversos, or "new Christians" as they were often
designated, were associated with strategic dissembling, and Jews became
synonymous with insincerity.

For all of the differences between the two paintings, version 2, like
version 1, shows a curious confounding of inner and outer. The color palette seems to suggest more unambiguously that Paul is clad, because the
torso is a vivid red and thus signifies, say, a leather jerkin molded to body
shape. There is a link to a visual tradition within which the natural body
gives itself over to the image of Roman military discipline. The figure is
clearly idealized, and the torso is firm and young.

In contrast, the body in version 1 is not idealized in the same way.
Rather, it appears vulnerable, inadequate to the future task of global impe-
rialism. It bears evidence of the contradictions and puzzles within the psychological and ideological forces the work seeks to resolve. It is an emblem
of both the literal Jewish body and the transcendental body of the new
Church. What is evident in version 2 is a shift to represent the universal-
ized body invoked by Paul. Nonetheless what this demonstrates is that the
universalizing gesture is normative, that the aging Saul becomes a militar-
ized Roman youth, the elusive ideal of the Narcissus perhaps, and a pros-
thetic image of Caravaggio's idealized self.

The expressive theatrics of the earlier canvas, with the pleading arms
of the intercessor from above and Paul's ostentatious gesture of blindness,
are here replaced by supine surrender. The blinding of this Paul is not so
much a shocking spectacle, but rather an emblem of the inner submis-
sion to the will of God. That work had explored the threat of castration
and the trauma of the event as Paul is "overborne" by the supreme will of
God. It is a scene of rape. Version 2 is perhaps more suggestive of seduction. Paul's arms yield in invitation. His closed eyes and the flush of red
on his cheeks tell of the inner landscape of the erotics of the moment. The
horse is not frightened; rather it gently probes the air in an almost explor-
atory manner, as if reining in its own power. The soft, dark muzzle has a
blaze of white across the nose that catches the light and defines the horse

against the dark ground of the canvas. This painting is all about the loss of boundaries, of mystery, and of rapture. The horse itself is no longer immaculately white; the animal is a piebald, bearing in its own markings the signification of ambiguity.

There are no supernatural witnesses to this scene, only an old attendant who like a midwife ushers the event into being while coaxing the horse into calm. The shocking planar extension of Paul's body into our viewing field is familiar from Caravaggio's experimental iconographies— say, the scene at the inn at Emmaus, where the outstretched arms of the demonstrative guest plunge us into the event. We do not witness these scenes; we experience them, as Caravaggio again confounds inner and outer, violating boundaries. Is the confounding of the absolutes "naked" and "clad" one trace of an erotics that destabilizes the limits of inner and outer?

Conclusion

My discussion of the converso has considered the implications of the rhetoric of sincerity for early modern discourses on ethnicity, and I want to conclude by briefly returning to the scene from *Titus Andronicus*. Shakespeare's play examines how the figure of Aaron is responsible for engineering the strategic downfall of Titus, using mutilation and rape as his instruments. Aaron is designated as "a Moor" and has in recent interpretations been characterized as African. I would suggest that this is in part because the racial discourses of the nineteenth century have overwritten the unstable languages of identity from the early modern era.[20] Shakespeare's construction of Aaron seems rather to draw on a complex of several rhetorics, one of which arises at least in part out of the early modern discourses on the converso Jew.

In making such a case it is easy enough to cite extra-textual and historical evidence; easy enough to assert that Aaron is, in the biblical account, the brother of Moses; easy enough to indicate that the historical Titus was the Roman general responsible for the sacking of Jerusalem and the suppression of the Jewish Rebellion in the first century. In such a logic, it seems inevitable that any figure named Aaron would be the sworn enemy of Titus.

More compelling for my purposes is the evidence internal to the play. When Aaron is held to account for his vile acts, the resolution that defines his speech is that while he will confess, he will not renounce his prior self. It is as if the unconscious of the play measures the Moor against the converso. Jewish identity in the Renaissance is as yet still coded primarily as a matter of belief, and in such terms Aaron is given the opportunity of conversion. However, contradictorily (and simultaneously) as the Moor, he takes his identity from an emerging somatics of race that excludes the possibility of conversion. After hearing a litany of Aaron's violent deeds, the Goth who interrogates him asks, "What, canst thou say all this and never blush?" To which Aaron bitterly replies, "Ay. Like a black dog, as the saying is."

The blush is, throughout the early modern era, cited as a natural sign of sincerity. Arising from within to appear on the surface, it cannot dissemble. However, Aaron's dark complexion makes the evidence of a blush illegible. His curt response is an accusation. He blames those whose representational practices fail to take account of him. As you name me, so I am. Because within dominant discourses, blackness is its own sign; because blackness has been established as a deficit; because common assertion allows him only that consciousness which is identical to his outside blackness; because his inner being has no trace, he boasts of his black deeds. As a result he confirms what others already knew. Aaron in the end has no choice but to be sincere—his inside is written on the surface of his skin.

2

Melody and Monotone

PERFORMING SINCERITY
IN REPUBLICAN FRANCE

Katherine Bergeron

I remember the first time I heard the voice of Sarah Bernhardt. I was sitting in the media room of the new Bibliothèque National. I called up a digitized file from the immense online catalog, clicked, and through my headphones came a sound I could never have imagined, uttering these lines by François Coppée:

> En ce temps-là, Jésus, seul avec Pierre errait,
> Sur la rive du lac, près de Génésareth,
> A l'heure où le brûlant soleil de midi plane . . .[1]

The poem was called "Un Evangile," a quaint imitation gospel relating a parable about a fisherman's widow who abandons her infant to help out an old beggar. But the topic hardly mattered. I was listening to something else. I thought I knew all about Sarah Bernhardt, but nothing I had learned prepared me for this sound. Trembling, pathetic, uncanny, her voice evoked in me that mixture of horror and fascination we often associate with the dead. Here, indeed, was a voice conjured from the past, but what I heard was not words. It was a more alien thing: a strange, murmuring cadence that sounded almost (but not quite) like singing. Through it the poem as such disappeared: form erased meaning, deed overcame word. What I perceived was close to the condition Adorno evoked when he used that enigmatic word *Rauschen*, the murmur or rustle of language: as he put it, this was "the experience of language itself speaking."[2]

It was the French language, of course, and my own situation as a non-native speaker no doubt contributed to the pleasurable sense of alienation I felt on that day. But some of Bernhardt's French contemporaries seem to have had the same reaction. A popular writer called Jules Renard described her voice in 1906 in terms surprisingly close to Adorno's. To watch Sarah, he said, was to experience not acting but something "more like the rustle of trees or an instrument's monotone noise." It was "perfect," he said, and at the same time "you hardly noticed it."[3] Freud was perhaps less eloquent but no less enchanted. Seeing Bernhardt perform for the first time as a young medical student in Paris, he reports a similarly powerful experience. The play he attended, an orientalist trifle by Sardou, may have bored him, but Bernhardt didn't. He wrote to his fiancée: "After the first words of her lovely, vibrant voice I felt I had known her for years. Nothing she could have said would have surprised me; I believed at once everything she said."[4] Together the two reactions are telling. Like Renard, Freud "hardly noticed" Bernhardt's acting, for in listening to her voice he felt something strangely familiar, like an uncanny effect of sincerity: he believed at once everything she said.

It is this effect of sincerity, and its peculiar French history in the era of Bernhardt, Renard, and Freud, that forms the subject of my essay. My starting points are a sound—an iconic voice of the French theater—and a question raised by that sound: what made it seem sincere? As a musicologist, though, I want to go further. I intend to follow Sarah Bernhardt's murmuring cadence beyond the theater, to consider a new kind of song that emerged on the French musical landscape during the same era—the long half-century known as the Third Republic. By staying with Bernhardt's remarkable recording of Coppée, and listening closely, as her contemporaries did, we should be in a position to appreciate the effect of that sound on a whole range of French performances in the years around 1900. As we shall see, the quality that Renard admired in Bernhardt's declamations would play an equally important role in shaping a modern concept of melody, which French musicians greeted much as Freud did: as a more believable, more sincere vocal art. Indeed, the surprising candor of this new song seemed to demand a different sort of name. The French chose a foreign word, and called it, simply, *le lied*.

Feeling What You Say

But let us return, for the moment, to the poem that started us down this path, Coppée's "Evangile." For Bernhardt was not the only one to have intoned those unlikely lines: there were others, too, who managed to record them for posterity. Take, for example, the actor Léon Brémont. Hardly known today, he was a popular figure in the Parisian theater of the 1890s, becoming even more visible after the unexpected triumph he enjoyed in the title role of a play about Jesus Christ. That success, oddly enough, brought him to the attention of Bernhardt, who hired him to play the role again, in 1897, in her own production of Rostand's hit *The Good Samaritan* (*La samaritaine*). The run turned out to be his crowning glory. Still, Brémont's lasting contribution to French acting came only later, in the many pedagogical studies he wrote after his retirement. The book I want to consider now was his most widely read: a little self-help manual he published in 1903 called *The Art of Saying Verse* (*L'art de dire les vers*).

Interestingly, there was a market for this kind of book. Declaiming verse before an audience was a hugely popular pastime in turn-of-the-century Paris, an entertainment of choice for both private salons and larger public theaters. Brémont was reaching out to younger actors, offering trade secrets and warning against common mistakes. The most basic error? For Brémont, it was the failure to distinguish between drama and lyric. What he called the *manie d'extérioriser*—the tendency to act everything out—had caused many an actor to ruin a poem in performance. And so he advised his readers to tone it down, using a telling musical analogy. Just as a great singer learned to "speak the song" (*parler le chant*), he said, a good actor had to know how to "sing poetry" (*chanter les vers*) (Brémont 1903, 39). In both cases the goal, it seems, was to neutralize performance in order to let words speak for themselves.

Brémont demonstrated the point by turning to Coppée's "Evangile." He chose an unusual method, too, sketching out two potential readings in musical notation—one bad, one good—to show actors more clearly what they should and should not do (Figure 2.1). A quick glance makes the differences obvious. In the first (a), the vocal line literally acts out the line, emphasizing the importance of every word with dramatic shifts of tone and register. The effect is, to my ear, a bit like a schoolteacher telling a children's story—an exaggerated sing-song. In any case, for Brémont, it was all wrong, because it brought out the wrong genre: an excessively melodious delivery, he said, suggested the anecdotal and the familiar. The proper way to read poetry was shown in the second notation (b). There, the expression was reduced to a single monotone. This kind of delivery, of course, had all the solemnity of a chant, suggesting the hieratic and the exalted. It was "truer" to poetry not (or not merely) because it was lofty, but because it drew attention to the purely sonic character of the words— to form, rather than content. Through this sort of intonation, Brémont said, the words preserved "their simplicity, their sweetness, their tranquility, their mystery—in short, their *poetry*."

Here, then, was a representation of poetry's truer voice, written as a kind of music. And yet, it has to be said: the resulting melody (b) looked and sounded surprisingly *un*musical, as if the notation were depicting that empty sound Mallarmé had once imagined from the flute of his dejected Faune: *une sonore, vaine et monotone ligne*, Mallarmé called it (a sonorous, meaningless, monotone line). The unmelodic string of A-naturals in the second example was both sonorous and pointless, like a neutral air with nothing to say. And that, of course, *was* the point. Only this kind

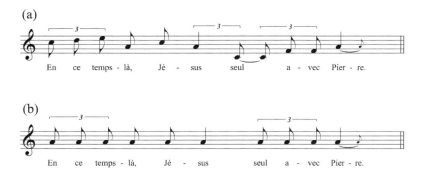

FIGURE 2.1. Coppée, "Un Evangile," declamation of opening line as demonstrated by Léon Brémont, *L'art de dire les vers* (1903) .

NOTE   (a) not recommended; (b) recommended

of delivery gave words the freedom to make their own sort of noise, like the natural rustling that Renard thought he could hear in Bernhardt's speaking voice. This sound was "perfect" precisely because it was neutral, occurring only when a volume of air passed through. The neutral monotone thus became the basis for a new kind of expression and, more importantly, a new sincerity effect. The poem ultimately became more sincere as the goal of declamation itself shifted from the expressive to the merely expressed. The truest reading was less about sentiment than sensation; less about saying what you felt than somehow feeling what you said— experiencing, through a neutral air, the physical reality of words, like a tree might feel a breeze in its branches.

Of course, it was something like this effect that I myself experienced at the Bibliothèque National as I listened for the first time to Bernhardt's recorded performance of Coppée. Indeed, Brémont's notation (b) matches Bernhardt's historic reading so closely that one can easily imagine him listening to the same record. And he might have. "Un Evangile" was one of several declamations Bernhardt recorded for French gramophone in 1903— the very year Brémont brought out his *L'art de dire les vers*. Figure 2.2 presents Coppée's opening lines as I heard them on that recording, and, while the resemblance is close enough to suggest a connection, it is impossible to know whether Brémont actually used the record as a guide. Still, we know of at least one other listener from the period who did use the record in this way, someone who transcribed Bernhardt's reading, line by line, in an effort to teach a lesson about proper French performance. The listener I am referring to was a French teacher called Marguerite de Saint-Genès, and I want to look now at her transcription, for it affords us another, more pointed view of what a sincere poetic performance might look like.

The French lesson I'm talking about appeared in an unusual place: tucked within the folds of a new magazine called the *Revue de phonétique*. This was a publication dedicated to the relatively recent science of experimental phonetics, and it featured lavishly illustrated essays, pitched to a specialist reader, covering every imaginable aspect of speech production. To reach a more general audience, it also boasted a neat educational insert—something the editors called the "Gramophone Course" (*Cours de gramophonie*). Once a month Saint-Genès would transcribe a recording by a famous actor into phonetic notation, offering it as a lesson in the finer points of French diction. Readers could learn to perfect their French

FIGURE 2.2. Musical transcription of "Un Evangile" by François Coppée, recited by Sarah Bernhardt (French Gramophone recording, 1903).

at home, simply by listening to records. Who did Saint-Genès choose for the magazine's inaugural issue? It was Sarah Bernhardt, of course, reading Coppée's "Un Evangile" (Figure 2.3).

The vocal transcription represented something like the "B-side" of Brémont's music notation. Where his efforts devolved on pitch, the relative rise and fall of the voice, Saint-Genès fussed over timbre, the nuances of spoken French, specifying them through a precise, alternative orthography. The phonetic notation was in one sense egalitarian, designed to make the sounds visible—and accessible—to the widest possible readership.[5] Indeed,

I

ǟn évājílœ

dœ Frāswá Koppé,

di par madam Sára Bernàr.   [5″]

lent

ā sœ tā la, Jézu, sœl avek pyèrœ, èrè,
súr la rív du lakœ; prè dœ jenézaretœ;
a l'èr u lœ brúlā solèy dœ mídi planœ;
kăt il vír dœvāt [é] unœ póvrœ kabanœ;
5 *la vœvœ d æ péèèr, ā lõ vwàlœ dœ dœyœ;*
ki s etè tristœmāt asízœ súr lœ sœyœ;
rœtœnā dā sèz yé, la larmœ ki lè muyœ;
pur bersé sõn āfā, e filé sa kœnuyœ.
nõ lwœ d el; kaɛé par dè figyé tufú,
10 *lœ mètr e sõn ami, vwayè sāz ètrœ vú.*   [48″]

sudē, æ dœ sè vyé, dõ lœ tõbó s aprètœ,
æ mādyā, portàt æ vázœ súr sa tètœ;
vēt a pásé, é dit a sèl ki filè :   [19″]

plus lent

famœ, jœ dwa porté sœ vázœ plē dœ lè;
15 *céz ǟn omœ, lojé dā lœ proɛē vilàjœ.*
mè tu lœ vwa; jœ süí fèbl e brízé par l ájœ.
lè mèzõ sõt ākòr a plú dœ mil pá;
é jœ sā byē kœ, sèlœ, jœ n akõplíre pá
sœ travay, kœ l õ dwa mœ beyér un obòlœ.   [22″]

lent

20 *la fam sœ lva sā dír unœ parolœ,*
lèsa sāz ézité, sa kœnuyœ dœ lē
e lœ bersó d ózyé u plœrè l orfœlē;
pri lœ vázœ; e s ā fut avek lœ mízerablœ.

FIGURE 2.3. "Un Evangile" by François Coppée, recording by Madame Sarah Bernhardt, as transcribed by Marguerite de Saint-Genès, *Cours de gramophonie*, in first issue of *Revue de phonétique* (1911).

with its use of the gramophone, and its emphasis on aural learning, Saint-Genès's teaching proved consistent with an entire philosophy of state language education in this period and the democratic ideals that came along with it. And yet the alternative writing was also strange—far stranger, at any rate, than Brémont's notation. In his example, musical symbols floated above conventional writing; in hers, phonetics took over, replacing familiar French with something impossible to read in the normal way. The only way to comprehend this gospel, in fact, was to sound it out. The notation thus promoted not only good diction, but what one might call a perverse kind of sincerity effect. Unable to recognize the words without uttering them aloud, the reader was forced to make her way through the text not so much by thinking as by feeling the words—this time quite literally—one phoneme at a time.

This exercise, moreover, offers even more direct evidence of what it might have meant to *chanter les vers* circa 1900. For the sensation of producing the nuances of speech, one sound at a time, is more or less what every singer feels when performing a song. And, indeed, we are not so far away from song at this point—at least, not from the kind of song the French seemed to have on their minds during this era. It may be a good time, then, to turn to music, to see what the not-quite-musical verses we have just witnessed might have to do with the new, more sincere art the French called *le lied*.

But I want to make the transition in two stages: first, by performing a little song experiment, based on Bernardt's reading of "Un Evangile"; and then, by looking at another song—a real one, this time—composed not long after Bernhardt had made her recording for French Gramophone in 1903. Taken together the two examples (one fictional, one real) should help to expose the values governing French expression at the beginning of the twentieth century, and allow us, in turn, to consider their larger cultural resonance.

Underscoring the Voice

The experiment I devised actually involves one final transcription of Bernhardt's voice, but with an extra element: a piano accompaniment. I wanted to see what might happen to Bernhardt's trademark monotone if it were experienced as part of an actual song (Figure 2.4). This is easier to

FIGURE 2.4. Musical transcription of "Un Evangile" by François Coppée, recited by Sarah Bernhardt (French Gramophone recording, 1903), with piano accompaniment by Katherine Bergeron.

hear in live performance, of course, but a glimpse at a piano-vocal score can nonetheless offer a clue. One can see by looking back to Figure 2.2, for example, that I have essentially changed nothing about Bernhardt's delivery; I have written the line exactly as I heard it on the 1903 recording. I just invented a piano part as a plausible accompaniment. On the page this makes the Coppée appear automatically more songlike. When performed, though, the effect is quite marvelous. With its naturally resonant chords the piano not only reinforces the harmony of the syllables; it also seems to give the pointless line a point. Heard with an accompaniment, in other words, the droning delivery begins to sound—unaccountably— much more like a "real" melody, as if Bernhardt had indeed meant to sing rather than speak those lines. And yet, even as it turns up the musical volume on the voice, the added piano manages to do something else: it also tones *down* whatever might have seemed strident, or even alien, about Bernhardt's originally high-pitched monotone. Through an odd sort of supplemental logic, the added music actually reduces the exteriority of the voice. By underscoring the monotone line, it offers a sense of direction that diminishes the perception of Bernhardt's reading as a "performance." The words, in effect, sound more natural, the rhythm clearer, the pitch somehow more true.

The experiment certainly suggests something about the close kinship between poetry and song during Bernhardt's era, when an actor's preference for "singing verse" came strangely close to a singer's tendency to "speak song," as Brémont put it. But it is not the formal resemblance that I mean to emphasize; it is the effect, a kind of "sincerity effect," as I have been calling it: the sense that uttering words in this way could somehow recover an essential honesty.

Why this sense should have prevailed in Bernhardt's time is a question I will leave for the end of this essay. For now, it is worth remaining with the question of song itself, for, as it happens, French critics of the period could be heard using the same terms when they struggled to explain the power of the new lyric art they called *le lied*. Henri Fellot, writing in 1904, praised it as "a more sincere, less showy art," a music that was both "more profound and more true because it dealt with intimate and eternally human things" (1904, 267). Georges Jean-Aubry, in an essay from 1916, went further, developing an elaborate analogy quite pertinent in the context. "Words," he began, "are tricky and untrustworthy things: certain men are capable of giving them a thousand different meanings. Since they are soft and resistant material; they can be stretched and molded at will; they're what you want when *you don't feel what you mean*" (1916, 237–38; emphasis added).

But music, he went on, that was different. Music was, in his memorable expression, "necessarily and fatally sincere." Why? As the one art that dealt most directly with emotion and sensation, music simply embodied feeling; its "essence," Jean-Aubry said, "was sincerity." By setting words to music, the *lied* as a genre was thus poised to recover the essential sincerity of verse. And yet not just any music would do. The French *lied* reflected an "uneasy modern sensibility," Jean-Aubry explained, with its "evasive and almost nonchalant" expression. That his musical ideal had something in common with my own very simple song experiment was suggested by a concluding comment. "It sometimes seems," he said, "that the composer has done nothing more than *underscore* the inflections of the poem, by following its subtle and floating contour" (1916, 240; emphasis added).

The composer who he claimed had brought this fatally sincere music to the French language was Gabriel Fauré. And for the last part of this essay, I want to turn my attention to him, both as a foil for Bernhardt and as a final example of what this kind of expression could mean. The *lied* I have chosen comes from a group of ten that Fauré began writing in 1906. He drew on poems by the Belgian symbolist Charles Van Lerberghe, and so Fauré called his collection, as Van Lerberghe called his book, *La chanson d'Eve* (Eve's Song). As we shall see, *La chanson d'Eve* offers a vivid example of the "uneasy modern sensibility" surrounding the French *lied*, through an allegory of origins that reveals, among other things, its deeper aspiration to sincerity.

To Sing Without Thinking

The desire is clearest in the final song, and so that is where I will focus; but an overview should help us get our bearings. The ten songs of the cycle together retell the story of Creation, though with a crucial twist. This time there is no Adam, no forbidden fruit, no other sin but speech. In the beginning God created only woman: Eve awakens in a dream of Paradise and, before she knows it, sings. Or, better yet, she experiences the dream resounding through her. "How it sings in my voice," she announces near the beginning, "this long murmuring soul of forest and spring!" Here, in effect, was the original *Rauschen*, the rustle of language, and her exclamation is both announcement and question. For Eve does *not* know how it happens. She "sings like a child," as one commentator put it; "sings without thinking" (Mockel 1904, 24).[6] Without thinking, that is, of what she wants to say. She simply utters her feeling and feels her utterance, wondering at all the new sensations—the sounds in her head, the breath on her lips. And, in this unintentionally resonant moment, the word (and the world) felt very good indeed.

This was, of course, a marvelous premise for a song cycle but, as Fauré tells it, the good feeling does not last long. You can imagine how it goes from here: Eve soon begins to think, to question, to bend her words (as Jean-Aubry might say) according to her will. But none of this will satisfy. She ends up asking more and more; her thought goes feverish, then benumbed. Predictably, as she sees her dream recede, the tale is nearly over. In the dark night of the ninth song, Eve is alone, desperate now for the lost murmur of Paradise ("I listen til it hurts," she cries). And, in the tenth, she finds what she is looking for, although essentially at her peril. For death alone will enable its return: she gets her wish by giving up her voice.

There is much to say about how Fauré's music deals with this symbolic narrative. There is much to say, as well, about the final song, which Fauré called by its opening words, "O Mort, poussière d'étoiles" (O Death, like stardust). I will point out just one feature—the most salient one, I think—that serves to convey, in musical terms, the truth of Eve's redemption. The evidence is right there on the surface of the score (Figure 2.5). The melody Fauré has written for the beginning of this song looks uncannily like something we have seen before: the not-quite-singing voice of Sarah Bernhardt. And yet, as I have said, it is not so much the formal resemblance that matters as what this singing stands for. In terms of the poem's symbolism, the flattening of melody into monotone represents the fulfillment of Eve's desire to return to an original state when language rustled through her without her knowing. But that desire—to make a song that would sing without thinking, a song that, as Renard might say, you "hardly noticed"—also informed the art of the modern French *lied*. Fauré is demonstrating, in song, the very conditions of this new art he had mastered, an art whose expression would be

FIGURE 2.5. "O Mort, poussière d'étoiles," final song of *La chanson d'Eve*, op. 95 (1906–1910); poetry by Charles van Lerberghe, music by Gabriel Fauré (beginning).

experienced as a nonexpression, as an instance of language itself speaking (to recall Adorno's apt phrase). And to that extent, we could think of *La chanson d'Eve* as his own little treatise on the *Art of Saying Verse*, a kind of extended musical lesson on how to speak, and act, sincerely.

Republican Sincerity

This lesson reaches out, though, to a broader point. The voices examined in this essay, from Bernhardt to Fauré, have revealed what I have called a distinct sincerity effect in French performance (and in the performance of French) in the years around 1900. And yet, while the recorded evidence offers a sense of what such an effect might have meant for performance, it does not quite explain why it mattered. It does not explain, that is, how the idea of sincerity had become such a virtue in itself in French music and theater, nor why at this moment in history. By way of conclusion I want to shift my focus, then, to speculate about this larger question.

And here it may be useful to return one last time to Jules Renard. In his remarks about Bernhardt cited at the beginning of this essay, there is an image, mentioned already a few times now, that deserves still more glossing. It is his description of Bernhardt's voice as something like "the rustle of the trees." In suggestively dispatching Bernhardt's voice to the countryside, Renard was doing more, I think, than making a pretty pastoral image. He was also making a kind of political statement, linking her art to a very different audience and a different kind of truth. This was, at any rate, familiar territory for a committed socialist like Renard, who by 1907 had become mayor of his provincial hometown and friend to two important republican leaders, Jean Jaurès and Léon Blum. In 1889 he had even helped found the *Mercure de France* as a venue for young writers who shared his political sensibilities. Like the so-called *plein air* painters of the previous decade, these were artists who self-consciously imagined their work not only in the space of the countryside but, as Philip Nord has argued, in the "language of republicanism" (1995, 187). To make their own art more democratic they wanted to become, above all, more honest.

This kind of talk was common in the early days of France's Third Republic. But what the historical context may help us to see is how such rhetoric served to shape a modern French concept of sincerity. A catalog for a one-man show by Manet put it best: "Come and see sincere work," it said, announcing both the painter's unorthodox manner and his democratic stance in the same breath. De Tocqueville had anticipated this rhetoric already in the 1830s when describing the influence of democracy on etiquette: democratic manners, he said, were "neither so tutored nor so uniform" as aristocratic ones, but they were often "more sincere." Some three decades later Ernest Legouvé would make the point more forcefully in his own study of modern French mores, defining sincerity not merely as the result, but as the duty, of democracy: "If the charm of the ancien régime was to be polite," he claimed, "the duty of democracy is to be sincere" (Legouvé 1878; cited in Nord 1995, 230).

As Nord has pointed out, the young impressionists took this duty to heart, representing a new kind of democratic subject by painting men in casual poses—with their feet drawn up—to show "the unmannered freeness of the milieu in which they lived" (1995, 230–231). But the writers of Renard's generation showed just as much diligence when they worried over the potential hypocrisy of their own work, and of the whole field they disparagingly called "literature." If Jean-Aubry considered words "untrustworthy things," he was not alone. Renard himself confessed it again and again in the pages of his journal. His greatest concern was "to seek true impressions, and to express, in precise language, feelings that have the taste of truth" (Renard 1960, 759–760).

Which brings us back to Sarah Bernhardt and, in a roundabout way, to Fauré. For it must have been this sense of sincerity, an impression of precise or truthful language, that Renard was talking about when he tried to describe the experience of her voice in his journal in 1906. It may be hard for us, in the twenty-first century, to hear the strange cadence of Bernhardt's declamations, or of Fauré's monotone, as something particularly honest or true. And yet if we do not try to hear them in this way we will miss a good deal of the point. Bernhardt, after all, once summarized the labor of the actor's art as nothing more than a "quest for truth" (1969, 78). And if Fauré made no such claims for himself, his music did, as we have seen. As a song cycle whose deliberately nonchalant melodies sought to instruct about the truest performance of the spoken word, *La chanson d'Eve*, in fact, tells us quite a lot. By rejecting all exaggeration, by attempting to return French utterance to a more primary state of feeling, of unpretentious oral sensation, the music performed a function not unlike the phonetic transcriptions of Marguerite de Saint-Genès: it encouraged a very distinctive "taste for truth," and a literal sort of verbal honesty. And, in an era when the French republic was putting massive resources into national literacy; and in an era, indeed, when Sarah Bernhardt herself would be awarded the Medal of the Legion of Honor for her work in spreading the French language across the world; this story of linguistic pleasure and desire—a story about tasting the purity of the mother tongue as it passed through unsuspecting lips—becomes far more resonant than we could ever have suspected.

3

The Irreconcilability of Hypocrisy and Sincerity

Frans-Willem Korsten

Appropriateness and Hypocrisy

All plays by Holland's most famous seventeenth-century poet and playwright, Joost van den Vondel, explore aspects of sovereignty—a fact that is perhaps to be understood in the light of the exceptional organization of the Dutch Republic. At the time, people tended to speak of this Republic as the (Seven) United Provinces: a term that was, and still is, more adequate. Of the provinces in the Low Countries that had risen against their rightful king, seven had decided to say farewell to that king, Philip II of Spain, and to stick together as a kind of confederation. The unity of that confederation was expressed by an abstract notion: the so-called Generaliteit. Each of the provinces remained sovereign, though. Its individual sovereignty was embodied by a council of representatives, the so-called States. These, in turn, chose representatives to the States-General. This was not a sovereign body at all, although by and large it did embody the Generaliteit. As such it even had some kind of sovereignty, especially with regard to foreign affairs. Yet, here, sovereignty could only exist on the basis of unanimity. Furthermore, the most powerful figure in the States-General, especially in the beginning, was the secretary of only one of the States, namely the province of Holland. Finally, there was the figure of the Stadholder, who was in charge of military affairs and who was supposed to safeguard internal order. Formerly, he had been the representative of the king; now he was appointed by the separate individual states. As one sees, in terms of sovereignty this is an exceptional situation indeed, especially because of the intricate web of different forms of representation.[1]

In the context of the history of the uprising and of the organization of the Dutch Republic, it will not come as a surprise that one important aspect of Vondel's explorations concerns the way in which the sovereign's responsibility could be tested or questioned. Another aspect concerns the way in which the sovereign was able to commit himself to his people in order to take care of them. Hypocrisy plays an important role in relation to the first aspect. Sincerity plays an important role in relation to the second. Hence, sincerity is not simply the opposite of hypocrisy. Instead, they each stand in a different relationship to sovereignty. This differentiation has important consequences for political theory and conceptions of democracy. In what follows I will consider hypocrisy and sincerity in their respective relationships to sovereignty on the basis of four plays by Vondel: *Lucifer, Salmoneus,* and *Faëton* on the one hand, and *Gysbreght van Aemstel* on the other. But let me emphasize first that my way of dealing with hypocrisy deviates from customary conceptualizations.

In general, hypocrisy is seen as an understandable yet corrupting factor in any organization or society—corrupting since it lacks the basic "appropriateness" or integrity that is needed for a system that works by, and adheres to, principles of justice.[2] One of the more important considerations of hypocrisy in the political realm, by Hannah Arendt in *On Revolution*, proves the point. Arendt asks herself why the concern with hypocrisy became an obsession for the leaders of the French revolution. At first, that obsession may seem a bit strange, so she states, because hypocrisy, in politics, is surely "one of the minor vices" (Arendt 1990, 100). Arendt immediately complicates this contention, however, when she adds that hypocrisy can also be considered as the vice of all vices, in the sense that it tries to prevent other vices from appearing as they are. Things become even more complicated when Arendt then relates hypocrisy to one of the oldest metaphysical problems, that of the distinction between being and appearance (Arendt 1990, 101), and more complicated still when she finally considers how politics is fundamentally threatened by such a thing as the "hidden crime": the crime that is not seen, let alone judged, by others. The principal requirement of politics, so Arendt states, is that any political act must be open to judgment, hence to witnessing. It is in this context that she considers the hypocrite to be a fundamental problem: "As witnesses not of our intentions but of our conduct, we can be true or false, and the hypocrite's crime is that he bears false witness against himself. What makes it so plausible to assume that hypocrisy is the vice of vices is that integrity can indeed exist under the cover of all other vices, except this one. . . . [o]nly the hypocrite is rotten to the core" (Arendt 1990, 103).

So, apparently, as long as there is some kind of centre or body that can be uncovered, hence judged as either true or false, or as long as there is a locus of integrity or deceit, politics is possible. But politics is fundamentally threatened when the core becomes entirely rotten.

A little later the metaphor of the "cover" is taken up again when Arendt goes back to the etymological root of the Greek word *hupokrités*, meaning the person of the play-actor. This actor becomes a *persona* as the bearer of a mask, or as a theatrical figure. That figure shifts into a juridical category in ancient Rome, when the *persona* becomes a "legal personality" (Arendt 1990, 107). In relation to Arendt's argument the point of this distinction lies "in that the unmasking of the 'person,' the deprivation of legal personality, would leave behind the 'natural' human being, while the unmasking of the hypocrite would leave nothing behind the mask, because the hypocrite is the actor himself in so far as he wears no mask" (1990, 107). Consequently, when the program of the French Revolution became to "tear off the mask" of hypocrisy, this was rendered difficult, or even impossible. It had to lead to the Reign of Terror, because it could not achieve its goal since the hypocrite does not really have a mask. He is an actor, the actor himself, who "pretends to be the assumed role, and when he enters the game of society is without any play-acting whatsoever." Here he becomes an odious figure because he claims not only "sincerity but naturalness" (Arendt 1990, 107).

Now, I have no argument with the contention that hypocrisy is, or can be, a societal danger, or that hypocrisy may threaten the very heart of politics. However, to consider hypocrisy as a kind of corruption or rottenness only is to overlook a distinct dynamics and a potentially positive force in hypocrisy. This positive force can be sensed when we consider how

Arendt's principal point is that the hypocrite cannot be unmasked. As a consequence, hypocrisy causes a fundamental sense of unease and propels a search for truth or integrity. Even if that search will never find its goal, it can be considered valuable, or necessary, in itself. In this respect hypocrisy may still be a threatening force, but perhaps it can also be a positive and driving force. Let me consider Vondel's plays in more detail in order to see how hypocrisy can indeed concern a positive dynamic and how it is not a fundamental kind of derailment of politics proper, but a functional and structurally built-in feature of any political system of representation. After that I will turn to sincerity.

The Representational Necessity of Hypocrisy and the Test of Responsibility

As we've seen, the Greek *hupokrités* came to mean "actor." It was derived, however, from *hupokrinomai*: "to answer" or "to formulate one's own standpoint." The reason that *hupokrités* came to mean actor, as in Latin *hypocrita*, is that in classical Greece the one speaker who told a story changed into two speakers who started a dialogue in order to tell something. Here lies the root of theatre. The shift in meaning from actor to dissembler and then to the modern hypocrite takes place mostly in the late Middle Ages. Now, whether we take the classical Greek meaning or the medieval one, for my argument it is important to see that both etymological roots of hypocrisy are relevant. The hypocrite is someone who has to answer, and answer to, another speaker as well as one who can put on a mask, or dissemble.[3]

Vondel's *Salmoneus* (1657) is named after its protagonist, the king of Elis. Salmoneus has decided that he must be a god. In the midst of specially organized festivities he will appear as Jupiter, and after this theatrical inauguration, his statue must be worshipped in the temple. Although the play is named after its protagonist, Bazilides is equally important as the captain of the king's guard. He wants to be loyal to the king as well as to the king's enemies, the priests. That does not make him a hypocrite. He becomes one when, in order to defeat the over-ambitious king, the archpriest explicitly asks Bazilides to play the hypocrite. This peculiar feature was so hard to swallow for most scholars that they decided to define Bazilides as a traitor.[4]

But that's not what he is. He is a dissembler. And the fact that Bazilides is asked to act like a hypocrite is meaningful on a different level. At the end of the play he saves the regalia and puts on the king's clothes. That is to say: he is not king, he only *acts* like one. But, tellingly, Bazilides can only legitimately restore order on the basis of a specific kind of representation. He is sanctioned by the archpriest as the representative of a supreme god.

In *Salmoneus*, then, hypocrisy does not threaten the social order. On the contrary, anarchy is prevented and social order is maintained as "good enough." There is also a connection between hypocrisy and a system of political representation. This connection may seem accidental, but it is of primary significance. In *Aesthetic Politics: Political Philosophy Beyond Fact and Value*, Frank Ankersmit, inspired by Machiavelli's idea of a "brokenness" in politics, argues: "We have to reject mimetic political representation not so much because it shows certain theoretical shortcomings, but . . . simply because it is not a theory of political representation at all. We can only talk about representation when there is difference—and *not* an identity—between the representative and the person represented" (Ankersmit 1996, 46).

True, when a representative is identical to the party represented, there is no need for representation at all. The representative differs—may differ substantially—from the ones represented. With respect to this difference I would like to widen the gap Ankersmit points out. There is a hierarchical jump that is brought about when the represented concede power to someone who may represent and rule them. Or, there is an ontological jump that occurs when the authority to represent is displaced from divine object to human subject.

Yet in emphasizing the split I do not want to downplay the element of similarity or identity that also remains present in the form of conformity. For besides distinction and difference, representation equally presupposes some conformity between represented and representative. Political representation is based, then, on the concurrence of both a gap and a conformity between represented and representative. My contention is that it is this concurrence that produces a built-in and functional hypocrisy within a political representational system. Any ruler will always have to present two faces. With the one he tells his subjects: "I am like you, and I am with you." With the other he says: "I am not like you, and potentially I am not with you."

If my argument is valid, this must imply that when hypocrisy is absent in a political system of representation, the system must be in trouble. This is indeed the case in Vondel's *Lucifer* from 1654. In this play angels revolt against a God who had first said the angels were his highest subjects and who has now chosen human beings as their future sovereigns. It is immediately apparent that heaven is not ideal here. Some scholars have even declared that this play is a failure as a Christian drama since it depicts heaven as a state.[5] In that state the angels emphatically claim to have legitimate rights. But almost immediately it becomes clear what kind of a political state this is, when the choir simply answers: "What right? Who ordains the law, may also break it" (line 922).

In order to avoid such a situation of political omnipotence, most thinkers on sovereignty have postulated a difference between the actual sovereign and the source of sovereignty. Even Jean Bodin, in his *Les six livres de la république* (1576), stated that the sovereign is sovereign under— and apart from—God. In the centuries that followed, thinkers such as Rousseau, Sieyès, and Guizot posited a split between the higher order, so-called sovereign by right, and the lower order, sovereign in practice. If the two kinds of sovereignty are conflated, the result is totalitarianism: a system that claims unquestionable legitimacy or else must lose all legitimacy.[6]

In such a system hypocrisy need not be simply absent, it may also become hyperbolic. It will then lead to a state of hyper-hypocrisy. In Vondel's play, God's incomprehensibility shows itself in discrepancies between statements or acts that cannot be brought back to a single source of meaning. Thus, God is either principally nonhypocritical or hyper-hypocritical. He cannot be hypocritical because to be a hypocrite is to act contrary to the authority of the law. Vondel's God *is* the authority of the law and cannot act contrary to himself. Still, there must be an innate discrepancy between the authority of the law and God in order for God to be able to act in violation of his own authority. This is why Vondel's God can be seen as hyper-hypocritical.

In the play this leads to subjects who keep on posing questions— relentlessly, restlessly, endlessly, desperately. No adequate answer is possible. Consequently, a considerable group of angels starts a civil war. In this way *Lucifer* tells us that when it is impossible for functional, political hypocrisy to exist, or when such hypocrisy has turned hyperbolic, the result is the collapse of order and social harmony. The ruler has become out of reach and out of touch: he cannot be questioned and tested in terms of *responsibility*.

Both the sustainability of a functioning order and the test of responsibility are central themes in another play by Vondel: *Faëton* (1663). The story is perhaps familiar. Phaiton is ridiculed by a bastard son of Jupiter for not knowing his father. So Phaiton asks his mother, who takes him to Phoebus Apollo. This divine father is so pleased to see his son that he promises to give him anything he might want to ask. His son asks to be allowed to ride the sun chariot for one day. Phoebus senses disaster but keeps his promise. Phaiton, on his way, almost instantly loses control and the earth catches fire as a result. The council of heaven comes together for emergency talks. These take a while—Jupiter especially hesitates and takes his time. At the very end, however, Jupiter decides to act: he mounts his eagle and kills the innocent young man, only barely saving humankind.

In the play, the sovereign Jupiter operates on two different political planes. On a strictly divine plane Jupiter is sovereign *in practice*. He rules the gods as chair of the divine council. Yet the council of the gods functions as the *source* of sovereignty—a source other than the sovereign-in-practice. In other words, there is a political system of representation in operation. Accordingly, it is no surprise that Jupiter acts hypocritically. After all he must satisfy or discipline subjects with conflicting interests. And indeed, in the second, third, and fourth acts we see the two faces of Jupiter at work in political maneuvers.

But the fact that we see this has huge implications for the second political plane. Jupiter is also the *source* of sovereignty with regard to the earthly, human order. As a hidden or absent supreme sovereign, Jupiter is a figure that human subjects simply have to obey, comprehend, and accept. Here Jupiter must function as the unquestionable fundament for the system of justice and power. This implies, however, that the trick of this play is to bring to light what should have remained hidden or absent, namely the divine source behind earthly political sovereignty. Once Jupiter has been brought into the light, he is no longer the unquestionable sovereign. He can now be questioned. One question, for instance, is why Jupiter waits until the very end—with the sun already setting—before killing Phaiton.

The question seeks a particular response, but it is really looking for responsibility. This becomes explicit at the end of the play. The choir urges Phaiton to speed up in order to reach the western hemisphere in time. But it is already too late. The eagle rushes forward and Jupiter kills Phaiton. This is then followed by a remarkable comment in the chorus's second antistrophe:

> A God who rules all should punish himself first
> [Een Godt, die 't al beheerst, / Bestraff'zich zelven eerst]

(Faëton, lines 1319–1320)

The text, here, directly addresses the question of divine responsibility. The answer that is suggested—God is responsible for everything that goes wrong and therefore should punish himself first—would have raised more than eyebrows, which is probably why Vondel addressed the issue allegorically. Nevertheless, the question stands, provoked by Jupiter's hypocrisy.[7]

Jupiter's hesitation to act points us toward the dynamics of conformity and separation. Jupiter has a bond with humankind, but at the same time he differs essentially from it. This is the structural source of hypocrisy, which in practice consists in the fact that Jupiter almost lets humankind perish, while saving what's left of it just in time to say that he saved it. The representational dynamics of conformity and split provokes a type of hypocrisy, then, that has a dual function. First, because of its possibility of dissemblance, hypocrisy is flexible and enables the sustainability of a social order—in this case the order in the socio-political world of the gods. Second, hypocrisy enables the establishment of a rule: the rule of questioning. That is to say, by revealing a discrepancy between the interests of the ruler and the ruled, hypocrisy creates an opening to question the ruler and, more importantly, to question his legitimacy to rule. On the basis of the rule of questioning, ruling powers can be tested and interrogated. In other words, they can be made *responsible*—to answer, answer for, and answer to. This is the second etymological sense of hypocrisy.

Such a process of questioning is potentially endless. In this regard, it is possible to compare the system of political representation to what Gilles Deleuze and Félix Guattari (1996, 112) call "the signifying regime of the sign," a regime that may well relate to Arendt's analysis of hypocrisy. A sign is a sign per se. It is hard to think of a sign as a mask, as if behind it we would get to the Real. Arendt's analysis of the hypocrite was that he utterly confounds the very distinction between mask and real, as a result of which he cannot be unmasked, and a search is propelled. Analogously, in a sign regime, signs keep referring to each other in an endless chain.

That leaves the question, of course, where such a system will find its meaning. Ultimately, so Deleuze and Guattari state, the endless chain refers to "a supreme signifier," which they metaphorically indicate as "faciality" and then specify as the face of some kind of despot. Arendt, in *The Human Condition*, would probably define it as "rule" in the sense of *Herrschaft*.[8]

The looking, threatening, and surveying face of a ruler, a despot, or of some Big Brother may provoke paranoia in the minds of subjects. With respect to paranoia and with regard to the inherent gap discussed above, the system of political representation necessarily contains an element of deception, but one that, I want to argue, provokes a positive kind of paranoia. Positive paranoia is adequate shorthand for the permanent vigilance that is required to constantly test and scrutinize representatives with respect to the nature of their responsibility.

This is where the concept of sincerity comes in. This positive paranoia does not mean that one should always mistrust representatives. The systematic necessity for hypocrisy in representational systems does not imply that representatives must be insincere. However, they cannot be both hypocritical and sincere at the same time. The reason is that hypocrisy and sincerity are not opposites; they relate differently to the idea of responsibility. Responsibility implies a demand. It requires that an account be given. Giving an account always takes place after the act and the fact.[9] The idea is to test rulers for what they have done, not for what they are doing at this very moment or for what they will be doing. It is, of course, possible to test current responsibilities of rulers from the viewpoint of the future, but this is a hypothetical situation in which, again, one is looking back. When rulers are considered in terms of here-ness and with regard to the effects their actions will have in the future, another rule is at stake, namely the rule of trust. This rule is based on sincerity. I turn to that concept now by way of yet another play by Vondel, his most famous one.

Sincerity and Trustworthiness in Relation to the Future

One could argue that a sound political system works only on the basis of some kind of an agreement, which ultimately implies trust—a trust that must be based on the sincerity of the parties concerned. But the fact that such political systems exist does not mean that sincerity is structurally built into such systems. Accordingly, it is hard to speak of structural or systematic sincerity, whereas one can speak of structural or systematic hypocrisy. Furthermore, unlike the affective neutrality of hypocrisy, sincerity cannot be considered apart from an internal, inherent passion or affective charge. Passion is considered here as both "a mode of thinking and a state of the body," as Susan James formulated it in her study of seventeenth-century philosophy (1997, 259). Because of this link to the body, sincerity is always a particular, subjective matter.

With regard to body and thought, and again unlike hypocrisy, sincerity works on the basis of a dynamics of conformity. As conformity of thought and body, the passion of sincerity cannot be strategic, since strategy implies a split. Any strategy implies a calculated distribution of goals and actions over time. Finally, put in terms of political representation, sincerity works counter to the idea that there is something to be represented. In fact, sincerity is immediately in danger of becoming corrupted if it raises the question of its motive: "What lies behind it?"—even if this is a so-called noble motive, such as care for a community. Sincerity appears to be more concerned with a kind of "care for self," an issue that Michel Foucault was much concerned with in the later years of his career. What is at stake in sincerity, however, is not an egotistical concern. The care of self that sincerity entails may have a distinct spin-off. It may be beneficial for an entire organization or society.[10]

All these issues concerning sincerity are at stake in Vondel's *Gysbreght van Aemstel*. First performed in 1638, it would remain Holland's most famous play for centuries to come.[11] The play starts with Gijsbreght, magistrate of Amsterdam, sighing with relief because God has freed the city: the enemy forces have ended their siege. However, Gijsbreght does not yet know that this is a ruse and that a band of enemy soldiers will enter the city hidden in a boat carrying firewood. An extremely violent takeover is the result. Close relatives of Gijsbreght and his wife Badeloch, including a niece who is head of an abbey, are raped and slaughtered. Whereas Badeloch constantly urges her husband Gijsbreght to flee, he wants to stay and in the end even wants to sacrifice his own life and that of his remaining people. Badeloch then asks a priest to pray for a solution, and a *deus ex machina* appears, in the shape of an angel who orders Gijsbreght to listen to his wife and escape. Instead of sacrificing everyone, he must take care of the remaining inhabitants of Amsterdam. This is indeed what happens—Gijsbreght and his small company of survivors go "elsewhere."

As many commentators have noted, the opening lines of this play— "Het hemelsche gerecht heeft zich ten lange lesten / Erbarremt over my, en mijn benaeuwde vesten" ["At long last divine justice has taken pity on me and my oppressed citadel"] (lines 1–2)—stand in sharp contrast to what is actually the case.[12] What most commentators ignore, however, is the fact that Dutch "gerecht" does not only mean "justice," but also "law" or "sovereign rule." As the play unfolds it becomes clear that God has not taken pity on the people of Amsterdam, has not taken care of them either, and has possibly treated them unfairly. Badeloch recurrently asks why God has forsaken the people of the city. The play then starts to investigate the language of martyrdom and sacrifice and quotes Tertullian's famous dictum from the third century that "the blood of martyrs is the seed of the church." Though a lot of blood is indeed being shed, the twist is that, on the advice or admonitions of Badeloch, Gijsbreght decides *not* to sacrifice himself in such a manner. It is not that he is tired of fighting; he decides to stop fighting and asks his people to trust him to lead them elsewhere.

To stop fighting is, obviously, a kind of action, but one that is often not immediately perceived as an action because it is an action-in-response. One of the issues that Patchen Markell puts forward in his fundamental article on the notion of action, on the basis of the work of Hannah Arendt, is that political action should not so much be conceived of in terms of conscious and effective acts ("The Rule of the People"). The question is whether the political act can open up new possibilities or be conceived of as a beginning of a new path (more on this later). This beginning is not something that can be chosen or produced at will. On the contrary: "whether your activity is a beginning is not wholly under your control: it is, instead, a matter of the character of the responses and reactions it provokes (or fails to provoke) in you and others" (Markell 2006, 10). Such a type of action is literally and structurally present in *Gysbreght van Aemstel*: scholars have been puzzled by the passivity of Gijsbreght, and some have even stated that Gijsbreght fails as a ruler.[13]

Indeed, Gijsbreght seems consistently to avoid action. Once he learns that the enemy is in the city, he shouts: "In order to have an overview I will go to the Scheiers-tower immediately; men, bring me my helmet and cuirass" (lines 850–851). Returning, he shouts: "Get my cuirass here, hurry men, bring weapons" (line 883), but still he does not fight. In the fourth act he is in the abbey just outside the city walls. Gijsbreght shouts: "The enemy is there! I'll run upstairs to protect the cloister gate as long as I can" (lines 1070–1071). But Gijsbreght escapes again and tries to organize resistance elsewhere in the city. Then, suddenly, in the heat of battle, he finds himself alone, "perplexed and numb" (line 1355). He sees a little cloud from which a voice says: "O Gijsbreght, will you forsake your niece Klaeris, and will you put your house, your wife and children in peril?" (lines 1360–1362). He finds an alleyway, crosses the river Amstel in a little boat, and climbs a tree—only to see the cloister burning. He helps to defend a bridge, and when that can be held no longer, he retreats to his castle.

There, on the bridge, he meets a representative of the enemy, who asks Gijsbreght to surrender. Suddenly the man who has avoided fighting in the previous acts now states that he would rather fight to the death. This sudden change in Gijsbreght's behavior is understandable in light of the fact that this play is an investigation into the dynamics of martyrdom. The question repeatedly posed by Badeloch is why God's innocent subjects are raped and slaughtered. Part of the answer is given by the reference to Tertullian's dictum that the blood of martyrs is the seed of the church. The slaughter of subjects in the present is justified, then, by a future destiny. This representation of the future in the present installs the dynamics of hypocrisy, something that does not satisfy Badeloch. She is concerned with the here and now, and wishes to resist the development of a history with a certain end—a history, moreover, that she considers to be unlawful and unjust.

With regard to these issues she very much resembles an intriguing conceptual figure in the history of Western thinking on sovereignty. I am referring to the figure of withholding called *katéchon*. It is best explained through Paul: in the second letter to the Thessalonians, Paul addresses a communal fear and despair. He assures the community that the day of the Lord will not come

except there come a falling away first, and that man of sin be revealed, the son of perdition; Who opposeth and exalteth himself above all that is called God, or that is worshipped; so that he as God sitteth in the temple of God, shewing himself that he is God. Remember ye not, that, when I was yet with you, I told you these things? And now ye know what withholdeth that he might be revealed in his time. For the mystery of iniquity doth already work: only he who now letteth will let, until he be taken out of the way. (2 Thess. 2:3–7)

That "what whithholdeth" (or "the one who now holds him back" in the New International Version) is called *katéchon* in the Greek original. On the one hand this *katéchon* upholds the law in order to withhold the evil forces of the lawless. Here it stands on the side of God. But in order for Christian history to arrive at its proper end, the evil one has to come. So in withholding the evil one, the *katéchon* is also withholding the necessary development of Christian history. Accordingly it also withholds God. That is why it needs to be removed—"taken out of the way"—in order for the day of the Lord to come.

The passage has been studied extensively in the field of theology and political philosophy. For Carl Schmitt, one of the most prominent scholars who paid attention to the *katéchon*, the figure acts as the historically embodied but ultimately divine, and by implication transcendent, basis of sovereignty.[14] However, in order to be able to contend with this, Schmitt has to ignore the fact that in the original text the *katéchon* also withholds divine power. Because both forms of the *katéchon* resistance are meant to safeguard earthly society from lawlessness and destruction, the *katéchon* is, in my view, an *immanent* political power—one that is neither a representative nor a ruler. This is what makes the *katéchon* relevant for my consideration of sincerity.

What makes the *katéchon* such a distinctive figure is that instead of ruling it acts in resistive response. In this respect, the opposing forces of lawlessness and divine violence define its activity. Yet they do not and cannot define the outcome of that activity. The activity of the *katéchon* is truly political in that it safeguards action as the type of "beginning" that Markell's reading of Arendt is concerned with: "Action, understood as a beginning, is an ongoing activity whose future is uncertain—and indeed whose past is in a certain sense uncertain as well, insofar as the character of one act as a beginning hangs on its future reception" (2006, 10). The uncertainty that Markell refers to is also produced by the fact that in relation to the forces of lawlessness and divine violence, there is an asymmetrical distribution of power at play. Analogous to what Foucault (2001) stated with regard to the *parrésiastés*—the one who speaks the truth—the *katéchon* is, principally, less powerful than its opponents. However, it is somehow more powerful in resisting the opposing forces because it is able to open up history or to keep it open. A final element of distinction is that the *katéchon* cannot and will not appeal to a legitimizing source outside of itself. Its ground is an immanent one. In other words, the figure of the *katéchon* is the figure of the here and now—of *haecceity.*

The primary *katéchon* figure in the play is Badeloch. She resents and resists both human lawlessness and the violence of divine passion. She will not accept that future destinies legitimize present violence. If the future history of the church is built upon or made possible by martyrs, this play offers the spectacle of rulers who withhold that history. When Badeloch asks her friar to pray and to call upon God to send an angel, she does so not to let a divine order be installed, but to save her husband and what is left of the community. Accordingly, the angel Raphael appears out of the blue and calls upon Gijsbreght to listen, not to God, but to his wife. Gijsbreght then lays down his arms—not in order to surrender, but to ensure that there will be no further casualties. He declares that the people must take the lead and assures them that "nobody needs to be afraid" (line 1877), because Gijsbreght and his family will guard the rear. Instead of ruling the people, he is now *with* his people.[15]

Thus, Badeloch and Gijsbreght do not so much fight against lawlessness. They attempt to keep the forces of the lawless at bay. They do not seek victory, they seek survival, not just of themselves but of the less powerful. This is where their sincerity lies. And perhaps we can see now that, whereas hypocrisy enables both political flexibility and a constant and critical questioning that tests rulers with regard to what they have done, sincerity concerns a love for a particular here and now in relation to an open future. Such love is not reactionary; it is a potential in that it constitutes openness to future possibilities. In relation to this openness toward the future, sincerity may imply a certain "turning away." In this play it requires a turning away from martyrdom, hence from a distinct conceptualization of Christianity. It also implies a turning away from the place where one once belonged. Considered more generally, sincerity must imply a turning away from forms of signifying regimes that need or imply some center of significance outside the particular situation of passionate bodies.

This does not imply that sincerity can do without a signifying regime. The signifying system that is at stake is defined by Deleuze and Guattari as a "passional regime." In it there is "no longer a signifier–signified relation, but a subject of enunciation issuing from the point of subjectification and a subject of the statement in a determinable relation to the first subject" (Deleuze and Guattari 1996, 127). Referring to the work of Emile Benveniste and his distinction between utterance and uttering, Deleuze and Guattari state that passion implies not just the coincidence of the subject that utters something with the subject that states something. Two different kinds of subjectivity are at stake. The enunciating "I" speaks in a nonreferential sense and reflects "its own use in the statement" (Deleuze and Guattari 1996, 130), as in: "I believe," "I assume," "I think." The stating "I" indicates, indeed, a state, as in: "I love," "I take care." In this context, sincerity makes trustworthiness possible, or the simple credibility of answers to questions such as "Can I believe and trust you when you state that . . . ?"

The consequences are considerable for signifying and political systems. Deleuze, re-reading the work of Benedict de Spinoza and David Hume, contends on the basis of the latter's work that "the major problem of the state is not a problem of representation but of credibility. The function of the state, according to Hume, is not so much to represent the commonwealth, but to turn the commonwealth into an object of credibility" (Deleuze 1953, 42; translation mine).

Implicitly two vectors are operative, here, that point in opposite directions. As an entity of representation the state's vector points back, to the ones represented. As an object of credibility the state's vector points forward, from the here and now into the future. Such an object of credibility is only possible on the basis of some kind of political sincerity. It appears, then, that this sincerity is irreconcilable with a system of political representation—and its inherent hypocrisy—because of the two divergent vectors. Let me wrap up my argument by considering a case in which the two are conflated.

Hypocrisy and Sincerity Conflated

In Vondel's *Lucifer* the rule of questioning turned into a questioning that ran wild. This hyperbolic type of questioning concerned God's behavior and was propelled by the fact that, in the play, God embodies two politico-moral orders. On the one hand God commits himself to the angels first and to humankind later. That is to say, at certain moments in time (in some kind of here and now), God is *with* his subjects. Here he should be sincere—acting in the here and now in relation to an open future. On the other hand, God's rule is embodied in different forms of representation. He appears as a hypocrite who would swap the angels for human beings. The fact that hypocrisy and sincerity are operative in the same body and at the same time in this play results in a state of suspicion. Such a state is not controlled on the basis of positive paranoia, but becomes, indeed, paranoid. Hence the relentless and compulsive questioning by the angels.

In this respect *Lucifer* contrasts sharply with what Claude Lefort describes as "savage democracy." Such democracy refers to a sound representational democratic system—one that is not based on consent or disapproval, but on real political struggle and the ability to question rulers directly with regard to any topic of relevance. Rulers will have to come out into the light, and this is precisely what the rule of questioning installed by hypocrisy aims to do.[16] But the savageness of Lefort's democracy does not concern, primarily, the past. Any real political struggle is concerned with tensions in the here and now that correspond with divergent routes for the future. This is where sincerity comes in. If human beings are really struggling with each other, and are doing so "savagely," the least one might expect is some kind of sincerity. Yet, again, this does not mean that hypocrisy and sincerity are operative on the same plane and within the same "economy," for then any social organization is threatened, as *Lucifer* shows. And it is not just the historical case of *Lucifer* that demonstrates the point.

Our current circumstances can be described as heavily mediatized. *Mediatization* originally meant the usurpation of one sovereign by another while the usurped one was allowed to keep its title.[17] This meaning of the word differs from what has been described by Baudrillard as mediatization (or by others as a media explosion). However, in the development of my argument, both meanings are relevant. The excessive appearance in and through media of modern rulers and individual subjects may result in a system of representation that infiltrates all layers and territories of society. Any individual who appears in a mediatized form immediately becomes the representative of something or someone else. As a result, the rule of questioning on the basis of hypocrisy starts to work. However, at our particular moment in time this does not lead to some kind of positive paranoia because of the fact that many Western societies are socio-cultur-ally strained and politically stressed. In the Netherlands, for instance, the multicultural society has been described by major parties and politicians as a failure—despite the considerable successes of Dutch multicultural society. In no more than three decades Dutch society has absorbed a sub-stantial number of people (since the 1960s more than 4.2 million people: between one-fourth and one-third of the population) with very differ-ent backgrounds and very different social circumstances. Of course there have been, and still are, tensions. How could there not be? Overall there has been no large-scale, recurrent violence. On the contrary. Whether one considers the situation in the daily street markets, the contributions of immigrants and their children to cultural life, or the way in which immi-grants are starting to appear on television, in sports, and in politics: the changes are enormous. The Netherlands of 2007 is in very few ways com-parable to that of 1977—and the changes are not for the worse.

Still, in this context mediatization à la Baudrillard may become dan-gerous. Every speaker who appears through the media and who comes from a certain group will almost immediately be considered not as a par-ticular figure—speaking from a here and now and able to open up a future—but as the political representative of some socio-cultural group. In short: mediatization, as a means of representation, becomes politically charged. As a result, it becomes hard for individual citizens (or groups) to relate to each other sincerely.

In the context of politically strained societies, massive mediatiza-tion may analogously lead to what was originally meant by mediatization, namely the usurpation of one sovereign by another. In this case it would refer to the usurpation of sincerity by hypocrisy. Sincerity would still keep its name and so-called title, then, but it would not be meaningfully oper-ative anymore. Still, Vondel's *Gysbreght* may offer insights into how to safeguard the figure of the sincere. The play shows us the possibility of a passionate, subjective choice for commitment. The play presents charac-ters who embody a particular and equally passionate resistance against the strategy of incorporating future destinies in the present. Or the charac-ters replace, in the words of Markell, "the unanswerable question of how to generate something (autonomy, spontaneity) from nothing (heteronomy, determination) with the more tractable question of how to sustain, intensify, and democratize the beginnings with which we are confronted" (2006, 12). Likewise, when the characters in *Gysbreght* appear to be able to "turn away" from reigning ideologies and centers of power, they do so to intensify their relationship with the less powerful. They are interested in the motives of powerful and violent others, but in the end keep focused on a here and now, and in doing so, they allow the here and now to be a potential—a ground for many futures.

4

The Rhetoric of Justification

THE PREPONDERANCE OF DECISIONS OVER RULES

Carel Smith

An Inconvenient Truth

It seems that one can hardly come up with a more apposite characterization of the legal profession than the topic of this book: the rhetoric of sincerity. Let me explain. In a lawsuit, the parties involved try not so much to persuade the judge of what, according to their sincere belief, really happened, nor is their alleged "call for justice" the expression of their deepest convictions of what would be a just and righteous sentence or judgment in the case at hand. Rather, lawsuits are settled on the basis of arguments. Solicitors, for example, demonstrate their professional mastery by convincing the judge that he or she has to adopt their point of view, that is, that their point of view is the one best vindicated by the rules that govern the lawsuit. Statements of fact, for example, have to be proven when contested. To prove a fact in court is a rule-governed activity: if a fact cannot be proven according to the rules of law, it is considered not to have happened—even if we all know it actually happened. So, whenever it is expedient for the overall argument, the solicitor will contest the facts. Litigations are, therefore, not about truth, but about *legal* truth.

In this respect, litigations are to be conceived not as exercises in sincerity, but rather as games—often serious and sometimes grim games. In fact, to ask whether the players in a game are sincere is a question that reveals a category mistake, for their sincerity doesn't matter at all. The only thing the players have to do is to play as well as they can. If sincerity plays any role in legal procedures, it is comparable to the sincerity of actors in the theater: lawyers argue *as if* they sincerely believe that their arguments are true. The title of this book, therefore, seems to be a perfect characterization of the legal profession: the sincerity of lawyers is a rhetorical one.

That, at least, *seems* to be the proper characterization of the profession of solicitors. It is in line with the popular prejudice that you can't trust lawyers, for they make straight what's crooked, and they turn the truth upside down. The prejudice is in line, at least, with an unsettling experience of mine when a textile entrepreneur, for whom I was working when I was an undergraduate law student, told me about a lawsuit he had won. When his solicitor brought the news that his case had finally been decided by the Supreme Court, he revealed to his lawyer that, now that nothing whatsoever could change the ruling, he felt free to tell him that his opponent should have won. "Try to avoid a lawsuit," my employer pointed out to me, "when you're right and the rival is wrong, for you could lose the litigation. But start a lawsuit when you refuse to comply with the agreement, although you legally should—for you might win the case by distracting the judge and the opponent with a flood of irrelevant facts, tons of paperwork, and a host of counterclaims."

That was an inconvenient truth of law. Although we were taught at university that the truth in law does not necessarily coincide with factual truth, this knowledge never struck me, nor my fellow students. We could all understand that there often lies a divergence between legal truth and factual truth. The disturbing truth that my employer made abundantly clear was that this divergence could deliberately be sought in court in order to win the case, not only by the parties involved, but also by the solicitors. Insincerity seemed to be king in court.

This glimpse into the factory of mundane justice made a deep impression on me. "Something is rotten in Law's Empire," or thoughts like these, must have crossed my mind—for I was young and utterly convinced that truth and justice were inextricably connected; that is, that justice is connected with *the* truth about what really happens in the world. The revelation of my employer moved the courthouse toward the space of theater, away from the solemn places that I connected with knowledge and wisdom: libraries, monasteries, and the university.

Nevertheless, I didn't blame my employer for handling the law expediently. That would have been to dismiss my employer's legitimate self-interest and his right to pursue it. Neither did I blame the solicitor who employed the law so cunningly. It was his professional duty to offer a partisan view on the case and to plead in favor of his client with all legal means. It was, therefore, *his* role to perform this way, whether or not he sincerely held true everything he argued. The courtroom may be a stage for solicitors, it seemed to me—but does this stage turn the *court* into a theater?

The Judge as Mouthpiece of the Law: A Longstanding Myth

What, then, about judges? Is it not their duty to administer justice, that is, to settle the disagreement or evaluate the accusation as disinterested and independent actors? Is it not their office to apply the law to the case at hand, even when their personal convictions are at variance with the legal settlement? Is not at least *one* actor in court—the judge—required to be sincere, that is, to perform according to a true belief of what the facts and the law require? If it is insincere to deliberately maintain a myth— if it is insincere to utter performative statements that are known to be at variance with the facts—then judges are insincere. But are they? I shall start with a myth.

It is one of the doctrines of institutional theory, and a consequence of the ideal of democracy, that the ruling power in democratic societies is the legislature, whereas the administration and the judiciary are subordinate powers that wield their authority in accordance with the law. This doctrine is famously expressed by Charles de Secondat, baron de Montesquieu, one of the founders of Western institutional theory. According to Montesquieu, the judges are practically inanimate beings who give voice or, more precisely, "mouth" to the law (*bouche de la loi*) (1949, 6, 301). They administer justice *according to the law*, that is, according to the rules issued by the legislature. Judges are, at best, *tools* of the law, linking law and case, not invent-ing new and better rules. They decipher the law and ferret out the facts of the case. Once they have figured out what the law prescribes, the ruling surfaces, as it were, after subsuming the facts under the determined rule.

In legal theory, this doctrine is known as *legalism*. Legalism flour-ished in the nineteenth century but came fiercely under attack by its end. In its primordial form, legalism is no longer accepted, on the grounds that it gave a methodologically false image of legal adjudication. Today, we all agree that the law is not complete, that its meaning is sometimes blurred, and that regulations may mutually clash. Whenever the judge encoun-ters such problems—in what are called "hard cases"—he has to consider the law in relation to a set of "background values" that are enclosed in the allegedly brute facts of legal history: statutes, precedents, legal practices, and institutions (Dworkin 1986). Such a construction or reconstruction of "the law" cannot be made by a mere tool, like Montesquieu's generic *bouche de la loi*, but demands a lawyer, who considers the law from an internal point of view, that is, as a participant in legal practice.[1]

Although the interpretation and application of the law in some way always involve judges' moral convictions and prejudices, it is posited that the law itself, as well as the institutions by and with which the law exists, offer sufficient constraints to prevent judges from going their own way.

Two Maxims of Legal Adjudication

Legal theory takes pains to reconcile the following apparently oppos-ing notions: that interpretation is a normative activity and that interpreta-tion must not deteriorate into inventing the law. Its calibration is sought in the development of methodological standards that enable judges to deci-pher the law's true meaning, on the one hand, and in demanding that the ruling is to be justified, on the other. To justify the decision is to justify the interpretation of the law. In the justification, judges account, besides other things, for the rule that underlies their decision, unfolding the rea-soning that has led to either the interpretation of an existing rule or the framing of a new one, which is nevertheless supposed to pre-exist in the body of law. The requirement of justification is thought to force judges to derive their premises and final judgment from the law only. The alleged sincerity of judges, then, is located in the justifications of their verdicts, reiterating and containing the *true grounds* of their decisions.

In this respect, current legal theory accepts one important method-ological assumption of legalism: the ruling is still conceived as the application of a rule of law to the facts of the case. Or to put it differently, the discovery of an apposite rule and the determination of the precise meaning of this rule are considered to *precede* the ruling. In short: *decision follows interpretation.*[2]

Here we meet, in my opinion, an ideologically animated premise of legal theory and practice. It is *postulated* that the rule precedes the ruling—and it *has to* precede the ruling, because of the political ideal of democratic sovereignty. This sovereignty demands that concrete cases must be decided according to the law's regulations, that is, according to prescriptions that, in one way or another, exist or pre-exist in the body of law. And it is this pre-scribed procedure of legal reasoning that seems to guarantee that the ruling is ordered by the law, and not by the contingency of the judge's whims.

But legal practice does not confirm this doctrine. Often, the decisive argument to interpret a rule one way rather than another is directed by the fairness of the ruling that would result, so that the decision could be said to *precede* the rule that serves as justification of the ruling. The maxim "decision follows interpretation" should, therefore, be complemented by the maxim "interpretation follows decision," together offering a better account of the reasoning processes that result in the ruling. To evince this thesis, I will discuss the decision of the Dutch Supreme Court in what is known as one of the "asbestos cases."

From Case to Rule

The legal issue addressed in this case, decided in 2000, was whether a shipbuilding yard could be held liable for the physical injury of a former employee more than thirty years after he had been exposed to asbestos, a notorious carcinogen. The legal problem here concerned the limitation period for damages like these. According to Dutch law (Civil Code, art. 3:330, para. 2), claims of damages for injuries caused by exposure to hazardous substances expire thirty years after the event that caused the damage. In its decision, the Supreme Court considered that the limitation period had been fixed at thirty years for the purpose of legal certainty, because employers and insurers have to make provisions in order to indemnify potential claims, and, therefore, they are in need of a limitation period that is neither too long nor too flexible. The legislature had explicitly rejected a limitation period spanning more than thirty years, partly because of the interests of employers and insurers, and partly because the injuries were supposed to reveal themselves within thirty years after exposure to hazardous substances.

But the problem with physical injury caused by asbestos is that the injury often reveals itself only after *more* than thirty years. As a result, a whole class of victims of hazardous substances—those who have been exposed to asbestos—is more often than not excluded from the opportunity to sue the company or (former) employer for the injury, a result that happens to be not only at variance with the legislature's intent, but also contrary to the principle of legal equality. The latter principle requires that like cases be treated alike; hence, to expel the class of asbestos victims from compensation that can be claimed by other victims of hazardous substances discriminates between these classes without justification.

In these preliminary considerations, the Supreme Court outlined the legal dilemma that had to be settled. In short, the question was, should the victim's claim be dismissed following the demand for legal certainty, or should it be assigned because of the principle of legal equality? According to the Supreme Court, this decision was entwined with the facts of the case. Although the principle of legal certainty entails that the ultimate limitation period of thirty years should be applied strictly, it allows for deviation from this rule in exceptional cases. The Supreme Court, then, enumerated seven circumstances that have to be taken into consideration when weighing and balancing the competing interests or principles in cases like these. The judges must take into account, among other issues:

- the type of damage (pecuniary or moral damage);
- whether or not the victim or relatives are entitled to benefits on account of the damage;
- the degree of reproach with which the author of the damage can be charged;
- whether or not the author is still able to defend himself against the claim.

In enumerating these and other circumstances, the Supreme Court actually referred implicitly to those facts of the above case that made it so unsatisfactory to apply the limitation period strictly.

It is the task of the Supreme Court to judge only the interpretation and application of the law by lower courts, not to settle a case finally: after its ruling, the case will be referred back to a lower court, which has to settle the case according to the Supreme Court's directions. In this case, however, the Supreme Court in effect judged—granted that the case satisfied all enumerated aspects—that it would be reasonable and fair not to abide by the limitation period of thirty years. The Court arrived at its decision not by interpretation in a strict sense, but by weighing and balancing both competing principles—the principle of legal equality and the principle of legal certainty. But the principles were not weighed and balanced in abstracto; the Supreme Court actually brought varieties of the case to mind and determined which circumstances were decisive in outweighing one principle in favor of the other. In so doing, the Supreme Court explicitly referred to the standards of reasonableness and fairness, asserting that in light of a mixture of some of the enumerated circumstances, the application of the rule was to be considered highly unreasonable and unfair and therefore should outweigh the demand for legal certainty.

Myth or Belief: Outside and Inside the Office

The reasoning process by which the Supreme Court arrived at its decision in the asbestos case is not an exceptional one, even if we acknowledge that many cases do not require the weighing and balancing of fundamental legal principles. But except for what are called "clear cases," most cases ask for judgment, that is, demand the weighing and balancing of different points of view or different interests.

It is lawyers' parlance to characterize the processes of weighing and balancing—that is, of judgment—as the weighing and balancing of the *principles* involved. In my opinion, the Supreme Court did not primarily weigh and balance competing principles, but *cases*, that is, a variety of cases similar to the case at hand, in order to decide which circumstances, or mixture of circumstances, no longer justified a strict application of the fixed limitation period. Seen from the angle of heuristics—the reasoning process—the judges focus on the case itself, asking which decision is the fairest one, all things considered, and it is *this judgment in advance* that serves as the starting point for the justification, which then grounds the decision in the verdict. The relative weight of these competing principles is, therefore, not determined first to settle the legal issue. It is the other way around: their relative weight is the *result* or *outcome* of the judgment that, under these circumstances, a strict application of the rule would be unreasonable and unfair. Or to put it differently, the law is as much determined by the ruling as the ruling is determined by the law. For cases like these, the maxim "interpretation *follows* decision" seems to characterize the heuristics of legal adjudication far better than the legalist's view on adjudication.

However, this view on legal adjudication seems to be at variance with the assumption of sincerity, for legal judgments are supposed to be based on the law, with the interpretation of the law not a justification in retrospect, but the verdict's very reason. To hold the maxim "interpretation follows decision," then, is to charge the caste of judges with being insincere, and to consider the legitimization of the ruling as mere rhetoric, not containing the true grounds of the decision, but solely those arguments that will presumably persuade the audience. The more effective the rhetoric of the judges, the more we will be convinced of their sincerity, that is, the more we will believe the rulings to be grounded in law-based reasons. The aim of the justification, then, would not be to account for the very reasons for the rulings, but, as it were, to wheedle the audience.

But this conclusion is, in my opinion, hastily drawn. It overlooks the complex interplay between the system of law on the one hand, and our legal judgments on the other. Although every complex legal system is underdetermined and different judges could therefore see, as it were, different "solutions" in hard cases as the result of differences in political and moral convictions and prejudices, this nevertheless does not justify the inference that they cannot be sincerely convinced of having the best *legal* arguments for their opinions—a belief that can even go with the simultaneous admission that other judges could have reached different but equally sincere opinions about what the law requires.

This may seem contradictory, but it can be explained as follows. On the one hand, hard cases only exist within a system of law. One could define a hard case as one in which the law offers different solutions to settle the issue. As such, it is the law that furnishes the arguments that could, in our opinion, justify a decision in one way or another. On the other hand, if we consider one solution to be more reasonable and fair than another, we will, in effect, be more convinced by the arguments that underpin this solution than by the argumentation that justifies the allegedly weaker solution. But this valuation will also affect the way we comprehend the law in general. The *reading* of statutes and case law will always be affected by our opinions of what we consider to be just and fair; that is, we will accommodate our reading of the law as much as possible to the decisions we think are best. As a result, we may be *sincerely* convinced that our judgment is ordered by the law itself and not prompted by personal preferences.

The paradoxical conclusion is, then, that judges' decisions are based on law, but that their understandings of the law are carried by their decisions. In the interplay between rules and decisions, the decisions have a slight preponderance over the rules, for in hard cases, the law is underdetermined. When at least two different decisions seem to be reasonable within the system of law, it is the judgment as to which one is best that directs the understanding of the law in this respect. In doing so, the intuitive judgment furnishes its own justification. If we are willing to compare the law to a house, we could say that the foundation walls are carried by the whole house (Wittgenstein 1972, 248). Like all institutional facts, law is a construction that carries itself: it exists in and by the acts and decisions of all participants, who, at the same time, are compelled by the system that they created themselves and that they continue to create.

Seen from an external point of view, it is a myth that the ruling is the application of a rule on the facts of a case: interpretation follows decision. But seen from the inside—as a participant who is subject to the practices, standards, and rhetoric of the office—it is the law, not the officials, that determines the ruling: decision follows interpretation.

Sincerity as a Function of Form and Procedure

It is a long way from judge to ruling. Between the person who administers justice on the one hand, and the ruling on the other, stand the multiple practices that constitute the judge's office. It is not enough to be a righteous person in order to become a judge. Handling the patchwork of law requires the mastering of techniques and the use of professional standards; the interrogation of suspects and witnesses asks for a vast semiotics of gesture and expressive style; and drawing up the ruling demands a keen awareness of how the words will affect the litigators, as well as society and the judiciary. To be a judge is to be naturalized into these techniques and practices.

This, I think, is sometimes forgotten—at least, *I* did not realize this when I was an undergraduate law student. Especially when the ruling affects us in one way or another, we ask for unmediated justice, the direct application of the rules of law that govern the case at hand. But justice has to be *done*: the facts of the case have to be determined, the locus of the crime visited, witnesses questioned, the evidence investigated, and all this within a procedural framework that ought to guarantee the litigants' equal procedural rights, to protect the immunities of third parties, and to see that the litigation is settled in due time.

Law is not the mere accumulation of rules directed toward subjects or citizens, providing rights and imposing duties; it is the interplay of different kinds of rules. As H. L. A. Hart rightly points out, law consists, on the one hand, of rules of obligation, or primary rules, that are concerned with the actions that individuals must or must not do. The rules of obligation are supplemented, on the other hand, with secondary rules that are all *about* primary rules. They specify the ways to recognize and change the primary rules and how they should be applied in concrete cases (Hart 1994, 95).

What, then, according to Hart, justifies judges' rulings when deciding cases of negligence, discrimination, or robbery? His answer is the facts of the case and a primary rule of obligation. But what justifies the vindication of the facts and the validity of this rule of obligation? The answer is: rules of a different character, that is, secondary rules, which guide the evidence of facts and the identification, interpretation, and application of the primary rules. These secondary rules consist of a whole body of standards, of which some are enacted, others are practices that exist as tacit knowledge, and still others are explicitly stated by the judiciary as guidelines for the interpretation and adjudication of statutes.

In short, legal adjudication is a rule-governed activity. The establishment of a rule of obligation is the result of a complex interplay of standards of adjudication; so is the ascertainment of the alleged facts of the case; and the final ruling is not the mere inference from this rule of obligation and the facts of the case, but a performative act in which ruling, rule, and facts—inextricably interwoven—come into being. Although the existence of those standards consists in their acceptance and use as standards of correct adjudication, it does not make the judge who uses them their author (Hart 1994, 145). To perform like a judge is to perform according to the ideals, techniques, and rhetoric that characterize the judge's office, standards that are incorporated through years of study, practice, and discipline.

It is theoretically possible, but not likely, for someone to be part of the caste of judges and to behave accordingly while still not adhering to the rules of the profession. Such a judge could end up like Paul Magnaud, known as "le bon juge de Chateau-Thierry" (1848–1926), who was offended by the notorious inequity of law and judicature. As a judge, he became immensely popular with workers and socialists for not enforcing the harsh labor legislation, judging solely by (his) standards of equity. In so doing, however, Magnaud ceased to be a judge, or, alternatively, inaugurated a different institution of a judiciary that administers justice, not according to legislation, but to moral intuition. But he himself proved the institution of "le bon juge" to be untenable. When he had been elected a member of parliament and became part of the legislative body, eager to reform the law, he could only do so under the (tacit) presumption of a subordinate judiciary, subject primarily to the law instead of the acute biddings for justice.

We all long sometimes for a judge like Magnaud, someone who is not bamboozled by form and procedures but grasps the matter at heart, until we realize that part of what justice is, at least in our society, *is* form and procedure. Judge Magnaud is as bad a judge as the bribable or partisan judge, despite their differences of disposition or ethical codes. The problem is that they do not behave like judges, that is, they do not enact the practices, techniques, and ideals that make up the profession of the judiciary. The same holds for the solicitor who, honest to her sincere convictions, argues in court that her client deserves the death penalty: being a solicitor is to behave like a solicitor.

The idea that a sincere performance is to perform according to one's true beliefs is both true and misleading. It is misleading because a true belief depends on circumstances, roles, contexts, and expectations. If the facts of a case are proven illegally—for example, if the testimony is acquired by torture—the existence of an "exclusionary rule" requires that both solicitor and judge must dismiss the evidence, regardless of whether or not these illegally proven facts actually happened. The judges' true beliefs of what happened are the result of testimony, arguments, and tests, all governed by procedural rules. Their "true belief" cannot be separated from the roles they are expected to play.

But the idea that sincerity and true belief are connected is, in some way, also correct. In court, one's true belief of what really happened depends on one's role. If a judge deliberately declares the accused guilty on the basis of illegally proven facts, the sentence will be based, paradoxically as it sounds, on a false belief of what happened, turning the performance of the judge into a false—that is, insincere—one.

I was right when I realized as an undergraduate that the courthouse is a theatre, a stage for the performances of solicitors and judges—but my accusation that their performances were *mere* rhetoric, in the sense that they only pivoted upon effect, not truth, was heedless. For legal truth, if not all truth, depends on form: at the very least on rules, procedures, and presentation.

5

Must We (NOT) Mean What We Say?

SERIOUSNESS AND SINCERITY IN THE WORK OF
J. L. AUSTIN AND STANLEY CAVELL

Hent de Vries

Stanley Cavell speaks of his personal encounter with J. L. Austin's 1955 William James Lectures at Harvard, which would be published posthumously in 1962 as *How to Do Things with Words*, as nothing less than a "conversion experience."[1] He ties this "experience," which seems no longer or not yet governed by rules or criteria, to the theme of "seriousness" and, by extension, "sincerity":

Austin's teaching was the occasion for me on which to ask, somehow differently from any way in which I had been able to ask it before, whether I was *serious* about philosophy—not quite as measured by its importance (to the world, or to my society, or to me), but as measured by a question I felt a new confidence in being able to pose myself, and which itself posed questions, since it was as obscure as it was fervent. It presented itself as the question whether I could speak philosophically and mean every word I said. Is this a sensible test in choosing a career? . . . And does it mean that I have—before I speak—to ask whether I am *sincere* in my words, whether I want all of their consequences, put to no matter what scrutiny? Who would say *anything* under such conditions? (Cavell 1996, 59–60; first emphasis added).

Does Cavell indirectly confess or prophesy here that we cannot say anything (or at least anything meaningful) under conditions where seriousness and sincerity are *fully* realized or realizable? And is this a lesson that Austin has taught us, albeit indirectly, unintentionally, and only when read against the grain? Is seriousness—and, by extension, sincerity—not a "sensible test" in human relations? Or are "seriousness" and "sincerity" simply not open to a "test" (at least not a "sensible" one)? And how can such questions be at once "obscure" yet also "fervent," if not necessarily "important"? How *does* one speak philosophically and still mean every word that one says? How, if this is what we feel we *must* do—if we "must mean what we say"—could we ever avoid or escape and disengage from speaking seriously or sincerely? How, if this is what we feel we *ought to* do, could we begin doing so, in word and deed?

Of course, we do say some things, and we do so all the time. "[L]ots of things will have been done," Austin says, even where a performative— an "act of speech" (1962, 20) to be distinguished from a statement of truth or falsehood—is infelicitous, which never means "without consequences, results, effects" (17). As Austin shows, "saying something is sometimes doing something" (Cavell 1994, 88) rather than, say, reporting or describing something. Moreover, saying something, even when and where we are competent users of a language, is often doing something inadvertently, unwittingly, unintentionally, with a slippage or side-effect of sorts.

Austin adds that there are cases in which to say and do things is to be subject—that is to say, exposed or vulnerable—to "possible ways and varieties of *not exactly doing things*"; in other words, of "not quite doing (or saying) something" (1962, 93; cf. 92). He suggests that this may be so even when and where we had intended our words to have an opposite effect (or sincerely thought and genuinely felt they might). This can happen in several ways, and every one of these unsuccessful utterances or infelicities needs to be clarified, he claims, "if we are ever to understand *properly* what doing things is" (271).

Cavell agrees with this overall diagnosis of the perils no less than the chances of speech, but he contests Austin's implication that there is a way of doing—or, for that matter, of understanding—things "properly." The possibility of misunderstanding, of "infelicity," "misfiring," or "abuse," belongs to the heart of the matter, he claims. But in what sense, precisely?

Cavell speaks of seriousness and sincerity as being, philosophically speaking, *unfathomable*, that is, immeasurable in terms of any worldly, social, or even subjective importance; and irreducible to any cognitive, normative, or existential register whose criteria or rules would leave us no room for doubt. On the contrary, the flipside of seriousness and sincerity is anxiety about their absence, a horror of posturing and masquerade; and, perhaps, also a terror at their presence, that is, at the claims they lay upon us, whose consequences we cannot foresee or whose foreseeable consequences we know or suspect we are unwilling—too weak—to bear.

In the limited space I have here, I cannot fully reconstruct what I take to be the most illuminating context for analyzing these matters, namely, Cavell's detailed discussion, in *A Pitch of Philosophy* and *Philosophical Passages*, of "the relevance, but inaccuracy, of what Derrida had to say about Austin" (Cavell 2003, xiii). As will become clear, the debate revolves around Cavell's conviction that the condition of so-called ordinary language philosophy is, first of all, its "intuition of the worldboundedness of language," which is to say: "Bound not necessarily to *this* world; and, as performatives are meant to show, not necessarily by reference" (1994, 118). Moreover, Cavell hastens to add, this is "worth saying if only to mark that the practice of ordinary language philosophy privileges the concept of a word as opposed to privileging the concept of the sign. This might be what the difference between my view of Austin and Derrida's view comes down to" (118). But how is it that words bind us to the world, whether this one or another? And how can they do so in a nonreferential (in any case, nondescriptive, nonassertive, neither veritable nor semiotic) way, and yet, in so doing, still be all the more serious and sincere?

In the remainder of this essay, I will concentrate on what Cavell, in this context and almost in passing, calls Austin's "theory of insincerity." Yet a few words indicating this striking controversy are in order, even though I hope to return to it elsewhere at somewhat greater length.

A Debate Revisited

In his remarkable essay "Signature Event Context" (1972) as well as in the extended argument of *Limited Inc.* (1988), Jacques Derrida depicts Austin (on Cavell's perceptive reading) as "attempting to track insincerity to its metaphysical roots, to attack metaphysics as an excuse for, a cover for, insincerity" (Cavell 1994, 103). This means that, according to Derrida, Austin has his own way of deconstructing a certain "logocentrism" that, on the latter's diagnosis, takes the form of so-called descriptionism (that is, of the descriptive or constative fallacy) and of verism. (All of them doctrines traced back to the logical writings of Gottlob Frege; the Vienna Circle's and Alfred Ayer's logical positivism; a certain evolutionary scheme of historical, social, and linguistic development; as well as to psychological compulsion.)

In order to understand the argument we need to establish what metaphysics means in this context and how its interrogation—inspired by Derrida's no less than Wittgenstein's—enables Cavell, as he says, "to go beyond" what he had earlier written in a chapter from *Themes Out of School* concerning "Frege's bearing on Austin's issue of the seriousness of assertion" (Cavell 1994, 185; cf. 95–96). Austin, it should be recalled, had translated Frege's *The Foundations of Arithmetic: A Logico-Mathematical Enquiry into the Concept of Number.* Yet, Cavell suggests, Frege's logical assumptions cast a much longer shadow on his translator's work. For all of Austin's opposition to logical positivism's conception of descriptionism and to Frege's verism, there would be a remaining sense and reference of the validity of "truth" that, Cavell surmises, tends to obscure Austin's far more telling (but forgotten, repressed) insight into the tragic condition or potentiality of all utterances and every act.

This tragic motif and motivation is, Cavell claims, based on a far more interesting Nietzschean inspiration in Austin's theory of performatives that goes virtually unnoticed by Derrida (who remains far more intrigued by the presumed prevalence of a conception of "force" and not merely "felicity," and would thus wrongly locate the Nietzschean impulse in Austin elsewhere [Derrida, 1972]).

According to Cavell, Derrida is not alone in this fateful oversight of Austin's tragic awareness of the necessary or, rather, unavoidable fragility of all intentions, utterances, and gestures (whether said or done or both). In fact, most of the analytical commentary on Austin's most famous text in the English-speaking world—and, indeed, Cavell acknowledges, his own earlier engagements with it as well—have either downplayed or overlooked this neurological point. Not even Austin himself seems to be taking it as much to heart as it deserves to be.

Cavell's whole essay is based upon the conviction that "Signature Event Context" and the "theatrical" debate with Searle that ensued, although it was heralded by some as the first serious encounter between so-called analytic and continental philosophy, have in fact "done more harm than good." For one thing, it established or served as an alibi for a suspicious view of Derrida's thought in professional philosophy (at least in representative philosophy departments in the English-speaking world) and, in the wake of Derrida's increasing influence in literary theory, allowed a too-restrictive reception of Austin's actual thought. All this, Cavell notes, "has helped perpetuate the thought that Austin underwrites some idea that language contains a general unified dimension of effect that can be called one of performance, and that he advances a general contrast between ordinary language and literary language." Yet "these ideas alone," Cavell continues, "are sufficient to destroy any contribution Austin's distinctiveness might lend in such discussions" (1994, 61).

Cavell's own assessment of Austin's "contribution" and "distinctiveness" intends to shift the discussion in an altogether different—and far more "difficult"—direction, one that would bring out his central concern with seriousness and sincerity whose all-too-indirect but crucial link with tragedy would need to be brought far more forcefully than has been hitherto realized. In Cavell's words: "My own feeling is that while Derrida found Austin philosophically interesting, even congenial, and Searle had found Austin useful and worth defending against Derrida's treatment of him, neither really felt that Austin's is a (philosophical) voice whose signature is *difficult* to assess and important to hear out in its difference. If what either of them says about Austin's ideas of language is right, then my question of seriousness, forced upon me by those ideas, is not only difficult to articulate, but pointless" (1994, 61).

Interestingly, Cavell goes on to explain that his reservations with respect to Derrida (and Searle) reiterate the ones voiced in his earliest defense of Austin (against Benson Mates's views) in the opening essay of *Must We Mean What We Say?* His unease over the conditions of seriousness and sincerity that are obscured in the early and recent assessments of Austin's work thus cuts across the divide of what seem to be two opposed schools of thought, whose "styles or voices or signatures" Cavell does not wish to regard as alternative or surmountable positions. Instead, more interestingly, he regards them "as forming the contesting, all but exhaustive, senses of the present, hence of the foreseeable future, of philosophy," as he notes in the foreword to Shoshana Felman's *The Scandal of the Speaking Body* (2003, xii). And the discomfort on Cavell's part seems only aggravated by the reception of Austin's work in literary, critical, or psychoanalytic (more precisely, Lacanian) theory, as seen in the writing of Eve Sedgwick, Judith Butler, and others.

But then could this debate between schools of thought that feed on disputation—and, it seems, must of necessity do so—ever be seriously and sincerely resolved by reasonable argument? Cavell suggests it cannot. And, perhaps unintentionally, no one demonstrated this more compellingly than Austin with his elliptical reference to the tragic.

The Tragic Hint: Rethinking Austin

But what would it require to live without the representationalist (descriptivist or verist) metaphysical backup, no longer using it as an "excuse" or "cover"? Would it allow or force us to live more seriously or sincerely, no longer living our knowledge and ignorance, do's and don'ts, likes and dislikes theoretically (as the representationalist stance would seem to imply), but instead in a more thoughtful, examined, responsible, and therefore lived (and who knows, more lively) way? Could this be done? Or is doing (or letting) not the mode and mood in which sincerity—and, by implication, seriousness—is found or founded? Is its mode and mood, if not motif, perhaps far more *tragic* (or, in philosophical terms, aporetic) than the philosophy of ordinary language (Austin), not to mention speech act theory (Searle) and their deconstructive detractors (notably Derrida), seems to suggest?

Cavell suggests that Derrida's scholarly omissions (beyond the lectures on speech acts) in taking stock of Austin's *How to Do Things with Words* "might not have been so costly had Derrida taken up the appearance, in the opening chapter of that book, of the citation—uniquely there in Greek, as if calling attention to itself—from Euripides' *Hippolytus*. Not that any other reader I know of *How to Do Things with Words* stops to wonder at it either" (Cavell 1994, 52–53).[2] In fact, Cavell confesses to having initially overlooked or underappreciated the literary citation himself. And no reference to it can be found in yet another deconstructive reading that he critically yet sympathetically engages with, Felman's book on Austin. As he ponders the reasons behind this near-total forgetfulness and, indeed, proposes the affect of "wonder" as the most appropriate—that is, serious and sincere—response to the oblivion of the citation, Cavell imagines the meaning it must have had for Austin himself. Perhaps we can comprehend the neglect of the passage if we realize that it almost "seems to make no sense to say that the deliberately superficial, witty, mocking Austin would be inscribing the relation of his work on performative utterances to the realm of the tragic" (Cavell 1994, 53).

I will focus here on Cavell's (and, albeit only indirectly, on Derrida's) reading of Austin in the second chapter of Cavell's *A Pitch of Philosophy*, and its parallel study in *Philosophical Passages*. Both culminate in the interpretation of a line from Euripides' *Hippolytus* (line 612)—ignored, Cavell claims, by even the most sophisticated readers of *How to Do Things with Words*, such as Derrida and Felman—which Austin translates as "my tongue swore to, but my heart did not."

This line, as discussed by Cavell, holds the key to a better understanding of the rhetoric of sincerity, a concept whose implications form a constant point of reference in his other work as well, most notably *The Claim of Reason*.[3] Not the least of the promises of Euripides' line is that it enables Cavell to explore in more detail what it means to "speak philosophically and mean every word" one says; it enables us to address, if not fully to answer, the question whether "I have—before I speak—to ask whether I am *sincere* in my words, whether I want all of their consequences, put to no matter what scrutiny" (Cavell 1996, 60; emphasis added).

Cavell leaves no doubt that "the cause of the neglect of Austin's citation from Euripides is a function of underestimating Austin's, let's say, seriousness" (1996, 181). This, more than anything else, would be the flaw in Derrida's (on Cavell's reading) selective, now appreciative, now overly dismissive reception of the theory of performative speech acts and the all-too-implicit allusion to tragedy on which it is based.

More broadly, Austin's sense of the tragic would allow us to ask what it means to live a philosophical theory—more precisely, to live one's theory and to do so *seriously* and thereby *sincerely*. I am not thinking, in this context, of the ancient topos of the *bios theoretikos* or of the reduction of life to theory, of living theoretically—which would mean, following ordinary usage, living hypothetically, and hence not really living at all. Rather, I assume a connection between the theme of our volume and what might turn out to be a specifically modern—though also classically tragic—problem. Specifically, I would like to ask to what extent living theory or living one's theory requires a certain acceptance (Cavell would say "acknowledgment") of truth, truthfulness, trust, and trustworthiness; indeed, of seriousness and sincerity. In this sense of "living philosophy" as living one's theory rather than merely having one, or of a theory sustaining itself only to the extent that it is lived and alive, Cavell's remarkable work is an indispensable guide.

Serious Swearwords

Insincerity is at the heart of the question of "infelicities," sometimes called "masqueraders," whose "misuse," Austin says, "engenders rather special varieties of 'nonsense'" (1962, 4). Infelicities are failed performatives; they indicate the ways in which a performative utterance, while neither a true nor false report or description, can still be "subject to criticism," for example, when I say "I promise" but do not intend to do what I say (25, 40; 44 for the reference to "insincerity").

Such a promise, says Austin, is an utterance (or rather "*act*") that is not "untrue" but rather *not done*, in the sense not only of "not implemented," but also of "given in bad faith" and thereby of having made a "false move" (1962, 11). Such an utterance may go wrong in two distinct ways. First, I may not have performed the act of promising correctly, in which case the performative "does not come off" or "is not achieved." Or, second, I may achieve the act but do so in ways that are "insincere." In other words, the infelicity of our utterance may be one of "misfiring" or of "abuse": in the first case, our performative act and the procedure it invokes are "disallowed" or "botched," rendering the utterance "void" or "without effect"; in the second case—that of insincerity—the utterance is just "professed," "hollow," "not implemented," or "not consummated" (16).

As he does so often, Austin hastens to add that these distinctions, while necessary, are not "hard and fast" (Austin 1962, 16). They do not contradict each other, since "we can go wrong in two ways at once." Moreover, they "shade into one another" and "overlap" to the point where "the decision between them is 'arbitrary' in various ways" (23). Interestingly, though, Austin worries that even his own theory of performatives might seem to imply that *merely uttering certain words on the right occasion or in the appropriate context does not by itself warrant seriousness.* But what more or what else could be needed? Do performatives, Austin asks, not require "the performance of some internal spiritual act, of which the words are to be the report" (1962, 9)? Put differently, is the theory of performatives not ultimately based upon some metaphysical understanding of *representationalism,* that is, of "verism" and the descriptive, constative, or "logocentric" fallacy after all?

True enough, a performative, Austin says, is a case of utterance whose sense is that to say something is to do something, "or in which *by* saying or *in* saying something we are doing something" (1962, 12). Furthermore, it is important to recall in the passage concerning the tragic dimension of ordinary language philosophy that, for Austin, the performative has a certain investment in (saying) words: that is to say, in "words," which are not merely representational or differential "signs" and whose "worldboundedness," we found, is not based on semantic reference of any kind. Hence Austin's striking claim, early on in the lectures, that "the act of marrying, like, say, the act of betting, is at least *preferably* (though still not *accurately*) to be described as *saying certain words,* rather than as performing a different, inward and spiritual, action of which these words are merely the outward and audible sign. That this is so can perhaps be hardly *proved,* but it is, I should claim, a fact" (13).

And yet, there is a certain privilege Austin attributes among the "necessary conditions" for the "smooth or 'happy' functioning of a performative (or at least of a highly developed explicit performative)" (1962, 14). He locates these conditions in the speaker's having "certain thoughts or feelings" and "intentions" (15, 15n.1). This latter appeal—but, apparently, not to something merely "inward" or "spiritual"—introduces his subsequent differentiation between what we could call *negative* conditions under which the performative is "not successfully performed at all, does not come off, is not achieved" (16). Examples abound. Austin mentions someone's entering a ceremony to be married while married already or his or her saying "I" without saying "I do." But he also distinguishes those cases in which, as he says, "the act *is* achieved, although to achieve it in such circumstances, as when we are, say, insincere, is an abuse of the procedure. Thus when I say 'I promise' and have no intention of keeping it, I have promised but . . ." (16). This differentiation calls, Austin continues, for the further distinction within the general category of "infelicities" between so-called misfires, on the one hand, and abuses, on the other (even though Austin urges us immediately *not* to "stress the normal connotations of these names!") (16). All of which requires us to consider "insincerities" as falling under "abuses," that it to say, "acts professed but hollow" (18).

Surely a promise, the very enunciation "I promise to . . . ," surmises Austin, "*must* be spoken 'seriously' and so as to be taken 'seriously'" (1962, 9; emphasis added).[4] Moreover, he continues, this not only holds for promises but is, "though vague, true enough in general—an important commonplace in discussing the purport of any utterance whatsoever. . . . I must not be joking, for example, nor writing a poem" (9).

What does this general requirement entail, imply, or presuppose? In what sense does it form a more than simply empirical, and hence near-transcendental, condition or near-logical necessity? Does this condition parallel—or is it *truth-analogous* to—certain requirements of constative statements? How does it hold even though the promise remains nondescriptive in any direct way (even though felicity and infelicity have no immediate or strict relation to truth and untruth)?

Austin begins by warning how we should *not* understand this relationship between uttered promises and the feelings, thoughts, and intentions that ought to— indeed, *must*—accompany them, and do so *almost* fatefully, compulsively, and obsessively (or, as Cavell will say, tragically). Intriguingly, Austin ironically echoes, even parodies, the sacramental language of the Anglican catechism in stating this erroneous view:

we are apt to have a feeling that their [i.e., these promises] being serious consists in their being uttered as (merely) the outward and visible sign, for convenience or other record or for information, of an inward and spiritual act: from which it is but a short step to go on to believe or to assume without realizing that for many purposes the outward utterance is a description, *true or false*, of the occurrence of the inward performance. (Austin 1962, 9)

That this is not the case cannot be "*proved*," Austin says, but is "a fact" nonetheless. Performatives, such as the acts of marrying, betting, bequeathing, christening, or, indeed, promising are "at least *preferably* (though not still *accurately*) to be described as *saying certain words*, rather than as performing a different, inward and spiritual, action of which these words are merely the outward and audible sign" (13).

Austin notes in a parenthetical aside that the "classic expression" of this latter idea can be found in line 612 of Euripides' tragedy *Hippolytus*, which Austin quotes: "my tongue swore to, but my heart (or mind or other backstage artist) did not" (1962, 9–10).

Cavell picks up on this citation as a key moment in his engagement with Derrida. The line also echoes throughout a whole succession of ancient and modern texts that are thereby obliquely inscribed in Austin's lecture. It is cited in Plato's *Symposium* and *Theatetus*, in Aristophanes' *The Frogs*, and in Aristotle's *Rhetoric*, a text that, Cavell suggests, might allow a reading of Austin that would allow one generally to "question a theory of language that pictures speech as at heart a matter of action and only incidentally a matter of articulating and hence expressing desire" (Cavell 1996, 159). The recent Loeb edition of *Hippolytus* renders the line as: "My tongue swore, but my mind is not on oath" (Euripides 1995, 185); yet another translation reads "My tongue swore, but my mind is unsworn" (Avery 1968). In the even more telling French translation of *Les belles lettres*, we find: "*Ma langue l'a juré, mon coeur s'est abstenu*" (Euripides 2003, 52).[5]

Why has the line been so memorable, both in antiquity and since? One commentator asks, "Why was this line so shocking?" and speculates: Is it because "it seemed to indicate that men could swear oaths with internal reservations?" (Avery 1968, 21). Or does the line, more broadly, summarize the philosophical, religious, and existential "contrast and conflict between inner truth and outer appearances . . . the enormous distance between what one actually is and what one appears to be" (25)? It thereby would anticipate not only the Platonic-Socratic concern with "contradiction," with "the tongue being safe from refutation, but the heart not being safe from refutation" (Plato 2004, 39), but also the debates and arguments concerning "private language" in Wittgenstein's *Philosophical Investigations*. Its echoes even reverberate in Hollywood's cinematic rendering of the liberating as well as disturbing observation that "the Matrix cannot tell you who you are."

Hippolytus's line is uttered, of course, by an actor on stage, in a theatrical play, a dramatic genre Austin "deliberately" excludes from consideration in elaborating the theory of performatives and illocutionary force, leaving it up to "a more general account" to situate all utterances more properly, including staged ones.[6] The line expresses Hippolytus's terrified response to the revelation, by her nurse, of his stepmother's adulterous and quasi-incestuous desire for him—after the nurse has first obtained his solemn oath under no circumstance to reveal the secret that he is about to be told. The line seals his fate as an "unhappy man" in his own eyes, and as a "seducer," with barely masqueraded "holy manner," in the eyes of his father. Both of them are unaware of the extent to which they are merely pawns in a hapless game that the gods—Aphrodite and Artemis and, more indirectly, Zeus and Poseidon—are playing with each other according to strict and strangely noninterventionist rules (Euripides 1995, 227). The citation is important for several reasons.

First, the example of *giving one's word*—of swearing, taking an oath, but especially promising—is Austin's privileged illustration of what is at stake in, what captures the essence and informal logic of, a performative *tout court*, what he calls an "explicit performative." Cavell agrees with

the widespread sense, and claim, that the act and concept of promising is not just one more among performative utterances . . . but that promising—even especially the promise to marry—is somehow privileged in Austin's view, naming as it were the fact of speech itself. . . . [I]n *How to Do Things with Words* Austin identifies speaking as *giving one's word*, as if an 'I promise' implicitly lines every act of speech, of intelligibility, as it were a condition of speech as such. (Kant held that 'I think' is such a lining). (Cavell 2003, xii)

Second, the quote is important in that Austin glosses Euripides' line as claiming that, in Hippolytus's invocation, the utterance "I promise to . . ." amounts to an internalized and self-imposed act of obligation and hence portrays "my" promise as putting "on record," Austin says, "my spiritual assumption of a spiritual shackle." Austin's implication is, of course, that this is *not* how the promise—or, for that matter, any performative—should be viewed, at least if we wish to block an immoral "let-out" (1962, 10) that undermines its very undertaking, aim, and effect.

An insightful commentator, Espen Hammer, notes that, in Cavell's reading of this gloss, "Hippolytus enacts Austin's suspicion that metaphysics can be used 'to get out of the moral of the ordinary, out of our ordinary moral obligations.'"[7] Or, as Cavell adds further in the passage to which Hammer refers: "Austin uses this distinction between tongue and heart as a type of the philosophical use of profundity (call it metaphysics) to exempt yourself, or exclude yourself, from the everyday responsibilities or accountabilities that make civilized life possible" (1994, 62).

But how does Hippolytus's statement "My tongue swore to, but my heart did not" render the absolute (Kant would say "categorical") imperative of obeying or fulfilling one's promise to be merely theoretical or "hypothetical," thus supposedly condemning it to being no longer a promise at all? Austin gives an explanation based upon a moral lesson, an "ethics of speech":

> It is gratifying to observe in this very example how excess of profundity, or rather solemnity, at once paves the way for immorality. For someone who says "promising is not merely a matter of uttering words! It is an inward and spiritual act!" is apt to appear as a solid moralist standing out against a generation of superficial theorizers: we see him [or are apt to see him, and this is our metaphysical "obsession," Austin suggests] as he sees himself, surveying the invisible depths of ethical space, with all the distinction of a specialist in the *sui generis*. Yet he provides Hippolytus with a let-out, the bigamist with an excuse for his "I do." . . . Accuracy and morality alike are on the side of the plain saying that *our word is our bond*. (Austin 1962, 10)

Only words, it seems, can stick and produce a noticeable effect in the world that is morally worth mentioning. Only words can bind, bond, or bend. Intentions (or in any case the "inward and spiritual" thoughts, acts, or feelings) remain—and must remain—ephemeral, disengaged, and perhaps disinterested.

But what, exactly, is the "let-out" and hence the "immorality" risked in this supposedly "metaphysical" conception? And why it is that *tragedy* should remind us of it? Is this because philosophy, "apt" as it is to seek "the invisible depths of ethical space," has thus far failed to give a reasonable account of the pitfalls and downside of such "space"? Or worse, can philosophy not produce an account of the grounds of its own making and design, trapping itself in its own web of mental constructions (that is to say, its representationalism, intentionalism, verism, spiritualism, or logocentrism; all of which are specimens of naturalism, idealism, or the constative fallacy)? Does not Austin overlook precisely the possibility that the dual perspective on the act of promising—the very distinction between "tongue" and "heart"—is not necessarily or exclusively a moral risk, but a chance (i.e., a risk worth taking and, indeed, always already taken) as well?

Austin says that he wants to "exclude such fictitious inward acts" (Austin 1962, 10)—that is, less fiction or theater as such than fictitiously

imagined and thus unrealizable acts)—from the very definition of promising, and hence from performatives that find their model in the paradig-
matic case of the promise (this means, again, virtually *all* performatives).
But can he relegate them to another context of study—the "general theory" of performatives, say—that could be safely bracketed or presupposed
here? Or does the quote from Euripides, on the contrary, indicate that
Austin already implicitly acknowledges the impurity or pervertibility of
all performatives, including the metaphysical and moral "let-out" they
presuppose?

The Unfathomability of Sincerity
and the Threat of Skepticism

Nothing, Austin suggests, and *a fortiori* none of the "other things
which are certainly required to accompany an utterance such as 'I promise
that . . . ,'" is, on closer scrutiny, described in the scene that Hippolytus
invokes. But what could Hippolytus's line imply in a nonconstative, nonassertive reading, beyond the dismantling of all apparent representationalism, verism, spiritualism, and logocentrism? What, in other words, are its
"normal concomitants" (Austin 1962, 10)?

In Austin's account, these concomitants are feelings, thoughts, and
intentions. But do they announce or impose themselves in more realistic
and everyday ways, as Austin believes they should?[8] To put it differently,
are these normal "concomitants" "fictitious," or are they *just as dubious*
(lacking seriousness and sincerity) as the literary and the theatrical, which
Austin *here and elsewhere* seeks to exclude?

The citation from Euripides is crucial to Cavell for yet another reason, since it makes clear that the potential misfiring or abuse of promises—of words as bonds—is one of age-old *tragic* dimensions. He cites
Shoshana Felman, from *The Scandal of the Speaking Body*: "If the capacity
for misfire is an inherent capacity of the performative, it is because the act
as such is defined, for Austin, as the capacity to *miss its goal* and *to fail to
be achieved*, to remain *unconsummated*" (Cavell 2003, xiv).[9] Yet Felman's
reading, Cavell suggests, "runs its own dangers of denying something in
Austin" (xiv). What she seems to be missing or glossing over (as does Derrida in *Limited Inc.*) is, Cavell writes, "Austin's horror of using, not to say

constructing, some metaphysical discovery as a cosmic excuse for moral chiseling, as in his example that takes a remark of Euripides' Hippolytus, 'My tongue swore but my heart did not,' as a way out of keeping a promise . . . as an excuse for having failed in a given case to do the best one might have done under the circumstances" (xv). Yet Austin is, Cavell points out, "perhaps falsely remembering Hippolytus's later behavior." For all his moral-metaphysical "let-out," Hippolytus nonetheless keeps his word to remain silent to the end, come what may (as a good Kantian *avant la lettre*). *He does not use the line as an excuse at all.* On the contrary, Cavell observes, Hippolytus expresses terror and implores pity, both of which are "some function of the knowledge that the most *casual* of utterances may be irretrievable: so my tongue swore without my heart—*nevertheless I am bound*" (Cavell 1994, 62).

Cavell seems to imply that Austin's view of performative misses (infelicities, misfires, and abuses) is one of near-misses, not the general derailment and the hilarity—the affront and "scandal of the speaking body"—they inspire. Yet Austin's sense of infelicity (here, of misfiring rather than abuse), Cavell nonetheless urges, should be distinguished from our common understanding of Freudian "slips" and "parapraxes" (Cavell 1994, 62; cf. Felman 2003, 56):[10]

An Austinian "misfire" is not a Freudian slip, because it is not essentially motivated. Yet Austin does investigate slips; that forms the project of his rediscovery of the importance of the concept of excuses, sketched in his notes called "A Plea for Excuses." There what emerges is that, in contrast to Freud's vision of the human being as a field of significance whose actions express wider meaning than we might care to be questioned about, Austin's vision is of the human as a field of vulnerability whose actions imply wider consequences and effects and results—if narrower meaning—than we should have to be answerable for. But then of what use is the difference without the sameness between them? And the sameness has to do with what might be seen as versions or visions of the speaking body. (Cavell 2003, xvi)

Whether infelicities, misfires, or abuses are slips of the unconscious or not (as Austin, on Cavell's reading, would seem to suggest), there is, for Cavell, something specific to *words*—to "speech arising as such," the "speaking body"—that remains strangely (even tragically?) distinct from actions and *doing things with words.*

We should try to understand why Hippolytus's line illustrates, for Cavell, that "the saying of words is not excusable the way the performance of actions is; or in a word, that saying something is after all, or before all, on Austinian grounds, not exactly or merely or transparently doing something" (1996, 104–5). Which is another way of saying the human voice—or human writing—and hence a certain concept of "absolute responsibility . . . tethered to a mortal" (1994, 64) retains a certain privilege in the general economy of being, acting, feeling, and so on and so forth. In Cavell's reading, Euripides' phrase shows that sayings and doings are not (fully) symmetrical or congruent, even when and where—and then often most painfully—they are in fact synchronic and hence seem to operate in tandem.

For Cavell, Hippolytus's line conjures up a possibility that Austin intimates but then leaves unexplored—indeed, shies away from—namely, the disturbing yet in a way liberating fact that we have no way of telling whether a promise is meant or intended to be kept. And since the promise is the best example of all performatives—perhaps, of all utterance—this simple but fateful fact reveals "the human as a field of vulnerability" in which all acts of speech and the actions they express "imply wider consequences and effects and results—if narrower meaning—than we should be answerable for" (Cavell 2003, xvi). Again, such infelicity, misfiring, or abuse is neither "essentially motivated" (as psychoanalysis claims) nor structurally random (as semioticians would seem to find). Based neither on hidden sense nor on explicit nonsense, it expresses a tragic possibility—and chance—of and for human existence, whose dimensions are unfathomable yet explain the aporia of all attempted seriousness and sincerity alike.

Austin suspects (but does not elaborate) that this fact by no means diminishes the weight our words acquire, whether we intend or desire this or not. He downplays the insight that if a promise—the word and act of promising—may not be what it seems or purports to be, this is precisely how it must and should be, that this is constitutive of the phenomenon of promising (or, by extension, of any utterance or act) and as such that this uncertainty should persist. The immorality risked by Hippolytus's declaring "my tongue swore to, but my heart did not"—which is a *cri de coeur* more than a statement with descriptive content—may thus be a serious risk: "Austin may be understood to have been drawn to and alarmed by this play of Euripides, in its study of the unfathomability of sincerity."

Parenthetically, Cavell establishes a further parallel: "That there are no marks or tokens . . . by which to distinguish the genuine or real from the false or fake is a way of putting Wittgenstein's discovery . . . that there are not what he calls criteria for distinguishing reality and dream, or, I add, animate and inanimate, or sincerity or seriousness and hollowness and treachery, hence no way of *blocking* the threat of skepticism" (1996, 102).

Hippolytus promises without knowing beforehand what the promise entails; he is enticed to be silent before being told what it is that he must remain silent about, a promise, he complains, that he makes "off guard" and by which he now feels "trapped through oath by the gods," which alone keeps him from "telling this whole story to [his] father" (Euripides 1995, line 655). One wonders why he lets things get this far. Could he have avoided this predicament? But then, Cavell seems to suggest, does one not always let things go too far? Or, as Derrida might have glossed, is a promise not always—and, from the moment one speaks, always already—made "off guard," that is to say, in less than complete awareness of its meaning (including its accompanying thoughts, feelings, and intentions), to say nothing of its consequences? Moreover, is one nonetheless not always bound by an absoluteness and categoricalness for which being "trapped" by nothing less than the "gods" is not such a bad metaphor after all? Who could—or would want to—be always on guard? Or give his or her word under the condition of complete transparency of "normal concomitants," guaranteed by saturated contexts and fully established conventions?

If we do too much knowing or calculating, thinking or feeling—in short, intending—we will be good for nothing, come to nothing, be available for nothing. In order to promise—or, more broadly and simply, to speak and write, or even be and act at all—we must for conceptual no less than existential and metaphysical reasons not only not (!) necessarily mean what we say, we must necessarily not (!) mean what we say. More precisely still: in order to "mean" what we say, we must not (fully and exclusively or transparently) mean what we say.

In speech acts such as promising (but promises, we found, reveal a more general truth concerning performative utterances as such), "precision," in terms of a pretended *unambiguity* of meaning, is thus *neither given nor to be aspired to.* This unamiguity of meaning is just like "making explicit," which, Austin says, is the "force" of how one's words are effectively taken by others. As imagined ideals, precision and explicitness—

rather than, say, the literary and the theatrical or the masquerade—must be excluded from Austin's analysis as less than pertinent to the understanding of seriousness and sincerity. Paradoxically, in matters of seriousness and sincerity, one can find precision and appropriateness only in (and through) imprecision and inappropriateness

This is the "aporia of sincerity" (as Jean-Luc Marion terms it in a remarkable essay, analyzing the locution "I love you," which is a "passionate utterance" and "perlocution" [Marion 2005, 124, 130, 132] if there ever was one): its groundlessness even in the face—or on the very basis—of grounds or reasons given (albeit infinite in number). This is also its "unintelligible bond," its *uneinsichtige Verbindlichkeit*, as Adorno said of the moral imperative, well beyond its Kantian form.

What remains, then, for Cavell's reference to Euripides' *Hippolytus* is that the play "may be thought of precisely as a tragedy of sincerity, that is to say, of the *inability to be insincere*, an inability *not* to be signed onto your words and deeds" (1996, 61). It is as if one's sincerity (like one's seriousness) were a matter of being "glued," neither to the world nor to others, but to oneself, to the "scandal" of one's being oneself, more precisely of being caught (indeed, "trapped . . . by the gods") in each of one's words (albeit those given "off guard," which amounts to most if not all of them). Put differently, it is as if, in principle and in fact, we have nothing else to call for. We are fatefully stuck with (or to) ourselves, not so much in the sense of unconsciously coinciding externally with some solemn internal (that is to say, spiritual-mental) deliberation in the depth of our soul, *foro interno*; but, more fundamentally, of being always already too late to reflect, to regret, to withdraw, to moderate, and, indeed, to be insincere.

Word-World Glue

I take the metaphor of being "glued to" ourselves—bound to our word—from Michael Fried's suggestive interpretation of the Wittgensteinian-Cavellian motif of "the everyday" (which *is* our being "glued" to the world) in *Menzel's Realism: Art and Embodiment in Nineteenth-Century Berlin*. Sincerity and seriousness, for all their tragedy and aporia, would, in this view, seem the most ordinary thing in our lives. While the context of Hippolytus's utterance is utterly dramatic and theatrical, it thus illustrates a mode of enunciation that, as it were, happens everywhere, everyday, into which we are fully *absorbed* (to borrow Fried's terminology), allowing no *theatricalization* and, indeed, no "escape," even if we try (which we must, no less fatefully, for the same conceptual and ontological reasons).

One is further reminded of Emmanuel Levinas's conception of responsibility in his second major book, entitled *Autrement qu'être ou au-delà de l'essence* (*Otherwise Than Being or Beyond Being*). Levinas evokes its "drama" no less than its "comedy" in terms of one's carrying the other not so much under but at—and as—one's skin. The skin is "glued" to me, beyond my initiative and consciousness, against my "interest" in a near-fatal, near-compulsive, and (as Levinas says) "obsessive," "traumatic," and in any case inescapably tragic manner. This makes the skin like the tunic given by the centaur Nessus, which managed, after all the heroic labors Hercules completed, to be the very thing that did him in. Like Hippolytus's fate, this reveals yet another element of the bond that our words impose on us, one that Cavell stresses over and over: the fact that their tragic nature is, for us mortals, *unbearable.*

Cavell notes that Austin himself seems eager to forget that Hippolytus apparently does not use the line ("my tongue swore to, but my heart did not") as an excuse at all, and in fact, as far as we can tell, he at no point seems to break his word on stage. On the contrary, Cavell observes, Hippolytus expresses terror and implores pity, both of which are "some function of the knowledge that the most *casual* of utterances may be irretrievable: so my tongue swore without my heart—*nevertheless I am bound*" (Cavell 1994, 62). And, lest we forget, even the gods—in Euripides' play, explicitly Poseidon—are supposed to keep their promises, even when they'd rather not to, since the promise's original intent is derailed.

More precisely, Hippolytus must stick to an oath about which one wonders whether he was ever at liberty to refuse to take it (steered as the entire course of action seems in this play by *deus ex machina*: first Aphrodite, then Artemis, at the opening and at the end of play, respectively). It is an oath that he can only forsake by sinning against at least one of the gods. He can only protect his integrity—his *sōphronein,* moderation or chastity (line 731)—by violating or casting suspicion on it at the same time. That is the aporia of his sincerity. Or, as Avery has it: "once he has taken the oath Hippolytus knows that he cannot explain his inner purity in any convincing way and that he has to let himself be judged by outward appearances.

These, although he does not know it yet, have been rigged by Aphrodite to bring about his destruction. His dilemma is that he must maintain these outward appearances to preserve the inward purity (part of which is his respect—*sebas*—for the gods). His statement is meant to be a cry of anguish at the recognition of his dilemma" (Avery 1968, 25).

In other words, "on Hippolytus's view of promising, the saying that our word is our bond proves a fatal *curse*," and in this sense exemplifies the "links of tragedy with moral necessities" (Cavell 1994, 62). In short, there is more to Hippolytus's exclamation than Austin allows or elaborates— although the mere fact that he inserts this passing reference to "tragedy" into his lectures is something that, for all its indirectness and underdetermination, should have prevented or modified some of Derrida's or, for that matter, Felman's conclusions.

It should be noted that Cavell, with reference to Felman's attempt to read "Don Juan with J. L. Austin," notes that Hippolytus's "anti-type" is, precisely, Molière's *Don Juan* and Mozart and Da Ponte's *Don Giovanni*, "for whom apparently no word is binding" (Cavell 1994, 62). Don Juan is "the compulsive promise maker and promise breaker," and hence, *pace* Felman, Cavell goes on to suggest, "Austin's nemesis, a figure for the chaos awaiting a social order forgetful of Austin's monitions" (Cavell 2003, xiii). But then, the scenarios for the type and anti-type, Hippolytus and Don Juan—the apparent promise withholder and actual promise keeper, on the one hand, and the apparent promise maker and actual promise breaker, on the other— are equally fateful, and the opposing protagonists are similarly "trapped" in a compulsive repetition of oath making and breaking that leaves no room for judgment in the singular case. They find no way to "let go" (Hippolytus) or to "give in" (Don Juan) and hence fail to loosen or tighten bonds where they could (or should). And yet, while "seduction"—including the seduction (or is it temptation?) of the tragic character—may well be part and parcel of Austin's prose and thinking (as Felman claims in her effort to extend his analysis into further and no less tragic domains), it nonetheless inspires a reservation that she overlooks and that Cavell expresses as follows:

But is it not worth trying to distinguish the laughter—and the attendant anxiety—caused in one who, like Austin, senses the bond of our words apt to be loosened beyond our understanding, from the laughter caused in another who, like Don Juan, finds the bond of our words apt to be tightened beyond reason, in each case destroying both obligation and pleasure? (Cavell 2003, xiv)

And is it not, precisely, the "laughter" and "anxiety" at this alternative loosening and tightening that tend to undermine morality and desire, that is to say, "obligation" and "pleasure"?

Dead Serious

Whether we like it or not, or know it or not, there is a dead-serious and quasi-mechanical or quasi-automatic quality, a near literalness or materiality and inertia, in the things to which we have become answerable. Therefore, Cavell reads Austin "not as denying that I have to abandon my words, create so many orphans, but as affirming that I am abandoned *to* them, as to thieves, or conspirators, taking my breath away, which metaphysics seeks, as it were, to deny" (Cavell 1994, 63).

This absoluteness has a temporal dimension, one that consists, paradoxically, in denying its passage or rather in making infinite its moment and momentum: "the price of having once spoken, or remarked, taken something as remarkable . . . is to have spoken *forever*, to have entered the arena of the inexcusable, to have taken on the responsibility for speaking further, the *unending* responsibility of responsiveness, of answerability" (Cavell 1994, 65; emphasis added). This element of infinity at the very heart of human finitude, Cavell concludes, is nothing but the condition of intelligibility, of making oneself intelligible to others as well as to oneself.

Yet this is not all there is to say. Regardless of his "terror" and our "pity," Hippolytus, for all we know, may, in speaking his line, very well 'intend' or plan to forsake his promise—or at least think and feel he has, inadvertently, done so already—while *de facto* keeping it nonetheless and holding his ground. As the goddess Artemis reveals at the end of the play, "He, as was right, did not fall in with her [Phaedra's] words, nor yet again, godly man that he is, did he break the firm bond of his oath" (Euripides 1995, 247). But Hippolytus, for his part, seems less sure of this when he responds to Theseus's anger: "As things stand, I swear by Zeus, god of oaths, and the earth beneath me that I never touched your wife, never had the thought. May I perish with no name or reputation . . . and may neither sea nor earth receive my corpse if I am guilty" (237). And a little later: "O Zeus, may I no longer live if I am guilty!" (237). But how could he himself, at least, not know?

This much is clear: for all we know Hippolytus may have never thought he wished (he did) or knew he did, given the fact that he leaves open the possibility that he may be guilty after all. And yet the "if I am guilty," which suggests lack of clarity and decision in this matter, stands next to Hippolytus's earlier assurance that "to this very moment my body is untainted by love. I do not know this act save by report or seeing it in painting. I am not eager to look at it either, since I have a virgin soul" (Euripides 1995, 221), or again, when he exclaims, "Why, when I am guilty of no wrong?" (253).

If he keeps his promise merely *de facto* and holds his ground, he would thus act not "out of duty," to use Kant's idiom, but merely "in conformity" with it; that is to say, in sync with absolute obligation or, in his context, with the divinely monitored oath (which, we saw, is a curse and a necessity). Would his act thereby be merely that of an actor (as if, even in the text and context of Euripides' play, he would be acting a role that is not his own)? Would it be seriousness or insincerity that he would lack in this scenario? Moreover, would he himself be able to tell whether he is serious and sincere? If we are to believe Austin as read by Cavell and Derrida, there are no criteria or rules by means of which we would be able to know or tell the difference with a reasonable degree of certainty. "With many procedures," Austin says, "for example playing games, however appropriate the circumstances may be I may still not be playing" (1962, 29). And a little later: "there may be nothing in the circumstances by which we can decide whether or not the utterance is performative [e.g., a promise] at all. Anyway, in a given situation it can be open to me to take it as *either* one or the other" (33).

We could go even one step further. Euripides' play *Hippolytus* and the telling line quoted from it demonstrate the tragedy and aporia of sincerity in that they reveal not just the fatefulness of promising but also—and simultaneously—the standing possibility, the remaining ability (perhaps, necessity) to be insincere. One has apparently or in fact has not (fully or not yet) signed onto one's words and deeds, after all is said and done, and this regardless of the "bound" and "terror" experienced or expressed.

Sincere Disengagement

Seriousness and sincerity require that we indeed grant and indeed cherish this semantic and ontological "let-out," which is a possibility for good and for ill, no mere escape from moral constraints and our answerability to others, the world, and ourselves. For one thing, we will want others to have wanted—that is, fully intended—their promise, rather than having made or even fulfilled it in almost fated, automatic, programmed ways. Put in psychological or psychoanalytic terms, such ways would be compulsive, obsessive, neurotic, regressive, and psychotic. The promise should not be made or fulfilled by the "unconscious," in other words, by the "body," but, however one spins the word, "spiritually" or, if you like, "freely." Its affect should be active, not passive, even though it can—and must—be "passionate" in the precise meaning Cavell gives to this term in his attempt to salvage yet another ancient (this time rhetorical rather than tragic) moment upon which Austin's text touches only in passing.

All of which leaves yet another, final question unanswered, namely: are sincerity and insincerity both *also* thinkable, or are they lived as *dis*engagement, retraction, disavowal, betrayal, indeed, *un-binding*? Austin somewhat unjustly considers this *dis*engagement to be merely a moral "let-out," that is, the necessary possibility of our being no longer able, let alone forced, to give or live up to what is or was a given word, a done deed. This is as if everything should in principle at all moments stand the test of (still) being willed (that is, claimed, acclaimed, or proclaimed) all over again, after all is said and done.

Asking what it means that human expressions can be pretended or imitated, staged or soliloquized, excused and reiterated—and all this either seemingly at will or unwittingly and while taken "off guard"—Cavell notes that this empirical or metaphysical given haunts each given word and

betokens, roughly, that human utterances are essentially vulnerable to insincerity and that the realization that we may never know whether others are sincere (I do not exclude the first person) is apt to become unbearable. (We might say that it returns philosophy's attention to the fact that human life is constrained to the life of the mind, such as it is). (Cavell 1996, 92)

This latter formulation may surprise. For one thing, it can hardly mean that, for all we know, we are captives of our own mind and its "life," which, say, would include its perceptions and ideas (as in solipsistic views of the mind or as in Berkeley's idealist conception of human knowledge, not to mention Schopenhauer's conviction that "the world is my representation"). In fact, the best explanation of the phrase is—with a decidedly Wittgensteinian streak—that "human life is constrained" to the life of the body, "such as it is." We are reminded of the Wittgensteinian dictum that this body (and its "life"?) is "the best picture of the human soul" (discussed at length in *The Claim of Reason*), but also of the decidedly Lacanian motif, recalled by Cavell in the foreword to Felman's book and cited with apparent approval: "A body is speech arising as such" (Cavell 2003, xiv; cf. 65).[11]

"Salaam"

Austin gives further telling examples throughout his lectures and philosophical essays of the uncertainties involved in every speech act or, indeed, *in all utterance*. These utterances hence inevitably include all those explicit statements entailing truth or falsity that Austin calls "pure," but also those that border upon the implicit and are expressive of so-called non-linguistic actions:

The situation in the case of actions which are non-linguistic but similar to performative utterances in that they are the performance of a conventional action (here ritual or ceremonial) is rather like this: suppose I bow deeply before you; it might not be clear whether I am doing obeisance to you or, say, stooping to observe the flora or to ease my indigestion. Generally speaking, then, to make clear both *that* it is a conventional ceremonial act, and *which* act it is, the act (for example of doing obeisance) will as a rule include some special further feature, for example raising my hat, tapping my head on the ground, sweeping my other hand to my heart, or even very likely uttering some noise or word, for example 'Salaam.' Now uttering 'Salaam' is no more describing my performance, stating that I am performing an act of obeisance, than is taking off my hat: and by the same token . . . saying 'I salute you' is no more describing my performance than is saying 'Salaam.' To do or to say these things is to make plain [to make explicit] how the action is to be taken or understood, what action it is. And so it is with putting in the expression 'I promise that.' It is not a description, because (1) it could not be true or false; (2) saying 'I promise that' (if happy, of course) *makes it* a promise, and *makes it* unambiguously a promise. Now we can say that such a performative formula as 'I promise' makes it clear how what is said is to be understood and even conceivably that the formula 'states that' a promise has been made; but we cannot say that such utterances are true or false, nor that they are descriptions or reports." (Austin 1962, 69)

But one wonders: how is it that raising my hat or (casually) saying 'Salaam' is not at least as ambiguous as bowing deeply before you? Surely, this enunciation is not something that just about everyone could plausibly and responsibly—seriously and sincerely—make at all times, irrespective of location and situation, from where and to whom the address is directed. Austin and his most astute readers have demonstrated that. Why cannot one tell in advance what will count as a greeting or an insult, as a welcome or farewell, as uprightness or irony, rapprochement or distancing? Just imagine someone more privileged walking in a French suburb—or, for that matter, into some Western military or even diplomatic facility—these days, saying 'Salaam,' and doing so provocatively or else innocuously, with the best of intentions. Depending on who speaks and why or how, there or anywhere else, a phrase that is a *sign* of peace might in fact constitute an act of hostility or, at best, insensitivity.

And, if this is the case, then saying 'I promise' ('take my word for it') is not, thereby, unambiguously promising (speaking the truth) either. Saying 'I promise' ('I assure you') does not—indeed, must not necessarily—mean 'I promise' (or that I can or will vouch for what I say).

Mutatis mutandis, this uncertainty affects our theoretical or meta-theoretical positions as well. The "life of the mind" we seek as we live our theory in a more than merely hypothetical mode—for example, in *doing philosophy seriously and sincerely*, taking it as a *way of life*—obeys the tragic logic Austin only mentions in passing and that Cavell unpacks with great consequence. Indeed, the "life of the mind, such as it is" might mean simply this: we may go for something, be onto something—and do so quite (or fully) seriously and sincerely—and yet *not know* or *fail to know* whether and how we can or will *do things with words*.

No Misunderstanding

A further, final, act of precision should be made here. The predicament of promising, which exemplifies and models any utterance in general, is not one of possible or even necessary misunderstanding. Its fatefulness is seated much deeper. In fact, the Euripides drama, as cited by Austin and explicated by Cavell, alludes to a far more challenging uncertainty than either knowledge or skepticism can fathom. Skepticism, in its respective affirmative or negative modes and moods, assumes still too much and remains tied to the very representationalist metaphysics of descriptivism and verism, positivism and logocentrism, that Austin—on both Derrida's and Cavell's view—so effectively enables us to undermine (even though he did not develop his own analysis to its full potential).

Why is Hippolytus's case of promising (as he says, without promising, strictly speaking) not one of "misunderstanding"? As Austin says: "It is obviously the case that to have promised I must normally (A) have been *heard* by someone, perhaps the promisee; (B) have been understood by him as promising. If one or another of these conditions is not satisfied, doubts arise as to whether I have really promised, and it might be held that my act was only attempted or was void" (1962, 22). Yet there is no doubt that, in this sense, Hippolytus has indeed promised. Neither he nor the woman servant questions that a promise was uttered. Therefore there must be other, more serious, doubts and backfires that make this dramatic scene tragic and, pace Austin, unintelligible to all involved as well as to all viewers, listeners, and readers. Call it a fateful necessity or—in the Jansenist theology and terminology that haunts Racine's adaptation of Euripides' play, *Phaedra*—predestination.

But, perhaps, tragedy simply exists in the fact that where the act of promising—or, for that matter, any other utterance—is concerned, so many things can "go wrong" and in more ways than one at once. Austin is at no loss for examples, suggesting that, for one thing, "we can insincerely promise a donkey to give it a carrot" (1962, 23). Further, tragedy may also convey an even more serious insight, Austin implies, namely that "the ways of going wrong 'shade into one another' and 'overlap,' and the decision between them is 'arbitrary' in various ways" (1962, 23). In other words, it would be impossible to tell whether or where we go wrong (misfire, abuse, become unserious or insincere), if we do.

And in the end, while all these combined "uncertainties" perhaps do not "matter in theory," it is, Austin observes, nonetheless "pleasant to investigate them and in practice convenient to be ready, as jurists are, with a terminology to cope with them" (1962, 24). But then what could *coping* mean here? Tragedy precisely seems to forestall any such solution, however temporary.

One need not look far to find examples—often hilarious ones—that hammer this point home and whose intellectual wit and potentially dead-serious implications leap out from these pages: "When the saint baptized the penguins, was this void because the procedure of baptizing is inappropriate to be applied to penguins, or because there is no *accepted* procedure of baptizing anything except humans?" (Austin 1962, 24; emphasis added); or, again: "Can I baptize a dog, if it is admittedly rational?" (31).

These seemingly rhetorical, unserious, and even insincere (but are they?) questions express a fundamental uncertainty that matters in more than merely theoretical or epistemological ways. And they do so not just juridically or canonically, but also ecclesiastically. Their unlikely subject illustrates precisely that uncertainty in utterance and acts, whether linguistic or not, extends even well beyond the range of semantic and pragmatic domains that we, so far, have considered ordinary (conventional and natural, normal and normative, thinkable and livable).

Yet the impossibility of answering these questions in any straightforwardly positive or negative way reveals not just a tragic necessity—namely to judge without certainty, without criteria—but also a chance. If nothing else, they entail the perspective of further expansion of human or animal rights just as they urge us to inquire what the human and animal mean both philosophically (indeed, metaphysically) as well as practically in the everydayness of our lives. Perhaps no more serious and sincere question could be raised.

Lessons in Exemplarity: Sincerity Come What May

What would a lived, living, that is to say, "life-" and at times, perhaps, even lively theory look like as it takes the motifs, modes, and moods of "seriousness" and "sincerity," well, seriously and does so—assuming now that this no longer comes down to the same—also sincerely?

At least two of many possible answers suggest themselves by way of examples. I take them both from Isaiah Berlin's remarkably pointed memoir of Austin in an essay that would have merited long discussion in its own right. In it, Berlin highlights two of his colleague and mentor's most surprising intellectual and personal qualities:

when he spoke, there appeared to be nothing between him and the subject of his criticism or exposition—no accumulation of traditional commentary, no spectacles provided by a particular doctrine—he often produced the feeling that the question was being posed clearly for the first time: that what had seemed blurred, or trite, or a play of conventional formulae in the books had suddenly been washed away: the problem stood out in sharp relief, clear, unanswered, and important, and the methods used to analyze it had a surgical sharpness and were used with fascinating assurance and apparently effortless skill. (Berlin 1973, 5)

As if to philosophize—and to do so seriously and sincerely—were first of all to speak on one's own account, at one's own risk, unaided by a hermeneutic horizon or methodological apparatus of sorts, then Austin's thinking would exemplify how one's words bind or unbind in ways that no reason or principle could anticipate, let alone regulate or control. It is as if one's words were glued to the "subject" or "question" at hand and in fact implied the disappearance of "writing" (to cite a topos that recurs and dominates in Western thought, from Plato's *Phaedrus* until its deconstruction in Derrida's *Dissemination*).

The second quality related by Berlin in this context is Austin's appreciation of intellectual rigor and fearlessness as it expressed itself not so much in a theory without context (or without reference to other texts), but in a theory without content (or, at least, without the content of the theory mattering as such). After a short-lived admiration for Marx and Lenin, Austin's "favourite examples of intellectual virtue" were, Berlin remembers, Darwin and Freud:

not because he particularly admired their views but because he believed that once a man had assured himself that his hypothesis was worth pursuing at all, he should pursue it to its logical end, whatever the consequences, and not be deterred by fear of seeming eccentric or fanatical, or by the control of philistine common sense. If logical consequences were in fact untenable, one would be able to withdraw or modify them in light of the undeniable evidence; but if one failed to explore a hypothesis to its full logical conclusions, the truth would forever be defeated by timid respectability. He said that a fearless thinker, pursuing a chosen path unswervingly against mutterings and warnings and criticism, was the proper object of admiration and emulation; fanaticism was preferable to cowardice, and imagination to dreary good sense. (Berlin 1973, 6–7)

Should we say that sincerity takes the form here of *parhessia*, as Foucault might have said? Are there parallels between the analysis of sincerity that we have followed here and the one Foucault propounds in *Fearless Speech* (2001), in an inquiry that dwells even more extensively than Austin's on Euripides' tragedies, the *Hippolytus* among them?

Or should sincerity, as Berlin summarizes Austin's view, be taken, if not as madness, then rather as a nearly absurd stubbornness? That Austin was willing to go quite far in his admiration for this pursuit of sincerity "whatever the logical consequences" can be gleaned from a further anecdote Berlin recounts. Probing the limits of ordinary language philosophy in search for naturalness and normalcy, Berlin recalls asking Austin:

Supposing a child were to express a wish to meet Napoleon as he was at the battle of Austerlitz; and I said "It cannot be done," and the child said "Why not?" and I said "Because it happened in the past, and you cannot be alive now and also a hundred years ago and remain at the same age," or something of the kind; and the child went on pressing and said "Why not?" and I said "Because it does not make sense, as we use words, to say that you can be in two places at once or 'go back' into the past," and so on; and this highly sophisticated child said "If it is only a question of words, then can't we simply alter our verbal usage? Would that enable me to see Napoleon at the battle of Austerlitz, and also, of course, stay as I am now, in place and time?"—What (I asked Austin) should one say to the child? Simply that it has confused the material and formal modes, so to speak? Austin replied: "Do not speak so. Tell the child to try and go back into the past. Tell it there is no law against it. Let it try. Let it try, and see what happens then." (Berlin 1973, 15)

Is sincerity both fearlessness and stubbornness, provided we can tell them apart? Are seriousness and the apparent lack thereof, like sincerity and insincerity, just two sides of the same coin, tossed up in the airy space of nothingness, where no criteria are given to help us orient our ways? Or do they mutually depend on one another, each affecting the other? Are they formally, analytically distinguishable at all? The example set by Austin—his own (as seen by Berlin) and Euripides' (in the lines from the *Hippolytus* cited in passing)—makes clear that no easy answer to these questions is readily available.

Such, in all seriousness and sincerity, might well be our fate, our tragedy, our predestination: namely, the more than merely empirical or psychological—and, perhaps, deeply metaphysical—fact that we have to hold on to (and be bound by) words, gestures, and meanings whose sendings and consequences, affects and effects, elude us and who thus render our commitments and obligations (to others and ourselves) ultimately *unfathomable*. Like reasons lacking grounds, but reasons nonetheless.

PART II

DECLINING SINCERITY

Can the Subaltern Confess?

PASOLINI, GRAMSCI, FOUCAULT,
AND THE DEPLOYMENT OF SEXUALITY

Cesare Casarino

> Indeed, just as light manifests both itself and the darkness, so truth is the standard both of itself and of the false.[1]
>
> BARUCH SPINOZA

Sincerity as Production of Truth: A Preface

Sincerity is the standard both of itself and of insincerity. Such a definition implies that sincerity has a tripartite structure, that is, a structure that is constituted by the relations among three terms: "sincerity," "itself," and "insincerity." Sincerity doubles itself here in its relation to itself. And it is only insofar as it posits itself in a self-relation that it relates at the same time also to insincerity. Put differently, sincerity provides the standpoint from which it is possible to speak and act either sincerely or insincerely. This is not a reversible process. Whereas, for example, I can speak and act insincerely from the standpoint of sincerity, I cannot speak and act either sincerely or insincerely from the standpoint of insincerity because there is no such standpoint in and of itself. Insincerity, strictly speaking, is a nonentity by itself.

There are, then, three distinct types of sincerity. Or, perhaps, sincerity has three different aspects. I would like to call these "sincerity," "insincerity," and "real sincerity" (or "the sincerity of the real"). The latter is that sincerity which is produced in an encounter with the real: it functions as the self-positing fiction that is indispensable for any confrontation between sincerity and insincerity. And, just like any other fiction, it has true and real effects. Sincerity and insincerity, thus, are mutually determining and constitute a dialectical binary opposition. Insofar as this opposition functions dialectically, it is founded on a foreclosure of the sincerity of the real, on a turning away from any encounter with the real.

This is another way of saying that sincerity and insincerity are the conscious and diachronic effects of an unconscious and synchronic sincerity of the real. For example, any form of parapraxis ought to be understood as a symptom of real sincerity, that is, as an index of that encounter with the real that constitutes the condition of possibility of any conscious speech act, sincere or insincere. And all three types of sincerity produce truth, or, more precisely, have a relation to truth, albeit in different ways and with different results. It is these different ways and these different results that concern me here.

In what follows, I sketch a possible articulation of the nexus of relations binding confession, sexuality, and subalternity—a nexus that, as I will try to show, presupposes a definition of sincerity as production of truth. In particular, I articulate this nexus by making my way through four specific texts—namely, Pier Paolo Pasolini's documentary *Comizi d'amore* (*Love Meetings*); Michel Foucault's review of that documentary entitled "The Gray Mornings of Tolerance" and his study *The History of Sexuality: An Introduction*; and Antonio Gramsci's essay "The Southern Question." My primary aim will be to show how the modern confessional subject and the modern sexual subject are produced at once by an oscillation between sincerity and insincerity, and by a foreclosure of the sincerity of the real. I wish to argue that real sincerity and its signs—that is, the forms of acknowledgment of, and of engagement with, an encounter with the real—index an altogether different and non-modern relation to the question of truth. They also point to an altogether different and non-modern form of subjectivity that is defining of the subaltern.[2]

Pasolini's Erotic Truth

In an emblematic moment of his 1964 documentary on the sexual mores of Italians—*Love Meetings*—Pasolini asks a handsome young man whether he is in favor of divorce, which at the time was not yet legal in Italy. The interviewee, who is surrounded by a throng of other young men, flatly answers: "No." When asked why not, he answers: "Because I am Calabrian"—Calabria being the southernmost region of mainland Italy. Far from being only a defensive response indicative of unrepentant patriarchal chauvinism, I take this to be also a politically astute answer to that modern and bourgeois technology of power which Foucault in *The History of Sexuality* calls "the deployment of sexuality" (1990a, 75–104).

In that work, Foucault concludes his arguments regarding the development of this technology of power with a critique of the project of sexual enlightenment, sexual liberation, and sexual tolerance that characterized the 1960s: "We must not think that by saying yes to sex, one says no to power; on the contrary, one tracks along the course laid out by the general deployment of sexuality" (1990a, 157). If one is to judge from Foucault's review of Pasolini's *Love Meetings*, which was written shortly after the publication of *The History of Sexuality*, this documentary foreshadows precisely such a critique. Foucault writes: "What pervades the entire film is not, in my opinion, the obsession with sex but a kind of historical apprehension, a kind of premonitory and confused hesitation with regard to a new system that was emerging in Italy—that of tolerance" (1998b, 230). To such a highly perceptive and largely accurate assessment of *Love Meetings*, I will add two indispensable corollaries.

The first corollary is rather obvious: namely, in formulating such an assessment of *Love Meetings*, Foucault points to Pasolini as a crucial precursor of the project that would occupy him during the last decade of his life. In other words, it is almost as if Foucault, as he was about to embark on an arduous investigation into the political genealogy of the relation between truth and subjectivity, was in search of potential allies and found such an ally precisely in Pasolini, with whom he felt an elective affinity.[3]

The second corollary is, perhaps, less obvious as well as more difficult to substantiate fully within the confines of this essay: namely, Pasolini's critique of the "deployment of sexuality" needs to be understood as part and parcel of his vexed, ambivalent, yet sustained engagement with

Gramsci's influential understanding of the Southern Question.[4] Importantly, this is an aspect of Pasolini's critique that Foucault almost entirely neglects. In what follows, I will also try to show some of the ways in which Pasolini's project in *Love Meetings* at once uncannily anticipated as well as significantly diverged from Foucault's own critical investigation of the modern sexual subject.

Love Meetings may seem at first an odd choice in this context for a few different reasons. First, if one is to look in Pasolini for substantive antecedents to Foucault's critique of the deployment of sexuality, it would make more sense to turn to those later works in which Pasolini will voice such a critique much more openly, bitterly, and ferociously. I am thinking, for example, of virtually everything Pasolini produced in 1975, the year of his death. I am thinking, in particular, of a film such as *Salò, or the 120 Days of Sodom*, as well as of the controversial essay "*Trilogy of Life* Rejected." There, in a moment of fierce sincerity and pitiless self-denunciation, Pasolini disavowed the utopian vision of unbridled sexual exuberance that he had produced in his cinematic investigation of medieval storytelling in films such as *The Decameron, The Canterbury Tales*, and *The Arabian Nights* (1987, 49–52).

Secondly, the genre and the format adopted by Pasolini in *Love Meetings*—namely, the documentary and the interview—would indicate that this film constitutes the apotheosis rather than a critique of the deployment of sexuality. In this film, Pasolini travels up and down the Italian peninsula mercilessly questioning people in the streets about sexuality, impertinently prying into their most intimate desires, annoyingly demanding the truth and nothing but the truth about sex. And, according to Foucault, such an imperative to speak the truth about sexuality, such an injunction to confess everything about sex, is the primary device in the deployment of sexuality. Yet, it is precisely because of the particular ways in which Pasolini handles the forms of the documentary and the interview in *Love Meetings* that this film constitutes such a crucial precursor of Foucault's project.[5]

Pasolini proves to be a very peculiar interviewer. To begin with, the questions he asks are often somewhat idiotic, as he himself sheepishly admits at one point in the documentary. Furthermore, at times he becomes quickly very bored with the inevitably predictable or pat responses as well as very impatient with the more hesitant or reticent interviewees. In those cases, he happily proceeds to answer his own questions, to provide the interviewee with the presumably right words, and to move right along to the next victim without further ado. Moreover, he seems to become most impatient, and even sarcastic at times, with those interviewees who take the interview and its injunction to confess very seriously indeed, while he is always far more attentive to those interviewees, especially children, who take the interview for what it is, namely, a game of truth that is best treated not seriously at all. For the latter, this game is an apparatus at once of power and of ideology whose main purpose is to interpellate the confessional subject. In short, its goal is to produce subjects incapable of not confessing. It is therefore a technology of both subjection and subjectivation whose siren-like allure must be resisted at all costs by being ignored *tout court*.

Pasolini finds it difficult not only to keep the equanimity that is appropriate for an interviewer but also not to express openly his sympathies for those interviewees who are unwilling or unable to play by the rules of the game and hence to fall into its subjectifying trap. Pasolini often exhibits indifference and disregard and at times even aversion and distaste for the means as well as ends of that eminently confessional genre which is the interview: to elicit, extract, and record the truth (means), so as to call into being a form of subjectivity for which truth will constitute forever after the absent cause immanent in its own effect (ends). Such disregard and distaste are not only negative, in the sense that they constitute reactions against the confessional subject, but also positive, in the sense that they point to and affirm Pasolini's true investments—which lie beyond that subject and elsewhere.

We begin to catch a glimpse of Pasolini's investments already in the preparatory notes for the documentary, in which he writes: "The questions must be stinging, malicious, impertinent, and fired point-blank . . . so as to wring from those interviewed, if not the truth in the logical sense, at least psychological truth. An expression in the eyes, a scandalized angry reaction, or a laugh, can say more than words" (Viano 1993, 123).[6] This ambiguous passage begs more questions than it answers. Leaving aside for the moment the dubious distinction between the "logical" and the "psychological," let us begin by highlighting the glaring contradiction that lies at the heart of this passage. The first sentence suggests that, ideally, one would want to extract the "logical" truth from the interviewees, but that, in reality, one will have to settle for *less*, namely, "at least psychological truth," or, in other words, at least a part if not the whole. Psychological truth is posited here as the consolation prize that awaits us once the attempt to attain the unattainable holy grail of logical truth has inevitably failed. The second sentence, however, suggests the opposite: psychological truth, which, it is implied, manifests itself in bodily gestures and affective states rather than in speech *per se*, in the end is more rather than less: "An expression in the eyes, a scandalized angry reaction, or a laugh, can say more than words" (123).

Pasolini is too precise a thinker for this contradiction to be dismissed simply as a momentary lapse in logic. This contradiction, on the contrary, is very precise, and constitutes a logical, structural symptom. If Pasolini ends up contradicting himself here, it is for a specific reason: he chooses a set of conceptual tools that are inadequate to the task that he has set for himself. Or, put differently, he attempts to express a qualitative difference by using quantitative categories, such as "more and less," or "part and whole." No matter how dubious or untenable the distinction between "logical" truth and "psychological truth" might seem, such a distinction does indicate at least that there are two types or levels of truth at stake here. And, precisely because they cannot be described in terms of quantitative difference without falling into contradiction, these types of truth must therefore indicate a qualitative difference. And if the difference between these two realms of truth is so difficult to define, this may well be because they are strictly immanent in one other: words and bodies, speech and gestures, verbal expression and physical expression inhere in one another inseparably, yet they do not necessarily express the same truths and certainly do not produce truth in the same way.

The point is that everything in the documentary supports the insight that is articulated—however inadequately—in the second rather than the first sentence of this ambiguous and contradictory passage: in *Love Meetings*, physical expression indeed constitutes "more" rather than "less." This is so, however, not at all in the sense that gestures speak more truth than speech acts do, or in the sense that bodies harbor the potential to unveil the *real* truth—that is, the truth of the real—while words do not. This is so, instead, in the sense that a corporeal excess is always attendant to and constitutive of any speech act. It is in the disparity and disarticulation between bodies and words instantiated by such an excess that the real may erupt and that a conception of truth may emerge that is altogether different from the one constituting at once the cause and the effect of the confessional subject. If Pasolini privileges such corporeal excess—in *Love Meetings* and elsewhere—he does so not because it speaks the truth and nothing but the truth about sex, but because it may afford a glimpse of a relation to the question of truth that is at odds with the confessional subject.

This is why in this documentary Pasolini for the most part uses the interview not in order to reveal—either in words or in bodies—that hidden truth of sex which is hidden by necessity and by definition. He uses it, rather, in order to plunge into that gaping abyss between words and bodies which opens up as soon as the physical presence, tactile behavior, bodily movements, facial expressions, or affective registers of the interviewees express a truth that can neither be hidden nor be revealed, a truth that can neither be affirmed nor be denied from the standpoint of confession. This is a truth, hence, that has little to do with sex as we know it. If it is bodies more than words that are at stake in *Love Meetings*, that is not because only bodies are sincere but because their corporeal and erotic semiosis often signals ways of being—and, indeed, forms of subjectivity—that are incompatible with the confessional subject.

Ultimately, the primary aim of *Love Meetings* is to capture what, for lack of a better term, I would like to call a non-confessional eroticism: this is not at all the eroticism expressed either in the act of confession or in the act of refusing to confess—since what is deployed in both those acts is specifically sexuality, regardless of the concomitant absence or presence of any form of eroticism. This is, rather, the eroticism exhibited in a radical inaptitude to confess—an inaptitude that constitutes a more uncompromising act of resistance to confession than even the sheer refusal to confess. In *Love Meetings*, Pasolini lovingly records the eroticism of those who have nothing at all to confess, of those whose truth will be no more than static interference in the voracious ears of confession.[7]

Gramsci's Pagan Subaltern

But who are these other subjects who are so impervious to the injunction to confess, who are so deaf to the hailing of sexual truth? In *Love Meetings*, they turn out to be subaltern subjects: either Southerners

or children, or both. In order to make sense of this crucial aspect of Pasolini's documentary, let us take a detour through both Gramsci and Foucault. Let us turn, first of all, to an illuminating moment in Gramsci's
discussion of the Southern Question. In the middle of his famous remarks
on the role played by intellectuals in the social life of the Italian South,
Gramsci argues that the clergy needs to be understood as an integral part
of the intellectual class, and he proceeds to distinguish sharply between
Northern Italian and Southern Italian clergy. Gramsci writes:

The Northern priest is usually the son of an artisan or a peasant; he has democratic sentiments and closer ties with the peasant masses; he is morally more correct than the Southern priest, who often openly co-habits with a woman, and he
therefore exercises a more socially complete spiritual office, that is to say, he is the
leader of all family activity. In the North the separation of the Church from the
State and the expropriation of ecclesiastical property has been more thorough-
going than in the South, where the parishes and convents have preserved or recon-
stituted a good deal of both fixed and moveable property. In the South the priest
appears to the peasant: (1) as a bailiff with whom the peasant comes into conflict
over the question of rents; (2) as a usurer who demands the highest rates of interest, and plays up religious obligations to secure the payment of rent or interest;
(3) as a man who is subject to common passions (women and money) and so spiritually inspires no confidence in either his discretion or impartiality. Confession,
therefore, has little significance, and the Southern peasant, though often superstitious in a pagan sense, is not priest-ridden. . . . The attitude of the peasant towards
the clergy is summed up in the popular saying: "The priest is a priest at the altar;
elsewhere he is a man like any other." (Gramsci 1959, 44)

After having listed the three different roles that the priest plays in the life
of the Southern peasant (namely, "bailiff," "usurer," and "a man subject to
common passions," that is, "a man like any other"), Gramsci interjects an
aside that constitutes almost a non sequitur—"Confession, therefore, has
little significance"—and then immediately proceeds unperturbed to discuss other matters. Despite its brief guest appearance, however, confession
may turn out to play a role of major significance in the drama between
North and South that is being staged in this passage.

   It is possible that the mention of "discretion" at the very end of the
preceding sentence functions as a catalyst or trigger for this flash of thought:
"(3) as a man who is subject to common passions (women and money) and
so spiritually inspires no confidence in either his discretion or impartiality.

Confession, therefore," etc. The fact that the sacrament of confession can-not function in the absence of absolute "confidence" in the priest's willing-ness and ability to keep his mouth shut may well constitute the missing link in this signifying chain, namely, that which introduces thoughts of confes-sion as well as relates them to what came earlier. It is possible also that for Gramsci the entire question of the social function of the clergy bears so obviously on the question of confession that the matter of their relations does not need belaboring—and hence the peculiarly offhand tone of the whole interjection. Either way, Gramsci does not elaborate further on this tantalizingly brief insight, which disappears from his reflections just as sud-denly as it had appeared in them—returning, thus, to those undetectable regions of thought from which it must have hailed in the first place.

Be that as it may, the point is that a thought that suddenly comes out of nowhere often is a thought that had been there all along in a form other than a fully actual one. It is a thought that comes not out of nowhere but out of an elsewhere of potentiality—and that points to such an elsewhere. It is what Gilles Deleuze—borrowing from Michel Foucault borrowing from Maurice Blanchot—calls the "thought of the outside." This is the thought produced when coming into contact with an outside of force rela-tions, that outside in which the agon between power and resistance cease-lessly unfolds.[8]

If this is the case—if, in other words, the abrupt, unannounced emergence of the question of confession in this passage reveals that this question had been there all along in a latent form as well as indexes a spe-cific point of tangency with relational networks of power and resistance—then it would seem as if Gramsci has identified the sacrament of confession as a crucial linchpin in the mechanisms of production and reproduction of subalternity. Confession constitutes here an apparatus of interpellation meant to guarantee the smooth reproduction of the relations of produc-tion, which include but are not limited to class relations.

Gramsci's point, however, is that this apparatus malfunctions in the Italian South and hence that there is nothing smooth about the reproduc-tion of such relations there: "The priest is a priest at the altar; elsewhere he is a man like any other." The Southern priest does not enable the type of transference required for true confession to take place and to do its job as a binding linchpin of subalternity. This is the important complex of power dynamics on which Gramsci has seized here: due to the decidedly worldly,

temporal, and, indeed, exploitative roles played by the all-too-human cler-
ical agents of divine transcendence, the sacrament of confession has little
hold on the subaltern subjects of the South. Its power of interpellation
among them, thus, is a very weak one at best. Gramsci's subalterns—who
are "superstitious in a pagan sense"—make themselves answerable to a
regime of truth altogether different and older than the one inaugurated by
the Church and articulated in its confessional interpellation.

Gramsci's powerful intuition has far-reaching consequences when
read in the context of Foucault's project in *The History of Sexuality*. One of
the central arguments of that work is that the deployment of sexuality is a
specifically modern and bourgeois invention whose success and effectiveness was crucially enabled by the subsumption and reformulation of much
older technologies of power, such as, above all, confession. Following its
sacramental codification by the Lateran Council of 1215, confession became
increasingly important as a procedure for the production of truth in all
realms of life. Since then, Foucault writes, "confession has spread its effects
far and wide." And this metaphorical locution, which is repeated several
times in *The History of Sexuality* and which turns confession into nothing
short of an infectious pandemic, cannot be taken lightly coming from the
writer of *The Birth of the Clinic* (Foucault 1990a, 59; see also 63). Since then,
Foucault declares, "Western man has become a confessing animal." And
this declaration, which constitutes at once an echo and a metamorphosis of
Aristotle's definition of man as *zoon politikon*, indicates the extent to which
Foucault understands the question of confession as one of the originary
bio-political questions (59). Most importantly, since then sex has been "the
privileged theme of confession" and confession has been "the general standard governing the production of the true discourse on sex" (126). In short,
the deployment of sexuality availed itself crucially of the modern secular-
ization and generalization of confession throughout the social field.

But if Gramsci is correct in his critical assessment (1) of the condition of possibility for the effectiveness of confession, first of all as a sacrament, leave alone as a generalized procedure for the production of truth;
and (2) of the lack or fragility of such a condition of possibility among
the subaltern subjects of the Italian South for whom, thus, confession
"has little significance," it would follow that the deployment of sexuality
too would have "little significance" among such subjects. I am suggesting
that without confession there can be no sexuality as we know it. Hence,

the subaltern subject is immune, or at the very least refractory, to sexuality understood as a modern and bourgeois invention. Such a subject is immune to that sexuality precisely to the extent to which it is also a non-confessional one, namely, a subject that does not come into being through an act of confessional hailing. Such a subject is deaf, indifferent, or otherwise resistant to interpellations in the name of truth.

Foucault does not take into consideration explicitly the possibility of such a form of subjectivity for which first confession and then sexuality would not signify very much or anything at all. Yet he does understand very well that for a long time a position of social subalternity implied a certain imperviousness to those bourgeois discourses and practices that go by the name of sexuality. In some of the most explicitly Marxian as well as Gramscian pages of *The History of Sexuality*, Foucault writes about the deployment of sexuality as an expression of "bourgeois hegemony." According to Foucault, the bourgeois "affirmation of the body"—which he defines as the affirmation of "a sound organism and a healthy sexuality"—constituted from the eighteenth century onwards nothing less than a powerful form of class consciousness (1990a, 126). The bourgeoisie first turned themselves into modern sexual subjects before exporting the deployment of sexuality to other class contexts, at home as well as abroad. In this sense, Foucault is elaborating further one of Marx and Engels's earliest and most crucial insights regarding the insidious novelty of the bourgeoisie as a class.[9] Foucault completes his argument by drawing the following conclusions:

Whence no doubt the proletariat's hesitancy to accept [the deployment of sexuality] and its tendency to say that this sexuality was the business of the bourgeoisie and did not concern it. . . . [T]he bourgeoisie endowed itself, in an arrogant political affirmation, with a garrulous sexuality which the proletariat long refused to accept, since it was foisted on them for the purpose of subjugation. If it is true that sexuality is the set of effects produced in bodies, behaviors, and social relations by a certain deployment deriving from a complex political technology, one has to admit that this deployment does not operate in symmetrical fashions with respect to the social classes, and consequently, that it does not produce the same effects in them. We must return, therefore, to formulations that have long been disparaged; we must say that there is a bourgeois sexuality, and that there are class sexualities. Or rather, that sexuality is originally, historically bourgeois, and that, in its successive shifts and transpositions, it induces specific class effects. (Foucault 1990a, 127)

I would like to suggest not only that the specific arguments we have found in Gramsci and in Foucault dovetail with and complement each other significantly, but also that Pasolini's documentary stands at the intersection of precisely such arguments. In this sense, this documentary's failures constitute its success: its often inconclusive and unrevealing interviews bear witness to the ways in which an archaic skepticism or even indifference toward the sacrament of confession is turned by Southerners into a weapon of resistance against a deployment of sexuality that is accurately perceived as a modern, bourgeois, and Northern import, whose not-so-thinly-veiled goal is subjugation *tout court*.

Foucault's Parapractic Sincerity

Let us return now to the Calabrian man I mentioned earlier. He understands perfectly well what is at stake in Pasolini's question: when asked whether or not he is in favor of divorce, he knows that by saying he is against it he has given the wrong answer, namely, that his opinion goes against the modern and supposedly progressive, liberated, and enlightened position on this matter. When Pasolini then asks him in effect why he has given the wrong answer, and he replies, "Because I am Calabrian," he is saying implicitly to Pasolini (who is recognizable as a Northern Italian by his accent) something like: "Your ideas on these matters are of no concern to us here down South—you can keep your sexuality, we don't need it, we don't want it." His answer, hence, constitutes the counterpoint of another very illuminating moment in the documentary.

At one point, we see Pasolini interviewing Oriana Fallaci, the Northern Italian journalist, essayist, novelist, and public intellectual who was going to become increasingly famous throughout the 1960s and 1970s because of her own controversial interviews, and who, after September 11, 2001, became increasingly infamous for her viciously racist diatribes against Islam. As soon as she starts waxing eloquent about the way in which working-class women nowadays enjoy a sexual freedom much like her own that was unbeknownst to them only a few years ago, Pasolini pointedly reminds her that this might be the case in Milan, that is, in the industrialized North. But what about the Calabrian proletariat? Caught off guard, Fallaci hesitates, smiles coyly, and then replies: "It's another planet."

Almost as a way of corroborating Fallaci's stark metaphor, the next sequence opens with a vast, bare, desert-like expanse: it could well be Mars, if it weren't for the miniscule figures of a man and a horse lost in the far distance. After an extreme long shot, the camera zooms in on an old Calabrian peasant plowing a field. Pasolini is there, ready to ask questions about the virtues of female virginity. This image of an immense, inhospitable, desert landscape, in which a lone human figure can barely be discerned on the horizontal plane of the horizon, will often return to haunt Pasolini, to the point of becoming something like an authorial signature. We will see it over and over again in subsequent films, such as *The Gospel According to St. Matthew, King Oedipus, Teorema, The Arabian Nights.* And every time it will be associated with the archaic, the mythic, the unconscious, the pre-historic, the pre-modern, the South.[10] In *Love Meetings*, in particular, this image is used to foreground what both this Northern Italian woman intellectual as well as these Calabrian peasant men are acutely aware of: Italy is one country divided into two planets.

In *Love Meetings*, Pasolini presents us repeatedly with a divided country. Pasolini is particularly keen to draw attention to divisions of age, class, sex, region, and language. The wide gap between, on the one hand, the modernized, relatively affluent, and largely urban and industrial North; and on the other hand, the traditional, extremely poor, and largely rural and agricultural South, captures Pasolini's attention above all other divisions. It is on this crucial point that I part ways with Foucault's otherwise very incisive reading of *Love Meetings*. Foucault writes: "Divisions between men and women, country people and city dwellers, rich and poor? Yes, of course, but especially between young people and the others" (Foucault 1998b, 230). The fact that the ubiquitous and glaring split between North and South escapes Foucault's usually attentive eyes is indicative of his desire to assimilate Pasolini's project to the concerns that will occupy him in *The Use of Pleasure* and *The Care of the Self.* Foucault proceeds to spend the rest of the review on the question of the social position of youth in Western culture, from ancient times to the present, in ways that resonate distinctly with those later works.

The point is that the question of youth is indeed a crucial one for Pasolini. But it is also a question that in *Love Meetings* is apprehended and articulated through the filter of the Southern Question. This question too, of course, is nothing new: it has been and continues to be possibly the thorniest political problem in Italy since the so-called unification of the country in 1860. And yet, *Love Meetings*, which was filmed right after the centennial celebrations of the country's unification, confronted this question at a particularly crucial moment in Italian history. The early 1960s were the years of the so-called economic miracle that marked the official entrance of Italy among fully industrialized countries. If the economic and cultural differences between North and South had constituted an old and long-standing problem, in the early 1960s such differences suddenly became starker than ever before. This was due to the fast-paced industrialization in the North and the lack of any comparable corresponding industrialization in the South. All of this is to say that in *Love Meetings* the Southern Question constitutes the indispensable key for understanding Pasolini's skeptical investigation into the deployment of sexuality.

It is the intersection of youth, sexuality, and the South—and especially the crucial role that Southern children play in the documentary—that concerns me here. At one point, Pasolini questions a child on a Southern Italian beach, after having had a not-so-edifying conversation with her parents, and then tells her that children like her have been the real surprise of the documentary. But what exactly surprises Pasolini? Is it that, unlike the adults, the children interviewed proverbially speak the truth? Is it that they are the only ones who are sincere? The opening sequences of the documentary provide compelling answers to these questions. I will focus on three key scenes. The first is the credits sequence, in which Pasolini interviews groups of children in the slums of the Southern cities of Naples and Palermo, asking them whether they know where babies come from; the second is the sequence immediately after the credits, which consists of a conversation between Pasolini and two other prominent intellectuals—the father of Italian psychoanalysis, Cesare Musatti, and the novelist Alberto Moravia; and the third is the sequence that begins the first section proper of the documentary.

Midway through the credits sequence, the passage from the South (Naples) to the deepest South (Palermo, the Sicilian capital) is sutured by a series of striking images. We enter Palermo through a low-angle shot framing the tall, imposing iron gates of a church compound, through and behind which we discern, far above in the distance, the desolate ridges and barren cliffs of the high desert plateaus that surround the city from the South, East, and West, and hold it tight in their arid, uncompromising grip. This establishing shot superimposes and brings together conspiratorially these two distinct yet similarly towering, oppressive, inimical, distant, and archaic powers—the Church, the Desert—in an emblematic image of geotectonic Catholicism. From the heights of such a shot, the camera begins its descent in a diagonal pan, sweeping down the steps in front of the church, beyond a cluster of palms, across the parvis, and stopping to frame a group of people in the middle of the square. It is as if the camera is following the path of an invisible or imaginary bird—a stork, perhaps?—flying down from the mountain peaks or from the bell tower and landing among children. Those are the children for whom the stork's existence and child-carrying duties constitute the perfect foil for not communicating with the adults and for not revealing anything at all about themselves, while making it seem nonetheless as if they are obeying the adult injunction to communicate, to reveal, to confess, to speak. Under the combined, ominous gaze of mountains and churches, these children are playing a different game.

The arresting opening images, whose radiant, masterful protagonists are the children of the slums of Naples and Palermo, must have captured Foucault's imagination to a high degree, if one is to judge from the fact that it is precisely with these images that he too opens his own review of the documentary. Here is the first sentence of Foucault's text: "Where do babies come from? From the stork, from a flower, from God, from the Calabrian uncle" (1998b, 229). And where does the "Calabrian uncle" come from? Who is he, anyway? This mysterious uncle is the visible trace left by a revealing parapraxis, one whose absent cause is nothing other than the Southern Question. Let us proceed gradually.

It is true that in the first sequence, in Naples, we witness a child who, when asked if he knows how he was born, answers that an uncle brought him. There is no indication, however, that this uncle is from Calabria: all that the child says is simply: *"Uno zio mio"* ("an uncle of mine"). It is perfectly legitimate, thus, to ask Foucault how he came to the conclusion that, somehow, this child's uncle was Calabrian. Much like Pasolini does when losing patience with his more clueless interviewees, I will take the liberty here to put words into Foucault's mouth and answer my own question. The adjective "Calabrian" is used only twice in the whole documentary and in much later sequences. It is plausible and even likely, hence, that it is from one or both of these sequences that Foucault extracts this adjective, so as to re-deploy it in a different context and with different effects.

We have already encountered these moments in the documentary: the first is the moment when the young man motivates his rejection of divorce by saying that he is Calabrian, thereby revealing that the Southern Question is determinative when it comes to these matters. The second moment, more importantly, is the point at which Pasolini criticizes Fallaci for her obliviousness to the Southern Question: "What about the Calabrian proletariat?" Pasolini asks. The two moments when the word "Calabrian" is pronounced in the documentary are not only the moments when the Southern Question is brought most into the foreground, but also the moments when the Southern Question is revealed to be that which is usually most in the background. Or, more precisely, it is that which *is* the background in the first place, namely, the object of systemic foreclosure, that outside of power and resistance which constitutes the unthought at the heart of thought. As Fallaci puts it, "another planet."

Paradoxically, Foucault extracts the adjective "Calabrian" exactly from those moments in the documentary that attempt to draw attention to the psycho-political mechanisms of negation to which he himself falls prey in his own text, which is almost as oblivious to the Southern Question as Fallaci had been fifteen years earlier. *Almost.* If I say "almost" it is because earlier I invoked parapraxis. It is to Foucault's credit that his foreclosure of the Southern Question is not so draconian as not to let the "Calabrian uncle" slip through its forbidding barriers and sit himself right next to God.

On the one hand, Foucault is remarkably blind to or seemingly unconcerned with the crucial role that the Southern Question plays in *Love Meetings.* On the other hand, Foucault saves himself in the nick of time with a parapractic somersault that inserts that signifier which most signifies at once the Southern Question and its foreclosure precisely there where it belongs most: in the mouth of a child who is as far from representing a modern and bourgeois sexual subject as, say, Palermo is from Milan—which used to be very far indeed in those days.

Foucault's brilliant lapsus—a lapsus of real sincerity, if there ever was one—binds youth, sexuality, and the South together indissolubly from the start. Thus, it reconfirms my conviction that it is above all such subjects who, as children and as Southerners, are in a position of subalternity at least twice over, that offer the most effective resistance to the injunction to confess, to the deployment of sexuality, and to the modern bourgeois sexual subject.

Parapraxis aside, let us delve further into both Pasolini's and Foucault's versions of these first sequences. Now I can quote in full the first paragraph of Foucault's text:

Where do babies come from? From the stork, from a flower, from God, from the Calabrian uncle. But look rather at the faces of these kids: they do not do anything that gives the impression they believe what they are saying. Delivered with smiles, silences, a distant tone, looks that dart to the left and the right, the answers to these adult questions have a treacherous docility; they assert the right to keep for oneself those things that one likes to whisper. The stork is a way of making fun of grownups, of paying them back in their own false coin; it is the ironic, impatient sign that the question will go no further, that the adults are nosy, they will not get into the circle, and the child will continue to tell the "rest" to himself. (Foucault 1998b, 229)

If these answers are eminently predictable and even banal, it is also the case that they do not matter in the least in and of themselves. It might be tempting for some, hence, to interpret Foucault's interpretation as suggesting that in these sequences it is bodies rather than words that really matter. Thereby one would risk falling into a certain kind of corporeal essentialism, bodily fetishism, or vitalism. Such discourses, I am afraid, have returned lately to haunt both academic and public discourses of all types: I take them as the supreme index of a fully realized regime of biopolitical production such as the one in which we all increasingly live.

That Foucault's text cannot be interpreted in this way is made abundantly clear, for example, by a remark such as "The stork is a way of making fun of grownups, of paying them back in their own false coin"—a remark that points to the specific relation between words and bodies articulated by these children rather than pointing to their bodies alone. If these children are pronouncing and enacting the word "stork" in such a way as to make fun of adults and turn such a word into the currency with which to pay them back, then here we are definitively in the realm of verbal expression and linguistic exchange. That is, we are in the realm of incorporated speech acts, rather than in the realm of bodily expression *per se*.

I would like to suggest that what matters most in these sequences consists of that gaping abyss between words and bodies that I mentioned earlier. This gap is at once instantiated and materialized by corporeal excess. Not that bodies matter more than words here. Rather, what matters most is the non-identity of bodies and words. This non-identity, however, is revealed by bodies rather than by words here. Even though these bodies and these words both function under their own specific and related regimes of truth, bodies and bodies alone indicate the disjunctive relation between such regimes as well as incarnate an outside of force relations through which another truth altogether may eventually emerge.

If these children at once speak a truth that can be confessed (i.e., what the adults want to hear) as well as express a truth that has little to do with confession (by hiding it teasingly in their elaborate gestural choreography), they also do more. They point to rather than turn away from, pry open rather than shut down, acknowledge rather than fore-close that immanent realm of force relations that had been there all along. Such a realm puts different regimes of truth in communication with one another, and enables as well as demands the production of any form of truth in the first place. These children do speak far more elo-quently—that is, really sincerely—through their physical interactions and bodily expressions than through the script they have learned to recite by heart. This is so not because the script is ineloquent or "false," as Foucault puts it, but because they turn such a script against itself by letting their bodies show that they know that they are reciting, that they are on stage, and that their words are encased by quotation marks in the first place.

Such corporeal excess indicates not only that many of these children know exactly where babies come from, but also that they know that the questioning adult knows that they know that truth. They know that he knows they are just putting up a show for his benefit. They know that he knows they are just having fun at his expense. Unlike those adults who take the injunction to confess seriously and react either positively or nega-tively to it, these children can be said, strictly speaking, neither to be lying nor to be telling the truth, neither to be sincere nor to be insincere. They make no pretense of speaking the truth and hence do not really expect to be believed, either. The game these children are playing is undoubtedly a very serious one. But the seriousness of this game is directly proportional to the fun they are poking at those games of truth through which the deployment of sexuality would hope to transform them all eventually into bourgeois adults.[11]

Pasolini's Subaltern Laughter

It is not a coincidence that Pasolini juxtaposes such child's play to the tedious adult seriousness of Musatti and Moravia—whose ponderous self-importance blinds them to the fact that Pasolini is making fun of them at least as much as the children were making fun of him during the credits sequence. In particular, Pasolini's sardonic assertion at one point that Musatti and Moravia are suggesting that his own documentary constitutes a crusade against ignorance and fear, a debunking of sexual taboos, as well as a desacralization of sex altogether, is nothing short of hilarious. For, if anybody holds sex as a most serious, all-important, and, indeed, sacred matter here, it is these two other intellectuals, who, unlike the savvy children, fall only too readily into Pasolini's trap.[12]

As far as Moravia is concerned, one needs only to peruse just about any of his novels to realize that his prurient and graphic obsession with sex is part and parcel of what Foucault aptly named the "great sexual sermon" of enlightened, liberal, bourgeois modernity. The self-righteous moralism of this sermon in preaching the virtues of sexual liberation is matched only by the sanctimoniousness of those retrograde and obscurantist powers that purportedly repressed our sexuality from the early modern era onwards by enforcing one sexual taboo after another. Jean-Luc Godard seems to share this assessment, if one is to judge by his dismissive and damning evaluation of *Il disprezzo*, Moravia's 1954 novel on which Godard based his 1963 film *Le mépris* (*Contempt*): "a nice, vulgar [novel fit] for a train journey, full of classical, old fashioned sentiments in spite of the modernity of the situation. But it is with this kind of novel that one can often make the best films."[13]

As for Musatti, the children contradict his predictions regarding the outcomes of Pasolini's inquiry in full. Musatti ventures to suggest that the interviewees either will not answer or will give false answers. All appearances notwithstanding, neither of these reactions describes the behavior of the children interviewed in the documentary. When Pasolini asks him whether he thinks that such reactions would be due to ignorance or to fear, Musatti explains that from a psychoanalytic standpoint ignorance and fear cannot be separated in any way. He says: "We hide certain things from ourselves because we want to defend ourselves from them, and hence we ignore them—which is precisely what happens with sex." Musatti supports his expectations of how people will behave when interviewed on the sexual question by invoking the mechanisms of repression. And, indeed, there are several interviewees in *Love Meetings* who behave according to this stereotypical script. Nothing could be further removed from such psychological dynamics, however, than what we witness taking place with the children. These children are neither ignorant nor afraid of sex, and they are certainly not hiding anything at all from themselves. If anything, they are hiding themselves from all of us; that is, they are defending themselves from the adults, and they do so out in the open and for all to see. Their behavior, in other words, does not bear the marks of repression here.

Musatti's version of psychoanalytic wisdom and Moravia's version of the enlightenment project do not work with these children. Indeed, such a wisdom and such a project do not even notice their existence. These children do not appear anywhere on Musatti's and Moravia's limited bourgeois radar, which can register nothing other than the dialectical tensions between sincerity and insincerity. The children are animated by a subaltern resistance to the injunction to confess that makes them all but invisible from the standpoint of Musatti's and Moravia's eminently humanist gaze. This gaze is trained instead to see and to comprehend only those subjects who already have been interpellated more or less successfully by the confessional imperative of the deployment of sexuality. Subalternity here is to be understood above all as a radical availability to the sincerity of the real, as an openness and an attentiveness to the force relations animating the outside. If history is what hurts, the nonsymbolizable real, the nonrepresentable outside, the subaltern incarnates a corporeal excess that is history's battleground.[14]

As Foucault will do more than a decade later, Pasolini draws attention to the following paradox in the opening sequences of *Love Meetings*. The earnest seriousness and missionary zeal with which the modern and enlightened bourgeoisie demands that sex be desacralized and liberated from centuries of repression by being put into discourse is attendant on and constitutive of that secular sacralization of sex which is the deployment of sexuality. No wonder, then, that this type of seriousness is often met and counteracted with levity, derision, or outright laughter by those for whose benefit it is supposedly meant. For laughter, of course, is often one of the most powerful weapons available to subalterns of all sorts.

As if precisely to undermine such pernicious seriousness and zeal, what follows the conversation with Musatti and Moravia marks a sudden shift in tone. The humorous, farcical, and ironic introduction to the first section of the documentary immediately undermines whatever pseudo-scientific pretensions this whole project had been granted during that conversation. Superimposed on a still shot of a young woman shown in profile with her mouth gaping open as if caught in the middle of laughter or while calling someone, we read in mid frame, as well as hear as voice-over, this title: "*RICERCHE I / GRANDE FRITTO MISTO ALL'ITALIANA*" ("First Research: Big Italian-Style Mixed Fry"). This title is followed by this paragraph (which is also heard as voice-over and which continues to be superimposed on the same still shot): "In which a kind of traveling salesman is seen going around Italy probing and polling Italians on their sexual tastes: and not so as to launch a product but with the sincerest purpose of understanding and of reporting faithfully."[15]

The tongue-in-cheek tone of the title preceding this paragraph suggests that neither the whole paragraph nor the declaration of sincerity contained therein ought to be taken too seriously. Neither sincere nor insincere, Pasolini here gives the lie to the sincerity-insincerity dialectical binary as well as to its various contemporary discursive deployments. On the one hand, he opposes the purported sincerity and disinterestedness of scientific discourse (e.g., sociological surveys, anthropological fieldwork, statistical research, public opinion polls) to the implied insincerity of business discourse, whose representative here is the salesman who conducts market surveys or who just wants to sell you something. On the other hand, he inexplicably does describe himself as "a kind of traveling salesman" all the same. This description raises many questions. For example, if he did trust the sincerity and disinterestedness of those scientific discourses, why not call himself a reporter, a journalist, a statistician, a sociologist, an anthropologist, rather than a salesman? Obviously, Pasolini feels not only that neither of these two discourses is adequate to his project but also that they are not so separate from one another in the end. To the extent to which the two terms of the sincerity-insincerity binary are mutually determining, one always implies, needs, and contains the other in order to function—and vice versa. Hence, Pasolini's project, and indeed his "sincerest purpose," seems here to consist precisely in ridiculing the whole sincerity-insincerity dialectic.

As if such a preamble were not enough, we hear in the voice-over the following statement (which, this time, does not also appear as written text in the shot): "In which it is seen first of all how Italians welcome the idea of this type of film and hence how they behave when faced by the idea of the importance of sex in life." And after a split-second pause, the deadpan voice-over delivers the clincher: "*'Molto allegramente'*—*nota del regista*" ("Very happily—Director's note"). How is one to take this cryptic corollary? Is it to be understood as the director's answer to the question implied in the preceding paragraph, namely, that Italians welcome the idea of this type of film as well as of the importance of sex in life very happily indeed? If this is what this note indicates, then it is undoubtedly dripping with sarcasm, given that immediately thereafter the first interviewees do not welcome the idea of this film happily at all. Or, is this corollary to be intended as a composer's notation in a musical score directing the performer's tempo? In that case, the director here would be indicating to himself and others that the rest of the documentary is to be shot, as well as perhaps to be viewed, in a very happy tempo. Whereas the specific meaning of this note may well be destined to remain undecipherable, the point is that the way in which it is framed and delivered is unmistakable: this is a joke. And this is a joke that ought to be taken very seriously as an attempt to offset and to poke fun at the seriousness of all those who, like Moravia and Musatti, feel the moral duty to strike a pose as subjects supposedly in the know as soon as that most grave of questions makes its appearance—sexuality. Echoing between the lines, one can hear Pasolini's subaltern laughter—a laughter that was one of the very few truly subaltern gestures that this self-declared and self-hating petty-bourgeois intellectual was able to muster.

The radical shift in tone in the opening of the first section of *Love Meetings* seems to function like a retroactive and complicit wink directed toward that credit sequence which had preceded the conversation with Musatti and Moravia. It is almost as if Pasolini is trying to convince the poor children of the Southern slums that he is much more like them than like those two boring old farts. It is almost as if he is attempting to strike a secret alliance with those subaltern subjects as well as to disavow any allegiance with the pontificating adult representatives of the intellectual bourgeoisie. The latter have learned how to confess with the proper words and want to teach us how to do likewise. Thereby they bind us as well as themselves all the more to the powers against which they think they are fighting. The former (the children) do not really care what words they speak, and hence their bodies can enact and display a sublime inaptitude to confess. This inaptitude points to other pleasures, other sincerities, and other truths—and puts them all beyond our reach.

7

Like a Dog

NARRATIVE AND CONFESSION IN J. M. COETZEE'S
"DISGRACE" AND "THE LIVES OF ANIMALS"

Yasco Horsman

> Seriousness is, for a certain kind of artist, an imperative uniting the aesthetic and the ethical.
>
> J. M. COETZEE, *Giving Offense: Essays on Censorship*

> With failing sight K. saw how the men drew near his face, leaning cheek-to-cheek to observe the verdict. "Like a dog!" he said; it seemed as though the shame was to outlive him.
>
> FRANZ KAFKA, *The Trial*

Only in Name

Upon its publication in 1999, J. M. Coetzee's novel *Disgrace* was widely read as a response to the hearings of South Africa's Truth and Reconciliation Committee (TRC).[1] As is well known, the TRC was established to facilitate a peaceful transition to democracy. During the proceedings, applicants giving a full disclosure of their past deeds could receive amnesty for politically motivated crimes committed during the apartheid years. Originally a quasi-legal, truth-seeking procedure, under the leadership of Anglican bishop Desmond Tutu the TRC became a ritual in which the country sought to come to terms with its past. Arranging meetings in which perpetrators confessed and victims forgave, it was believed, could achieve some sort of reconciliation and establish a *common humanity* that was thought necessary for the country to heal from its past wounds and become a functioning democracy.

The first part of *Disgrace* can be read as a thinly disguised allegory about the scenes of confession and forgiveness that were a central part of the TRC hearings. When it is discovered that David Lurie, a professor at the Cape Technical University, has had an affair with one of his students, Melani Isaacs—an affair that borders on abuse—he has to appear before a committee convened to consider her complaint. The committee suggests that Lurie has a chance to keep his job if he is willing to confess his deeds and show remorse. Although he is willing to confess and plead guilty to the charges leveled against him, he stubbornly refuses to show remorse. Arrogantly declining to read the complaints made against him, he simply chooses to quickly declare his guilt. "I am sure the members of this committee will have better things to do with their time than rehash a story over which there will be no dispute," he tells the committee. "I plead guilty to both charges. Pass sentence and let us get on with our lives" (Coetzee 1999a, 48).

Pleading guilty, however, is not enough for the committee. "There is a difference between pleading guilty, and admitting you are wrong," a member of the committee tells Lurie. According to a committee member, admitting one's guilt involves more than uttering a few words: it requires that these words come "from one's heart." By assenting to the charges too quickly, Lurie gives the impression of accepting them without acknowledging their implications. "Professor Lurie says he accepts the charges," a committee member says. "Yet when we try to pin him down on what it is that he actually accepts, all we get is a subtle mockery. To me that suggests he accepts the charges *only in name*" (Coetzee 1999a, 54).

In making a distinction between the utterance of words and a serious and sincere admission of one's wrongdoing, the novel points to a paradox at the heart of confession. To be recognized as an admission of guilt, a confession depends on a series of conventional procedures and well-known formulas, such as "please allow me to express my sincerest apologies." The conventional nature of the phrases, however, implies that they can always be uttered in an empty, insincere, or even mocking way.[2] Because a confession needs to be perceived as sincere and heartfelt, it has to be *supplemented* by an ostentatious show of sincerity. A confession, in fact, relies on a "theater of sincerity" that forces the confessor to publicize the veracity of his apology.

The drama of the first sixty pages of *Disgrace* revolves around David Lurie's explicit refusal to engage in the theater of sincerity and to play the role that is expected of him. "I have said the words for you," he exclaims during his hearing, "now you want more, you want me to *demonstrate their sincerity*. That is preposterous." An insistence on sincerity, Lurie argues, is out of place in the legal sphere. "That is beyond the scope of the law . . . I appeared before an officially constituted tribunal, before a branch of the law. Before that secular tribunal I pleaded guilty, *a secular* plea. That plea should suffice. Repentance is neither here nor there. Repentance belongs to another world, to another universe of discourse" (Coetzee 1999a, 58).

In pointing out the religious overtones that accompany the insistence on sincerity, Coetzee—if we can assume he is speaking through Lurie—seems to be echoing a reproach that was often made against the TRC, namely that by insisting on the ritual of confession, repentance, and forgiveness—and its promise of restoring a common humanity—it had effectively Christianized what was originally a secular, legal process.[3] By relating its religious overtones to the problem of sincerity, Coetzee also returns to an argument that he had made in his essay "Confession and Double Thoughts," first published in 1985. In this essay, Coetzee argues that the demand for a confession to be sincere implies that it is structurally interminable, because the motivation behind every confession—and thereby its claim to sincerity—can always be subjected to further scrutiny. Every ostentatious demonstration of sincerity can potentially be supplemented by a demonstration of the sincerity of this demonstration of sincerity—raising the spectre of an infinite regress. Because there is no limit to the suspicion that a demand for sincerity can raise, the only way a confession can find an ending that is not arbitrary, Coetzee argues, is by presuming a moment of grace or absolution.[4]

Indeed, when Lurie loses his job because he refuses to fully participate in the ritual of confession, he seems to lose more than just his social position. His departure from Cape Town and settling with his daughter Lucy on her farm is described as a *fall from grace*. Living in rural South Africa, an effectively lawless zone, Lurie retreats into a state of what the novel terms "disgrace without term" (Coetzee 1999a, 172).

The novel, then, consists of two parts that are separated by a fall. The second, much longer part of the book is a dramatization of the psychological and philosophical implications of this fall. In this essay, I will relate this story of a fall to the particular mode of writing that Coetzee adopts in *Disgrace*. As many critics have pointed out, *Disgrace* marks a break from Coetzee's earlier novels in that it is "more bluntly realistic" (Head 2006, 100). Whereas his earlier works, such as *Foe*, *Waiting for the Barbarians*, and *Dusklands* were characterized by metafictional devices that seem to resist referential readings, *Disgrace* appears to engage "seriously" with the reality of post-apartheid South Africa. This shift in style could be seen as a response to the critique that was mounted against Coetzee's novels of the 1980s, namely that their non- or anti-realistic nature effectively blocked a serious and sincere engagement with politics.[5] Yet, as I will demonstrate in this essay, rather than accepting realism wholeheartedly, *Disgrace* points to the paradoxical nature of realism's "seriousness" itself. I will first look at the second part of *Disgrace*, which tells of Lurie's life after leaving Cape Town, its university, and his home, and then discuss a few passages from Coetzee's *The Lives of Animals*, a small book that came out shortly after the publication of *Disgrace*, but whose two chapters were delivered as the Tanner Lectures at Princeton in 1997–1998.[6] Read together, these books pit confession against narrative, as the difference between an integrity that relies on a declaration of sincerity and a mode of writing that is serious in its refusal to be sincere.

Disgrace Without Term

The implications of Lurie's fall from grace are manifested stylistically in an obvious shift of tone in the second half of the book. Whereas the first part of the novel is constructed as a plot-driven, tightly structured page-turner whose suspense relies on its movement toward an expected *denouement*, namely the hearings of the tribunal, the second part seems to consist of a series of loosely connected events that in no way give the impression of heading toward a climax.

This lack of direction and sense of disorientation in the narrative result from various stylistic choices Coetzee has made. Parts one and two are both written in the present tense, thus avoiding the impression of hindsight usually evoked by the past tense. Yet passages in the first part predict events in the second part. Lurie's final visit to Melani Isaacs, for example, is introduced with "He would see her one more time," suggesting the voice of a narrator who tells the story with a foreknowledge of its ending. This clear sense of an impending conclusion, however, is completely absent in the second part of the novel.

For example, the single most crucial events, the rape of Lucy and wounding of Lurie by three burglars, comes unannounced. Furthermore, the novel leaves it unclear whether the consequences of this event will ever fully be over. Despite the insistence of her father, Lucy refuses to report the rape to the police and press charges, giving up all hope for a future moment of justice. When she finds out she is pregnant, she decides to keep the baby and seek protection as the second wife of Petrus, her former employee, who was perhaps involved in the attack. Lucy accepts having hit rock-bottom and decides to live her life, as she herself puts it, "at ground level. With nothing. Not with nothing but. With nothing. No cards, no weapons, no property, no rights, no dignity. Like a dog" (Coetzee 1999a, 205).

Jobless, homeless, and with no social position, Lurie also seems to have lost all direction. He wanders aimlessly on his daughter's farm, "losing himself day by day" (Coetzee 1999a, 121). The project he had embarked on after his departure from Cape Town, the writing of a chamber opera based on Byron's last love affair—at first a rather narcissistic rewriting of the Don Juanism that had helped bring him down—seems to be slowly disintegrating, indicating that high drama is no longer capable of capturing the reality of his fallen state. The reality of post-apartheid rural South Africa, Lurie muses, is that there are simply "[t]oo many people, too few things. What there is must go into circulation . . . [it is] just a vast circulatory system to whose workings *pity and terror are irrelevant*" (98; emphasis added). The dignity of the tragic mode, with its culmination in a moment of catharsis, a cleansing through empathy and fear, no longer suffices to describe this situation.

The second part of *Disgrace*, then, is set in a world and written in a mode in which closure, in the psychological and narrative senses, is unlikely. This state is ironically announced in the first part of the novel. In one of the last classes he teaches in Cape Town, shortly before his fall, Lurie explains the grammatical tense of the perfective, the tense "signifying an action carried through to its conclusion" (Coetzee 1999a, 71). It is exactly this perfective tense, and the temporal perspective it implies, that is absent in the second part of the novel.

Disgrace does, however, conclude with a scene of mercy, and perhaps even of absolution or salvation. In the final chapter, Lurie decides to volunteer at an animal welfare clinic in Grahamstown, assisting Bev Shaw in the killing of old, blind, crippled, maimed, or homeless dogs whose "term has come." While engaging in what he calls "mercy killings"—giving stray dogs a dignified end—Lurie learns to offer the dogs "what he no longer has difficulty in calling by its proper name: love" (Coetzee 1999a, 219). Toward the end of the novel, Lurie finds himself, to his surprise, utterly involved in this process, feeling empathy and pity for the dogs he helps to die, finding some sort of redemption in the humility that this task requires. This newfound humility coincides with another resolution Lurie makes earlier in the chapter: to include a dog in his chamber opera, mixing the human singing voice, which he had stated emanates from the soul, with the earthly barks of an animal.

This ending reads like a rather traditional moment of closure in which Lurie reconciles himself with the idea of having to live "like a dog," as his daughter had done earlier. By immersing himself in this task he gives up his arrogance and misguided sense of dignity to learn the importance of empathy. According to this reading, *Disgrace* ends as a traditional realist novel, which, as D. A. Miller reminds us, typically concludes in a psychological resolution in which the main character gives up some illusions and comes to a newfound insight. Many critics of *Disgrace* do indeed take such a newfound insight as the "lesson" that the novel teaches its readers.[7] The story of Lurie's fall would then be a story of an arrogant academic who learns the simple lesson of the importance of empathy. As Jane Taylor has suggested, the novel's ending echoes eighteenth-century debates on the importance of "sympathetic imagination" as a necessary corrective to the arrogance of human reason. In her essay Taylor cites Adam Smith, who argued in *The Theory of Moral Sentiments* that this capacity of sympathy is a necessary supplement to the technological and economic reasoning that effectively separates human beings from the natural world (Taylor 1999).

According to this reading, the ending of *Disgrace* presents us with a secular equivalent of the scene of reconciliation that the TRC aimed for. But instead of being reunited with *humanity*, Lurie learns to accept that he is part of the natural, *animal* world. By participating in mercy killings, he accepts that he shares a fundamental condition with animals: mortality.

This realistic sense of closure, however, is undermined by the fact that we, as readers, cannot be sure how *seriously*—in the strong sense of the debate on speech acts mentioned in note 4—we should take this secular equivalent of redemption-through-mercy and the plea for sympathy on which it relies. Earlier in the novel, addressing the students of his seminar on romantic poetry, Lurie had explained that Byron's poem on Lucifer should be considered a failure because it attempts to evoke sympathy for a creature whose very fallen nature bars us from fully sympathizing with him. Lucifer is a creature who "lives among us, yet is not one of us" (Coetzee 1999a, 34). These remarks could be taken to apply to *Disgrace* as well: although focalization lies consistently with Lurie, it is very hard to feel for this fallen creature. Rather, the novel maintains a distance from Lurie's words, frequently using the figure of dramatic irony, highlighting the difference between the intention behind a character's words and the reader's reception of them. As critic Michael Gorra, writing in the *New York Times*, observes, "Coetzee makes us understand, but not sympathize with Lurie's intellectual arrogance" (1999). Indeed, Coetzee's writing style has often been castigated by critics for its cold, cerebral, and skeptical idiom that blocks our sympathetic identification with Coetzee's main characters. The novel itself, then, cannot seem to adopt the very attitude that it prescribes in its conclusion.

This raises the question of the *sincerity* of the ending of *Disgrace*. Is this a heartfelt, sincere plea for sympathy and pity, one that refuses to draw boundaries between human beings and animals? Or is it an ironical demonstration of the impossibility of sympathizing with a fallen creature, highlighting a discontinuity between reader and character, culminating in a parody of forgiveness and reconciliation? This latter reading is suggested by the alterations Lurie makes to his chamber opera. By including a dog, Lurie's opera seems to turn into a farce, with the barks of the dog mocking the dignity of the human singing voice, provoking in his audience not pity and empathy, but a cynical laughter. Both readings, though equally plausible, are mutually exclusive. The text itself offers no definitive clues as to which reading should prevail since its temporal structure precludes a moment of retrospection. There is no meta-narrative level that would allow for an extra-diegetic narrator to make an overall judgment. Indeed, upon finishing the novel we are left with the question whether Lurie's case has indeed now been closed, or whether we have just been confronted with an impossibility of finding closure.

The Bottom Has Dropped Out

Similar problems of seriousness were raised by *The Lives of Animals*, a short book published shortly after *Disgrace* that contains Coetzee's two Tanner Lectures delivered at Princeton University in 1997–1998. These lectures, entitled "The Philosopher and the Animals" and "The Poets and Animals," deal explicitly with the human capacity to empathize with animals and could therefore be read as a postscript to *Disgrace* that might provide us with a key to its reading. Yet, rather than presenting us with a straightforward philosophical argument, Coetzee's lectures take the format of a fictional story about a novelist named Elizabeth Costello who gives talks at an American college. Costello's lectures consist of a passionate defense of animal rights: she repeatedly calls the meat industry a "crime of stupefying proportions" (Coetzee 2003, 114) to which we can only remain blind by an act of willed ignorance, a semi-conscious decision to block out our knowledge of the horrors committed in slaughterhouses all over the globe. Costello compares this mindset to that of the citizens of Treblinka, Auschwitz, and Dachau during World War II, whose denial of Nazi atrocities in their midst was in fact complicit with these acts.

Costello combines this scathing attack on the consumption of meat with a rather traditional defense of the moral value of literature, which she contrasts with that of philosophy. Philosophy's reliance on metaphysical distinctions between animals and human beings has traditionally blinded us to the plight of animals, Costello argues. From Aquinas's idea that the souls of animals die with their bodies to Descartes's definition of the animal as a biological automaton, all philosophies about animals amount to the idea that whereas humans are godlike, animals are like *things*, a view that effectively justifies their mistreatment. Literature, however, relies not so much on rational thought as on our capacity of "sympathetic imagination." Since, as she states, "[t]here is no limit to the extent to which we can think our way into the being of another," and hence our sympathies can be extended to animals as well, literature teaches us to open ourselves to the suffering of animals and awakens us to the horrors committed against them (Coetzee 2003, 80).[8]

Given the rather principled stance of this argument, it is no surprise that it is not delivered philosophically, but takes the shape of a literary work. Its fictional nature, however, inevitably raises questions as to the seriousness of the arguments presented. It remains unclear whether the book itself—or indeed the author J. M. Coetzee—subscribes to Costello's views, or whether they are merely cited or perhaps even mocked by the work. This latter reading is, again, made possible by the novel's style. In *The Lives of Animals* Costello hardly emerges as a sympathetic character: she is narcissistic, grandiose, short of temper. Since focalization throughout the book lies consistently with Costello's son, whose feelings about his mother are ambivalent, we are put at a distance from her. Furthermore, as Marjorie Garber observes, *The Lives of Animals* is remarkably close to a minor genre of literature, that of the campus novel, commonly a satirical genre in which conflicting ideas are put "in play by characters who—precisely because they are 'academics'—can be relied upon to be unreliable." Their sincerity is by definition undecidable. "Sincerity," Garber concludes, "assuming it to be a value, cannot be assumed in this contest of faculties. We don't know whose voice to believe" (1999, 79).

For many readers of *The Lives of Animals*, this ambiguity was taken as a refusal on Coetzee's part to take responsibility for the views proposed by the book. Philosopher Peter Singer, for example, calls Coetzee's adoption of the fictional mode "evasive," since he presents principles without committing himself to them. Similarly James Wood argued in the *London Review of Books* that "[t]he frame story allows Coetzee to share ideas while obscuring his overt possession of them" (2003). This formulation is precise in its misreading, for it is exactly the notion of being "in possession" of ideas that is challenged by the book. In the final pages of *The Lives of Animals*, when Costello is driven to the airport by her son, she confesses that she is not sure whether she can truly adopt her views as being her own. Her convictions are not so much opinions that she subscribes to, but rather thoughts that have come to her, like fantasies or dreams. Costello tells her son,

I no longer know where I am. I seem to move around perfectly easily among people, to have perfectly normal relations with them. *Is it possible*, I ask myself, that all of them are participating in a crime of stupefying proportions? Am I fantasizing it all? I must be mad! Yet every day I see the evidence. The very people I suspect produce the evidence, exhibit it, offer it to me. Corpses. Fragments of corpses that they have bought for money. (Coetzee 2003, 114)

She continues to illustrate her predicament by repeating her comparison with the Holocaust:

It is as if I were to visit friends, and to make some polite remark about the lamp in their living room, and they were to say, "Yes it's nice, isn't it? It's Polish-Jewish skin it's made of, we find that's the best, the skin of young Polish-Jewish virgins." And then I go to the bathroom and the soap-wrapper says, "Treblinka—100% human stearate." Am I dreaming, I say to myself? What kind of house is this? (Coetzee 2003, 115)

This passage indicates that Costello's belief in the importance of animal rights cannot be reduced to a position that she wishes to defend. Her thoughts on animals are articulated in the conditional, presented as a question that is probed or a possibility that is explored fictionally, metaphorically, in a scene that is conjured up by her imagination.[9] Yet even for Costello herself it remains unresolved whether this imagined scene provides grounds for accepting her views as true—or indeed whether they are actually hers. The passage even raises the question whether the evocation of the Holocaust rhetorically serves as an argument against the meat industry, or whether Costello's struggle against the meat industry is an allegorical way of understanding the Holocaust.[10]

The Lives of Animals was later included in *Elizabeth Costello: Eight Lessons*. In the first chapter, entitled "Realism," Costello relates this undecidability to the genre of the realistic novel. Realism, according to Costello, should not be defined in referential or mimetic terms, but as a crisis in reading that is provoked by the worldly, secular nature of realistic writings. Realistic novels, Costello suggests, typically offer no clues as to whether certain key passages should be read referentially or allegorically. She illustrates her point in a reading of a Kafka short story, "A Report to the Academy," which, again, dramatizes the issue of the distinction between human beings and animals as it tells of an ape who speaks to a learned society and asks to be adopted as a human being. Kafka's text, Costello argues, invites an allegorical reading, yet it remains unclear whether it should be read as an allegory of a man pretending to be an ape who wants to be a man—in short, as an allegory on the animality of human beings—or whether it is really an allegory of the humanity of animals. Kafka's text itself offers no reliable key that would allow us to make a definitive interpretation.

We live in a time, Costello concludes, when words on a page no longer proclaim "I mean what I mean," making it impossible to distinguish allegory from realism, seriousness from playfulness, and, finally, human beings from animals. She concludes: "There used to be a time, we believe, when we could say who we were. Now we are just performers speaking our parts. The bottom has dropped out. We could think of this as a tragic turn of events, were it not that it is hard to have respect for whatever was the bottom that dropped out—it looks to us like an illusion now" (Coetzee 2003, 19). This passage teaches a theological lesson: in a secular world, when we can no longer believe in an immortal soul—when our "bottom has dropped out"—there is no transcendental ground that would enable us to distinguish ourselves from animals. This is combined with an important semiotic insight: without an extra-textual reference point to ground us, closure—as a final coupling of signifier and signified—has become impossible. There is no key that we can use to decipher the true and final meaning "behind" our utterances. We are forever haunted by the idea that we may simply be "speaking our parts," repeating empty phrases without knowing their "true" meaning.

These two lessons are—again—related in the story of a fall. Or to be more precise, of the falling away of a bottom, a *ground* on which one can safely land, and in its stead is the opening of an abyss. To Costello, this drama teaches a moral lesson of humility. But the scene in which this lesson is taught no longer resembles that of a tragedy. It does not culminate in a final, cathartic, and redemptive moment of closure that evokes pity and terror.

Perhaps, then, the story of a fall evokes laughter rather than a sense of tragedy. Laughter, as Paul de Man has argued in "The Rhetoric of Temporality," is our response to the fall we experience when we stumble over the groundlessness of our language (1971, 208–228). Like Costello, de Man suggests that there is something to be learned from this experience, as it undermines our earlier misguided sense of dignity. This lesson, however, can not be subsequently appropriated as a form of knowledge that we "possess," or an insight that we own and can share with others, since it is taught only as the breakdown of our earlier assumptions. As de Man puts it, to learn this lesson we all have to go down ourselves (1971, 214).

The Croaking of Frogs

Coetzee, then, opposes two ways of approaching the question of sincerity and, indeed, two modes of writing. On the one hand, there is the first-person confessional. This mode relies on an explicit, theatrical demonstration of its sincerity, which, in the final analysis, depends on trust in a moment of grace. On the other hand, there is the radically secular writing of the realist novel. The realist novel, written in the third person, can offer no guarantee of its seriousness, or even a key to its reading. This latter form of writing—particularly when it raises *serious* issues—is nevertheless continually confronted with the demand that authors declare their sincerity. Coetzee encountered this demand when critics of *The Lives of Animals* castigated him for not "seriously" "outing" himself as a confessed animal-rights advocate. Elizabeth Costello is similarly asked to confess in the final, dreamlike chapter of the book, when she finds herself outside a gate that she can only pass when she states, to the so-called boards who decide whether she will be allowed a passage through, what she *honestly* believes. "We all believe," the gatekeeper tells her, "we are not cattle." She answers, "I am a writer, it is not my profession to believe, just to write. Not my business. I do imitations, as Aristotle would have said." And she adds to these words—perhaps cynically, perhaps sincerely—"I can do an imitation of belief, if you like" (Coetzee 2003, 194).

When she later returns to a dormitory where the people who were denied passage through the gate are kept, a woman tells her that she is mistaken to take the issue too seriously. "Who knows what we truly believe," the woman tells her. "It is here, buried in our heart . . . buried even from ourselves. It is not belief that the boards are after. The effect is enough, the effect of belief. Show them you feel and they will be satisfied" (Coetzee 2003, 214).

It is unclear whether Costello takes this advice to heart. When she returns to the gate one last time, she tells the boards of a memory that stems from her early youth in Australia, a memory of the sound made by frogs at the beginning of the rainy season. It is because of the frogs' indifference toward her, she adds, that she believes in them. One of the board members tells her that this story resembles an allegory with the frogs embodying the spirit of life, which is what she as a writer believes in. Costello answers, enigmatically, that this may be the case for us, but not for the frogs: "to the frog itself it is no allegory, it is the *thing* itself, the only thing" (Coetzee 2003, 217). This answer leaves the boards, and indeed us readers, in suspense as to whether the croaking noise of the frogs is itself an allegory for the unreadability of our innermost beliefs, or an allegory for the silly sounds we tend to produce when asked to play our parts in a theater of sincerity.

Putting Sincerity to Work

ACQUIESCENCE AND REFUSAL
IN POST-FORDIST ART

David McNeill

On the face of it, "sincerity" might seem an unpromising point of departure for a discussion of contemporary art. Conceived by Lionel Trilling as a "congruence (of) avowal and actual feeling" (1972, 1), that is, as a correspondence between (outward) behavior and some (inner) authentic core, the concept seems of little use in a world in which Cartesian assumptions concerning the subject have well and truly passed their use-by date. Postmodernism's decade-long housekeeping exercise consigned any number of terms tainted with essentialism to the lexical rubbish bin, and "sincerity" appears a fine candidate for such treatment. While a romantic or expressionist artist's sincerity might once have been considered of paramount importance, to ponder whether Andy Warhol was sincere when he painted his 1970s society portraits would be to miss the point. Lionel Trilling wrote an obituary for the term in 1972, and sincerity seemed destined for relegation as merely one among many rhetorical postures available to (for example) the writer or the politician. The cynical catch phrase, "if you can fake sincerity you can fake anything," is merely an indicator of sincerity's declining fortunes and its loss of privilege.

Oscar Wilde anticipated this more than a century ago. His novella *The Portrait of Dorian Gray* can be read as a rumination on the artistic value of sincerity. Here the dissolute rake, Lord Henry Wotton, is credited with the view that

> the canons of good society are, or should be, the same as the canons of art. Form is absolutely essential to it. It should have the dignity of a ceremony, as well as its unreality, and should combine the insincere character of a romantic play with the wit and beauty that make such plays delightful to us. Is insincerity such a terrible thing? I think not. It is merely a method by which we can multiply our personalities. (Wilde 1998, 117)

And further:

> the value of an idea has nothing whatsoever to do with the sincerity of the man who expresses it. Indeed, the probabilities are that the more insincere the man is, the more purely intellectual will the idea be, as in that case it will not be colored by either his wants, his desires, or his prejudices. (8)

Thus construed, sincerity serves as an impediment to the breadth of expression and to its intelligence; it is equated with subjective prejudice, self-interest, and restricted perspective. Art, properly conceived, is artifice, not a window onto the spiritual morphology of its author.

Wilde's epitaph is pertinent, if a little premature. "Sincerity" takes a late but important curtain call in 1953 as the presiding value invoked by Vladimir Pomerantsev in his influential essay, "On Sincerity in Literature" (2004). This manifesto, published in *Novy Mir*, served as a significant catalyst to the Soviet cultural "thaw" that paralleled the de-Stalinization announced at the Twentieth Party Congress in 1956. For Pomerantsev, a novel in which the hero lives and breathes production quotas is insincere because it is shallow, inauthentic, and undialectical. Pomerantsev launches an attack on writers who offer a fictive world coextensive only with "the struggle waged at the nation's metallurgic factories for the optimal use of blast furnaces" (2004, 2). Sincerity is identified with the capacity of artists to resist placing their talents at the service of state ideology. It is here that we might find a way of understanding a certain zombie-like persistence that has marked the refusal of sincerity to lie down and die. Without doubt it lacks the kind of corporeal substance that it once enjoyed. It is the purpose of this essay to attempt to map its current spectral form.

There is a story, perhaps apocryphal, that the American minimalist Donald Judd was once questioned about the responsibility of artists to comment on such political issues as U.S. involvement in Nicaragua. He replied, so the story goes, that the artist had this responsibility "just as dentists do." The answer is a clever one, but it also feels slightly unsatisfactory. This may be because it seems to endorse, tacitly, the partitioning of professional and private lives in a manner that might insulate artistic practice from the rigors of political accountability. It implies that, just as the dentist will restrict any activism to a realm beyond the dental chair (in which disinterested science holds sway), so too will artists embed their political activism somewhere beyond the boundaries of an autonomous sphere of aesthetics. A question inviting a response about the specific obligations of artists is returned in the form of a general statement about human responsibility *tout court*.

Regardless of whether the suggestion that political expression is properly confined to a world beyond work can fairly be laid at Judd's door, it is a view that is even less tenable now than it was many years ago when he offered his smart *aperçu*. Apart from anything else, the thrust of First World labor policies in the era of empire seems to be toward an erosion of any distinction between a public place of work and a private space of leisure.

It is hardly news that work practices in the so-called developed world are appearing increasingly disorganized and decentered. Casualization, work at home, sweatshop labor, and the exploitation of precarious migrant workers all conspire to render obsolete the spaces in which labor has traditionally been inclined to represent itself. The vestigial guarantees of security that were purportedly enjoyed in the era of "fordist" capitalism are disappearing under the impact of individual contracts, offshore tendering, just-in-time production, and large unemployed reserve armies of labor. More often than not, these changes are orchestrated under the rubric of "flexibilization."

Labor struggles in Australia, as in much of the developed world, have frequently focused on just these transformations, and it must seem tempting at times to join the calls for a return to sedentary and routinized working conditions, if only through nostalgia for the surety that we imagine these conditions once offered. There are countervailing arguments, however. A number of political theorists and activists have suggested that the truly progressive stance might be to push for the recognition of all forms of immaterial and social labor and to reward them in the same manner as their more visible workplace counterparts. Thus, against an attempt to contain and confine labor within its traditional boundaries, is opposed a struggle for the realization of the total social ubiquity of productive (including immaterial) labor in all of its diverse forms.

Antonio Negri and Michael Hardt are only the best-known proponents of the view that what is called "globalization" should best be seen as the attempt by capital to follow labor power down its chosen path of deterritorialization and away from traditional forms, structures, and sites of production. For Negri and Hardt, it is time for new political subjects (the "multitude" or the "precariat") to insist on the primacy of immaterial labor. They have a right to think new thoughts and to create new things, against the protocols of mindless and repetitive work that were brought to such a high level of refinement in the assembly lines of late capitalism. Accordingly, there can be no turning back, either to indentured labor with its promises of minimum financial security, or, more broadly, to an inclusive sense of national identity, with its promises of physical security against global terror. For Hardt and Negri, in a passage from *Empire* that has become somewhat notorious, "Productivity, wealth, and the creation of social surplus (today) take the form of cooperative interactivity through linguistic, communicational, and affective networks" (2000, 294). Work is no longer done on "stuff"; instead it is done on social relations, and it produces only "services," "symbols," and "affects" (Hardt and Negri 2000, 293).

Many commentators have taken the postulation of an omnipresent "smooth space" of capital to be little short of risible, and it is not difficult to see why. However, if we disallow Negri and Hardt's expansive global claims and view their work instead as a more closely focused regional study pertinent only, or principally, to the economically powerful states of the North Atlantic and their settler culture derivatives, we might conclude that their work offers some reasonably well-tempered tools for the production of new forms of understanding. In particular, their work can help cast light on the point at which creative labor as aesthetics, and creative labor as *work*, may overlap and interpenetrate.

The belief that work is taking more fluid, creative, and precarious forms has prompted some writers to suggest that the social and institutional separation of art and productive labor is under some considerable pressure and that these once quite separate spheres are becoming co-extensive, or, less strongly, that they are beginning to overlap like a Venn diagram.[1] The work on the proliferation of "immaterial labor" and on the increasing importance of the "general intellect" that has emerged over the last decade (and which is sourced in a hitherto obscure passage in Marx's *Grundrisse*) remains evocative in spite of the many shortcomings that have been attributed to it.[2]

Of course theories of labor alone do not enable us to account with any precision for the performance of aesthetic practice in the political domain. By analyzing some of the tactics that artists employ to depart from their enclaves and contribute to the "general intellect" and this politics of labor, I want to suggest ways in which progressive labor theory might be enhanced by acknowledging, and even learning from, particular forms of creative work.[3]

Rather than working out of labor theory on the one hand or art theory on the other, I want to take this opportunity to examine the interdisciplinary production of a concept. In order to do this I will first flesh out what I see as the continuing relevance of the elusive term "sincerity." I wish to establish how a concept of sincerity is operational within a contemporary labor politics in order, then, to show how a critical reorientation of this concept—a "re-partitioning," as Rancière might have it (2004, 7–47)—occurs in the work of some contemporary artists.

Autonomy Versus Engagement

Before doing this I wish to offer a caveat against an increasingly prevalent critical position that has emerged in recent years and that, if taken seriously, effectively forecloses on the disinterested investigation of a kind of medial creativity situated equally in labor and in art practice. I will let the English art historian Claire Bishop stand as representative of this tendency because of the exposure granted to her position in the journal *October*. Her essay "Antagonism and Relational Aesthetics" is an assessment of the kinds of work endorsed by Nicolas Bourriaud in his curatorial practice and in his influential book *Esthétique Relationnelle* (1998). Bishop's aim in this essay is to applaud artists whose work "acknowledges the limitations of what is possible as art" and "subjects to scrutiny all easy claims for a transitive relationship between art and society" (2004, 79).

None of this would be particularly contentious were it not for an opening gambit that associates relational or immersive art (art that requires, and is incomplete without, some form of collective audience participation) with "the marketing strategy that seeks to replace goods and services with scripted and staged personal experiences" (Bishop 2004, 52). Bishop adopts her perspective on contemporary marketing from American business studies rather than from Hardt and Negri's analysis of affective labor. This might have helped foster her concern that art that ventures too far from its sanctified spaces will run the risk of collusion with ersatz marketing practices. However, the point needs to be made that all experience requires a *mise en scène* of some sort and that "scripting and staging" cannot in themselves be taken as evidence of the proximity of the inauthentic, somehow construed.

Bishop also expresses skepticism about the heterogeneity of the audiences that are privileged to experience relational works, and in this she is hardly alone. Art writers often invoke the elitist caste of art audiences in moments of guilt or self-doubt, frequently citing surveys (such as Bordieu's) in support of their concern. Accordingly the generosity and conviviality of much relational work is seen as akin to what I have elsewhere described as the generosity that capitalism extends to those that it recognizes as its own through gifts like frequent flyer points, loyalty discounts, and so on (McNeill 2005, 126). For all this, it is nevertheless salutary to bear in mind that the category "art audience" is not a class descriptor. We cannot take for granted that the person standing next to us at an art gallery shares our views, has an income similar to ours, or has had a similar education. In short, Bishop tries rather too hard to discredit proponents of any art that strays into the muddied realms of social relations, especially as they play out in the world beyond the art gallery.

In my view Bishop's is not the elitism of the Frankfurt school (the preservation of a zone of critique and non-resolution), but is rather a conservative policing action designed to ensure that the world of high art remains safely insulated from all else that is quotidian. Art's purported autonomy does, after all, have chameleon-like properties that enable its invocation for a variety of ends. In what follows I wish to avoid the prejudicial assumption of this autonomy in order to explore the possibility of a more heterogeneous deployment of, for want of a better phrase, aesthetic creativity. In doing so I am cognizant of, and take heart from, the many attempts in contemporary philosophy to foreground the virtues of "illicit" disciplinary transgressions and of various tactics that might be character-

ized as promiscuous and inclusive or, to revive an old Latin term, "maca-
ronic." Finally, any case that takes as its point of departure an opposition
between "art" and "society" will most likely bear the taint of such a foundational category mistake. It is, after all, the equivalent in aesthetics of
opposing apples to fruit.[4]

Sincerity as a "Relation of Production"

So, having offered this caveat as a kind of pre-emptive inoculation,
I wish now to return to some of the characteristics of post-fordist labor.
In the contemporary working landscape, traditional forms of workplace
surveillance no longer do service as the most secure foundation for a disciplinary regime. The time clock cannot capture the kinds of labor that
so many of us commit to when we check our emails at six o'clock in the
morning on our wireless laptops. Nor can it be assumed that an open-plan
office full of workers riveted to their monitors is a productive space in any
traditional sense. A recent UK survey apparently revealed that IT workers
spend up to 40 percent of their office time doing their own private work
on-line, in a kind of contemporary recasting of what, twenty-five years
ago, de Certeau named *la Perruque*.[5]

This leaves the modern corporate manager with the problem of measuring the intensity and efficacy of all the various off-site or on-line performances, if only for purposes of retention or promotion. As the work
force scatters into the nooks and crannies of domestic space and civil society, dedication becomes so much more difficult to quantify, and indeed
the only plausible candidate for measuring sublimation and identification
is, arguably, atavistic. Thus "sincerity" is conscripted more and more frequently as an adjunct to the traditional technologies with which the productivity, fealty, and dependability of employees are measured. Sincerity
re-emerges in the post-fordist environment in the form of a supplement of
the kind that Slavoj Žižek addresses in his analysis of Rob Reiner's film *A
Few Good Men*.

This is a film that deals with an investigation into the death of an
American Marine who, it transpires, was killed by his fellow soldiers
because he refused to enter fully into the spirit of the Marine Corps. He
committed no offence for which he could be discharged, but his behavior

was of a kind that failed to demonstrate the requisite belief, commitment, enthusiasm, and "sincerity." This surly but ill-defined refusal to totally acquiesce is described in the film as a violation of "Code Red." It is the inability or unwillingness to adopt an attitude of total constancy and belief as measured by a suite of individually trivial behavioral and participatory performances. Žižek asks rhetorically: "Where does this splitting of the law into written public law and its unwritten obscene reverse come from? From the incomplete 'non-all' character of the public law: explicit public rules do not suffice, so they have to be supplemented by the clandestine 'unwritten' code aimed at those who, although they do not violate any public rules, maintain a kind of inner distance and are not truly identified with the 'community spirit'" (1993, 98).

As for public law, so too (perhaps) for the rules that govern our working lives—an increasingly dispersed and invisible workforce can only produce anxiety among the managers entrusted to oversee it. Such anxiety, as it becomes more unsettling and urgent, is alleviated by ever more hyperbolic demands for expressions of employees' allegiance. Hence it is no longer enough to work in an organization: one is expected also to identify more and more closely with its programmatic appendages such as the ubiquitous "mission statement."

As labor has become more decentered, the pressure to participate and perform belief in the policies and ambitions of the employer-institution increase. New protocols have developed to facilitate the performance of corporate sincerity. Active committee involvement, willingness to work on-call, participation in on-the-job retraining schemes, team-building exercises (from work dinners and parties to boot camp "bonding" courses), ambassadorial proselytizing on behalf of the home institution, and, where possible, loudly boasting of the amount of work done outside the workplace have all become more or less *de rigueur* in modern institutional life. All that is missing is an oath of allegiance and a uniform, though we should perhaps note that many chain workers employed in service industries already do have to suffer these impositions.

As a number of the Italian theorists of post-fordist capitalism have argued, the flight from the workplace is in no way a flight from work. Indeed, some view "flexibilization" as simply an attractive euphemism for the extraction of ever higher rates of unpaid labor. In any case the evacuation of traditional spaces of production does raise several interesting questions in relation to the oft-noted tendency of much contemporary art to locate itself outside the art gallery, that is to say, its own traditional site of reification and commodification. The flight from the gallery space has exercised critics, curators, and practitioners considerably in recent years. Bourriaud, Grant Kester, Marc-Olivier Wahler, and many others have written about certain seismic rumblings that appear to indicate a kind of deterritorialization of, and in, the art world that seems analogous to the atrophying of sedentary and concentrated work sites in civil society at large. Many readers will have their own examples of artists or art collectives that prefer to work beyond the sanctified and surgical space of art galleries, and I would like to discuss a couple of Australian examples. I wish to do this, not so much in order to imply a symmetry between the flight from the workplace and the flight from the gallery *per se* (others have done this), but rather in order to return to what I have already called "spectral" sincerity. My aim is to specify what I see as both a tactic and a precondition for the kind of art and labor coalescence that is currently exercising so many contemporary commentators.[6]

Case Studies, Gentrification, and the Bourse

The Sydney collective Squatspace was formed during the Sydney Olympics in 2000 to organize guerrilla events in support of an inner suburban squatting initiative. They worked from a vacated shop front, facilitating a number of exhibitions dealing with urban renewal and real estate development. At the time of the Olympics the city governors inaugurated a strategy in collusion with local property developers for "opening up" the suburb of Redfern. This area to the immediate south of the central business district was identified with its long-term indigenous Australian inhabitants. The campaign to move them out of the area in order to make way for trendy apartments, office space, and boutique retailing was accompanied by systematic police harassment, media vilification, and claims of uncontrollable crime stemming from a heroin culture and the breakdown of traditional aboriginal structures of familial authority.

This campaign was relentless, and it was successful in producing a public perception of the area both as dangerous and as an obstacle to inner-city gentrification. Following a campaign on behalf of a community-based model of urban renewal in an adjacent district, Squatspace committed themselves to a series of projects addressing the class and race underpinnings of urban development. For example, in the large and depressed regional city of Newcastle, they opened a shop-front real estate agency advertising deserted retail spaces to a presumptive squatter clientele. The storefront configuration accurately mimicked the presentation of realtor offices on shopping streets throughout a country that consistently employs the real estate market as an index to economic health in general.

Although many of the members of Squatspace are art and architecture graduates, they do not, by and large, present their work in art galleries. A colleague and I recently invited them to participate in an exhibition of "disobedient" art and they agreed, but only in order to use wall space to recruit visitors for a bus tour of Redfern. During this tour they invited local community leaders to talk with the tour group in order to redress the largely negative and threatening view of the area disseminated in newspapers and on television. The tour included a visit to a modest but poignant memorial site where a young black cyclist had died during a police pursuit. In circumstances not dissimilar to those that triggered the more recent French events in 2006, there was a local "riot" in response to the death—a response that the media both relished and exaggerated.

The relationship between urban development and progressive art is not always one of mutual indifference or repugnance. The process of "renovating" impoverished suburban communities has on occasion followed a fairly precise trajectory that starts with artists searching out cheap studio space and *lumpen* ambience, and ends with restaurants, designer shops, and renovated loft apartments: in short, all the trappings of what the real estate industry has come to call, rather grandly, "lifestyle." This story has been repeated in cities as diverse as Paris, New York, London, and Beijing, and in each instance artists have served as a kind of unwitting mercantile avant-garde. Squatspace knows how easily artists' lifestyles can be transformed into a *gemütlich* commodity. They therefore insulate their practice against bohemian contamination, not by masquerading as workers in some romantic fashion, but rather by extruding social relations beyond and across the borders of the art world.

My second example is the Sydney-based artist Michael Goldberg, who is fascinated with the world of on-line speculation. Like so many others of his ilk he has made money and lost it again, despite an intensive campaign of self-directed apprenticeship in the intricacies of trading. In effect he has written off his losses as research costs for entrée into a world that has supplied him with suggestive new directions for his work as an installation artist. The resulting project, "catchingafallingknife.com," was shown at Sydney's Artspace gallery in November 2002, and it marked a significant transition in his thematic concerns. Goldberg's previous work, done both in Australia and in his native South Africa, focused on the unveiling of suppressed histories in a manner that had been almost militantly regional and site specific. Thus his shift to a theme that is paradigmatically global marks him very much as an artist who is of his moment.

It would be difficult to imagine two more antithetical professions than those practiced by share traders and artists. Traders, as popular wisdom has it, are social parasites who produce nothing of any tangible value. Artists, according to the same source, take a collective stand against the world of greed and avarice. The broker is a soft target for literary vilification. Tom Wolfe, Martin Amis, and Bret Easton Ellis have all constructed larger-than-life monsters from the figure of the cocaine-fuelled speculator of the 1980s, and every recession or bursting "dot com" bubble offers more ammunition against those who make a living through trading in abstract numbers. For example, the erstwhile Malaysian prime minister, Mahathir, blamed anonymous currency speculators for the entire Southeast Asian economic collapse on the eve of the new millennium, on the grounds that they had transgressed the Islamic law (*Riba*) forbidding usury. He hastily introduced national currency controls in violation of the spirit of economic globalization, and the Malaysian economy managed to survive the recession comparatively unscathed.

It would seem that such critics have a point. The entire thrust of globalization is based on a fundamental sleight of hand that enables investment funds to travel at the speed of light in search of new markets and cheaper labor. At the same time, workers in Third World sweatshops are prevented from travelling to countries in which their work would be more fairly remunerated. The increasing speed and mobility of capital plays against the containment of labor power, and new opportunities for the extraction of surplus value are generated as a result. As many commentators have noted, the market is itself determined by a volatile mix of greed and fear such that a tremor in confidence on Wall Street can cause a fiscal earthquake in Argentina or Thailand.

However, the caricature of the avaricious speculator with his (rarely her) Armani suit and ponytail is an atavistic leftover from the last century. International currency exchange deregulation and the enthusiastic adoption of on-line trading has meant that the typical trader is now more likely to be a part-time amateur with a little spare money and a lot of wide-eyed optimism. One only has to check out the "self help" and "how-to" shelves in a local bookshop to get a sense of the extent to which this particular demographic is burgeoning. The appeal is, of course, little different from that which has motivated gamblers from time immemorial, and indeed there might well be a significant crossover between amateur traders and those of us who regularly buy lottery tickets or bet on horse races. Both groups also have in common the fact that they almost invariably fail to achieve the dream of effortless riches.

Web trading exponentially magnifies the euphoria and the paranoia that was once contained within traditional trading houses and *bourses*. Chat rooms run on wild speculation about imminent profit statements, take-over bids, national budgets, and war scares. Hysterical responses in any part of the world, what Manuel Castells has described as "information turbulences" (1996, 105), can rapidly infect the entire system, with potentially dire consequences for populations far removed from the source of rumor. Indeed, as Muhatir claimed, it does appear as if it was panic of this kind that generated the crisis in Southeast Asia at the end of the last century, marking it as capitalism's first cyber-bust or virtual recession.

"Catchingafallingknife.com" featured the artist trading on-line in News Corporation shares or, more accurately, share derivatives called "warrants." These transactions took place in real time for the four-week duration of the exhibition. Goldberg sat atop a platform made of scaffolding in a large darkened room eerily lit by desk lamps and the glow of data projection. Three wall-sized video projections followed the progress of the shares in the form of various graphs, lines, and charts. The work also included a constantly updated website that allowed public access to the project and its progress via a chat room and dialogues conducted between the artist and the Internet analyst-activist Geert Lovink.

Goldberg alerts his audience to the fundamental act of faith at the heart of the speculative mentality. This is the belief that if the long- and short-term histories of the market are exhaustively and expertly analyzed, they will reveal recurring patterns that can be mapped geometrically and can then serve as the basis for prediction. Goldberg has studied the ways in which these predictors have evolved over the last century, and it is his firm belief that they are taken up or rejected on grounds that are, in essence, aesthetic. Thus, for example, the "Gann" system of anticipating "bear" or "bull" markets uses geometries rooted in the golden mean (1:1.618) and the Fibonacci series. The original Japanese "Candle Chart" is accompanied by poetically named accessories such as "morning star" and "paper umbrella," which, formed by price action, can be interpreted to give a picture of developing trends.

For this reason the chart projections could be viewed as a form of painting in real time, authored by tens of thousands of unwitting collaborators spread across the globe. Indeed, in an earlier work the artist had treated them in just this manner by transcribing them into large wall murals. However, Goldberg does far more than aestheticize the visual technologies through which late capitalism transforms the laws of supply and demand into forms that are anonymous, abstract, and often beautiful. More significantly, he draws our attention to the fundamental instability of the boundaries that separate taste and affluence, patronage and profit.

To raise investment capital for "Catchingafallingknife.com," he advertised in share trader chat rooms for a group of "entrepreneurs" who would stake the project. Three speculators, who may well have had no comprehension of contemporary art in its various digital, interactive, performance, or installation guises, invested a total of fifty thousand (Australian) dollars. While he certainly informed them of his intentions, it was still possible for the audience, and indeed for Goldberg himself, to harbor the suspicion that these anonymous venture capitalists were in it purely for the profit. Why, then, would they give money to the artist rather than simply trade the shares themselves? The answer is that Goldberg was able to present himself as a competent trader and, more importantly, he could stay on the job throughout the day for four weeks and could thereby take immediate advantage of small- or large-scale fluctuations in value.

In setting the situation up in this way, Goldberg was quite deliberately making problems for himself. For example, if he had lost all the money capriciously, he would have been guilty of exploiting sponsors who had backed him in good faith. Conversely, if he made a significant profit for them his performance could appear complicit with those practices of speculation from which he wished to maintain an ambiguous distance. Curiously, it was difficult to visit the work in progress without feeling some disappointment at the incremental losses that steadily accumulated. The criteria by which the work was to be judged were, at best, unclear, as mercantile and aesthetic success entered into a kind of duplicitous collusion. The knife that Goldberg attempted to catch was double-edged. His skills as a trader and artist were both up for critical assessment, and it was not easy to partition the two. It was this sense of awkward compromise, or at least of a fondness for the object of his critique, that imbued the work with much of its edginess. For Goldberg it would have been too easy, not to say disingenuous, to play the role of an artist-observer operating, in some sense, "above" the abstract but powerful world in which he had chosen to immerse himself.

From the Greenhouse to the Garden:
The Escape from Sanctified Space

The inclination to work beyond the (literal or presumptive) confines of gallery space is hardly new, for it was, after all, one of the principal characteristics of much conceptual and installation art in the late 1960s. Further, such work from this period has recently been interpreted as a kind of anticipation (in art) of the subsequent post-fordist evacuation of the sedentary workplace. I have no wish to dispute this historical claim. However, what I believe to be more novel in instances such as the two I have described is the kind of studied indifference to the question of whether the activity is best described as art, that is to say, an apparently blasé lack of concern with aesthetic status. In such cases the work travels through an art gallery only in order to gather an audience. The loaded gallery space is occupied, as it were, under a kind of flag of convenience. Where site-specific artists might once have argued vigorously for the aesthetic qualities of their work, many of the politically motivated individuals and collectives that have emerged in recent years seem instead to adopt a genuine disinterest in the aesthetic status of their work. And it is this, I suspect, that makes their work, in Brian Holmes's term, properly "post-vanguard" (2005, passim).

No one with any interest in contemporary art can have failed to notice its rapid and exciting expansion in the last decade and a half. In quick succession, the contemporary art of the ex–Soviet bloc of Africa, and of China has elbowed its way, if not to center stage, then at least into the chorus of exhibitions with the least pretension to global coverage. Prior to this ecumenical expansion, it was all too easy for those with an interest in contemporary art to imagine that the cultures of the North Atlantic possessed a near monopoly in the field; now, however, it is almost impossible to imagine that anyone ever believed in a singular, exclusively European conception of what it means to be modern. This alone marks the last fifteen years as the most exciting, fecund, and provocative period in the history of modern art. However, none of this means that these processes of cultural globalization have produced a level playing field on which all cultures can evenly compete for critical attention and financial reward. The very exhibitions in which this global expansion has occurred are, by and large, deployed in, and curated for, the old putative centers. Thus, these centers still hold.[7]

This globalized art world can be approached, if only from a particular perspective, as little more than the institutional expression of diverse mercantile, curatorial, and state interests that triangulate to form phenomena such as biennales, art fairs, auctions, and advertisement-laden art journals. Viewed in this way it could be plausibly argued that this institutional matrix enshrines and protects precisely those social relations of production founded in (intellectual and material) private property that Marx so long ago identified as the fundamental structural underpinnings through which the forces of production were orchestrated and given form.

It may therefore be timely to remind ourselves of what Marx said about the dialectic of social relations and forces of production in the famous and somewhat notorious passage of the 1859 preface to *A Contribution to a Critique of Political Economy*. There he claims that social relations of production serve to foster productive forces in the emergent stages of a particular mode of production, but that as these forces evolve, their capacity for effective deployment is increasingly fettered by these social relations which (as the form in which privilege and power are enshrined) do not share the same proclivity to evolve (Marx 1977b). Many examples of this tendency have been offered up by those who believe capitalism is drawing toward its historical twilight, from the deployment of new technologies of reproduction that seem shackled in the expression of their potential by copyright laws (the juridical "reflection" of entrenched social relations) to debates about the patenting of botanical and biological material and the restrictions applied to the manufacture of cheaper generic pharmaceuticals.

Everywhere we turn it seems that new technologies are restricted in their application by the dictates of state, church, or law. The technologies of art production are also subject to evolutionary and even revolutionary transformation, and it may be that the traditional venues for the production and consumption of art are no longer best suited to the emerging forces of artistic production. When the gallery "fetters" new, relational art forms, the producers of these forms are faced with the choice of siting their work elsewhere (the option chosen by Squatspace) or treating the gallery as a "legacy environment" that can be treated playfully or made strange. This is the path that Goldberg takes.

The Politics and Aesthetics of A-sincerity

Practitioners like Goldberg and the members of the Squatspace collective are not sincere in their commitment to art making as such, but neither are they truly insincere. There is no postmodern irony or cynicism here; instead there is just a pragmatic determination to work with one foot in, and one foot out of, an art world that is defined in terms of some set of necessary and sufficient conditions, or as Claire Bishop might put it less vigorously, a micro world with limits and borders that demand respect. These artists, and increasingly many like them, do not commit to subversion from within, but instead adopt a posture similar to what the curator Marc-Olivier Whaler has described as "oscillation" (2006, 41). They operate neither strictly "in" nor "out" of the art world. Neither do they appear particularly exercised by the precariousness of their location.

Instead they adopt a kind of pragmatic *a-sincerity* that enables them to take advantage of art world resourcing and of its accompanying critical apparatus when they feel it is appropriate or useful, without thereby acceding to its demands for acquiescence, fidelity, and attention. They play neither the good (committed) artist, nor the mischievous rebel within. Their fields of inquiry take them beyond this game. They choose the option that Paolo Virno and Brian Holmes have described as "exodus," understood as an "engaged withdrawal" designed to promote an "alliance between general intellect and political action" (Hardt and Virno 1996, 196; Holmes 2005, 60). The grammatical trope that best describes this feral commitment is that of the *palinode*, understood as a poetic assertion that is immediately withdrawn or denied.

What I characterize as a relationship of agnostic a-sincerity toward the art world as an institutionally and ideologically bordered structure is symptomatic of a movement from critique to engaged withdrawal, a withdrawal that gestures toward a world in which "art" becomes enmeshed with the totality of social relations and disavows its current, bounded utility as a signifier of intellectual capital. A-sincerity is not an aesthetic tactic for survival within the art world, but rather the opposite. It assists its practitioners in deploying their artistic skills as part of the "general intellect" and thus in staging sets of relationships that, in Rancière's terms, make possible a new "partitioning of the sensible" (Rancière 2004) in our understanding of what art is, where it lives, and what it can or should do.

I am, of course, suggesting that this refusal to identify with the institutional and ideological trappings of the art world might serve as a model for a more ubiquitous and general tactic of disidentification. No doubt the broad generality of immaterial labor has judged—and will continue to judge—the efficacy of this tactic in the interpolative calls for allegiance that it experiences more frequently and more intensely, day by day. I have argued that the performance of sincerity plays a crucial role in "cohering" post-fordist labor. Sincerity is used as an index of "surplus" commitment, which in turn is employed as an indicator of surplus value. Performances of sincerity and of insincerity may register on the corporate (or aesthetic) Richter scale, but a-sincerity might be somewhat more difficult to measure, domesticate, or police.

When Sincerity Fails

LITERATURES OF MIGRATION AND THE
EMBLEMATIC LABOR OF PERSONHOOD

Leslie A. Adelson

Emblematic Subjects and the Ties That Bind

For a political economist such as Saskia Sassen, migrant laborers in the late twentieth century become "emblematic subjects" of a global economy dating to the 1970s (2000, 216; 1998, 55–76).[1] For most studies and stories of globalization, the figure of migrant labor does appear indispensable as both social referent and rhetorical conceit. Yet the emblematic labor of literary configurations of migration in the same period is more difficult to discern. While much scholarship continues to presuppose an authentic migrant self who suffers indignities, celebrates hybridities, or even performs postcolonial tricksterisms sincerely, this essay proposes an interpretive alternative for evaluating the social deixis of personhood that so often seems to prevail in transnational literatures of migration. Precepts of sincerity associated with first-person articulations by migrants in particular often rely on categories of experience and identity that do more to hobble rather than hone our grasp of the emblematic labor that figures of migration perform in the literary realm. Even in the extraliterary realm of social relations, as Karl Marx serves to remind us in his account of commodity fetishism, value—which pivots on relations between people, history, and things—"does not have its description branded on its forehead; it rather transforms every product of labor into a social hieroglyphic" (1977a, 167).

May personhood itself be considered, not as the enabling ground of sincere feeling and authentic voice, but as a "social hieroglyphic" of sorts? The following remarks entertain this question with some reflections on the emblematic labor of personhood in the present age of globalization, with special emphasis on the presumed ethnic identity of migrant voices in fiction. This essay takes issue with the common presupposition that personhood and sincerity are necessarily bound to each other as rhetorical conceits in even fictional accounts of transnational migration today. Rather than taking as a given the sincere expression of migrant identities as a self-evident trajectory of this literature, the arguments here turn a critical eye to what precedes any putative claim to sincerity as a correspondence between inner truth and outer expression. If the semblance of personhood in literatures of migration labors toward something other than sincerity in this sense, what labor does the fiction of personhood serve?

The global economy Sassen has in mind is "characterized by a rapid growth of transactions and institutions . . . outside the framework of interstate relations" (1998, 100), and migrant laborers acquire emblematic status at "frontier zones" of capitalist development where national domains and a global economy interact (2000, 216). The political economist conjoins, as K. Anthony Appiah observes in his foreword to one of Sassen's books, "a discourse about global capital and the discourse of migration" by reconceiving the latter "as the globalization of labor" (Sassen 1998, xiv). What is at stake for Sassen in this conceptual shift from migration to labor, especially since she does not understand globalization to mean the erasure of national domains? By emphasizing labor rather than migration in studies of global capital and demographic mobility, Sassen highlights structural processes of economic transformation that "the language of immigration and ethnicity" obscures (1998, 87 passim). She hardly treats immigration and ethnicity as inoperative terms, but her mode of analysis exceeds any experiential perspective on migration and ethnicity as social frames of reference.[2]

Like Sassen, I pursue a mode of analysis that exceeds an understanding of labor as an experiential property of migrants as characters or authors. Recalling Arjun Appadurai's emphasis on the social practice of imagination as a pivotal "form of work" in "the new global order" (1996, 31), I ask what forms of imaginative labor fall to a literary text when the story of Turkish migration turns on entanglements with capitalist reconstruction in Germany after 1945.[3] This figural coupling of capital and labor indexes, not a political agon of predictable Marxian contours, but a relational nexus that warrants interpretive scrutiny. It will prove more protean than proletarian. This is not to suggest that the literature of migration produces fluid or hybrid identities as a cultural innovation. Instead, as seen in my primary literary example of the German literature of Turkish migration, the very sign of ethnicity begins to be reconfigured. What abstract forms of labor and capital does an analytical rhetoric of experience, identity, authenticity, and sincerity obscure under these circumstances?

"A small master folk sees itself in danger: one has summoned forces of labor, and human beings are coming," writes Max Frisch (1976, 374). While Frisch's dictum is often invoked in discussions of migration in Germany, one would not know from such commentary that Frisch indicts Swiss resistance to envisioning a national future that reflects the reality of Italian labor migration. The fact that Frisch was speaking about Italians in Switzerland in 1965, not Turks in Germany, is less significant for my present purposes than the categorical authority that has come to inhere in his assertion. When Kien Nghi Ha invokes Frisch in a study of Turkish migration and postcolonial ethnicity, he does so in a manner characteristic of others: "By pinning these people down . . . as a flexible 'industrial reserve army,' these human beings were dehumanized" (Ha 1999, 20).[4] What circulates in repetitive distinctions between "forces of labor" and "human beings" is the reminder that competing regimes of incorporation are at play in the social scene of migration and cultural narratives ensuing from it.[5] Frisch's ghost alerts us that structural tensions in the process of incorporation form the crux of stories about transnational migration to Europe since the 1950s.

If the globalization of labor proves a richer structural grid for Sassen than a personalized discourse of migration allows, Frisch and those who cite his pronouncement as if its import were self-evident regard the category of "human beings" as having both broader scope and greater value than "forces of labor." This is not a tension I intend to resolve. Literatures of migration, however, foreground abstract forms of imaginative labor and cultural capital that are enabled by conceits of personhood in pivotal ways. These conceits often revolve around ethnicity and gender, rhetorical figures of social deixis without which the story of Turkish migration cannot seem to function.[6] The relevance of these figures for migration narratives is by no means self-evident. Far more analytical curiosity about these social referents as strategic nexuses of narration is warranted if cultural innovations in the literature of migration are to become intelligible. The seemingly self-evident quality of Turkish figures in Germany is often enmeshed in fables of migration in which ethnicity and gender are presupposed as figural categories of personal identity and organizational frames of social reference. What labor functions actually accrue to such figures and frames?

Against migration studies that recast the story of postwar demographics from a sociology of labor to cultures of identity, Levent Soysal cites Frisch's emphasis on personhood as representative of a broad and unfortunate shift in perspectives on migration (L. Soysal 2003, 496–497). Soysal's main point is that "an elementary story of exclusion" predicated on frameworks of ethnic identity and cultural difference overlooks "processes of incorporation" in play (499). For this reason, the anthropologist considers the recurring figure of the *Gastarbeiter* (guest worker) in migration studies an anachronism that reproduces a familiar ethnocultural paradigm rather than attending to newly transnational labors of incorporation. Levent Soysal cites the sociologist Yasemin Soysal (1994; 2002) in this vein. As the latter observes, "Guestworkers become *symbolic* foreigners"[7] (Y. Soysal 1994, 135; L. Soysal 2003, 500).

Here two clarifications are in order. First, to call figures of guest workers "symbolic" has a very different analytical thrust from Sassen's designation of migrant laborers as "emblematic subjects" of globalization. By Sassen's account, migrant laborers late in the twentieth century participate in structural changes that the discursive figure of migrant labor indexes. According to both Soysals, guest workers become symbolic figures precisely because the ethnocultural paradigm attaching to them cannot index the changing sociality of migration. Second, doing without the figure of ethnicity altogether is an exaggerated response to the analytical blind spots of a focus on identities cohering or conflicting as cultural blocs. The discourse of incorporation need not oppose all possible discourses of ethnicity, only those relegating community to the straitjacket of anthropomorphic identity and inherited cultures.

Instead of considering ethnicity or even gender through an experiential or even ideological lens, this essay refocuses attention on such figural markers as strategic sites where imaginative labor and cultural capital in the literature of migration transform the meaning of *ethnos* (the ties that bind) rather than representing the content of any particular ethnic identity. If emblematic subjects index structural transformations afoot in the labor of migration and symbolic figures have lost their ability to index the changing sociality of migration, what sorts of social subjects do we encounter in the rhetorical conceits of personhood that palpitate transnational literatures of migration today?

Cultural Capital and Its Indexical Remainder

Work by Rey Chow and John Guillory is conceptually instructive where literary cultures of migration are concerned. In her study, *The Protestant Ethnic and the Spirit of Capitalism*, Chow categorizes "ethnicity as alienated labor" (2002, 33). She takes liberal manifestations of multiculturalism and feminism to task for subscribing to "the philosophical foundation of individualism" (154). By her account, this foundation favors the conceit of "an inviolable human subject" (32), thereby obscuring abstract structures of labor and commodification that call ethnic and gendered subjects into being as social forms of alienation rather than personhood.[8] This conceit inheres, not only in universalist paradigms of ethnicity as cultural heritage to be passed on as embodied identity, but also in oppositional paradigms of ethnicity as political resistance to be articulated as a critical voice.

Citing instead the capitalist production of ethnicity as an ambivalent index of social relations, Chow situates "our contemporary culture of protest . . . within the framework of a prevalent work principle" (2002, viii). With Max Weber as her muse, Chow argues that "the protestant ethnic"—the ethnic subject whose calling is to protest injustice—is called forth as an event intrinsic to rather than outside capitalist modes of interpellation (43 passim).[9] On these grounds she faults ethnic studies (especially in the United States) for presupposing that "protestant" ethnics represent a kind of proletarian consciousness necessarily "engaged in a struggle toward liberation" (40–41). On the same grounds she chastises scholars who approach the migrant or minoritarian experience of otherness presupposing "that ethnics are . . . aliens from *elsewhere*" (34). Ethnicity becomes, according to Chow, a flexible social mechanism for producing an internal boundary between what is considered valuable, on the one hand, and "foreign and inferior" on the other (34–35, 137).

In the German literature of Turkish migration, figures of ethnicity mark the site of many forms of imaginative labor, not a few of which bedevil the internal boundary concerning Chow. Figures of ethnicity in tales of migration sometimes enable new modes of affiliation rather than reproducing familiar patterns of differentiation. Protest may or may not be a central feature of this configuration. Chow's refusal to treat "ethnicity as a thematic concern" (2002, 51) is nonetheless compatible with the structural approach to Turkish figures I favor. The literature of Turkish migration by and large also intervenes in German culture from within rather than from "elsewhere."[10] Like Sassen, Chow treats anthropomorphic constellations of ethnicity and gender as emblematic subjects of social transformation involving the labor of migration. These are neither the symbolic subjects of migration studies decried by Yasemin Soysal and Levent Soysal nor individuals of any make, though human beings are interpellated by them.

Unlike Sassen, however, Chow is interested in cultural narratives in which "the turn toward the self, especially the ethnic self," functions "as a form of production" rather than representation (2002, 111). This leads her to identify a form of mimicry overlooked in postcolonial theory associated with Homi K. Bhabha, namely, "the level at which the ethnic person is expected to come to resemble what is recognizably ethnic" (Chow 2002, 107). For Chow, the protestant ethnic "must both be seen to own her ethnicity and to exhibit it repeatedly" in a problematic process of "*self-mimicry*" (112). Noting "the overwhelming popularity of self-referential genres, such as autobiographies, memoirs, journals, and diaries, in contemporary cultural politics," Chow radically questions the presumption of liberatory consequences attaching to such genres where ethnic subjects are concerned (112–113).[11]

These criticisms of ethnic mimeticism in capitalist production resonate with my critique of the self-evidentiary status ascribed to Turkish figures in German culture and literature (see Adelson 2005). Most of the literary texts in that genre are also written as first-person narratives from which one might conclude that the self takes center stage. Yet two basic precepts of my work point to phenomena for which *The Protestant Ethnic* cannot account. First, the Turkish figures at stake are by and large not protestant ethnics as Chow defines them. The German literature of Turk-ish migration does not revolve around identity politics, certainly not the type that Chow targets for critique in the United States and Great Britain. Minority subjects often resort to self-referential modes, Chow observes, as if they were "performing a confession in the criminal as well as noncrimi-nal sense." Socially interpellated as inferior, they proclaim their selfhood almost religiously, "as if it were a crime with which one has been charged" (2002, 115).

In the German literature of migration (including the novella to be discussed in the next section), one often encounters migrant characters that feel they are about to be accused of a crime. Even when this motif comes into play, conceits of selfhood do not necessarily serve the confes-sional functions that Chow ascribes to them in other contexts.[12] Even first-person narratives in the literature of migration can be dramatically at odds with presumptions of selfhood in an ethnic or humanist vein. Second, for all her insights into ethnicity as a form of labor, Chow does not interrogate the production of "ethnic community," a term she uses casually.[13]

By contrast, I argue that literary narratives of Turkish migration imaginatively labor to reconfigure tropes of ethnicity and gender under-writing the cultural capital of migration. To be sure, this approach to labor also exceeds the thematic emphasis on industrial labor that prevailed in guest worker literature prior to the 1990s. Attending to a less familiar form of labor now allows us to recognize how literary cultures of migration begin to re-imagine what it might mean to belong to an ethnoscape (as distinguished from an ethnicity) in the rapidly changing worlds of our day. To recall Appadurai's seminal if elusively metaphorical coinage, an ethnoscape is "the landscape of persons who constitute the shifting world in which we live" (1996, 33), not a cultural heritage that can be embodied.

Until now I have used the term "cultural capital" loosely for val-ues, beliefs, predispositions, and affects that lend greater purchase to some public stories of migration as compared with others. By contrast, John Guillory engages post-Marxist theories of value to illuminate institutional aspects of debates about canon formation that an ideological emphasis on minority representation obscures. Transnational migration and German contexts are far removed from Guillory's study, *Cultural Capital*, where the term denotes first and foremost "a problem of access to the means of liter-ary production and consumption" (1993, ix). According to Guillory, turf wars over the literary canon in terms of inclusion *versus* exclusion fail to grasp deep structures of school curricula and their social effects. The contents of the canon are not the real issue in such battles, he contends. "The canon debate signifies nothing less than a crisis in the form of cultural capital we call 'literature'" (viii). Guillory aims to clarify the nature of this crisis, in dialogue with canon debates in the United States and post-Marxist theorists such as Pierre Bourdieu, by rethinking how economics, aesthetics, and social relations are entangled in institutional processes regulating judgment and access. I foreground only limited aspects of Guillory's argument that shed light on a problem of representation relevant for my own inquiry. Notably this concerns cultural capital, a term that Guillory wields with greater conceptual precision than I have done thus far.[14]

At the heart of "the liberal . . . critique of the canon," Guillory identifies "a confusion" between political and visual representation (1993, vii–viii). One can readily agree that the experience of Turkish migration has enjoyed little social capital in Germany, and German readers usually expect literature by authors identified as Turks to represent the experience of migration. Guillory's approach to the relationship between commodities and works of art indicates that such observations cannot grasp the deeper cultural significance that accrues to the literature of migration. Defending Bourdieu's sociology against the charge "that it reduces the cultural field to a reflection of the economic" in spite of its post-Marxist critique of "economism," Guillory nonetheless finds that Bourdieu's distinction between "an economic logic" within the cultural field and "narrowly economic interests" of the market is insufficient to address the nature of cultural capital (Guillory 1993, 326–327). This form of capital always entails an illogical "remainder," which Guillory identifies as "aesthetic experience" (327).

His understanding of this remainder stems from his argument that no object, "not even the commodity," can be reduced to exchange value as a universal measure of equivalence (Guillory 1993, 325). The crux of the matter, for Guillory, is a structural tension between use value and exchange value: "The double discourse of value emerged as a way of assimilating the fact that exchange in the market really does function as an epitome of social relations . . . but as the site of the objective disharmony of these relations. . . . The 'logic of equivalence,' according to which every exchange is supposed to be an *equal* exchange, denies the crucial fact revealed in the market, that social relations do not *make sense*" (326).

The aesthetic effects of Turkish figures in literary texts yield "a remainder" in Guillory's terms, I suggest, something out of step with the logic of representation to which cultures of migration are often held. The figural image of migration and what such images represent are not bound to each other by equivalence. This reminder proves especially helpful when we consider Aras Ören's depiction of Ali Itir, a would-be guest worker in Germany who emerges in fiction as neither a person nor a thing, but a remainder where cultural capital resides. This calls into question both the interiority of feeling and the exteriority of expression on which precepts of sincerity conventionally rely. The discussion at this juncture thus revisits a luckless Turkish laborer who figures centrally in Ören's early and emblematic novella, *Bitte nix Polizei* (*Please, No Police*).

Ali Itir and the Transformation of *Ethnos*

The novella was written but not published in Turkish before being translated for German publication in 1981.[15] As the prototype for a series of novels that Ören authored under the near-Proustian rubric of being "in search of the present," the German version marked the tale's original publication. As I have observed elsewhere (see Adelson 2005), the Turkish *Gastarbeiter* is both an outdated stereotype and a stock figure in cultural fables of migration. Why does the male figure of ethnic labor associated with Turks in Germany exert such spectral force in spite of its anachronistic status? Perhaps this ghostly icon performs some other kind of labor than what we have customarily attributed to it as a cipher for capitalist exploitation or ethnic anomie. Reading *Bitte nix Polizei* with this possibility in mind proves worthwhile, for this early text begins to recast in literary form the imaginative terms of labor and capital forged by migration. Ören's tale of a woeful Turkish laborer and capitalist reconstruction in Germany indicates that there was more to the labor of migration than meets the eye well before globalization loomed large on public horizons.

Born in Istanbul in 1939, Ören represents a different perspective from many younger writers on the topics of national politics, Cold War antagonisms, and transnational migration. He does so without actually representing the guest worker experience. Although the author often characterizes his life in Germany as a "private exile," as the title of a published lecture series on his aesthetic production records (*Privatexil: Ein*

Programm?), his decision to move to West Berlin in 1969 also predates the military coups that prompted many intellectuals to seek refuge in Germany. Earlier the fledgling author had concentrated on theater work, mostly in Istanbul, but also in West Germany and Berlin. A permanent move to Berlin for personal reasons brought scattered jobs in industry, restaurants, and theater.

Ören enjoyed some success as a literary author in Germany when he published in 1973 an extended prose poem featuring Berlin. This "mosaic of working-class experience" (McGowan 2000) depicted the entangled lives of Turkish migrants and German laborers in the Berlin neighborhood of Kreuzberg, known as Little Istanbul; it was so well received that a major media station adapted it for television. According to Rita Chin, Ören was later hired to edit the first daily Turkish-language broadcast in the Federal Republic (2002, 63). Since 1996, Ören has served as the editor-in-chief of a major station's expanded Turkish program. His novels, short stories, and poems are now published mostly in German and Turkish, with some translations available in English and Dutch (Chiellino 2000, 466). Never involved in publishing enterprises that formally gave rise to "guest worker literature" in the 1980s, this author is nonetheless perceived in Germany as the emblematic "protagonist" of that phenomenon (Hohoff and Ackermann 1999, 2–6; Suhr 1990, 226; Heinze 1986, 62). This has something to do with the self-evidentiary status ascribed to Turkish figures in the public sphere, but it also has something to do with how one understands the relationship between labor and ethnicity in Ören's transnational tales of class history.

Scholars find that a "Marxist perspective" early on gradually yields to an emphasis on ethnic identity and multiculturalism (McGowan 2001, 297).[16] By some accounts, the novels "in search of the present" signal "the exhaustion" of Ören's original political project (McGowan 2000) or an abandonment of realism in favor of fantastically fluid identities (Hohoff and Ackermann 1999, 10). Most scholars resort to anthropomorphic conceits of identity to argue for one interpretation or another regarding a given text or the writer's oeuvre. For Yüksel Pazarkaya, another Turkish-born writer who has played a significant role in Germany's media landscape since the 1960s, "the identity question" is central to Ören's depiction of life "between two worlds" (1986, 19–20). Irmgard Ackermann calls Ali Itir a typical victim of labor migration and the novella "exemplary" in its "realist depiction of a migrant's fate" (1997, 21). By one reckoning, Ören's labors from the early 1970s into the early 1980s "demonstrated a fundamental rethinking of what constituted German identity" (Chin 2002, 46). Others are inclined to see a search for personal identity as central to the writer's work whether the writing is considered subjectively authentic or radically anti-realist. Hohoff and Ackermann present both views in one article.

Several scholars make the important observation that stories of Turkish and German laborers converge in *Bitte nix Polizei*. But when one reads the convergence through an anthropomorphic filter alone, the novella is reduced to "the pyschogram of a neighborhood that has lost its humanity" (Hohoff and Ackermann 1999, 7) and Ali Itir to a human victim of social circumstance: "homeless, isolated, and lost" (Suhr 1990, 232). In these approaches we recognize Max Frisch's conundrum. Competing regimes of incorporation are clearly at stake in the novella and its reception, but conceptual confusion prevails when one tries to read Ali Itir as a human being subjected to the cruel constraints of economic migration. How else might we read this literary figure of ethnic labor as an emblematic subject of late-twentieth-century migration?[17]

In some ways, Ali Itir does fit the male stereotype of Turkish abjection in Germany. Driven by economic need to migrate, this character is desperate for work in December 1973 after a week of fruitless searching. Unable to communicate with Germans or even other Turks, including the married relatives who shelter him, he is emotionally bereft. Ever fearful of German police and their dogs, he wants only to work so that he may realize his dream of personhood in Germany. When he lands an odd job shoveling snow off a factory courtyard, he ecstatically envisions long employment, if only the weather cooperates. Laid low by human interventions, this migrant laborer is accused of causing the death of a German man and raping a German woman in the story, which concludes with the Turk's disappearance. The final chapter describes police attempts to identify a corpse found in one of Berlin's infamous canals.[18] Driving through Kreuzberg with a loudspeaker, the police display a "phantom image" of the person found and a mannequin dressed in the clothes of the dead man, "presumably a Turk" and possibly the "victim of a crime" (Ören 1983, 87; 1992, 128–129). The young woman who had filed rape charges against an unidentified Turkish assailant claims to recognize the man in the "display dummy," but no one believes her (1992, 128).[19] Though Ali

Itir resurfaces in various guises in Ören's series of novels, his sudden erasure is left unclarified by the novella. For some inclined to read Ali Itir as a pathetic cipher of abjection, a migrant laborer trapped in a downward spiral of bad luck and inhuman conditions, suicide seems a self-evident conclusion.[20] What is wrong with this picture?

Economies of Personhood

Economic motifs are surely key to *Bitte nix Polizei* (Mani 2002, 118). Ali Itir is desperate to earn hard cash as a means to acquire personhood, to leave behind his status as "a nobody."[21] This is another way of saying that this figure, as a character, lacks capital in any form except for the small amount of money he earns shoveling snow. Peppered with words from a semantic field linking "non-person," "person," "personality," "personnel office," and "personal identity card," the text underscores this thematic link between money, personhood, and the symbolic legitimacy accruing to those who have them. Brigitte Gramke is the young German who accuses the foreigner of raping her, and she too is driven by a desire for symbolic capital. Although she earns something as a hairdresser's apprentice, she imagines she could earn more by prostituting herself, as her older sister does, and thus gain the personal stature her parents and boyfriend deny her. Humiliated by an unsuccessful attempt to be accepted as a sex worker at a brothel, Brigitte tries her luck with Ali, whom she approaches on the street and persuades to take her to his relatives' apartment, where the rape occurs and no money changes hands.

Unlike this act, later documented in police protocols in spite of "a few things that don't match up" in the telling (Ören 1983, 79; 1992, 118), another rape of pivotal importance to this story of migration goes unreported, and this rape too is narrated in reference to an economy of labor. During the Allied occupation following World War II, Brigitte's mother had belonged to those legendary "women of rubble" whose raw physical labor cleared the ruins of war to make way for reconstruction. This was paid work, necessary for survival. Events that transpire in December 1973 prompt Mrs. Gramke to recall, but only to herself through flashbacks, how the German man who had been appointed the women's crew boss traded sugar and cigarettes for sexual favors and sometimes raped members of his crew in dark cellar ruins. Never a willing trader in this economy, Mrs. Gramke recalls her rape at Ernst Kutte's hands. "I wanted to scream, but I couldn't get a sound out. Defending myself was senseless anyway, he was stronger and I needed work and vouchers for food rations" (1983, 57; 1992, 84).

All these economies of labor, violence, and legitimacy converge in the figure of Kutte in 1973. Now Mrs. Gramke's elderly neighbor, the former crew boss walks his dog on a snowy street in early morning. When he slips and falls, unable to right himself, Mrs. Gramke recognizes his plight but "in a strange mood of revenge" leaves him be, hoping that "the swine" will freeze to death (Ören 1983, 11; 1992, 10). By the time Ali Itir happens upon him, Kutte is "a whining heap of misery out of fear and pain," his tears "like frozen chickpeas" (1983, 37; 1992, 53). Although the foreign laborer wants to help, fear overwhelms him when he hears "police" from Kutte's lips and other people starting to gather around. (The title of the novella derives from this.) Able to flee the belated scene of a crime he did not commit, the Turk is believed by German bystanders to have beaten up an old man, who dies as a result of whatever transpired, a "murder" victim according to the rumor mill.[22]

These converging story lines of material needs and ethical ambiguity may highlight, as some propose, a shared humanity binding Germans and Turks together more than any differences drive them apart.[23] Such readings are compatible with indictments of capitalism and xenophobia as social systems depriving individuals of their basic humanity. In a different analytic register I argue instead that the textual economy of the novella hinges on abstract functions accruing to Ali Itir as a "non-person."[24] Some see his fate as tragic because this migrant laborer remains a "nobody" without any capital. This perception shifts once we recognize that Ali Itir—as a literary figure of ethnic labor—is best understood as a commodity. This figure's capacity to index the cultural capital of migration pivots on this distinction.

Illogical Remainders and Literary Form

If ethnicity becomes a form of alienated labor under capitalist conditions late in the twentieth century, then (as Chow demonstrates) ethnicity is a commodity indexing abstract social relations. But not even commodities, Guillory tells us, can be reduced to exchange value as a universal measure of equivalence, for something illogical remains. Cultural capital is Guillory's term for this remainder, which points to ways in which the commensurability of economic value is befuddled by the incommensurability of social relations. The aesthetic effects of Turkish figures in literature at times yield such a remainder, something out of step with the logic of representation to which cultures of migration are usually held. *Bitte nix Polizei*, which many readers find unquestionably realist in its representation of working-class history and labor migration, lends itself especially well to such a contrapuntal reading.

There are numerous allusions in the text to human beings performing various types of labor. Mrs. Gramke and a Turkish woman clean office buildings for a living, and Mr. Gramke went from lucrative tailoring to "rationalized" ironing before being replaced by unskilled laborers (Ören 1983, 60; 1992, 88). Vegetable vendors, street cleaners, trash collectors, and sex workers people this story in lesser roles as well. What labor falls to the ethnic figure of Ali Itir as a commodity rather than a would-be person? As a character, this figure portrays his labors as anything but alienating, for he sees an immediate relationship between money to be earned and dreams to be realized. On a thematic level this underscores market principles and ideologies of personhood, though the migrant's dreams dissolve predictably into nightmares instead. Yet this anthropomorphic figure of ethnicity requires further scrutiny for three reasons.

First, Ali Itir is not a guest worker at all. Deemed medically unfit to participate in the recruitment program, he has entered the Federal Republic on a tourist visa and resides there as an illegal alien.[25] Holder of a valid Turkish passport, he *can* claim personhood on grounds of citizenship. This is important because his figural role in the narrative turns on the uncertain status of the labor he performs, not the personhood he desires.[26] Second, because of his illegal status, Ali Itir circulates in the novella as no mere commodity, but rather as contraband. He is explicitly interpellated as such when a Turkish leftist tries to explain how legally traded goods become "contraband" (*Schmuggelware*) when "individual persons" attempt to deal in commerce otherwise handled by the state. "You are contraband (*Schwarzmarktware*)," the orator declares (Ören 1983, 23; 1992, 30–31).[27]

Disappointed that this educated person has not really helped him at all, Ali Itir nonetheless receives his proper designation in this scene. Dipesh Chakrabarty's assessment of the sublation of difference in commodities is helpful here: "Commodity exchange is about exchanging things that are different in their histories, material properties, and uses. Yet the commodity form, intrinsically, is supposed to make differences—however material they may be—immaterial for the purpose of exchange. The commodity form does not as such negate difference but holds it in suspension so that we can exchange things as different from one another as beds and houses" (Chakrabarty 2000, 655). Difference is thus neither "external to capital" nor "subsumed" by it (671). In Guillory's terms, something illogical is suspended in cultural capital, which cannot be grasped in terms of equivalence. The figure of Ali Itir indexes this remainder, a network of relations that are not subject to open trade or direct representation precisely because no equivalence applies. Despite decoy exchanges in the novella—Ali Itir receives day wages and buys socks, for example—the touching tales at issue in the novella are not narrated in a register of exchange.[28] As a figure in reference to which stories that don't "match up" can nonetheless be articulated, Ali Itir falls between the cracks of representation on yet a third level.

Unlike the self-confessional genres that Chow targets for critique, *Bitte nix Polizei* proceeds mostly by third-person narration, multiple focalization, interior monologues, and reported discourse. The sole exception occurs almost immediately, when the voice of narration speaks as an "I" to mention a dream. This seems only a teaser, since the narrator never speaks as an "I" again. This "I" is neither omniscient by grand abstraction nor identifiable by anthropomorphic attributes. Though provided with many anthropomorphic features by contrast, Ali Itir teeters along a spectrum between a first-person medium of interior monologue and third-person status in objectified narration.[29]

The precariousness of his role as person or thing is exacerbated when he disappears altogether, only to be resurrected (and this only perhaps) as a "phantom image," a "display dummy" with which police hope to reconstruct lived circumstances resulting in death. The text's central conceit of lived histories brought to a standstill—frozen or suspended in matter—culminates in this phantom image, which literally displaces Ali Itir as an individualized character from the narrative. It is *as if* he had disappeared. Other rhetorical figures drawn in keeping with this central conceit include Kutte as a wooden marionette, Brigitte's boyfriend as a built monument, Mrs. Gramke as a "woman of rubble" in a group photo, and "a huge plastic doll in a wedding gown" in the bedroom where the disastrous encounter with Ali Itir occurs.[30] Lived histories that crystallize into frozen images in this winter landscape are suspended in ice. "It looked as though the entire neighborhood had frozen and held its breath from so much cold" (Ören 1983, 25; 1992, 33).[31]

Amidst so many frozen and suspended histories of desire, shame, fear, rage, and violent transgression, one image of life brought to a standstill nearly leaps off the page with renewed vitality. Mrs. Gramke recalls being raped by her crew boss in the ruined cellar through the medium of interior monologue. Where we might expect a forceful image of something frozen, we read, "Together we fell onto something soft." The woman's interior monologue opens up into an external perspective on this scene by means of indirect discourse and reported speech. Only from this external perspective can we identify this "something soft" and understand how it can be simultaneously dead and alive: "Suddenly a few kids were standing at the entrance, I heard a boy with a deep voice say that he knew where the dead horse was, and another boy screamed: 'There it is, up ahead, it's even moving.' The kids ran out of the cellar screaming, and the boy with the deep voice called after them: 'You dummies, you know a dead horse doesn't move!'" (Ören 1983, 57; 1992, 84).

As a genre the novella famously "flourished in Germany," and Goethe's definition of its structural cornerstone holds that a novella turns on a mysterious event. This is an event that is "unheard of" but takes place nonetheless, something that takes the reader by surprise but follows from what has been recounted (Cuddon 1991, 641–642).

The dead horse that moves qualifies as such an event, and Ören's novella pointedly draws our attention to the illogical status of something that has nonetheless transpired. Other mysterious events (Ali Itir's disappearance, for example) are weighted more heavily in terms of plot, but the dead horse that moves is emblematic of the indexical economy on which *Bitte nix Polizei* hinges. The equine figure of life in death does not represent the rape but gestures toward it, and only a disaggregated voice of narration alerts us to the gesture at all. The story of this violation under the guise of capitalist reconstruction is not recounted in sincerity as authentic experience, but as a relational nexus of illogical remainders. If Kutte and his victim fall onto something soft in a bombed-out cellar, things have hardened considerably by the time Ali Itir enters the scene. No equine corpse points to social relations that don't quite add up in 1973. This indexical labor falls

instead to Ali Itir as an ethnic commodity, a phantom image alerting us to
the cultural capital of transnational migration.

As one scholar observes, the main story lines involving Ali Itir and
the Gramke family converge in two pivotal scenes, Kutte lying on the
street and Brigitte lying on a bed (Şölçün 1992, 26–27). How are these
scenes and story lines related? Do they converge in equivalence after all,
or do these tales of Turkish migration and German reconstruction touch
in some other way? Much speaks for convergence in the first sense, since
histories of economic need and sexual transgression appear encoded in
street and bedroom alike. Both women are raped and both men portrayed
as rapists. Mrs. Gramke is partly responsible for Kutte's death, and her
daughter is partly responsible for Ali Itir's disappearance. Both women
conceal the truth about their relationships with these men from others—
Brigitte by lying to the police, and her mother by purchasing a funeral
wreath for Kutte, for which she plans to prepare a nice ribbon that reads:
"*To our dear neighbor, a final farewell*" (Ören 1983, 86; 1992, 127). As the
actual turning point in the novella, the violent transaction between the
hairdresser's apprentice and the illegal alien stems initially from a reversal of fortune for both. Ali Itir can respond to Brigitte's proposition only
because he has just been paid and envisions himself en route to personhood, and the young woman approaches him only because her efforts to
achieve personhood have been spurned by organized sex workers. Most
important, Ali Itir utters the title phrase when he tries to silence both the
fallen man and the frightened woman. What then speaks to anything but
a mirroring of equivalent experiences?

The answer lies in the relationship between events that are narrated
and figures in reference to which such narration becomes possible. Ali Itir's
role as a phantom image is crucial here. As the narrator predicts, the young
woman will remain ill at ease, even after reporting her assault to the police,
"because even the recording of an event (*Tathergang*) is not enough to produce an offender (*Täter*)" (Ören 1983, 81; 1992, 121).[32] Yet Ali Itir's situation
is not to be envied, the narrator elaborates: "Although he had a passport
and thus officially existed, he did not exist after all, on the other hand,
because as an illegal, he did not officially exist. He existed only in the
police report: as an unidentified offender" (1983, 83; 1992, 123).

The illegal alien's status as a non-entity is underscored earlier
in the text when his relatives and their building manager confirm for

police that only registered residents in fact live in the Turks' apartment. This refrain denotes a course of action with no identifiable agent but an indexical phantom. If Brigitte's police report yields an event without an agent, her mother's story has an offending agent who goes undetected because the rape is never reported. The case of the daughter seems, nearly exactly, the mirror opposite of the mother's. Yet Mrs. Gramke's story goes unreported only to legal authorities and those with whom she cultivates social relations. Readers are privy to what transpires in the darkness of cellar ruins. Our access to these events is enabled in the first instance by an equine figure that draws our attention to something beside itself. At a greater remove from the event, the phantom figure of migrant labor assumes this structural function in the narrative overall.

In a chain of indirect references this phantom figure keeps pointing elsewhere, to events and relations that never resolve into equivalent images or coherent ethnic communities as multiculturalist representation defines them. Ören's configuration of a would-be guest worker indexes frozen histories of crime, shame, exploitation, fear, anger, and revenge and restores movement to them. Ali Itir functions as a rhetorical figure in reference to which an untellable German story of capitalist reconstruction can be told, all logical expectations of personhood in the service of sincere expression to the contrary. This is the cultural capital of Turkish migration to which Ören draws our attention as early as 1981. While conceits of ethnicity, gender, and sexuality enable the telling of this tale, Ali Itir is best understood as a strategic nexus where imaginative effects of migration only appear to congeal into something resembling a person who suffers so sincerely. This emblematic conjunction manifests as a specter of capitalism, which haunts a national history and a globalized economy in disaggregated ways. *Bitte nix Polizei* weaves a spectral tale of complex social histories that only appear tailor-made for the men and women compelled to wear them. Male and female, German and Turk, such characters are display dummies in which the hopes and fears of a changing transnational economy of *ethnos* are suspended, as if on ice.

PART III

SINCERITY AS MEDIA EFFECT

A Feeling of Insincerity

POLITICS, VENTRILOQUY,
AND THE DIALECTICS OF GESTURE

Jill Bennett

In Mediality

For two video works in the early 2000s South African–born artist Candice Breitz worked with amateur singers struggling to master songs in a foreign language. In *Karaoke*, Tamil, Russian, Spanish, and Vietnamese speakers perform the song *Killing Me Softly* in a New York karaoke bar, their ten performances screened simultaneously on monitors surrounding the viewer. Each singer, striving to embody the words in accented English, interprets the lyrics—"killing me softly with his words"—with a conventional range of gestures: the small movements of eyebrows and contractions of facial muscles that serve to express emotion, personalizing the song by imbuing the words with feeling. For *Alien*, Breitz worked in Berlin with foreigners who had recently arrived in the city, asking them to learn popular German songs. In the final piece the audio track of the performances is deleted and replaced with a version by a native German speaker, in a way that is never fully lip-synched, so that again the work dramatizes, as Breitz puts it: "the battle to possess language as opposed to being possessed by language" (Beccaria 2005, 22).

In capturing the process by which a given language and form of linguistic expression is incorporated from an exterior source, Breitz is concerned neither with mastery of language, nor with linguistic ineptitude, but with an interaction within language. Her focus on gestural performance, intensified by the ultimate erasure of the singer's own voice in *Alien*, manifests a subject's inner dialogue with this "received" language, rather than its use as a communicative tool. Breitz's characters are not actors with language at their complete disposal, but are, in the terminology of Giorgio Agamben, "suspended by and in their own mediality" (2000, 58), so that the work essentially makes visible the dynamic of being in a medium.

Such a dynamic is vividly evoked in Mark Crispin Miller's acute description of President Bush tackling a speech: "His eyes go blank as he consults the Teleprompter in his head, and he chews uneasily at the corner of his mouth, as if to keep his lips in motion for the coming job, much as a batter swings before the pitch. Thus prepared, he then meticulously sounds out every . . . single . . . word, as if asking for assistance in a foreign language" (2001, 6). Crispin Miller's *The Bush Dyslexicon: Observations on a National Disorder*, from which this account is taken, is one of a growing number of texts that catalogue not just the infamous malapropisms and linguistic stumbles of George W. Bush, but precisely his struggle with language as this is manifested in face and body. In Bush's case this struggle has a particular televisual presence; micro-gestures are immediately registered in the static head-and-shoulders shots that often frame the president, so that as words fail him, there is always something to fill the gap. As Jenny Edbauer has observed: "The President appears and suddenly something goes wrong. He stumbles. He squints. His mouth opens, but the words won't come. And when they do come, they are wrong. His body jerks just a little, but the camera magnifies the small flinches until they appear larger than life" (2004, 1). This is a phenomenon exploited by filmmaker Michael Moore in the sequences of *Fahrenheit 9/11* (2004), which highlight the plastic transformation of Bush's body in the moments before and between speech—the moments that are of course invariably more eloquent than the speech, and that are so visually compelling that they provide unusually good traction for Moore's voiceover, allowing the sequence to go beyond satire into a gestic comedy.

These two examples—and Breitz's and Moore's work generally—

have led me to think more about the significance of gesture as a component of linguistic performance, and in particular about the critical, often political strategy of reducing a performance to its gestural elements through a process of extraction and recombination. Such an expansion of the discussion of the performance of language seems to me important in the light of the difficulties that post-structuralist thought poses for the concept of sincerity, which always implies a certain understanding of the relationship of the subject to language.

Critical theory has effectively upset the very foundations of an investigation of sincerity by calling into question the ontological basis for defining an act or speech act in terms of a congruence of avowal and actual feeling or belief. Where language is conceived as a tool wielded by a subject who "does things with words" [in J. L. Austin's formulation (1975)], there is at least the possibility of being true to oneself in speech. But post-structuralism undermined this view of language in the service of subjectivity, offering instead variations on the notion of a self brought forth by and through language. Now it's possible to affirm that words "do things with us"; expressions don't conform to the will of individual agents—nor does belief necessarily precede avowal. As certain theories of performativity have proffered, ideations may themselves be produced through expression, so that we may come to believe something only in the act of avowal.

It's not surprising, then, that the discussion of sincerity has refocussed on the semiotics of appearances, not just on an academic but also on a popular level. Sincerity is readily understood as an effect of speech or performance, rather than something that is inhabited in any deeper or more ethical sense. What is generally missing in the analysis of such surface effects is, however, a discussion of the experience of speaking belief, of "doing language" in Toni Morrison's phrase (1993), or indeed of feeling oneself to be doing it.

As Judith Butler points out in her book *Excitable Speech* (1997), doing language is not the same as doing something *with* language. It is not about a speaker creating an effect with language, but about being within language in a certain sense: language that confers a speaking position upon us, that is given or inherited, but that nevertheless must be interiorized and spoken. This interiorization or making-over of language to the self occurs through what Denise Riley calls the "ventriloquy of inner speech" (2005, 6), which in itself occasions affect, not merely as a component of the drama of the speech act (saying it with feeling) but in and around the reception of language within the speaker, in as much as there can be an experience of "linguistic emotion" (102). Linguistic emotion in this sense is an immaterial experience that arises out of the process of interaction with—or within—language. This might encompass feelings arising from the struggle to produce language, the sensation of feeling it run away, linguistic embarrassment, or linguistic pleasure.

Riley's idea of language—an inhabited domain filled out with the plenitude of a speaker's emotion—on the one hand disposes of any radical opposition between the notion of language shaping subjective experience, and on the other hand disposes of language under the control of the subject. Language is, in her formulation, neither our master nor our instrument, but "amiably indifferent" to us (2005, 7). Hence it exerts a torsion on us that becomes visible as a struggle in the Bush imagery and in Breitz's work.

Such an approach to language offers the possibility of exploring the affective and political dimensions of sincerity without reaffirming a hidden interior experience as a substrate—and ethical guarantor—of expression. We might, in this vein, remap the emotional dynamics of sincerity on another axis altogether from the one that indexes avowal to inner belief. We could then consider instead the relationship of a subject to a speech act and its associated bodily expressions in a way that allows us to see how a sincerity effect might arise not merely from a convincing expression of belief and feeling, but also from the way language is inhabited and the extent to which this is captured in media.

In visual terms, gesture is a fundamental element of this process—gesture understood not as non-linguistic, but as Giorgio Agamben puts it, as a "forceful presence in language itself" (1999b, 77). As a component of the performance of language, gesture does not simply animate or give emphasis to speech; it is often at odds with the function of communication. In his essay "Kommerell, or On Gesture," named for the German critic Max Kommerell, Agamben develops a notion of gestic criticism building on Kommerell's description of a "dialectic of gesture" (1999b: 79). This dialectic manifests in the face, which can combine two registers, the solitary and the communicative, engaging in conversation even as "it seems to tell us the history of solitary moments" (78). According to Kommerell, "Even a face that is never witnessed has its mimicry; and it is very much a question as to which gestures leave an imprint on its physical appearance, those through which [a subject] makes himself understood, or, instead, those imposed on him by solitude or inner dialogue" (1956, 36).

A more empirical account of this tension emerges in the experimental studies of psychologist Paul Ekman, the well-known expert on lying, who tells us that "the face is equipped to lie the most and leak the most" (Ekman and Friesen 1969, 98) because it is not only the vehicle for expression or projection of emotion, but also where affect is manifested in a more immediate and direct way. When Ekman observed groups of people watching gory videos, he noted that all subjects—regardless of cultural background—tended to display the same affect, that is, until they became aware of others watching them, at which point they would modulate their expression, and the emotions displayed would differ. Emotion can thus be understood as having a social dimension; it is displayed or projected feeling. By contrast, what the psychologist Silvan Tomkins labelled "affect" (what others term "basic emotion") is a pre-reflective biological experience: "affects are primarily facial behaviors and secondly outer skeletal and inner visceral behavior" (Tomkins and Demos 1995, 217). Thus, according to Tomkins and Ekman, affects have generic characteristics or facial signatures. For example, Tomkins describes fear-terror as "eyes frozen open, pale, cold, sweaty, facial trembling with hair erect" (95).

Emotion, on this model, is a potent but inherently unreliable component of the linguistic performance of sincerity. Unlike affect, emotion can be faked; it is, by definition, for another. Kommerrell's dialectic potentially brings affect and feeling into play in this scenario by envisaging a sphere of solitary expression that inhabits language as a counterpoint to the outward address. Gesture, he argues, never exists only for the other; "indeed, only insofar as it also exists for itself can it be compelling for the other" (Agamben 1999b, 78). Hence the capacity to sustain this image of an inner life in tandem with—and often at odds with—external communication may serve to convince us of a person's sincerity. This occurs not through the perfect confluence of words and emotion, but by revealing a struggle with the feeling or experience of something we might call insincerity.

Riley reminds us that language is often felt by its speaker to be incorporated imperfectly, so that even in the moment of truth telling and transparency we may feel insincere; for Kommerell it is gesture that escapes from us in this way: "The beginning is a feeling of the 'I' that, in every possible gesture, and especially in each of its own gestures, experiences something false, a deformation of the inside with respect to which all faithful presentation seems a curse against the spirit" (Agamben 1999b, 79).

The critical function of media (film, video) arises from the capacity to capture gesture and to reveal this dialectic—a dialectic that effectively presumes an incongruence of inner belief and external expression—and that is understood as enacted through a "feeling." Feeling here is not the complex organization of affect that we call emotion, but precisely the moment of awareness of affect through which the self is experienced—experienced as a deformation of itself.

In this sense, to capture gesture is to capture a face or body sustaining a feeling of insincerity. This feeling does not precede its exhibition in media. It is not a property or characteristic of an individual, revealed by or made the subject of media; it is a function of "being in a medium." An artwork or film thus exhibits and exposes gesture in its mediality. To do this is to enact critique in a particular way, scrutinizing the body to reveal, not so much what language wilfully covers up or denies, but the point at which language fails—for the gesture, as Agamben argues, is essentially always a gesture of not being able to figure something out in language (1999b, 78).

A criticism that reduces expression to gesture realizes the condition of "not being able to figure something out in language" as an event or moment *within* language rather than its breakdown or malfunction. Such a critique has particular purchase in the contemporary context where images of leaders can function effectively by registering a struggle with language, which doesn't always yield readily to the speaker. If the fantasy of linguistic triumph and domination is the televisual presidency of the *West Wing*, the reality is the triumph of Bush, Reagan, and the right-wing populist Pauline Hanson in Australia, who have each in different ways capitalized on linguistic ineptitude. They are not successful in spite of their stumbles, malapropisms, and misadventures with language, but almost because of them, as Brian Massumi (2002) noted of Reagan.

Sincerity/Exposure

Figureheads like Bush and Hanson understand and exploit the appeal of down-to-earth plain speaking, but there is more at stake here than identification with the home-spun persona, which serves as a housing for a particular form of expression centered in the gesture of not being able to figure something out in language. In the 1990s Pauline Hanson found-ed a briefly popular neo-nationalist political party, One Nation, pitching her campaigns in opposition to the slick rhetoric of politicians, which she saw as perpetrating lies. Fuelled by a desire to embody truth in politics, Hanson was undaunted by her incapacity to either speak or comprehend the language of policy, politics, and economics, which she sought to com-bat with the simple fact of her honest conviction—with her sincerity, in other words—and this made her very difficult to subdue with argument. In a now famous interview on the TV news program *60 Minutes* in Octo-ber 1996, she was accused of xenophobia. Thrown off balance because she didn't understand the word, she blanched and countered with the clipped response "please explain." This phrase is now commonplace in media-speak, if not ordinary language, as a compound noun (news reports might say "the government has been issued with a 'please explain'").

Hanson's catch phrase, coined in a moment of linguistic embar-rassment, was a forced improvisation—a slightly pained, arch response to someone who had tried to catch her out with fancy words. It was what Agamben refers to as a "gag," that is, "in the proper meaning of the term, indicating first of all something that could be put in your mouth to hin-der speech, as well as in the sense of the actor's improvisation meant to compensate a loss of memory or an inability to speak" (2000, 59). This gag functioned as an embodied expression within a language game, and its real currency was not as a descriptor, but as a gesture. Even when it is used in the media it remains in parentheses because the words have solidi-fied in the voice and body of Pauline.

A large part of the reason for this was the intervention of sound artist Simon Hunt and his drag persona Pauline Pantsdown, who stood against Hanson in the 1998 federal election. As a drag act emerging from the con-text of Sydney gay performance culture, Pantsdown had recorded a song using samples of Hanson's own voice and the recognizable phrase "please explain." This first recording essentially took the rhetoric of the right-wing xenophobe and, in the Weimar cabaret tradition, changed the object of the ranting so that Pauline now became a gay activist (Bogad 2005, 172–175). The song "Back Door Man" might have remained within gay subcul-ture and minority radio had Hanson not sought an injunction.

During the race for the senate, Pantsdown released a second record-ing that had considerable mainstream success—a catchy rap song with a dance beat, titled "I Don't Like It." Hanson did in fact utter this same phrase when asked her view of Sydney's Gay Mardi Gras parade, though Hunt actually created the sound bite through a complex and laborious process, cutting up Hanson's distinctive voice, syllable by syllable, and altering the pitch to create perfectly phrased sequences with appropriate tone, timbre, and affect. The lyrics were not purely satirical but put words into Hanson's mouth:

> I don't like it, when you turn my voice about.
> I don't like it, when you vote One Nation out.
> My language has been murdered, my language has been murdered.
> My shopping trolley murdered, my groceries just gone. (Hunt 1998)

This process was effective because, as Hunt observed, Pauline was given to speaking in what appeared to be pre-formed sentences or phrases (1998). Her speech, in a certain sense, already sounded ventriloquized.

This tendency to deliver words in solidified chunks has the effect of reducing their signifying function. Pauline's words didn't readily carry meaning, but when embodied and performed with their characteristic edge of defiance, resentment, and resistance, they were effective as "linguistic gestures." Their apparent sincerity was not a function of their iteration, nor of the performance of projected emotion, but of what Anna Gibbs, in her formative analysis of the Hanson phenomenon, identified as the presence of competing affects (2001). By this she means sensations of distress or anxiety that are themselves at large in the voting population.

Pauline Pantsdown was arguably Hanson's most tactically efficacious opponent in the 1998 election, where the major political parties made the mistake of assuming that the One Nation phenomenon could be stopped with words, and that Hanson's "not being able to figure something out in language" would prove self-defeating. In the event, attacks that focused on content—that tripped her up with polysyllabic words or trumped her with facts—were iterations that merely played to her claim to be the disenfranchised voice of the people. Hunt's modus operandi was to challenge this claim to authenticity by attaching epithets like "please explain" or "I don't like it" to the body of Pauline in order then to set them loose. Once free they began to plague Hanson on the campaign trail, ringing out in places like shopping centers.

In the Pauline Pantsdown recording, Hanson was confronted with the deformation of self to which Kommerell refers. It induced a form of trans-body linguistic embarrassment. The characteristic of this is, as Riley notes, not a feeling of being exposed, but a feeling of *wrongful exposure*. One is revealed not as one's true self, but as a self engaged in mimicry, in other words, as inauthentic. This was the ultimate lie for the politician who believed that her voice was the marker of her sincerity, that it expressed an irreducible truth guaranteed by the depth of her conviction (Stratton 1999).

Affective Politics

How then, can we think about "gestic criticism" through media more generally in these terms? The feeling of "wrongful exposure" induced by Hunt in and around Hanson is a media event; it is an affective moment sustained by media. Its effect lies in confronting a subject with a feeling of insincerity. This is a particular mode of exposition—an exposé without the conventional grounding in evidence; not one that exposes fabrication or a misplaced belief in a politician's sincerity, but an exposé that actually induces a feeling.

Michael Moore's documentary strategy is interesting in this regard. As his detractors are quick to point out, he strays readily from the facts, but that could be seen as an issue of methodology. This is particularly true in the 2002 film *Bowling for Columbine*, which is, I would argue, more radical than *Fahrenheit 9/11* in its deviation from a more empirical approach to political exposé. *Fahrenheit 9/11* pursues evidence, such as digging up concealed information to discredit the Bush family; *Bowling for Columbine* searches for ideas, explanations, and theories—but more than this, it addresses a politics in which belief is no longer indexed to empirical truth in a simple or demonstrable way.

The primary conceit of *Bowling for Columbine* is the enactment of the incomprehensibility of gun violence and the failure of contemporary America to account for it. Moore himself personifies the national befuddlement, setting out on a quest for answers. The image of America congeals around a series of corporeal signs—bodies performing actions that exceed the banal self-descriptions of performers and witnesses: from the

Michigan Militia and their calendar girls posing in combat gear, to the hunting dog who shot someone in the leg. These sequences are run against the moments when speech fails the victims or witnesses of violent crime— or when a Colorado home security consultant starts to expound a theory of how Columbine has changed the way we talk, only to find he can't in fact talk at all about Columbine without choking up.

One segment in particular examines the function of the gag in relation to belief in the contemporary political dispensation. A rapid succession of clips from current affairs TV bulletins announcing a flurry of plagues and threats, spooking the American public in shopping malls, homes, and the outdoors, cuts abruptly to the White House pressroom for a presidential announcement. Bush delivers his lines, slowly and deliberately, with enough lip chewing and blinking to break up the flow of his announcement that the Justice Department has issued a blanket alert in recognition of a general threat: "It's not the first time the Justice Department has acted this way. I hope it will be the last, but given the attitude of the evildoers, it may not be." The sequence closes with another abrupt cut to two seconds of a film noir sequence of a woman stalked by an unseen predator, her eyes and then mouth opening wide with what Tomkins would identify as fear-terror.

As Moore highlights, there is no information to impart here. The only effect of the announcement is to induce fear or anxiety—an affect without an object to attach itself to. This is, as Massumi puts it, politics "addressing bodies from the dispositional angle of their affectivity, instead of addressing subjects from the positional angle of their ideations" (2005, 34) so that it is no longer concerned with adherence or belief but with direct activation.

This shift away from an engagement with beliefs or ideations was in some respects pre-empted by Michel de Certeau in the *Practice of Everyday Life* (1984), where he noted that complicity in politics between politicians and voters has displaced belief. Voters now generally acknowledge that the rhetoric of political campaigns is unbelievable, but at the same time they assume that the managers of the political apparatus are moved by convictions and knowledge. The implications of this for the representation of belief are quite tangible; there is no appeal to voters' beliefs yet there must be a manifestation of believing, at least in a self-contained media domain. De Certeau suggests that what comes into play here are citational mechanisms, since belief is no longer "expressed in direct convictions, but only through the detour of what others are thought to believe" (1984, 188). Hence opinion polls (over and above the content of a politician's rhetoric) convince us of their believability. Slavoj Žižek has made similar arguments to the effect that belief can function at a distance. There has to be some guarantor of it, though the guarantor may be displaced, never present.

The scenario of threat that informs contemporary global politics has made the absence of any guarantor of belief much more palpable, particularly as it operates under the sign of the precautionary principle. Actions are justified on the basis of an imagined future and the threat of a force that hasn't yet acted or revealed itself; there can be no empirical basis for this argument since it is hypothetical, and the proposed action seeks to prevent the imagined dangers from ever being realized. The "guarantors" that inform policy through secret security briefings are now literally invisible to us. The politicians to whom they speak now themselves embody belief, revealing themselves to be touched by dark truths known only by insiders.

This economy of threat has given rise to a performative sincerity in which politicians appeal not to shared belief but to shared anxiety, grounding this in their own sense of conviction. Hence, in a *Newsnight* interview in February 2003, Tony Blair gushed: "Dangers are there, and I think it's difficult sometimes for people to see how they all come together, but it's my honest belief that they do come together, and . . . it's my duty to tell it to you if I really believe it, and I do really believe it. I may be wrong in believing it, but I do believe it." On the face of it, this kind of impassioned iteration of belief trades on a conventional sincerity [for example, Trilling's (1972) "English" form of sincerity that turns on duty rather than self-exploration] that is in practice readily acknowledged and dismissed by Blair's political opponents, such as then Liberal leader Charles Kennedy, who described Blair's support for war as "sincere" but misguided.

If Blair's persuasiveness really rested on belief, however, it would surely matter that he "may be wrong." Such a concession is possible—perhaps even masked—in the face of the overwhelming urgency of affect, which is what is really in play here. Blair is in fact exasperated and under pressure at this point in the interview—and it is his own mounting distress that functions as what affect theorists call an amplifier.

The dynamic in operation here is quite distinct from the kind of self-conscious emotional accenting of a speech that Blair, the orator, employs very well on occasion. It is not performative in the same sense, nor does it work in terms of a confluence of emotion and semantic expression; rather it proceeds from the divergence or imperfect fusion of affect and speech. Blair isn't distressed about terrorism specifically at this precise moment; he is distressed about not being believed, about his sincerity evaporating into mimicry.

Affect is, according to Deleuzian theorists like Massumi, an intensity embodied in autonomic reactions on the surface of the body as it interacts with other entities; it precedes its expression in words and operates independently. According to Tomkins, affect extends beyond individuals, and it does not pursue the same goals as either drives or cognitive systems (1962). In this sense it does not cohere with individual or psychological motives and so undermines a model of sincerity predicated on correspondence. Affect is the essential amplifier of other drives, however, "because without its amplification nothing else matters and with its amplification anything else can matter" (Tomkins and Demos 1995, 355–356). So while it is characterized by urgency and generality, it can readily attach itself to new objects and words since it has no fixed relation to an object.

Media

The media—as theorists like Gibbs and Massumi have demonstrated—constitutes vectors for the migration of affect, and for new attachments and collisions. This is why Massumi argues that affect modulation is a key factor in the operations of power (2002, 42). It is also why we can no longer think of sincerity as performed and framed by the media, as something that emerges from the regulated, controlled, and predetermined flow of emotion. Affect is potentially in play—in the dialectic of gesture—before words are delivered and before an emotional narrative is developed, and even before what we might call a feeling is sustained.

In this sense, affective presence in language is not a function of dramatic expression or of the speaker's capacity to marshal emotion and convey words with feeling. It arises from Kommerell's "linguistic gesture": "the stratum of language that is not exhausted in communication and that captures language, so to speak, in its solitary moments" (Agamben 1999b, 77).

Hence, Jenny Edbauer (2004, 12) has argued that the disruptions of expectation that characterize Bush's rhetoric cannot be understood in terms of broken lines of meaning. Bush's efficacy, she suggests, is not locatable in the indexical meaning of speech but in moments of affective intensity. His failure, like Blair's distress or Hanson's embarrassment, does not accent the script (as an appropriate expression of sympathy might), but instead plays off it as a counterpoint.

In the opening credits of *Fahrenheit 9/11* we see members of the Bush administration receiving attention to hair and make-up in what stands for the 9/11 moment. Bush is the most fidgety and anxious. He appears to be in dialogue with an off-screen presence, but the sequence is cut to emphasize the noncommunicative, solitary nature of his gestures. The muted voice of a technician emanates from the foreground, saying "testing, oval office." Isolated in the mid-ground, stuck behind the desk, Bush bobs up and down in his chair, looking oddly like a ventriloquist's dummy. He tries out a few expressions, in a tentative fashion, and appears self-conscious, aware of his own gesture. The gestural comedy that Kommerrell says always threatens to break out of the dialectic of gesture is happening.

What Moore draws our attention to is the voluble activity at the level of gesture that occurs in the gap in speech or the moment before speech— precisely the element of the Bush spectacle that works most effectively. Bush is not so much "gone missing" as Moore implies in his subsequent voiceover; regardless of where his mind actually is, the spectacle is one of presence and activity because gesture is an activity within language. In the words of Agamben, it is "speechlessness dwelling in language" (1999b, 78).

Moore willfully over-reads such images, tracking Bush in the Florida classroom where he sits after receiving the news of the World Trade Center attack, supposedly unable to speak or move until someone gives him direction. But as Riley notes, even when speech is literally given to us from outside, it does not enter the body in the manner of an immaculate conception, because the body itself is within language (2005, 6–7). The ventriloquy of inner speech and the process of incorporation of language are essentially interactive, so what is really at stake is the manifestation or visibility of an interaction. The satirical figure of the puppet-politician misses the aspect of inner dialogue, which is precisely where affect comes into play.

This interaction, however, must be understood as a function of both being in language and being in media. The televised close-ups that frame Bush in this kind of context readily capture gestural dialogue, but also, in the process, a sense of the dislocation of affect [what Massumi has identified as the "autonomy of affect" (1996)]. It is this autonomy and impersonality that deprive affect of the ethical value required to guarantee sincerity; it can only reveal to us the inauthenticity of self. But this is why it is fundamental to a critical strategy in media.

Within such a strategy, the reduction to gesture (already operative in Bush's delivery) must be combined with a geography of affect that traces its movement in separation from individual subjects. This may in fact entail the recontextualization of imagery that many people find problematic in Moore's work, insofar as he substitutes intermedial resonance for the kind of causal argument that is conventionally expected of a political documentary. I'd like to address this first via Breitz's work, in which the steps involved in reducing work to gesture—and also tracing its migration across different media—are much more explicitly demonstrated.

In her *Soliloquy Trilogy*, protagonists of three well-known Hollywood movies are cut away from the scenes that make the narrative legible. Dropping in a monochrome black screen, Breitz recompiles clips of these characters speaking (though now without evidence of others present in conversations), with the effect that every word, sound, and gesture acquires a prominence and intensity. With no context to absorb or make sense of a gesture, the soliloquy intensifies into a spiralling word flow. As Marcella Beccaria has noted, language loses not just its external context but its "transcendental angst and inner necessity," taking on an almost psychotic quality as it degenerates into solipsistic babble (2005, 43). No longer psychological, spoken language becomes, as Beccaria puts it, "solidified matter." We might also say that it becomes pure intensity: affect characterized by urgency and lack of attachment. It is *purely* intensity at this point to the extent that it is disarticulated from motives or drives.

In a vein similar to *Soliloquy*, Breitz turns to her two companion conversation pieces: *Mother* and *Father*. Here, six Hollywood stars perform motherhood (and a further six fatherhood), digitally extracted from their respective movies and reassembled as twitching and fidgeting against a black backdrop so that their incidental gestures of distress, betrayal, self-pity, and loss of esteem are transformed into symptoms. Julia Roberts's eye roll, stripped of context and repeated with a digital twitch, looks hysterical—and when orchestrated with gestural sequences, performed in similar isolation on the other five screens, appears contagious. Hunt achieves a similar effect with his sound collage of Hanson's voice, which crescendos with the repetition of the phrase "please explain," as if Hanson herself is the symptom. Breitz's character ensemble recalls the medieval *sacra conversazione* in which holy figures don't so much converse or interact as perform gestures directed toward the viewer; the logic of conversation operates at the level of gestural echo. The repetition of a gesture, of a specific movement or utterance, works to highlight its mediality and reduce its signifying capability—and in this recombination and proliferation what unfolds is a geography of gesture, so that we see the migration of gesture and associated affect across screens.

This construction of an intermedial tableau in which gestural performance is isolated against a black background might be seen as the digital filmographic inheritance of the atlas of images known as *Mnemosyne* (1924–1929), undertaken by the German art historian Aby Warburg, of which Agamben has also written (1999a). The atlas was for Warburg a means of doing art history without words, "an instrument of orientation" (Michaud 2004, 277), tracking the emergence of figures at different points in a history of representation and tracing their migration into different cultural domains, genres, and media. On large panels stretched with black cloth, he arranged images exhibiting formal or gestural similarities from disparate sources: photographs of classical statuary, news clippings, magazine advertisements, maps, and amateur snapshots, all of which were then rephotographed in these new combinations.

This cartographic approach, plotting the irruption of figures across time and space, was an attempt to understand monumental pictorial forces in terms of a larger cultural memory and to trace the energetic currents that animate history. Thus, each irruption of a gesture or formal component is revealed as expressing a tension and carrying an emotional charge. As Georges Didi-Huberman has argued, the displacement that occurs in the cut and montage process effects the transformation of the symbol (the iconographic entity) into a symptom, charged with energy or affect (2001, 637).

Unlike the art historical inquiry that begins with the formal components of a gesture, *Bowling for Columbine*, led by its political agenda, is concerned with the movement and intensification of affect through media, which in turn coheres around corporeal signs and expressions. As in Breitz's work, the reiterative nature of recut sequences of current affairs bulletins produces a discomforting intensification of affect. Fear is amplified and perpetuated by its own feedback loop, to the point where its objects are comically inadequate to its intensity and force.

On one level, of course, Moore's pastiche is a send-up of the overexcited pitch of current affairs TV—but while the tone of such media presentations can always be questioned, it is notoriously difficult to attack them on the facts. As Žižek wrote of the implied racism in the reportage of the Hurricane Katrina aftermath, the problem is not that reportage is untrue, it is rather that the motives that make people say things like "black men are looting our shops" are false (2005). Thus, we are dealing with "lying in the guise of truth." Moore makes effectively this same point, frustrated with the media focus on the violent aspects of South Central Los Angeles and with the propensity for fear to falsely attach itself to proximate objects. It matters not if the reports of deadly escalators, spiked candy, and Africanized killer bees are true, or whether scenes of black men arrested on the reality show *COPS* really happened, because the underlying fear is untrue; it's a pathological ideological condition, in Žižek's terms, insofar as social antagonisms are projected onto a black male figure or its equivalent in the bee world.

To expose the insincerity (as opposed to the hyperbole or exaggeration) of the endless stories of black violence or the threat of terror and disaffected teens, therefore, requires some disarticulation of affect and expression. But Moore is unable to achieve this in interviews or by uncovering the motives of specific actors (for example, he interviews the director of *COPS*, who turns out to be a liberal). There *are* no lies, no cover-ups, no bad intentions to expose; there is no underlying insincerity in this sense. Exposing false intention is arguably not a good strategy in documentary film unless you have an Enron-scale conspiracy. As a film strategy it is unaesthetic, liable to be entirely narrative-based, and often bogged down in detail. This is the reason that the story of the Bush family in *Fahrenheit 9/11* is relatively boring as film, however satisfying politically. It's factual; you need only see it once.

Bowling for Columbine is more aesthetic, more exhilarating for the fact that it runs its critique at the level of medium or mediality itself; that is to say, it focuses on the way that affect is propelled and regenerated through media—on the process of affect contagion itself. Moreover, it derives criticism from a comedy of gesture: a sphere, which Agamben argues is beyond psychology and, in a certain sense, beyond interpretation (1999b, 80). Criticism in this domain cannot amount to readings of underlying motive; it can only function by and through the reduction of work, speech, and expression to their gestural components. This takes us not to the level of drives and motives—or to the drama of emotion—but to the level of affect, revealing the free-ranging movement of affect (in media and across bodies) and its incongruent attachment to, and irruption in, the self.

By converting iterations into symptoms—as gestural or linguistic performances characterized by repetition rather than signification—*Bowling for Columbine* traces not just moments of anxiety, but also the larger migratory forces that propel its movement through media and culture. The frenzied proliferation of images in the "fear sequence" carries a force to the degree that it mimics the behavior of affect itself, amplifying narratives and precipitating an on-going quest for objects. Such a quest is explained by Tomkins [and, in turn, by Gibbs and Angel (2006)] as a function of objectless fear:

Objectless fear is a prime source of more fear of fear because the lack of an identifiable frightening object characteristically prompts an accelerated quest for the unknown source. The longer that source cannot be identified, the greater the probability that fear will be repeated and so provide a trigger which is no more likely to be identified than was the original source. In this case one becomes more afraid just because there is now fear of fear and because one doesn't know what one has feared, has tried too hard and too fast to discover the unknown source. Such speeded attempts become additional sources of free-floating fear. (Tomkins 1991, 541–542)

The migration of fear is traced through the Columbine saga, which produces its phobic object (Marilyn Manson) and then, via enhanced school surveillance regimes, a panoply of danger signs, all on the order of kids with baggy pants or wild hairstyles. None of these signs are themselves the triggers for fear; they can only be understood as effects of fear already at large. What is exposed here is the mimetic contagion that characterizes the speeded attempts to find the source of fear—fear's insincerity, in fact.

Conclusion

Fear, like xenophobia, has in recent times produced its own politics of sincerity. As columnist Zev Chafets wrote in relation to the Iraq war, "war calls for sincerity—or at least the appearance of [it]" (2002). It is thus notoriously difficult to oppose with cynicism. This is no doubt because the purity of motive that is implied in sincerity transcends the political. Hence, Pauline Hanson grounds her ethics in an appeal to something outside political discourse. Similarly, with the War on Terror, support is marshalled on ethical rather than political grounds. The antiwar position gains momentum once it can be wrested from politicians with political motives and grounded instead in the conviction of the military mothers— an extra-political expression of opposition from deeply felt experience.

This is where *Fahrenheit 9/11* plays out according to a more conventional narrative, defeating those who play for political and economic advantage with the sympathetic and apolitical figure of Lila Lipscomb— the grieving military mother who at the end of the film goes to Washington. It is, in this sense, a character study: duplicitous, self-interested politicians counter posed with authentic experience and the voice of those with kids on the frontline. *Fahrenheit 9/11* is about the politics of war in which a narrative is already in play. *Bowling for Columbine* is about the politics of fear—about affect itself and its transmission and magnification in media. There, sincerity (as the confluence of avowal and belief or feeling) is no basis for critique for the same reason that it transcends or simply sidesteps politics: it is neutral with regard to content (Pauline Hanson was sincere but xenophobic and some argued Tony Blair was sincere but wrong). More than this, the expression of belief and of emotion in congruence with speech is an effect of performance. It is learned behavior, so it can be genuine or simulated.

The problem with sincerity is not that emotion/conviction can be faked, but that the truth or falsity of it cannot be revealed in media. To overcome this problem we need an expanded conception of language, combined with an understanding of the way language is enacted in media.

By shifting emphasis from the congruence of emotion/belief/avowal to the autonomy of affect, I am not simply arguing that primary affect is a more valid guarantor of truth. Affect operates according to a different economy; "the skin is faster than the word," as Massumi says (2002, 25)—and it is this that creates the conditions of possibility for a dialectic of gesture: a relational analysis of being in language, rather than a moral evaluation of a performance.

The autonomy of affect is readily captured in media, eased by the fact that, according to Tomkins, its primary site is the face. Hence, Tomkins argues that the self is located in the face, not in language (1962; 1991 passim). This does not, of course, imply that we should look for the truth of the subject in the face. As Agamben argues, criticism that focuses on the sphere of the gestic goes beyond psychology and beyond interpretation. We are not, then, concerned with reading meaning into gesture, which is ultimately futile; as Riley notes, good liars and good truth tellers are one and the same (2005, 92–93).

But there is a sense in which the self can be exposed in media, if not as sincere, as insincere, in the moment of encountering itself in gesture. As Kommerell saw, and Michael Moore, Pauline Pantsdown, and Candice Breitz each in different ways realized, the "disjunction between appearance and essence" that emerges in this encounter "lies at the basis of both the sublime and the comical" (Agamben 1999b, 79).

To capture in media a feeling of affect—or a linguistic emotion— may be sublime, but it is also a source of pleasure, even joy. Perhaps, then, the concept of linguistic emotion may be extended to encompass a form of critical pleasure, arising from a "gestic" critique in a medium that doesn't simply register affect but induces it: a feeling of aesthetic satisfaction?

Derrida on Film

STAGING SPECTRAL SINCERITY

Michael Bachmann

In an interview with *Cahiers du Cinéma*, the French philosopher Jacques Derrida compares the act of writing to the projection of a movie: "When I write a text, I 'project' a kind of film, I have the project and I project it. . . . That's what cinema is, incontestably" [Quand j'écris un texte, je 'projette' une sorte de film. J'en ai le projet et je le projette. . . . C'est du cinéma, incontestablement] (2001a, 82).[1] This image relates twice to a logic of spectrality. First, cinema—at least for Derrida—is a medium with an overtly spectral structure. It projects image-bodies that are neither living nor dead. Like ghosts, the apparitions on the screen linger in between presence and absence. Second, Derrida's comparison of writing and cinema destabilizes the source of his project(ion). Just as the projector is not the origin of film, the writer is not the origin of ideas.

But like a director, he is concerned with their *mise en scène* (i.e., with putting them on paper in a particular order and style). In writing, Derrida arranges a "parade of spectral powers" (*défilé de puissances spectrales*), that is, he works on the rhythm and tone of his discourse (2001a, 82). Such an arrangement affects the import of the "projected" argument. The terms used by Derrida primarily gain their meaning due to the way in which they are distributed throughout a specific text. According to

Marian Hobson, they are "functions" rather than "lexemes" (1998, 8).[2] Each *mise en scène* may thus alter the concepts it stages.

In the interview from which I have quoted above, the rapprochement of philosophy and cinema highlights this iterability or difference in repetition. A "projection of thoughts" is neither anchored in the philosopher nor stabilized on screen. In the spectral space of cinema, concepts are revealed to be unstable entities: as ghosts, they are always already open to change.[3]

While—according to the logic of so-called deconstructive reading—this holds for any concept, Derrida has participated in three films that make the spectrality of his concepts explicit. Here we encounter ghosts admitting their ghostliness, thus leaving us with the question of how to grasp (or "film") them: "Comment filmer un spectre qui dit: je suis un spectre?" (Derrida 2001a, 84). In my contribution to this volume, this "ghostly" question serves as a starting point for rethinking the notion of sincerity. Looking at Derrida's cinematographic appearances, I try to outline what could be called a "spectral sincerity."

For this reflection I look to three films in which Derrida has played a major part. Two of these are documentaries: Safaa Fathy's *D'ailleurs Derrida* (1999), and *Derrida* (2002) by Kirby Dick and Amy Ziering Kofman. Working before these films came out, English director Ken McMullen made an experimental fiction film called *Ghost Dance* (1983). Without neglecting the documentaries, my discussion concentrates on this work. I will argue that in all three films, Derrida on film—poised between his image and its "other"—is staged, and stages himself, as ghost(s). He thus assumes a spectralized author-position, authorizing his philosophical discourse in the form of a "spectral sincerity" that seeks to escape conventional binaries such as truth and fiction.[4]

Spectrality of the Sincere

The term "spectral sincerity" is deliberately ambiguous: It refers to a *spectrality of the sincere* as well as to a possible *sincerity of the spectral*. Its first meaning might not surprise, especially in the context of theories commonly named "deconstruction." Many texts by Derrida describe the logic of spectrality mentioned above and relate it to various concepts such as truth, testimony, or confession. Troubled by this logic, these concepts can never exclude their "others." Accordingly, something supposedly sincere—philosophy, for instance—is necessarily haunted by the possibility of being insincere. Derrida reflects on this particular haunting when trying to conceive a "History of the Lie." He states that his theses on the lie could be utterly wrong; still, it would not be a lie "unless I did it on purpose" (2001b, 67). Derrida thus claims to be sincere even if he is not telling the truth about the lie.

It is impossible, however, to qualify the sincerity of this claim. Only a few sentences later, the philosopher admits: "One will never be able to prove anything against the person who says, 'I was wrong but I did not mean to deceive; I am in good faith,' or, alleging the always possible difference between the said, the saying, and the meaning-to-say, the effects of language, rhetoric, and context, 'I said that, but that is not what I meant to say, in good faith, in my heart of hearts; that was not my intention; there has been a misunderstanding'" (2001a, 68).

For structural reasons, then, we may never know if someone is actually being sincere or not. In this respect, the claim to sincerity becomes a rhetorical practice to authorize a narrative, to "make" or perform its "truth."[5] By declaring that one is sincere, one might reinforce the credibility of one's own discourse. But what about someone who—like Derrida in "History of the Lie"—concedes that an irreducible virtuality haunts his words, thus "spectralizing" the sincerity of his rhetoric?[6]

The Derrida of Ken McMullen's film *Ghost Dance* makes a similar concession. Asked by a student (played by actress Pascale Ogier) whether or not he believes in ghosts, Derrida answers: "That is a difficult question. Do you ask a ghost if he believes in ghosts? Here, the ghost is me" [C'est une question difficile. Est-ce qu'on demande à un fantôme s'il croit aux fantômes ? Ici le fantôme, c'est moi].[7] This self-portrait of the philosopher as *fantôme* points to the second meaning of "spectral sincerity," that is, to a potential sincerity of the spectral that concerns the difference between someone talking about ghosts and someone talking about ghosts while insisting on the possibility of being one.

In *Ghost Dance*, Derrida improvises, or at least claims to do so, on the question of spectrality. He continues his dialogue with Pascale Ogier as follows:

As soon as I am asked to play my own role, in a filmic scenario that is more or less improvised, I have the impression of letting a ghost speak in my place. Paradoxi-

cally, instead of playing my own role, I let a ghost ventrilocate me without knowing it. [Dès lors qu'on me demande de jouer mon propre rôle, dans un scénario
filmique plus ou moins improvisée, j'ai l'impression de laisser parler un fantôme
à ma place. Paradoxalement, au lieu de jouer mon propre rôle, je laisse à mon insu
un fantôme me ventriloquer.]

These few sentences build up various tensions: between knowing and believing (having an impression), between one's own place and the realm of
ghosts, and between acting (playing a role) and ventriloquy. For now, I
wish to focus on the latter distinction, which at first glance seems to imply
a "naturalistic" concept of acting.

As is well known, naturalism in the theater—I am referring to nineteenth-century European theater, though naturalistic acting still exists
today (in method acting, for example)—attempted to produce an illusion of reality. Actors consequently tried to sincerely believe in what they
were doing, that is, they sought to identify completely with the characters
they played (Fischer-Lichte 2005, 10–11). Ventriloquy, on the other hand,
uncannily divides the subject. It produces a ghostly voice, which seems to
emanate from a different source than the performer's vocal organs. Either
there is a puppet, or the belly appears to be speaking (as in the literal sense
of the term "ventriloquy"). Thus, ventriloquy works against the illusion
of a unified self. If it is opposed to acting, then acting—as the "other" of
ventriloquy—may indeed relate to the naturalistic idea of embodiment,
where actor and character supposedly are one.

(Im)Possible Improvisations:
Acting and Ventriloquy

An opposition between "acting" and "ventriloquy" is not that easily
drawn, however. In *Ghost Dance*, they do not form a stable binary. Rather,
acting and ventriloquy haunt each other for various reasons. First of all, a
non-naturalistic acting style dominates McMullen's film. This is especially
apparent in the case of Pascale Ogier. When she asks Derrida if he believes
in ghosts, her manner of speaking suggests that she repeats a sentence from
a script. The actress forms the French words—*Est-ce que vous croyez aux
fantômes?*—slowly and with distinct pronunciation, as if she were talking
to a non-native speaker. Her face, which is shown in a close-up, remains

strangely inert. During the scene with Derrida, Ogier's acting style fore-grounds the differences between actress and character (although it would be impossible to "truly" distinguish them). She acts, one could argue, as if possessed by the ghost of her role. In a way, her text becomes a ventrilo-quist, speaking through Ogier's puppet-like appearance.

Derrida, while supposedly improvising, acts in a very different man-ner. The scene during which he talks about the question of spectrality takes place in his office at the Ecole Normale Supérieure in Paris, where he taught from 1964 to 1984. This setting differs remarkably from his first appearance in the film, only a few minutes earlier. The student played by Pascale Ogier bumps into her supervisor (John Annette) while walking through the streets of Paris. The unnamed professor is on his way to meet Jacques Derrida in a bar called Le Sélect, and he literally forces the young woman to come along. "Pascale is my problem student," he explains to his French colleague. The American professor hopes that Derrida might be able to help Pascale write her thesis, the problem being that she has no idea what to write about.

Their encounter at Le Sélect is filmed and edited in the conventional style of a fiction film. It starts with a long shot, establishing the location. The rest of the scene, namely the dialogue between Derrida and Ogier, is organized according to the shot–reverse shot principle, with alternating close-ups of each speaker's face. By contrast, the office scene at the Ecole mainly consists of a four-minute sequence shot, showing the philosopher behind his desk. The very length of this sequence shot adds to the effect of improvisation since it leaves the development of Derrida's argument intact. It retains and, through their accumulation, accentuates the abrupt pauses, word repetitions, and disruptions that are typical markers of oral-ity. Furthermore, the philosopher's remarks are interrupted by a seemingly unscheduled phone call. All this makes his talk about spectrality appear spontaneous, especially since the alleged improvisation takes place in the natural habitat, as it were, of his office.

Nevertheless, the scene at Le Sélect, due to its fiction-like editing and dialogue, introduced Derrida as a character played by Derrida. Thus, the distinction between acting and ventriloquy collapses for a second time. Except for the presence of Pascale Ogier, the office scene could be an interview from any documentary film; but since *Ghost Dance* integrates it into a fictional framework, the improviser Derrida is inextricably bound to the actor Derrida. Moreover, his ventriloquy originates from the attempt to act, as he puts it: *de jouer mon propre rôle*. "Instead of playing my own role," the philosopher says, "I let a ghost ventrilocate me. . . ." And while he appears—through the means of improvisation—more natural and self-identical than Ogier, he insists on being haunted or ventrilocated by other selves: "Precisely because I believe that I am talking in my own voice, I let the voice of the other contaminate it parasitically; not just the voice of any other, but of my own ghosts" [Précisément parce que je crois parler de ma voix, je la laisse parasiter par la voix de l'autre; pas de n'importe quel autre mais par mes propres fantômes]. By explicitly using the word "play" (*jouer mon propre rôle*), Derrida highlights the break between actor and character that allegedly naturalistic acting seeks to prevent. As an actor, he tries to represent himself. That is one of the reasons why Derrida's selves become ghostly and return to haunt him. The attempt to *play* one's own role, even if it is done "sincerely," necessarily produces this spectrality. In trying to represent oneself "authentically," one's self always already returns, like a *revenant*, on the level of representation.[8]

My reading of *Ghost Dance* relates this spectral return of selves to the idea of improvising. In the office scene, Derrida claims that the filmic scenario was *more or less* improvised. I want to pay attention to precisely this "plus ou moins" through another instance of Derrida's improvising act. In 1995, Derrida participated in a conference called *Applied Derrida*, organized by the University of Luton in the United Kingdom. He did so only on the condition that his contribution would be "totally improvised" (Derrida 1996, 213). According to Derrida, deconstruction is something that resists being a method, school, or program. It dwells ghostlike at the margins of disciplines and methods. The philosopher's insistence on improvisation may thus be understood as an attempt to undermine the logic of application, namely that of Derrida himself being applied. Shortly before his talk at the Luton conference, which took place in the form of an interview, he ran into director Ken McMullen. Derrida said that the filmmaker "reminded me of the moment, a few years ago, when he asked me to answer a question before the camera, while he was shooting the film *Ghost Dance*. The question was 'What is improvisation? is an improvisation possible?' I had to improvise of course, and I said 'No, an improvisation is absolutely impossible'" (1996, 213).[9] During the shooting of the film as well as at the conference, Derrida encounters a situation in which—at one and the same time—he does and does not improvise.

In Luton, he explicitly stages this paradox by bringing notes with him that he shows to the audience but promises not to use. According to him, they are "fake, just to reassure myself so that I can pretend to have notes" (Derrida 1996, 215). Furthermore, Derrida's comments come after a great many papers concerning his concept of deconstruction and its possible (or impossible) applications: "Everything has been said and, as usual, Geoff Bennington has said everything before I have even opened my mouth. I have the challenge of trying to be unpredictable after him, which is . . . absolutely impossible; so I'll try to pretend to be unpredictable" (215).

Geoffrey Bennington, who is mentioned here, has not only worked on Derrida; he has worked with him. In 1991, the two authors published a book called *Jacques Derrida* (Bennington and Derrida 1993). The idea behind their conjoint work is a simple yet productive one: Bennington tries to deliver a comprehensive explication of Derrida, while Derrida attempts to contradict him. Hence, the Luton conference already marks Derrida's second effort to be unpredictable "after Geoff."

The *Jacques Derrida* book consists of two texts, one by each author. Bennington's "Derridabase" takes its title from the domain of informatics. He endeavors to systematize Derrida's thought "to the point of turning it into an interactive program which . . . would in principle be accessible to any user" (Bennington and Derrida 1993, 1). Derrida rightly points out that such a program would render himself, as Derrida, dispensable. Therefore, he declares it a matter of life and death to subvert the system that "Derridabase" describes. This cannot be done, however, by exposing a potential difference between his "system" and Bennington's account of it. If it were possible at all to establish a "law of production of every past, present, and why not future statement that I [Derrida] might have signed" (29ff.), the philosopher would be deprived of his future(s). For that reason, Derrida, like a computer virus, infiltrates the program of "Derridabase" with the intention of overriding its functionality. To do so, he places his contribution, "Circonfession," in the margins of Bennington's text. There, Derrida undertakes the attempt to write "improbable things" that Bennington "will not have been able to recognize, name, foresee, produce, predict, *unpredictable things* to survive him" (31). For Derrida, it thus becomes vital to improvise—the Latin root of the word is *improvisus*, the unforeseen. It becomes vital to exceed the logic of "Derridabase" and escape the system, as it were, of his own thought.

The Ghosts of the Other

At the same time, Derrida reminds us, such an escape or improvisation is "absolutely impossible." In the office scene from *Ghost Dance*, he tells Pascale Ogier that, while improvising, his own ghosts return to ventrilocate him: "It is they that will answer you or that might have answered you already" [Ce sont eux qui vont vous répondre, qui vous ont peut-être déjà répondu]. Regarding the "plus ou moins" of improvisation, this sentence might be read in two different yet closely related ways: Derrida's ghosts might have answered already because the "law of his writings" has said everything before he "has even opened his mouth," and they will continue to answer according to the same law. In this respect, ventriloquy makes improvisation impossible. It provides the return of thoughts that have been thought before.

Yet, this return—the return that ventriloquy provokes—is a ghostly one: "I let a ghost ventrilocate me" [Je laisse un fantôme me ventriloquer]. In *Specters of Marx*, Derrida affirms that spectrality allows for something to concurrently be "repetition *and* first time." He therefore considers the "question of the event as question of the ghost" (1994, 10). Ventriloquy, in this respect, makes improvisation possible. When Derrida's ghosts return through him, they are repeated; but paradoxically, they are repeated for the first time. "The ghosts," he says in McMullen's film, "do not come, they return; they are *revenants*, as we say in French. This then supposes the memory of a past which has never had the form of presence" [Les fantômes ne viennent pas, ils reviennent, comme on dit en français, ils sont des revenants. Ça suppose donc la mémoire d'une passé qui n'a jamais eu la forme de la présence].

If the ghost returns from a past that, eluding the form of presence, has always already been other, then thoughts—in a *ghostly* return—may never be the same. According to the spectral logic that I have described at the beginning of this contribution, they necessarily carry their other within. Neither at Luton nor in the office scene of *Ghost Dance* does Derrida follow a written script exactly. Hence, he improvises (or pretends to improvise) against the impossibility of doing so. Whereas McMullen's film stages Ogier as an actress who is apparently ventrilocated by a written text, the office scene shows Derrida as a ventrilocated improviser.

At a later point in *Ghost Dance*, Derrida further explains the connection between spectral ventriloquy and otherness. He relates it to Sigmund Freud's distinction between mourning and melancholia, as formulated in Freud's 1917 text of the same title ("Trauer und Melancholie"). Derrida mentions the French psychoanalysts Nicholas Abraham and Maria Torok, who have elaborated a theory of psychic phantoms in relation to the work of mourning. According to Freud, in successful mourning, we idealize the dead. Thus, we negate the otherness of those who have died by assimilating them into our memories. Torok and Abraham distinguish this assimilation or introjection from the concept of incorporation, which is connected to unsuccessful mourning or melancholia (Abraham and Torok 2001, 260–267). There, the one who has died is given a crypt in the body like that in a cemetery or temple. Not being assimilated, the dead one continues to lodge in us as a radical other: "He is able to speak for himself," Derrida says in the film, "he can haunt or ventrilocate our own body, our own discourse" [Il peut parler tout seul, il peut hanter ou ventriloquer notre propre corps, notre propre discours].

Therefore, the ghosts that answer Pascale Ogier might say something, through Derrida, that is absolutely foreign to him. A "truth" might speak through him that—due to its radical otherness—neither he, Derrida, nor his "law," "Derridabase," can grasp. It is "not only our unconscious, but the unconscious of an other, that plays tricks on us, that talks in our place" [C'est non seulement notre inconscient, mais l'inconscient d'un autre qui nous joue des tours, qui parle à notre place]. This brings us back to the other tensions, apart from *acting* and *ventriloquy*, introduced right at the beginning of Derrida's (if it is Derrida's) answer to the question of spectrality: "I have the impression of letting a ghost speak in my place . . . without knowing it." One may never know if one is actually being haunted. It is a matter of belief, of having an impression or not, because the ghost is there where the I cannot reach it. It is the other—the unconscious, for instance—that, precisely due to this not knowing, has always already invaded and spectralized the place of the self. Here again, the spectral is related to the (im)possibility of improvisation. In *Derrida*, the 2002 documentary by Kirby Dick and Amy Ziering Kofman, the voiceover narration uses an excerpt from an unpublished interview with Derrida: "And there where there is improvisation, I am not able to see myself. I am blind to myself. And it's what I will not see, no, I won't see it. It's for others to see. The one who is improvised here, no, I won't ever see him" (Dick and Kofman 2005, 93).[10] While improvising, one does not meet his or her other; it lodges ghostlike within the self. Accordingly, Derrida leaves the question of spectrality—*Est-ce que vous croyez aux fantômes?*—suspended: "I do not know," he tells Ogier, "if I believe or if I do not believe in ghosts" [Je ne sais pas si je crois ou si je ne crois pas aux fantômes]. However, it is this suspension, the undecidability of the spectral question, that, for Derrida, opens up to spectrality: "But I say: Long live the ghosts" [Mais je dis: vive les fantômes].

Spectral Stagings: The Deaths of Pascal Ogier

Ghost Dance accentuates the otherness of the spectral by a spectral *mise en scène*. When Derrida speaks about Freud's theory of mourning (and its elaboration by Abraham and Torok), he is absent from the screen. His words seem to continue the talk delivered in his office. However, the film includes them some thirty minutes later, while the camera pans along an empty wall in the London apartment of a young woman called Marianne (Leonie Mellinger). Derrida is heard only in the voiceover; his image does not appear. The camera movement stops when it reaches Marianne leaning against the wall. By this means, Derrida's voice, disembodied as it were, is connected to her. The simultaneity of male voiceover and female image-body is the only time that Marianne and the philosopher "meet" throughout the film.

Such a simultaneity could be used as a narrative device to suggest how one is haunted by his or her memories and fantasies. In Alfred Hitchcock's *Psycho* (1960), for instance, Marion Crane (Janet Leigh), while driving by herself to the Bates Motel, hears the voices of her lover and her boss. In *Ghost Dance*, however, the connection between Derrida and Marianne belongs to yet a different register of spectrality. Since the narrative does not directly relate them to each other, the voiceover becomes what it is talking about: a ghostly repetition of a past that has never been present, and a spectral ventriloquy. Regarding this last point, spectrality is emphasized by Ken McMullen's editing. The simultaneity of Derrida's voice and Mellinger's image-body makes it undecidable who ventrilocates whom.

Although Pascale and Marianne do actually meet in the movie, they are also related in a spectral way. A striking example is the end of the office scene that I have been discussing. There, Derrida changes into the "non-naturalistic" acting style typical for *Ghost Dance*. Turning his head with a knowing smile, he slowly asks Ogier if she believes in ghosts. "Yes, now, yes," Ogier says. "Now yes, absolutely." During this answer, her face is filmed from various distances with the shots superimposed upon each other. Finally, they fade into an image of Leonie Mellinger's Marianne, who is thus spectrally connected to the ghosts—the various faces—of Pascale.

In 1984, only a year after shooting *Ghost Dance*, Ogier died of a heart attack. It was shortly before her 26th birthday. More than a decade later, Derrida—in his conversations with Bernard Stiegler, published as *Echographies of Television* (2002)—talks about the experience of watching *Ghost Dance* again, long after Ogier's premature death. It was at a screening in Texas, where suddenly "I saw Pascale's face, which I knew was a dead woman's face, come onto the screen. She answered my question 'Do you believe in Ghosts?' . . . 'Yes, now I do, yes.' Which now? Years later in Texas, I had the unnerving sense of the return of her specter, the specter of her specter coming back to say to me—to me here, now: 'Now . . . now . . . now, that is to say, in this dark room on another continent, in another world, here, now, yes, believe me, I believe in ghosts'" (Derrida and Stiegler 2002, 120).

A spectral response, Derrida asserts in *Archive Fever*, must always be possible. For him, it is the very condition of history and culture that the ghost continues to respond without responding, "like the answering machine whose voice outlives its moment of recording" (Derrida 1988, 62).

Informed by a technology and inscribed into an archive, the spectral response comes from a "time out of joint," to use Hamlet's phrase. If the philosopher declares, in *Ghost Dance*, that his ghosts have answered already and will continue to do so, this also refers to such a spectral temporality. "Cinema," he says during the scene with Ogier, "is the art of letting the ghosts return" [l'art de laisser revenir les fantômes]—one reason being that a film may be watched over and over again: "Once the image has been taken . . . it will be reproducible in our absence, because we know this *already*, we are already haunted by this future, which brings our death. . . . We are spectralized by the shot, captured or possessed by spectrality in advance" (Derrida and Stiegler 2002, 117). Thus, it is necessary to return once more to the question of unpredictability.

Derrida improvises—"more or less"—only during the shooting of *Ghost Dance*. The film, or so it seems, can merely repeat the improvisation, thus making it impossible once again. Still, every screening—like the one in Texas—is a singular event, different for each spectator. Although the ghost of Pascale Ogier responds from a time out of joint ("quel maintenant?"), its haunt is historical. It belongs to a specific moment because the singular experience of the spectator is bound to his or her here and now. Thus, the spectral response remains—to a certain extent—unpredictable. It is, to quote once again from *Specters of Marx*, repetition as well as first time, "since everyone reads, acts, writes with *his or her* ghosts, even when one goes after the ghosts of the other" (Derrida 1994, 139).

Cinema: The Art of Conjuring Ghosts

The Derrida of *Ghost Dance* talks extensively about cinema, spectrality, and psychoanalysis. He even sets up an equation, according to which cinema—in conjunction with psychoanalysis—constitutes a science of ghosts: "I think that cinema plus psychoanalysis equals a science of the ghost" [Je crois que le cinéma plus psychanalyse égale science du fantôme].[11] This equation stages three relations. The first one, between spectrality and psychoanalysis, is dominant in McMullen's film. While explaining the theory of mourning, Derrida describes how a "spectral truth" keeps returning from the unconscious without ever becoming presence.

In *Ghost Dance*, no elaboration is explicitly made on the second connection, that between psychoanalysis and cinema. However, it has been inscribed into film theory from the very beginning. This seems at least partly due to the quasi-simultaneous emergence of psychoanalysis and cinematography. Walter Benjamin, for example, is among those who describe the new technology with vocabulary provided by the new science. In his famous essay on "The Work of Art in the Age of Mechanical Reproduction" from 1936, Benjamin introduces the notion of an *Optisch-Unbewußtes* or "optical unconscious" (1969). The camera,

Benjamin asserts, might show us what we cannot perceive in daily life: "Its lowerings and liftings, its interruptions and isolations, its extensions and accelerations, its enlargements and reductions, introduce us to unconscious optics as does psychoanalysis to unconscious impulses" (1969, 239). Here, the camera serves as a tool to restrain the realm of ghosts, to explore what otherwise could not be perceived. In a text he has published on Safaa Fathy's film *D'ailleurs Derrida*, Derrida takes up the notion of optical unconscious but reads it against the grain. He talks about what the spectator of a film "perceives without realizing it" [ce qu'il perçoit sans s'en apercevoir] (2000, 97). This is an optical unconscious as well, affecting the viewers and haunting them like the spectral truth of psychoanalysis.

The third connection staged by Derrida's equation is that between spectrality and cinema. As a technique of reproduction, film is marked by an intrinsic virtualization: "we are spectralized by the shot" (Derrida and Stiegler 2002, 117). Once our image is taken, it belongs to what Derrida calls a visible invisibility, meaning "the visibility of a body which is not present in flesh and blood" (116). This kind of spectrality, again, haunts film theory. It resonates with what André Bazin thought about the cinematic appearance of the actor. Writing on the differences between "Theater and Cinema," the French film critic claimed that the invention of cinematography introduced a "middle stage" between presence and absence: "It is likewise at the ontological level that the effectiveness of cinema has its source. It is false to say that the screen is incapable of putting us 'in the presence of' the actor. It does so in the same way as a mirror . . . with a delayed reflection, the tin foil of which retains the image" (Bazin 2005, 97). In this way, Bazin tried to defend cinema against the theater. He wanted to show that the actor's "mirror appearance" was present enough to substitute for the physical presence of the actor, as it is associated with theater. For Bazin, as well as for a dominant cinematographic practice, it was (and is) important—one could argue—to exorcise the ghost of cinema's spectrality, to stabilize the reality effects of film, and to let the actor become "flesh" again. Thus, conventional horror films aim at making their ghosts "real." Nowadays, digital technology succeeds in the photo-realistic representation of any ghost that we might imagine. By contrast, a spectral *mise en scène*—like that in Ken McMullen's *Ghost Dance*—accentuates the uncanny moments between absence and presence, documentation and fiction, by which movement it catches the film itself, which then tries to implode these binaries by deliberately staging in-betweenness.

Sincerity of the Spectral

The ambiguous title of Safaa Fathy's documentary *D'ailleurs Derrida* plays with the notions of displacement and otherness ("Derrida's Elsewhere") while also promising closeness to its subject ("Apropos Derrida").[12] This ambiguity determines the structure of Fathy's film. She brings Derrida to various places that relate to the philosopher: Algeria, for instance, where he was born, or Southern California, where he taught at the University of Irvine. Still, even for a spectator who knows these places, it becomes nearly impossible to distinguish them. They are never named, and the film continually changes location. Through this movement, *D'ailleurs Derrida* unsettles the borders between familiarity and otherness, as well as between here and there. In a scene right at the beginning of the film, the visual metaphor of the mirror underscores this destabilization: Derrida walks along an office building but is seen exclusively in its large reflective windows.

André Bazin, when describing film as a "mirror . . . with a delayed reflection" (2005, 97), employs this comparison in accordance with a long tradition of Western thought, a tradition that regards the mirror as a symbol for truthful or naturalistic representation. However, this metaphoric use downplays the implicit otherness of the mirror image. By contrast, Derrida's reflection in *D'ailleurs Derrida* manifests its otherness. Since the philosopher *moves* along the office building, there is no continuity of his image: it is interrupted, again and again, by the window frames. Each time Derrida passes from one window to another, his reflection (and therefore Derrida "as such," because he is only seen as reflection) vanishes and returns in a distorted way. Fathy's film uses this visual metaphor to "produce" a displaced Derrida who is identical yet different to himself. This illustrates the theorization of "ailleurs" that the philosopher has given a minute prior to the mirror scene. "The elsewhere is always beyond a border" [l'ailleurs est toujours au-delà d'une limite], Derrida claims, before going on to specify that this border lies within ourselves: "one carries the elsewhere in one's heart . . . the elsewhere is here" [on a l'ailleurs au cœur . . . l'ailleurs est ici].

This "elsewhere in one's heart" can be related to the "spectrality of self," as described in my discussion of *Ghost Dance*, and likewise to the question of acting. This becomes clear in an essay on *D'ailleurs Derrida* that Derrida has written about playing his role in that film. The essay's wording already reflects a familiar otherness of self since the philosopher refers to his apparition on the screen as "the Actor": "Even though the Actor interprets and plays me . . . he is not me, he thinks me as little as he reflects me. He betrays me" [Même si l'Acteur m'interprète et me joue . . . il n'est pas moi, il ne me réfléchit pas plus qu'il ne me reflète. Il me trahit] (Derrida 2000, 74). However, according to Derrida, it is precisely this betrayal that makes a "faithful representation" possible. In his essay on Fathy's film, he uses the notion of *trahison* in an ambiguous way. On the one hand, the Actor betrays Derrida because they are not the same; on the other hand, he betrays him like someone betrays a secret, revealing the "truth," as it were, about Derrida: "The truth, if it exists, gives itself in the singular experience of betrayal" [La vérité, s'il y en a, se donne dans la seule expérience de la trahison] (97).

Through literally distorting the philosopher's image, the mirror scene of *D'ailleurs Derrida* emphasizes the division between this image and a Derrida who necessarily remains other, even to Derrida. "It may very well be," he writes, that "the division between the Actor and me . . . faithfully *represents*, in truth, to a certain degree . . . the division between myself and myself, between more than one me" [le divorce entre l'Acteur et moi, il est fort possible qu'il ait fidèlement *représenté*, en vérité, jusqu'à un certain point . . . le divorce entre moi et moi, entre plus d'un moi] (Derrida 2000, 75). Fathy's film, in other words, highlights the "spectrality of self" and the division "in one's heart." Like Ken McMullen's *Ghost Dance*, the mirror scene from *D'ailleurs Derrida* stages Derrida in between presence and absence, thus making him at the same time identical to and different from (i.e., neither identical nor different) himself, or his selves. Hence the film visually exposes that the distinctions between other and self collapse. In this movement, which recalls the movements between acting, ventriloquy, and improvisation that I have described for *Ghost Dance*, the Derrida on film acquires a spectral sincerity that is the sincerity of the spectral.

This sincerity is constantly *ailleurs*, displaced to a familiar elsewhere, like Derrida's image in the office windows. Thus, it does not produce the illusion of a stable discourse that could be connected to the "inner truth" of a self-conscious, unified subject. Instead, spectral sincerity relates to a "faithful representation" of the division "in one's heart," exposing the discontinuities of self. Through spectral sincerity, one authorizes his or her self—as well as the discourse associated with it—as open and hospitable toward the haunting of the unpredictable other. Therefore something may still happen, even after one's death.

"The thinking of the specter," Derrida writes in the last footnote of *Specters of Marx*, "signals toward the future. It is a thinking of the past, a legacy that can come only from that which has not yet arrived—from the *arrivant* itself" (1994, 196).

12

Documenting September 11

TRAUMA AND THE (IM)POSSIBILITY OF SINCERITY

Alison Young

According to the etymology of sincerity, there are two crucial components in its meaning: "of one growth" (meaning unmixed), and "that which is not falsified." Any mixing of elements risks falsity as well as producing adulteration or contamination. Falsity is obviously the demeaned term in the founding binary opposition true/false, and sincerity is therefore asserted, through its oppositional rejection of the adulterated or false, as truthful. Thus, sincerity aligns itself with legitimacy, since the legal process is founded upon the very notion of speaking true testimony, mirrored by the obligation on the part of the judge or jury to deliver a verdict (*verdict* deriving from *truth-speaking*). Falsity, on the other hand, is criminalized as perjury. Adultery can dissolve the union of marriage and was previously prosecuted as a "criminal conversation." Sincerity therefore is embedded in legal and social processes, while the aura of the legitimate underpins the very notion of sincere discourse.

While its etymological origins posit sincerity as existing in simple opposition to insincerity, its operations are far more complex than this would suggest. The purpose of this essay is to examine the extent to which sincerity and insincerity are implicated within each other, rather than separated in opposition. It proposes that each is immanent in the other, their oppositional construction necessitating that their meanings must be inter-dependent and inextricable.

Different genres have varying reputations for sincerity. The memoir is assumed to be the product of sincere recollection: controversy has arisen when various literary memoirs were revealed to be imaginary rather than the recollections of the authors.[1] The legal judgment is not expected to be inflected by irony or to include fabulous detail unsupported by the evidence admitted into trial. The genre of the joke, however, allows the author to make statements that she knows are untrue for humorous or ironic effect. Magazines such as the *National Enquirer* in the United States are understood to contain outrageous stories with little relation to what is "true." Such genre expectations and affects of sincerity and insincerity are pursued within this chapter with reference to texts belonging to two distinct genres: the report of a governmental commission of inquiry and a short documentary film.

The reputation and capacity of these genres for sincere representation are also considered in the context of the effects and affects of trauma. It is often said that survivors of trauma lack the ability to resolve their experiences through representation. That is, they continually re-live the traumatic event without imagination; they cannot work through its effects by rendering it subject to the processes of the imagination. This may mean that the traumatic event cannot be written, spoken, or recorded. In the wake of a traumatic event such as the attacks of September 11, certain genres seem to lend themselves to the sincere representation of disaster—hence the dearth of "September 11 jokes" and the condemnation of those whose comments about the event breached assumed generic representational boundaries.[2] This chapter investigates the conventional separation of sincerity from insincerity (the unified from the hybrid) in relation to the legacy of trauma in two attempts to generate sincere representations in the wake of the unimaginable.

The Unimaginable Disaster

New York has always imagined itself, has always made itself into an image, and in the aftermath of September 11 the city continued this practice with memorial images flooding the city. Furiously asserted images and slogans of nationality. Flags, stars-and-striped souvenirs. Angry tattoos burned into flesh. Messages on walls, stencils on sidewalks. The "Portraits of Grief" printed each day in the *New York Times*—thumbnail sketches of the missing and the dead.[3] If the event's aftermath began in those handmade, impromptu posters and graffiti, it is an aftermath that continues almost seven years on. That it has always been characterized by a drive to memorialize has been noted by others.[4] But less remarked is a different type of image: a series of representations produced not in the immediate pain of loss but in the difficult interim space of the succeeding years—a time of "present pasts," as Andreas Huyssen calls them (2003)—whose imagery is the product of a struggle between memory and amnesia, trauma and resolution. Of these aftermath images, this essay analyzes the *9/11 Report* (2004), the Final Report of the National Commission on Terrorist Attacks upon the United States (also known as the 9/11 Commission); and also a short film by the Mexican film director Alejandro González Iñárritu. Both attempt to document the attacks, and both attempt to "work through" the suffering caused by the events. Both are unquestionably "sincere" texts—but such a statement assumes a straightforward conceptualization of sincerity as opposed to "insincerity," readily achievable irrespective of circumstance. My analysis of these two texts seeks to reveal both the limits of this oppositional approach to sincerity and the effect of seeking sincerity in narration after trauma.[5] Cathy Caruth has shown that "to be traumatized is precisely to be possessed by an image or an event" (1995, 4–5), with trauma serving not to record the past but to register "the force of an experience that is not yet owned" (151). Shoshana Felman adds to this the observation that the traumatic event, in that it "registers a belated impact," has a haunting function, historically returning and repeating itself "to the precise extent that it remains *un-owned* and unavailable to knowledge and to experience" (2002, 174). Post-traumatic narration, then, locates itself in uneasy tension between the compulsion to recount the traumatic event and the impossibility of achieving an account that is capable of encompassing it. My reading of the two selected texts considers them within the parameters of the limit-case for narration constituted by the traumatic event of the September 11 attacks.

Genre, Judgment, and Sincerity: The *9/11 Report*'s "Day of Unprecedented Shock and Suffering"

Fourteen months after the attacks of September 11, the U.S. Congress established the National Commission on Terrorist Attacks upon the United States, also known as the 9/11 Commission. Its remit was "to investigate facts and circumstances relating to the terrorist attacks of September 11, 2001," including those relating to intelligence agencies, law enforcement agencies, diplomacy, immigration issues and border control, the flow of assets to terrorist organizations, commercial aviation, the role of congressional oversight and resource allocation, and other areas deemed relevant by the Commission (National Commission 2004, xv). In sincere pursuit of such a wide-ranging remit, the Commission reviewed "more than 2.5 million pages of documents and interviewed more than 1,200 individuals in ten countries. . . . [It] held 19 days of hearings and took public testimony from 160 witnesses" (xv).

The resulting massive *9/11 Report* was designed to determine the location of "fault lines within [the United States] government" (National Commission 2004, xvi).[6] To this extent, the *9/11 Report* arises out of the process of judgment, a juridical interrogation of facts, the hearing of testimony, and the determination of fault. Judgment is thus its organizing purpose. And yet its sincere efforts are situated within a profound ambivalence about judgment in the wake of September 11. For where legal judgment depends primarily upon notions of precedent and analogy, the *Report* is constructed on the edge of an abyss: the narration of an event beyond imagination and analogy. As the Commission states in its preface, "September 11, 2001, was a day of *unprecedented* shock and suffering in the history of the United States" (National Commission 2004, xv; emphasis added).

Its ambivalence about judgment is so pronounced that the *Report* retreats from the assignment of responsibility at almost every point where it might arise.[7] Actual criticisms are few, even at points where there would seem to be a clear connection between first responders' actions and the deaths of individuals in the towers and on the planes.[8] "We write with the benefit and the handicap of hindsight," states the Commission (National Commission 2004, 339), hindsight being the acuity gained through retrospection and an essential part of the process of judgment. But here it is a dangerous faculty to be used with caution lest it distort the narration of the event. Indeed, for the Commission, hindsight is *a limit upon judgment*: "we asked ourselves, before we judged others, whether the insights that seem apparent now really would have been meaningful at the time" (339). At the same time, however, the Commission deploys hindsight in the form of an unblinking retrospective gaze that seeks to detail the unfolding of the attacks. In further demonstration of its refusal to lay blame, these attacks are even at one point characterized by the *Report* as a lightning strike: "no analytical work foresaw the lightning that could connect the thundercloud to the ground" (National Commission 2004, 277), thus constructing the attacks as an act of God that comes out of the blue with devastating effects.[9] In such a metaphor, the attacks are a weather event, a cataclysmic force of nature. And although it is a commonplace that thunderclouds can lead to lightning, the thundercloud that was the Al-Qaeda plot is somehow different, resistant to any analysis: unpredictable, unpreventable, *unprecedented*.

In my reading of the *Report*, I want here to analyze not so much its substantive findings, but rather its struggle to represent the traumatic event of September 11 itself. What is striking about the *Report* is the way in which it engages in a paradox: the trauma of September 11 is held at bay for the Commission by its detailed recounting of the event, just as the response to a wound can be the desire to probe it, to pick at its scab, to re-open it. The *9/11 Report* does not just return to the wound that is September 11, *it inhabits* that wound, oscillating between judgment and narration, prescription and description.[10]

In its narration, in unexpected contrast to its identity as a fact-finding government document, the genre of the *Report* is that of the thriller or mystery novel.[11] Chapter 1 is a fiercely immediate account of the hijackings with a strong emphasis on the experiences of the passengers on the planes. The *Report* includes many quotations from transcribed phone calls; the names of passengers and flight attendants are given, as are the names of relatives that they had called.[12] The passengers are characters with identities, families, and emotions, rather than statistics in a tally of loss. Every factual detail known about the planes is given in the *Report*, and given with a precise clock time for its occurrence.[13]

The opening chapter begins by locating the event in calendar time and in meteorological detail:

Tuesday, September 11, 2001, dawned temperate and nearly cloudless in the eastern United States. Millions of men and women readied themselves for work.

Some made their way to the Twin Towers, the signature structures of the World Trade Center complex in New York City. Others went to Arlington, Virginia, to the Pentagon. Across the Potomac River, the United States Congress was back in session. At the other end of Pennsylvania Avenue, people began to line up for a White House tour. In Sarasota, Florida, President George W. Bush went for an early morning run.

For those heading to an airport, weather conditions could not have been better for a safe and pleasant journey. Among the travelers were Mohammed Atta and Abdul Aziz al Omari, who arrived at the airport in Portland, Maine. (National Commission 2004, 1)

This opening is both folkloric and cinematic. It manages to give the now-notorious date both specificity and fabled timelessness. It deploys a convention well known in the establishment of a cinematic narrative: that of showing key protagonists going about their usual activities or locations in a state of equilibrium or tranquility (with such normality poised on the verge of disruption).

Having created a sense of ordinary life about to meet with disaster, the *Report* goes on to detail the seemingly insignificant but retrospectively crucial moments in which disaster was *almost* averted. For example, with the hijackers Atta and Omari about to board planes in Portland, the *Report* then relates how Atta was selected for extra screening by a computer program, the first of several of the hijackers to be singled out in this way. The text raises the possibility that a security measure might actually ensure security, only to confound that in its next sentence: "the only consequence of Atta's selection . . . was that his checked bags were held off the plane until it was confirmed that he had boarded the aircraft. This did not hinder Atta's plans" (National Commission 2004, 1). From the very first page, then, the *Report* sets up the attacks as both inevitable and as always already subject to human intervention. Security checks become "turning-points," moments when the narration could have moved in a different direction. Disaster ultimately arises because the *potential* of these turning-points was not realized.

The entwined proximity of salvation and inevitability of disaster are conveyed most strongly in relating the events on board United Flight 93. As is well known, United 93's passengers attempted to regain control of the aircraft, which ultimately crashed in a field well short of its assumed targets (the Capitol or the White House).[14] In its detailed narration of the passengers' attempt to regain control of the plane (captured by the cock-pit voice recorder), we can detect the *Report*'s wish that at least this one aspect of the story could have been different. It is only five minutes from the beginning of the passenger revolt till the plane crashes, but the sense of this particular hijack *almost* turning out differently haunts the text: "The hijackers remained at the controls but must have judged that the passengers were only seconds away from overcoming them" (National Commission 2004, 14). Similarly the *Report* can sense a different ending "only seconds away" from the one that must instead be related, a parallel narrative that did not get the chance to enter the text.

After this intense narration of the entire event as it unfolded within the planes, the *Report* then swerves backwards in time with a series of five chapters detailing the history of both the role of Osama Bin Laden and counter-terrorism measures in the West. In fact, these chapters constitute a prolonged anachronic deviation in the narrative sequence, which both suspends the suspensefulness of chapter 1 and also intensifies it, by withholding the details of the attacks on the Twin Towers and the Pentagon. After this hiatus, the prehistory narrated in chapters 7 and 8 accelerates the story as it rushes toward its apex.

At this point, the *Report* reverts to the dual tone that characterized chapter 1, that of dreadful longing for a different outcome. Just as the *Report* commenced its narration of the hijackings by recounting successive missed opportunities to stop the hijackers from boarding, so the narration of the collision of the planes with their targets is preceded by a statement that sets up the sense of yet another turning-point whose potential was never realized:

"The system was blinking red" during the summer of 2001. Officials were alerted around the world. Many were doing everything they possibly could to respond to the threats.

Yet no-one . . . looked at the bigger picture; no analytical work foresaw the lightning that could connect the thundercloud to the ground.

We see little evidence that the progress of the plot was disturbed by any government action. . . . Time ran out. (National Commission 2004, 277)

The *Report* then returns to the present tense of the attacks, and a lengthy detailing, as close to minute-by-minute as it can manage, of their unfolding in New York and Washington, D.C. Entitled "Heroism and Honor," it is imbued with melancholy. Where chapter 1 commanded the affect of the thriller through its run-up to the collision and explosion of each plane, chapter 9 pretends no urgency. The planes are in the air; their destinations are now a *fait accompli*.[15]

Sincerity, Trauma and the Unimaginable Event

Throughout the *Report*, the notion of the unprecedented nature of the attack is mirrored by repeated statements as to the utter unimaginability of the event.[16] Comments to this effect are scattered throughout the opening chapter, but they are featured more prominently in Chapter 9, where the Commission finds itself assessing the actions of the emergency service providers after the planes struck the towers. Political theorist Jenny Edkins notes that "it is already hard to remember how unimaginable it [the manner of the attack] was before it happened" (2004, 250). The lapse of some few years has not reduced the scale of the leap required to encompass the event's occurrence: although it is hard to recall how unimaginable the attacks were, we have not forgotten the *fact* of their unimaginability. Indeed, for the 9/11 Commission, the reiteration of that fact causes profound tension in the *Report*'s desire to narrate without judgment: first, because that unimaginability means that the *Report* is continually telling the story of something outside invention and narration; second, because that unimaginability functions as an important alibi in the investigation of fault. For, if it was unimaginable, the attacks could not have been planned for, predicted, or prevented.[17]

This quality of the event's utter unimaginability hangs over much of the *Report*'s narrative. While emergency services personnel were in some ways able to grasp the nature of the disaster (assessing rapidly, for example, that it would be impossible to put out the fire and that a rescue mission for civilians was the only option), its *scale* turned out to be beyond their ready reckoning:

In the 17-minute period between 8:46 and 9:03 a.m. on September 11, New York City and the Port Authority of New York and New Jersey had mobilized the largest rescue operation in the city's history. Well over a thousand first responders had been deployed, an evacuation had begun, and the critical decision that the fire could not be fought had been made.

Then the second plane hit. (National Commission 2004, 293)

Again, the Commission refuses any possibility of assigning fault in relation to operational decisions at the World Trade Center on that day, evoking the unimaginability of the disaster as the rationale for all actions undertaken. For example, in one of the most striking instances of bad advice provided during the disaster, after the first plane had hit the North Tower and before the second plane's collision with the South Tower, an announcement was made over the public address system in the South Tower, telling individuals that the problem was confined to the other building and that they should return to or remain in their offices (287–288). Upon hearing the announcement, many individuals remained in place on higher floors, and others who had begun to descend the stairs "reversed their evacuation and went back up" (289)

Unable to question the person who made the announcement (he died in the South Tower's collapse), the Commission comments that "clearly . . . the prospect of another plane hitting the second building was beyond the contemplation of anyone giving advice" (National Commission 2004, 288), a view endorsed by one of the fire chiefs who stated that such an eventuality was "beyond our consciousness" (289). And later, although such consciousness had already been ripped through by not one but two planes flying into the World Trade Center, the idea that the towers might not withstand the impact of a jet airliner was also outside conscious thought: in the *Report*'s words, "No one anticipated the possibility of a total collapse" (291).

Thus not only were the attacks events that in their execution and planning exceeded the ability of existing security procedures to detect and prevent them (as set out in chapters 1, 7, and 8), they were also events that existed outside of consciousness even as they occurred, their unimaginability rendering them wholly surreal at every moment of their unfolding. The attacks are related as both inevitable and preventable; capable now of being known in all their substance (hence the painstaking recounting of all details), yet then "beyond consciousness"—a move that underscores both the *Report*'s uneasiness about judgment in the wake of trauma and its striving to imagine sincerely the unimaginable disaster.

The *9/11 Report*, then, is both constituted and structured throughout by means of a series of ambivalences. It is an inquiry designed to assess "fault lines," yet it refuses the assignment of responsibility, characterizing the attacks as akin to an act of God and beyond imagination. It seeks to limit hindsight, yet is driven to look backwards, fascinated by the sight of the unimaginable event inching ever closer to the actual. It must recount an event already completed, yet cannot shake the conviction that the ending might still have been otherwise. It foregrounds its dual dependency upon judgment and narration, and it shows the unbearable consequences of both in the (re)presentation of unresolved trauma. And, within its hundreds of pages, it is possible to trace the trauma that inhibits the *Report*'s sincere representation of the event: the very notion of unimaginability signals the idea that the United States government and security services were not, in fact, secure.

The trauma of September 11, for the 9/11 Commission, is located not just on the calendar date, but in those months preceding it, during which "no analytical work foresaw the lightning." The recognition that governance was not under control, that the United States was not secure, and that forthcoming events were "beyond imagination" all demarcate a primal scene in which foresight is lacking and all that will remain in the future are the melancholic judgments of hindsight. As such, the *9/11 Report* is always already traumatic. This is not to imply that the *Report* is insincere; rather, it is to acknowledge that it is unable to achieve its aim (the documentation of the event) by virtue of the event's status. Its performance of sincerity takes place both within the textual framework arising from trauma and within a complex interconnection with *in*-sincerity. Trauma demands repetition but inhibits representation; sincerity demands truth-telling but is constrained by its institutional status as a commission of inquiry.

The limits of such investigative public bodies have been established by others: "sincerity" understood as "stating the truth" is an institutional and discursive impossibility for any commission of inquiry. To that extent, the *9/11 Report* is a text existing within the constraints of its institutional authorship, as a commission of inquiry made up of government-appointed politicians representing each of the two dominant American political parties. For some,[18] it is a matter simply of noting the limits of these institutional constraints; for others,[19] the Commission's silence on certain aspects of the attacks has been parlayed into claims that such silence constitutes evidence of government conspiracy and cover-up. However, it is important to note that in the narrative of constrained authorship there exists a nostalgic desire for the possibility of *un*-constrained authorship—for an investigator (whether an individual or a commissioned panel) to generate a discourse metaphysically full of truth-telling capacity. Indeed, it underscores the very notion of "truth" as both limit and end against which all other values must be measured (and must fail). It has been my aim, in reading the *9/11 Report* for its textual traces of trauma and its narrative tropes and turns, to acknowledge its institutional authorship without privileging that as the originary source of the *Report*'s form. Rather, my reading has emphasized the *Report*'s repeated ambivalences and hesitations as symptoms of trauma or evidence of the limits of sincerity as it is conventionally conceived, illuminating instead a sense of sincerity that intersects with its derided other, insincerity.

Trauma, Cinema, and Sincerity: *11' 09" 01*

Such intersection of sincerity and insincerity can also be found, albeit in a rather different form, in a short documentary film relating to the attacks. Where an absence of vision constitutes the paralyzing primal scene of the *9/11 Report*, a different crisis animates this cinematic response to the events of September 11. The Mexican filmmaker Alejandro González Iñárritu had made a series of still photographs in the days after September 11, which he called *Blinded by the Light*. The series was refused publication for being out of step with the spirit of the times.[20] The experience of these photographs being withheld from publication informs the short film that Iñárritu went on to make for the French film producer Alain Brigand, who in 2002 commissioned eleven filmmakers, each from a different country, to direct a short film in response to the events of September 11.[21] Iñárritu's film thus in part derives from *a criminology of the image*, in which legitimacy can be both awarded to and withheld from an image. However, what interests me here is not a question of censorship. Rather, Iñárritu's vanished photographs constitute an image of absence underlying the ways in which the plural cinematic relations between sound, image, and editing order the attachment of subject to object—of the one who looks to that which is seen, and which will foreground the possibility of an ethical response to the demands of *witnessing catastrophe*.

The films, and the project as a whole, were imagined (as Alain Brigand put it) as a cinematic "reflection . . . responding to images with other images" (2002).[22] The project has met with some fierce criticism, and, to date, it has not been released for cinematic distribution in the United States.[23] For many, the very notion of the project seemed objectionable; for others, it was Iñárritu's contribution that was singled out. One film critic commented that "the callowness of youth doesn't excuse (though it probably explains) [the] unremitting monstrosity" and "hideous self-conceit" of Iñárritu's film (Matthews 2003).[24]

The film begins with a darkened screen. There is no moving image, just a black screen against which is overlaid the sound of voices speaking indistinctly, repetitively. For a time it might almost seem as if something has broken down. Cinema is the art of the moving image in light, and a film whose image is dark and static seems to be a failure of cinema, evidence only of the disappearance of the image. This image of absence is accompanied by the sound of voices, belonging to the Chamulas Indians of Chiapas, Mexico; they are chanting a prayer for the dead. Faint musical sounds underscore the voices. Suddenly, the viewer's suspension before the darkened screen is interrupted by the flash of an image, which is on screen for the briefest of instants. It is a shot that cuts through the darkness, placing an image on the screen and just as quickly removing it again. The viewer registers more the flash of its presence and a sense of motion than any content. The flashes increase in duration, and the content becomes discernible: they are images of people falling or jumping from the towers of the World Trade Center.

Paralleling these flashes is the sound design. Iñárritu used "found sound," segments from recordings and media broadcasts from around the world on that day, incorporating hundreds of them into the film to aurally regenerate the event and compress it into only a few minutes of cinematic time.[25] For the audience, this sound repeats and accelerates the experience of those at the time who watched, looked, and witnessed. Such accelerated repetitions have the character of trauma, dwelling on and in a memory without resolution or respite.

The event is primarily narrated through these found sound segments. We hear a radio announcer read the weather forecast, just before the roar of the first plane comes in overhead. From that point, the soundtrack jostles with exclamations of shock and disbelief as screams compete with journalists' attempts to describe the sight of the World Trade Center. The falling bodies return, now no longer flashes but shown for an increasing duration until the announcement of the towers' collapse is related against a black screen, whereupon several different consecutive shots of the falling are shown and the sound increases in volume until it is a massive rumble: chaotic, impenetrable, and deafening.

Silence suddenly cuts into the noise, punctured by two visual sequences. First one tower falls; then the next. The bright daylight is shocking after the black screen. The towers' descent seems both astonishingly fast yet at the same time in slow motion, in contrast to the preceding flashes. The chanting voices of the Indians return against a black screen; but the black slowly dissolves into white, and the Indians' voices merge with orchestral string music. Written text emerges out of this white screen, in Arabic and then in English, asking, "Does God's light guide us or blind us?"[26] Two dazzling white lines of light eclipse the screen; the music swells to a climax, and leaves only the voices in prayer, which are cut as the screen returns to black with the end of the film.

Iñárritu's film constitutes a deeply disturbing viewing experience. With the screen an enormous darkened rectangle, the spectator's eyes strain for something to look at, but each lighting flash of image produces a painful visual jolt. And the film's alternating blackness of screen and shocking images of the moments just before death heighten the film's sounds. To the extent that cinematic spectatorship involves an entire phenomenological raft of effects, Iñárritu's film is a *sensorium* of sonic and visual trauma.[27] Its impact arises out of a tension between two opposing structural tropes within it: on the one hand, the cohesion derived from its compression and acceleration of the narration of the event, and, on the other hand, the effects of its dislocation of the traditional cinematic unity of sound and image.

Thus, although deeply unconventional in many ways, Iñárritu's film retains a strong narrative structure, progressing through the before-during-and-after of the event, and deploying elements such as the Indians' prayer, the music, and the progression from black screen to white as a means of generating a redemptive narrative for the viewer. Iñárritu has stated that his intention was to allow people "to experience catharsis"—that is, to resolve the trauma—and his sincere desire for it to constitute a "tribute" implies that he anticipated the film would provide some kind of memorial or solace after trauma.[28] Certainly, the film builds up an extraordinary amount of tension that is slightly dissipated by the end of the eleven minutes. But as a viewing experience it is devastating rather than consoling because of its reconfiguration of sound, image, and editing.

Iñárritu's film foregrounds the dual dependency of the viewer upon cinema as a *sound-image* and excises the one from the other so that each medium runs riot within the cinematic text. It is no coincidence that the images used by Iñárritu are the ones that were said to have the most impact on viewers at the time and that were, like Iñárritu's own, quickly withheld from circulation in the media.[29] Iñárritu's film takes those repressed images and presents them, joltingly, in response to the viewer's desire for something to look at when faced with the darkness. As befits traumatic images, they appear as flashes, out of synch with any unifying narrative, and, in cinematic terms, discomfitingly out of synch with the events narrated in the soundtrack. The images of falling people start to appear before the planes hit the towers: to that extent they constitute visual premonitions of aural experiences yet to come. The soundtrack records the thunder of the towers' collapse before they are shown falling on screen; the images thus return as traumatic visual repetitions of what has been heard. Sounds occur within the film detached from any image at all, and the final images of the towers falling play out in silence.

Such a dislocation of sound and image results in a destabilized viewing position. The viewer is located at the moment of the disaster and experiences it as trauma. As Iñárritu has stated, his intention was "to put myself and the audience in the shoes of those who were inside those buildings, waiting for the unpredictable." Located *within* the crime scene, *within* the buildings, the images of the falling address the spectator both as the one who waits to see what happens, and as the one who falls. In his stated desire to provide a memorial tribute, Iñárritu's intentions are wholly sincere, but it is a memorial born out of a primal scene in which his photographs disappeared from the public sphere and return as cinematic lacerations that crack the screen separating the spectator from the disaster on display. As such the film exists in a moment of paradox: in representing the narration of disaster as a narrative that cannot be narrated, that is unpresentable, the film de-legitimates the claim of documentary narrative to recount the event as it occurred. Such delegitimacy is inevitably sundered from sincerity, which (as noted earlier) aligns itself with legitimacy, truth, and documentation. Arising from the criminalized images that were refused publication, Iñárritu's documentary film is profoundly partial, shattered, and shattering. In its formal construction, then, it constitutes a sincere performance of the inevitable insincerity of the documentary form in relation to the representation of the traumatic event.

Sincerity in the Aftermath of Disaster

For the reader of the *9/11 Report* and the viewer of Iñárritu's film, the sincerity of the authors of these texts seems beyond question. Both the report and the film speak with urgency, authenticity, and earnestness—their "sincerity effect" cannot be doubted. And yet such sincerity should still be in doubt: the poststructuralist insistence on the "death of the author" certainly seems to remind us of the disjunction between an author's intentions and any resulting textual product. Similarly, the sincerity of a text should not simply be equated with textual authenticity. Sincerity is not something that can necessarily be "read off" a text, as if there exists a direct relationship between a word (or image) and the emotional condition of its author. It should rather be asked whether texts can embody the sincerity of their authors and whether they can succeed in delivering the *sincerity affects* their authors seek. As my earlier emphasis on form and genre would indicate, it seems more fruitful for a poststructuralist inquiry to investigate the extent to which there can be a *sincerity of things* in addition to the perceived sincerity of individuals. Sincerity is always staged, performed, and enacted (although the very notion is counterintuitive to sincerity's semantic register, since "staged" sounds "forced" or "fake"), and thus is dependent upon a textual inscription for its effects upon the reader or viewer. Attributions of sincerity therefore rely upon the successful textual *rendition* of sincerity. In the conventional association of sincerity with metaphysical or emotional states and effects, it is easy to overlook the theatricality of sincerity.

In this essay I have taken the interdependence of authors and texts seriously, shifting from the conventional association of sincerity with an emotional subject in order to look less at the sincerity of people and more at the sincerity of *genres*. In the context of the aftermath of September 11, the association of sincerity with a speaking subject or emotional actor would lead us to examine only what the 9/11 Commission or Iñárritu said about the tasks they had undertaken. If, however, we think instead about the sincerity of genres, we can raise questions about the affective relationship to trauma and the aftermath of disaster created by the genres of the two texts. The report of a governmental inquiry is a juridical text, the juridical being inextricably associated with truth-telling, integrity, honesty, objectivity, and so on. The short documentary film is a subjective text, in that it is the product of one person's viewpoint; it orchestrates image, music, and editing into a highly particularized form. But it is also an objective text through its claim to document the event, its use of "found sound" from the news media, and the archival aspects of the images it includes. The government report therefore seems to claim sincerity through its truth-telling and fact-finding dimensions, the short film through its status as documentary.

Genres thus appear capable of confirming sincerity. However, if we move from the general characteristics of their generic forms, are these particular texts "sincere"? On the one hand, as discussed above, yes, both are sincere. But, on the other hand, the *Report*'s textual sincerity is a paradoxical one: it is sincere in its aims, but they are aims arising from the unacknowledged trauma at its heart, in the insecurity of security. The *Report*'s sincerity is thus partial, and partiality is, as I noted at the outset, an attribute of insincerity, since sincerity is about wholeness and unity. The short film's sincerity is also staged through a series of paradoxes: it is documentary, and yet highly personal; it is archival, and yet partial; it is the viewpoint of one filmmaker, and yet it speaks from a multiplicity of places.

Both texts are paradoxical, but their sincerity affects derive from very different post-traumatic symptoms. The *Report* of the 9/11 Commission narrates the event in order to re-live it. Its sincerity derives from the continual repetition of trauma: not the trauma of the attacks of September 11, but the traumatic realization that security procedures are always already insecure. As such, its narration seeks to close off and repress that realization by means of a prescriptive sincerity that judges even as the Commission asserts the impossibility of judgment in the aftermath of disaster. In contrast, Iñárritu's short film does not dwell on the difficulties of judgment: it is born out of judgment, out of the experiences of being judged (censored) and of mediated watching and witnessing a crime. It is a forensic inquiry, just as the report is. But it opens itself (and the viewer) to a place that is always here and elsewhere—multiple, split, fragmented.

In this way, the film puts the very act of witnessing in tension and inter-section as a traumatic event requiring a response in which sincerity is both necessary and impossible.

We might say, then, that this essay has traced the difficulties of achieving sincerity in the wake of trauma, and that a reading of two texts made in these interim years after disaster has revealed the unavoidability of the mood of conditionality (through which we acknowledge these texts as "sincere, but . . ."). In the tension of exceptionality we can see sincerity as conditional upon the insincere: implicated in, rather than oppositional to, insincerity. The diagnosis of sincerity thus asks the wrong questions, in that it situates sincerity in an oppositional, exclusionary relation and seeks a zero sum answer, whereby a text or genre is or is not sincere. Instead, the limit case provided by cultural or legal responses to disaster allows us to acknowledge that such texts both are and are not sincere: we have reached the *aporia* of sincerity, one occasioned by the legacy of trauma.

Being Angela Merkel

Maaike Bleeker

In her contribution to this volume, Jane Taylor locates the appearance of the notion of sincerity in the context of Western modernity and points to the relationship between the concept of sincerity and the representational order. The concept of sincerity emerges as a result of our difficulty of dealing with some of the implications of this representational order, in particular with the problem of knowing the relationship between a person's inner motivation and her or his external performance. The promise presented by sincerity, one might argue, consists largely of the illusion of a "natural," self-evident, or given bond between inner motivation and outer performance. That is, the promise presented by sincerity consists of an illusion fundamentally at odds with that which makes the order of representation possible in the first place. My own contribution is about this complex relationship between representation and sincerity in contemporary politics.

Playing the President

In his entry on "representation" in Lentricchia and McLaughlin's *Critical Terms for Literary Study*, W. J. T. Mitchell observes that representation has been the foundational concept *par excellence* in aesthetics and semiotics, while it has for the last three hundred years also formed the cornerstone for political theories of sovereignty, legislative authority, and the relation of individuals to the state. We now think of representative government and the accountability of representatives to their constituencies as fundamental postulates of modern government. One obvious question that comes up, then, Mitchell observes, is the relationship between aesthetic or semiotic representation (which he describes as "things that stand for other things") and political representation (which he describes as "persons who act for other persons"). Mitchell writes:

> One obvious place where these two forms of representation come together is the theatre, where persons (actors) stand for or "impersonate" other (usually fictional) persons. There are vast differences, of course, between Lawrence Olivier playing Hamlet and Ronald Reagan playing the role of president—the difference, say, between playing and real life; between a rigid script and an open, improvised performance; or between an aesthetic contract and a legal one—but these should not blind us to the structural similarities of the two forms of representation or to the complex interaction between playful fantasy and serious reality in all forms of representation. (Mitchell 1995, 11–12)

With his comparison between Lawrence Olivier playing Hamlet and Ronald Reagan playing president, Mitchell reformulates political representation—which a little earlier he defined as "persons who *act for* other persons"—in terms of role-playing (Olivier playing the role of Hamlet and Reagan playing the role of president). Mitchell then proposes this comparison in terms of role-playing as an example of the structural similarities between aesthetic representation and political representation. There are vast differences between representation in the theater and representation in politics, he observes, yet these differences should not blind us to the fact that they are structurally similar.

One might argue that Ronald Reagan's success as politician did indeed result to a large extent from his ability to play the president. And this success is not an isolated instance either. But it is something else to say that for this reason Reagan's political performance illustrates the *structural similarities* between representation in the theater and representation in politics. Wasn't the idea behind representational government that we vote for politicians not because of how well they play the politician, but because of how well they represent our interests and act according to them? Or, to put it in Mitchell's terms, wasn't the idea behind representation in politics that we vote for politicians in order that they *act for us* in ways that are in accordance with our beliefs and interests, not because they play the role of politician so well?

On the other hand, it might be argued that when it comes to actual political practice, many people do indeed vote for candidates that most convincingly play the politician. Seen this way, Mitchell's comparison does make sense, albeit not as an illustration of structural similarities between aesthetic representation in the theater and representation in politics. Instead, one might argue, Ronald Reagan is the example par excellence of the *structural confusion* that can be seen at work in the way representation in politics functions. This structural confusion is my subject here. I am especially interested in how this confusion is supported by persistent anti-theatrical sentiments that can be seen at work in responses to both theater and politics. These anti-theatrical sentiments, I will argue, blind us to what the structural similarities between representation in the theater and representation in politics actually are.

This structural confusion is illustrated by one of the most passionate political statements of the very first years of the twenty-first century, which is Michael Moore's *Fahrenheit 9/11*. In this film, Moore plays with the comparison between theater and politics right from the beginning, when he introduces Al Gore as the tragic hero sincerely playing the role he is destined to play, as opposed to George W. Bush, who plays "mere theater" and wins his audience by deceit. The movie begins with documentary footage showing the celebration of Gore's victory in Florida during the presidential elections in 2000. We see Gore triumphant ("God Bless you Florida. Thank you!"). We hear dramatic film music and Moore wonders: "Was it all a dream? Did the last four years not really happen?" Country music kicks in and we are back to reality. It did happen, and Moore is going to explain to us why. "It was election night 2000 and everything seemed to be going as planned." State after state projects Gore as the winner, including Florida. But then, suddenly, out of the blue, "something called the Fox News Channel" projects Bush instead as the winner in Florida. From this moment on, Moore suggests, the only thing the good guys could do was step back and witness treachery take its course. Moore points to the close relationships between George W. Bush and the man in charge at Fox (Bush's first cousin John Ellis), between Bush and the governor of the state of Florida (his brother), between Bush and the person responsible for the vote counts in Florida (the chairwoman of his campaign), and between

Bush and the members of the Supreme Court (the friends of his father George Bush senior). Gore is the tragic hero brought down by their deceit.

Moore shows American politics to be theater. In this theater, Gore is the good guy who sticks to his role and performs it in a way that Lawrence Olivier playing Hamlet could not better. We see Gore during the joint session of the House of Representatives and the Senate, the meeting that was to certify the election results. Gore, in his dual role as outgoing vice president and president of the Senate, presides over the event that would officially anoint Bush as the new president. An exemplary tragic situation. If any congress member wants to raise an objection, the rules insist that she or he has to have the signed support of at least one senator. Protagonist Gore, on a raised stage, faces an audience of merciless senators. One congress member after another steps up and tries to change Gore's tragic fate, but in vain. Not one senator supports their objections, and they stand powerless. When one of the members of congress remarks that she does not care that her objections are not signed by a senator, Gore responds by stressing the importance of obeying the rules. He plays his role to the very end and heroically accepts his tragic fate.

Bush's behavior, too, is framed in terms of theater, albeit in a very different way. After a prologue of about ten minutes dealing with the controversies surrounding Bush's "election," Moore begins his account of the events surrounding September 11th with a sequence of short fragments related to the television appearance in which Bush announced the invasion in Iraq, alternating with the film's credits. We see the major political players preparing themselves for the show like actors, having their costumes arranged and make-up applied by assistants. Other, lesser gods have to improvise and take care of these things themselves. There are light checks and technical checks. The atmosphere is somewhat tense. The actors are nervous. One actor worries whether the protagonist will remember his lines. They make jokes, mocking their nervousness about going on stage. "Make me look younger," one of them says. It seems that he himself would be the first to acknowledge this is a hopeless undertaking. The main actor makes faces to the camera. The screen turns black and *Fahrenheit 9/11* begins with a black screen and a soundtrack of fragments of the September 11th attack and moments following.

Moore's montage highlights the similarities between politicians and actors preparing for a show. It also highlights the difference between Bush as the serious and self-confident president on TV and the preparations involved in producing him as such. Moore shows politics to be theater. "You see," his film says. "It is all staged." I could not agree more. But, when it comes to Bush, *Fahrenheit 9/11* not only points to the similarities between politics and theater. It also shows politics to be "mere theater." Moore's rhetoric recalls this old anti-theatrical prejudice in which theater is equated with falseness, artificiality, and exaggeration as opposed to something more true, more authentic, and more sincere, something to be taken more seriously precisely because it is *not* theater.[1]

Crucial in this respect are the moments of the Bush tape right before Moore cuts to the black screen, the moment that Bush begins to make faces. Moore must have been most happy to discover this footage, for it performs an important function in the construction of his anti-theatrical rhetoric. In Moore's montage, these moments are the culmination of the preparation process, or the moment it goes over the top. We see Bush squint into the camera and then Moore cuts to black to contrast Bush making faces with the sounds of the September 11th documentary material, as if to oppose Bush's media circus to the real thing that cannot be adequately represented by media images. Or perhaps is not allowed to. Or should not. As the ungraspable moment of truth amidst a world that is "mere theater" and in that respect utterly insincere.

Imagine Moore had cut the Bush tape earlier. Then, too, we would have seen politicians like actors preparing for their show. Politics would similarly have been shown to be theater. But it would have been much more serious theater. The final moments showing Bush making faces are instrumental in turning the situation into "mere theater": theater that mocks its audience behind their backs or perhaps even in their faces. Bush made his faces to a camera and he can be expected to know that what he does will be seen, and will be seen by the people he is supposed to represent. These moments show his behavior is not only theater, it is also bad theater. It is theater that does not take itself seriously as theater, and therefore can hardly be expected to be taken seriously by others. This montage sets the tone for the shock Moore wants to induce with the rest of his film, a shock that the montage anticipated, cutting directly to the black screen combined with the soundtrack of eyewitnesses responding to the horror of September 11th. The screen remains black for the duration of a full minute, during which time we hear the sound of planes crashing into buildings, sirens, and people screaming. When finally images light up again from the black, we see faces of eyewitnesses expressing horror and fear. It is as if we cut from Bush's performance to his audience sitting in the dark, responding with horror to what they see: be it either Bush making faces or the very real consequences of his theater of make-believe.

Covering Up Confusion

I share much of Moore's critique of the Bush administration and admire him for the persistence and energy with which he investigates and exposes the hidden history of the second Gulf war, as well as other atrocities committed by this regime. Nevertheless, I think his anti-theatrical rhetoric is quite problematic and counterproductive. This is not only because as a theater professional I think it is not fair to equate theater with Bush's bad acting. More important than that, rejecting Bush's political performance for being "mere theater," and therefore not to be taken seriously, is missing the point. The problem is not that politics is theater. The problem is that politics is theater but we don't want to know it.

Moore shows us a leading actor on the world stage who finds it necessary to make faces to the camera just seconds before he is going to announce a war that will destroy the lives of hundreds of thousands of people. This is insulting, irresponsible, and shows a shameful lack of respect. Bush's behavior can be taken as a sign of a marked distance between his performance as a public person and his personal feelings. His behavior can thus be read as a sign that points to the insincerity of the seriousness performed during his speech, to the fact he is doing something one might call acting. Yet, this insincerity, this acting, is not what is problematic about his behavior as a politician, nor is insincerity what is so problematic about his politics. On the contrary, this kind of insincerity is the foundation of representative government.

In representative government, politicians represent other people: the people who voted for them. People vote for politicians so that these politicians may act for them and represent their interests and convictions. Within this political system, Bush is not supposed to act on his own inner impulse, but in a way that is in accordance with the interests of those he represents. What is needed, therefore, is not that he say what he thinks is sincere and true to his inner beliefs, but rather that we can trust what he says. What is required in politics is not sincerity or authenticity but reliability. One of the problems with Bush's political behavior is that it is not reliable. This is also what the rest of Moore's film demonstrates. Moore shows us how we are being deceived by George W. Bush; how he and his collaborators make us believe lies about connections between Saddam Hussein and Al-Qaeda, about the existence of those famous weapons of mass destruction, and how these lies serve Bush's interests rather than the interests of his voters. However, in framing his unreliability in terms of its being mere theater, Moore's rhetoric suggests that the problem of Bush's politics comes down to that of a mimetic gap between the character (Bush the president) and the actor (Bush the person). Ironically, this gap is actually one of the very few things that is *not* a problem about George W. Bush.

Moore's anti-theatricality supports a kind of double twist that covers up the structural confusion at work in the practice of politics. What I mean is this: although in actual political practice people tend to vote for those candidates who most convincingly play the role of politician (instead of those who will represent their interests best), this is usually not how these very same people will motivate their choice. It is quite the opposite. Usually people will argue that their candidate is not playing a role at all, which is why he or she deserves their support. This happened, for example, in a famous Dutch case of politics meets theater: the unstoppable rise of Pim Fortuyn. "Finally a politician who says what he means," many people said. People valued Pim Fortuyn not for playing the politician so well, nor for the way in which he represented their interests. Instead, they valued him for what they perceived as his being himself, that is, being sincere, just as they valued him for saying how it is, rather than for the way he represented their interests or beliefs. Yet, one might wonder: would these same people have voted for him in such large numbers if what he said had been "how it is," but had not represented what they believed? Would they even have recognized it as "how it is" if it had not represented their point of view?

Blame It on Bush

How then do we know the good guys from the bad guys? How do we recognize the right political candidate? At this point, *Fahrenheit 9/11* again presents an interesting example. When discussing the dubious role of President Bush with regard to the Bin Laden family in the days after the attack, Moore uses a montage of fragments from detective movies to demonstrate what kind of role the president and CIA should have played.[2] These fragments of fiction film are presented to us as self-evident examples of what would have been normal and right. A little later, Moore wonders what would have happened if Clinton had arranged a trip out of the country for the McVeigh family days after the Oklahoma City terrorist bombing. What would have happened to Clinton if that had been revealed? For an answer, he shows a film fragment in which a furious crowd screams, "Burn them, burn them," while some of them come forward with a torch, presumably to set fire to those who have caused their rage.

Fahrenheit 9/11 presents people acting in films as a frame of reference through which to read and understand the behavior of political actors. In the very first scene of *Fahrenheit 9/11*, Gore, as the embodiment of a dream of hope, is associated with the world of film in images that stage him as a movie star among other movie stars. We see fireworks, a crowd of cheering fans, we hear dramatic film music and the voice-over remarks: "Look, there is Ben Affleck. He is often in my dreams. And the *Taxi Driver* guy. He was there too. And little Stevie Wonder. He seems so happy like a miracle had taken place." The question: "Was it all a dream? Did the last four years not really happen?" explicitly frames this as what should have been reality as opposed to the Bush administration as a bad dream. Bush is shown to be stumbling over his lines, not knowing how to act, and incapable of more than a bad imitation of being a cowboy at his ranch in Texas. Bush is the one who needs the make-up, the hairdressers, the camera and light assistants in order to do what to Gore comes naturally.

The anti-theatrical rhetoric of *Fahrenheit 9/11* thus supports a conflation of role models presented by film and what is natural and self-evident. Film is not just a frame of reference, it is presented as a frame of reference that helps us recognize what is normal and what is right. In opposing Gore as a natural-born actor to Bush's political act as bad acting and therefore a sign of make-belief, *Fahrenheit 9/11* invites an understanding of Gore's acting in terms of the paradoxical promise presented by Hollywood movies, namely that what we see is the behavior of a brilliant actor who is not acting at all, the promise of an actor who is sincere.[3]

Gore is not just playing his role well, he *is* his role—or at least, this is what *Fahrenheit 9/11* suggests—and therefore he is the right candidate, the candidate that deserves our support. Bush, on the other hand, is a bad actor and therefore a bad politician who is deceiving us. Yet would Bush's politics have been any better if he had been a better actor? Near the end of his film, Moore wonders:

I have always been amazed that the very people forced to live in the worst parts of town, who go to the worst schools and who have it the hardest, are always the first to step up and defend that very system. They serve so that we don't have to. They offer to give up their lives so that we can be free. It is remarkable, their gift to us. And all they ask for in return, is that we never send them into harm's way unless it is absolutely necessary. Will they ever trust us again?

Bush—this much Moore's film makes clear—has misused the trust of the people who do the dirty job for him. He has lied to them and misused them for a war that serves first and foremost his own interests. His lies have very serious consequences for them and millions of other individuals around the world, as well as for the position of the United States in the world. Moore's film shows how they have been deceived and in doing so performs a function one would hope independent media would fulfill. Yet one thing his film neither explains nor questions is why people trusted Bush in the first place. Why did they believe and support him, especially if he was such a bad actor? And if it is the pivotal problem that his political act was "mere theater," wouldn't Gore's good, natural acting have evoked an even greater problem? Does this good, natural acting not make it even more difficult to see what kind of theater he is playing?

Useful here is the distinction between "theatrical" (used to describe a particular quality of some action or object, either its belonging to the theater, or its being theater in the sense of its being staged), and "theatricality." Tracey Davis (2003) traces the emergence of theatricality as a separate term, and locates this emergence in the eighteenth century. At that time, theatricality as a separate term is used to denote a communicative effect that results from perceiving something as being theater, staged, make believe. Theatricality as communicative effect therefore does not necessarily mean that what we see is staged, but that it is perceived as if it were. Michael Fried comes to a similar understanding based on Diderot, using "theatricality" to describe the effect of an address that makes a viewer aware of her or his being implicated in what is seen. Diderot, writing about visual art and dramatic theater, is not in favor of such effects and comes up with several suggestions of how to stage scenes on paintings or in the theater in such a way as to look more natural. To do so, he explains, it is important to take into account the point of view of the audience and stage one's scenes in relation to this point of view, yet in such a way that this point of view does not become too obvious (Fried 1980).[4] Theatricality points attention to precisely this point of view implicated within what is seen. Doing so, it destabilizes the illusion of a point of view marked by absence, a point of view from which we can see things as they are and recognize what is "natural" and "self-evident," and what is not.

Political Acting

Moore's observations near the end of his film point to responsibility, and, rightfully so, he locates this responsibility with "us." It is "we" that sent young people to the war that Bush, "our" political representative, started in "our" name. He may have deceived "us" concerning his true intentions and the ways in which he and his friends would personally benefit from this war, he may have lied to "us" about the connection between Hussein and Al-Qaeda and kept silent about his own connections to the Bin Laden family, and he may have exaggerated the threat posed by Iraq and its supposed connection to international terrorism. But all of this does not change the fact that in order to do so, he needed to convince "us" that war was what was needed. He needed to make it look like the right thing to do. And so he did. Even if he got this support on false grounds, unmasking him as fake, as "mere theater," does not help to understand how this could happen nor how we can prevent this from happening again. Instead of blaming it all on Bush's "mere theater," we had better take this theater that is politics very seriously and try to understand how it works, and this means taking into account how this involves "us."

This relationship between what convinces us as being right—as how things are, as being more than just acting—and our culturally and historically specific point of view presents one of the greatest challenges to representational government today. That is not because this political system cannot deal with differences in point of view, but because many people find it difficult to deal with the implications of the system on this point. At the core of the problem lies the difficulty of accepting the fundamentally theatrical character of the political system. The idea of representational democracy is fundamentally theatrical in the sense that it is not based on political actors acting on their own accord but on politicians acting for others and representing their interests or, at least, having to give the impression of representing the interests of those they represent. At this point, the theater and theatricality actually present a useful model for understanding the implications of representational democracy. This is not to point to the falsity of political behavior, as Moore does, but rather to understand how political representation works, or could work. It involves a reconsideration of what is at stake in political representation and what kind of acting is involved. More precisely, it involves a reconsideration of political acting in relational terms. What this could mean was the subject of *Deutschland 2* by German/Swiss theater collective Rimini Protocoll.

The idea of *Deutschland 2* was to enact in real time an entire session of the German parliament, lasting from nine in the morning until around midnight. This enactment was to take place in the former building of the parliament in Bonn, the place where the parliament used to reside before it was moved to Berlin after the reunification of East and West Germany. In this building, Rimini Protocoll was to bring together a large group of nonprofessional actors, each representing one member of parliament. All of them would wear headphones through which they could hear a live telephone broadcast of the actual Bundestag session as it was taking place in Berlin at the very same time. The performers in Bonn would then on the spot perform what they were hearing.

Deutschland 2 was carefully prepared and preceded by extensive casting sessions in which people interested in participating were asked to explain whom they would like to represent and why, all of which was filmed. But then, at the last moment and with everything prepared for the big event, the president of the Bundestag withdrew permission to use the former Bundestag building. He argued "dass durch den speziellen Programmablauf des Projects im ehemaligen Plenarsaal das Ansehen und die Würde des Deutschen Bundestags beeinträchtigt werden" [that the proceeding of this particular program in the former assembly might pose a threat to the standing and dignity of the German parliament] (Malzacher 2002). Journalists were eager to point out that "Die Sorgen des Bundespräsidenten waren ünbegrundet. Die Kopie macht das Parliament nicht lächerlicher als das Original es selbst manchmal tut" [The president of the parliament did not need to worry. The copy would not

make the parliament any more ridiculous than the original does at times]
(Heine 2002). Both the critique of the president and this way of refuting
his argument miss the point in that the performance was not about showing the Bundestag or the members of parliament to be ridiculous. Not
only were the performers very serious about representing their representatives as appearing sincere, but also, and more importantly, this discussion about whether or not the performance made the parliament appear
more ridiculous than it already was misses the point when it comes to
understanding what exactly would be happening in this performance and
whether it might be a threat to the standing of the parliament.

In itself, copying can hardly be considered a threat to the parliament's
reputation. Copying is often a sign of admiration, a motivation several
participants of *Deutschland 2* suggested. Although the practice of copying
may raise questions about the relationships and differences between copy
and original, one thing it usually does not question is the standing of the
original. The standing of Elvis Presley or Madonna is not questioned by
the wannabes imitating them, not even by crowds of them. These imita-
tors only increase their standing. What then is the problem? What is the
problem with this very serious enactment of the parliament? At the same
time but from a different point of view, this amounts to the question: what
is so interesting about doing a very serious enactment of the parliament?

The problem, or at least part of the problem, I would argue, is that
Deutschland 2 is *not* a copy of the parliament. It is a different staging of the
same play. This second staging, more explicitly than the first one, shows
politicians to be actors representing others. Importantly, "representing"
here does not mean "imitating." The makers of Rimini Protocoll chose to
enact in real time a session that was going on at the very same time. The
performers did not see (nor had they seen) the session they were enacting.
They only heard what "their" politician was saying and were asked to speak
this text aloud and act according to it on the spot. What they were asked to
do was produce the external performance that according to them would fit
the text they heard through the headphones. Their acting, therefore, is not
a matter of imitating the performance of others (in which case the problem would be that of the mimetic gap between actor and character), but is
instead closer to what happens in the film *Being John Malkovich*.

In this film, one of the characters discovers by accident a door that
leads into John Malkovich's consciousness. Whoever goes through this

door can be Malkovich for fifteen minutes. How this is possible remains a mystery, and we don't get to know anything about Malkovich. Instead, we witness what happens when various people *are* him. During their fifteen minutes of fame, the people inside Malkovich can make him act according to their wishes. They direct his performance, while at the same time others witness this performance as being the behavior of Malkovich. This is also what makes the choice for Malkovich so interesting. Being John Malkovich means to be an actor. Malkovich is the enigmatic performer whom most of us will only know through the characters he has represented on screen. We only know him (or think we know him) through the ways in which he has represented others. That is, he exists for us only in the ways in which he has had others speak through him and made his behavior correspond to the intentions, ideas, and assumptions of those he is representing.

Deutschland 2 shows that being a politician is like being John Malkovich. Like actors embodying Shakespeare's lines, these performers embody the speakers of the lines they receive through their headphones. Of course, knowledge about the various politicians speaking can (and most likely does) inform us about how these performers will embody them. Yet, the behavior of the participants of *Deutschland 2* is not an imitation of what these politicians are doing. It is an embodied interpretation of how these politicians say, or may say, these lines. The performance thus represents the political representatives in Berlin by means of what might be called *sincere simulation*. The representatives of the people's representatives act as sincerely as possible, not according to their own intentions, but to the presumed intentions of those they represent. This means that the actors incorporate a point of view about these political acts, including assumptions about what would look convincing, true, and right. *Deutschland 2* also— and this probably is the more disturbing part—invites us to look at the behavior of the actual political representatives in Berlin in similar terms.

Deutschland 2 deploys theater and theatricality as a "critical vision machine" to point to the relationship between political actors, their performances, and their point of view.[5] Theater here is not a matter of spectacle, exaggeration, or make-believe, but a matter of becoming aware of how we are implicated within what we see and how we see it, and how this in its turn is implicated in the performance of others addressing us. *Deutschland 2* shows political representatives speaking the words of others and enacting them and in ways that correspond to assumptions about what will look right, true, and convincing from the point of view of those represented by them. The result is an uncanny vision of representational politics as it actually is. Rejecting the uneasiness thus evoked on the grounds of its being "mere theater," false, or a copy does not explain this uneasiness, but instead reinstalls such binary oppositions as theater/reality, true/false, or original/copy—binaries that are threatened and undermined by what is shown.

How Ironic

Being John Malkovich means to be recognized by others as John Malkovich. Typically, the first person in the film who goes through the door to be Malkovich discovers who he is when he/Malkovich looks in a mirror. This "mirror stage" moment tells him who he is and invites him to identify with what he looks like from a position outside himself. Being John Malkovich means that your behavior will be seen as the behavior of John Malkovich. It also means being confronted with the look of others looking at you as being Malkovich. Understood as a metaphor for political acting, *Being John Malkovich* presents a warning to "us." Malkovich exists in the ways in which he acts for others or the ones he represents, and since these others are different people all the time, this means that being John Malkovich means being confronted with the fact that how others will see you is not only a matter of your own sincere, or insincere, behavior at this very moment, but also results from what others, in the name of Malkovich, have said and done earlier. Similarly, political acts are always preceded by other acts performed in the name of those represented and by other political performers. These political acts cannot be justified on the grounds of the good intentions of the performers, nor can unmasking the behavior of political representatives as insincere serve as an excuse for those who have supported these acts and allowed them to happen in their name. All too easily, the claim of having been sincere or having believed somebody to be sincere can be (mis)used to avoid responsibility and justify (assumed) naïveté.

What is needed in today's globalized world is an awareness not only of how politicians' behavior incorporates points of view, but also a conception of "us" in relational terms. This means acknowledging that "we" exist as a political body with a history of actions that we may or may not approve of or know about, but that are nevertheless part of how "we" are being looked at by others. In this situation, pointing at Bush as the bad guy who failed to see it coming and took America to war for his own benefit may be helpful in the sense that it confirms the critique of many people who have long disagreed with Bush's politics. At the same time, however, it directs attention away from a more profound problem, namely the question as to whose interests are served by this particular reading of the events.

At some point in *Fahrenheit 9/11*, Moore uses two short fragments of a television interview by Larry King with Prince Bandar, the Saudi ambassador to the United States. In Moore's montage, these fragments draw attention to the close relationship between the Bin Laden family, the Saudi-Arabian government, and the Bush family. The fragments support Moore's claim that Bush may have been insincere concerning his motives for the war against Iraq and that his official rationale was "mere theater." In the interview, Prince Bandar, who knows the Bin Laden family well, is asked if he also knows Osama Bin Laden, and he answers: "He is the only one I never . . . I don't know him, well, I met him only once." Prince Bandar is clearly struggling with the right way of putting it, very much aware of how his words will be read by the television audience, very much aware of the theatricality of the situation and the role he plays. When Larry King asks him about the circumstances under which he met Osama Bin Laden, Prince Bandar answers: "This is ironic. In the mid '80s, if you remember, we of the United States were supporting the Mudjahedin to uh, liberate Afghanistan from the Soviets. He came to thank me for my efforts to bring the Americans, our friends, to help us against the atheists, the communists." Larry King answers: "How ironic. He came to thank you for helping bring America to help him. And now he may be responsible for bombing America." Prince Bandar's words are carefully chosen. Bandar's way of putting it, as well as Larry King's response, frame Osama Bin Laden as the ungrateful protégé who has turned against his benefactor, a reading in line with the official U.S. reading of the September 11th events. What is left out is whose interests were served by supporting the Taliban in the first place. Why did "we" support a regime like that? Framing support to the Taliban in terms of "helping" obscures the fact that this support was a matter of strategic calculation and interest for the United

States. The fact that many people in the United States seem to be unaware of these facts is sad, ironic perhaps, but by no means an excuse.

Prince Bandar's words present his U.S. television audience with an image of "us" in which the evocation of sincere intentions directs attention away from the theatricality of the situation and prevents us from looking at U.S. foreign policy in terms of a role played on the world stage. If something is to be called ironic here, it is that in this interview, the U.S. support for the Taliban is used to stage the United States as victim. If something is to be called "ironic" it is the miscalculation that "we" could support the Taliban as well as a whole series of questionable regimes without this ever having repercussions for how the rest of the world will look at the United States. This is the political theater that is our reality. Do we dare face it?

Saying Everything and Affected Self-Disclosure in the Works of Reinaldo Arenas and Hervé Guibert

Reindert Dhondt

A necessary condition of all social interaction, and of a cooperative activity in particular, is a certain degree of trustworthiness in speech that cannot be deduced from the content of an assertion. This we call sincerity. In a private face-to-face conversation, sincere expression requires of the hearer a willingness to listen attentively. In social psychology, strategic impression management implies that we present ourselves as being straightforward: a non-deceitful and uninhibited declaration is supposed to guarantee a true understanding of the other. Even when the speaker seems to act spontaneously, but repeatedly exaggerates, dramatizes, improperly breaches confidences, or seeks self-abasement, his interlocutor will turn his or her eyes away and the rhetoric of sincerity falls short. Apart from the reliability of the speaker, the hearer's disposition or communicative expectations play a central role in the determination of uprightness. The importance of the speaker's attempts to regulate his perception on the social stage is ironically illustrated by the following aphorism of the French *vaudevilliste* Tristan Bernard: "Men are always sincere. They change sincerities, that's all" ["Les hommes sont toujours sincères. Ils changent de sincérité, voilà tout"] (Bernard 1926, 164).

People are usually poor judges of the degree of sincerity of their discussion partners, and less so in more indirect contacts. It has become almost a commonplace to assert that at the root of all good writing lies a certain sincerity of conviction. Since the Romantic movement, auto-biographical writing has been recognized as an important testing ground for polemics about selfhood, authenticity, and sincerity. Of all "egodocu-ments" (Presser 1969, 277–282), autobiography is without any doubt the most highly developed form of the unremitting activity of self-inquiry and self-promotion and supposedly the most sincere of all literary genres. In critical discussions of what Georges Gusdorf has called "the requirement of a clarification of the inside" ["l'exigence d'une mise au net du dedans"] (1991, 73), the notion of an allegedly honest intention, which is supposed to guarantee the unvarnished truth of the writing, has played an often unquestioned role in the sealing of an "autobiographical pact" between author and reader (Lejeune 1989, 3–30). This pact implies that the auto-biographer makes a sincere endeavor to understand and to come to terms with his life. But in order to achieve this textual sincerity on which the reader's judgment depends, the author is sometimes obliged to disregard the sincerity conditions in social interaction. Indeed, most readers will feel suspicious about an unusual degree of sincerity in memoirs and auto-biographical texts because it turns social insincerity and indiscretion into a necessary evil. With the purpose of drawing a sincere self-portrait in the eyes of the readership, the author paradoxically needs to transgress a number of social conventions, including the sincerity requirements with respect to speech acts or the general representation of the self.

The dismissal of authorial intentionality by the New Critics and Roland Barthes's claim of "The Death of the Author" had far-reaching implications for autobiographical writing because every pre-existing sub-ject was presented as a mere illusion: after all, a text can be perfectly sincere without having an intention to be so. Since Barthes's time, many theoreti-cal frameworks have supplanted an author-based perspective with a reader-based poetics of autobiography. Deconstructionist critics such as Paul de Man, who published "Autobiography as De-facement," warn us against any facile assumptions of transparency of autobiographical texts as a reli-able record of the past by drawing our attention to their rhetorical nature. De Man proposes to see autobiography not as genre *sui generis*, but as "a figure of reading or understanding that occurs, to some degree, in all texts"

(1979, 921). According to de Man, the rhetorical figure that presides over self-writing is that of prosopopeia, literally, "to confer a face" or "to make a mask" (*prosōpon poiein*), the figure by which poets address and lend their voice to something or someone inanimate, such as an ancestor or literary precursor, so that a sort of dialogue with the dead is established.

We should not be surprised, then, to find de Man declaring that this trope of address is "the very figure of the reader and of reading" (1986, 45). The so-called autobiographical moment happens when the two subjects involved in the process of reading determine each other by a substitutive exchange (de Man 1979, 921). In his tropological deconstruction, de Man demonstrates that the author reads himself in the text, but what he sees in this "specular" moment is no more than a mask. Inevitably, the autobiographical subject is dissolved into words: "Death is a displaced name for a linguistic predicament, and the restoration of mortality by autobiography (the prosopopeia of the voice and the name) deprives and disfigures to the precise extent that it restores. Autobiography veils a defacement of the mind of which it is itself the cause" (930).

De Man illustrates his thesis with reference to an exemplary autobiographical text, William Wordsworth's *Essays upon Epitaphs* (1810). Autobiographical discourse always contains the epitaphic because it echoes a "voice-from-beyond-the-grave" (De Man 1979, 927). Autobiographical personae are so "disfigured" that they could be said to die, their personal narratives becoming a kind of funerary discourse. Just as literary history is often seen as a reading practice that stems from a "desire to speak with the dead" (Greenblatt 1988), life-writing is frequently inspired by a claim for restoration of mortality: the fact that so many autobiographies have been published only posthumously suggests that the writers want the period of time between the completion of their life-story and the end of their worldly existence to be overlooked.

Moreover, some autobiographers preface their text with the assurance that they can honestly write as if they were already dead. The death mask they put on is, in some cases, a kind of *laissez-passer* for indiscretion, social criticism, and even theatrical self-display. At the same time, the impossible mediation between the world of the living and the hereafter confers a certain authority on the dead that excludes every possible objection in advance—or as the saying goes: "Never speak ill of the dead." The substitutive trope of prosopopeia de-faces the dead at the very moment it gives them a face. But the everlasting problem with death, especially when it is invoked rhetorically as it frequently is in post-structuralist theory, is that it leaves space for all kinds of revenants or ghostly returns, the more so as the death announcement of the author as "persona poetica" is wrapped up in an obituary notice of his empirical counterpart or "persona pratica" (Croce 1919, 129–138). According to the "horizon of expectations" of the reader (Jauss 1982, 23), an autobiographical text may generate disapproval of the author's alleged sincerity. In this chapter I shall examine how an excessive openness and outgoingness risks undermining the autobiographical pact and the sincerity that it implies.

Sincerity in the Face of Death

I will examine this risk of sincerity by concentrating primarily upon the projects of self-revelation of Reinaldo Arenas and Hervé Guibert, two authors who at first glance seem to have very little in common apart from the similar circumstances in which they died and the autobiographical content of their fictional enterprise. As a Cuban subversive intellectual who was considered a counterrevolutionary by the Castro government, Reinaldo Arenas (1943–1990) suffered literary marginalization as well as political confinement and, after having been repeatedly imprisoned, finally succeeded at the beginning of the 1980s in leaving his Latin American homeland for the United States. His multi-talented *confrère* Hervé Guibert (1955–1991), a notorious media personality in France toward the end of his life, began his brief career as a photographer, scriptwriter, and critic for *Le Monde*. Apart from their different backgrounds and literary styles, both authors had in common a love for working in the tricky zone where life and fiction meet: they continually and deliberately blurred the boundaries between reality and fiction, between truth and falsehood. Just a couple of months before their final suicide attempts they each wrote a highly polemical work with an unmistakable autobiographical bias in which they not only revealed their "genuine" identities, but also divulged the most intimate secrets of their acquaintances. This singular kind of witnessing narrative explicitly conceived for publication can obviously be compared to last wills and testaments or the famous deathbed confessions that contain startling disclosures.

Since fictionality is a necessary part of the autobiographical process, it is not my aim here to enter into any simplistic fact-versus-fiction debate about life-writing. It would be pointless to waste time on trivia like factual mistakes or simplicities when one is reading a book written against death, the ultimate antagonist. Rather, I want to examine how both authors hold on to the right to "say everything" while at the same time undermining the sincerity of their autobiographically inflected narratives.[1] Although it might be tempting to regard the elusive concept of sincerity as akin to truth-telling, the question of veracity or literal accuracy is completely insignificant at the origin of the autobiographical gesture. According to Régis Jolivet, it is only possible to prove that one is willing to be sincere, but sincerity as such is not demonstrable: "Sincerity is not verifiable by demonstration, neither by someone else, which is evident, nor by oneself. . . . The only possible sincerity is that of the immediacy and, as such, it excludes all narration and analysis" ["La sincérité n'est pas vérifiable par démonstration, ni par autrui, ce qui est évident, ni par soi-même. . . . La seule sincérité possible est de l'immédiat et, comme telle, exclut la narration et l'analyse"] (1950, 28; translation mine). Being clearly aware of the irrelevance of factual data to sincerity, some autobiographers are uncompromising in their outspokenness on behalf of truth. In one of the first paragraphs of his *Confessions*, Jean-Jacques Rousseau describes himself as crystalline and affirms that sincerity is the only law that regulates his literary enterprise in the making. The French critic Jean Starobinski underscores in this respect that sincerity refers primarily to a conformity between speech and gesture, between writing and emotion or memory: a sincere self-portrait, he notes, "requires not that language reproduce a pre-existing reality but that it produce truth freely and without interruption" (1988, 198). The etymology of the Latin word *sincerus* ("without wax," "clear," "sound") reminds us that the absence of dissimulation is at stake, not cold objectivity. According to Lionel Trilling, sincerity, defined as "congruence between avowal and actual feeling" (1972, 12), appears with the emergence of the modern world from the medieval, characterized by the rise of an individualistic culture and an unprecedented social mobility. Trilling notes that sincerity is itself paradoxical, becoming a truly social virtue only as it becomes a theatrical performance. Sincerity, when practiced because society requires of us that we abstain from pretending, inevitably leads to self-concealment and masquerade: "We play the role of being ourselves, we sincerely act the part of the sincere person, with the result that a judgment may be passed upon our sincerity that it is not authentic" (11). The social stage, especially within a totalitarian context, is indeed the principal locus of insincere role-playing.

Self-Scrutiny and Saying Everything

As Trilling observes, in some national literary traditions, sincerity does not only imply telling the truth about one's inner self, but also consists of an intemperate and unmediated exhibitionism in revealing obnoxious thoughts and morally or socially reprehensible actions (Trilling 1971, 58). Rousseau accused Michel de Montaigne of counterfeit sincerity because the latter had "sinned" by omission and excessive discretion. In his *Essais* (1580), Montaigne retained the right to privacy in some matters on the grounds that a sincere and unadorned self-portrait—"entire and wholly naked" ("tout entier, et tout nu")—is not possible (2007, 27). Arenas and Guibert radicalize Montaigne's project, rejecting his occasional modesty by breaking most conventional barriers. They reject all kinds of artificial masquerade or pose in order to provide a truthful and adequate account of their personal lives, lapsing sometimes into what many readers will see as indecency. Nevertheless, they cannot refrain from providing a fictitious *veritas* because their writing is mannered, contentious, and at times even baroque. Their autobiographies also reveal a growing awareness that in order to be scrupulously honest about their conduct in life they must admit that they cannot always distinguish between reminiscences, events of their own invention, and what actually happened: their memory is finite as well as fallible.

Throughout their eventful writing careers, Arenas as well as Guibert regularly alternated novels filled with invented characters and events with thinly disguised autobiography. Diagnosed as HIV-positive at the end of the 1980s, both authors committed their own private lives to paper in a desperate attempt to write against time and death. From the point where the ominous specter of AIDS makes its entry into the text and where this is confirmed by a biographical note on the back cover and other paratextual indications, it becomes almost impossible to read their work in total disregard of their common thanatological fate. After having contracted the syndrome, they wage a truly furious race against death to complete their works-in-progress.

The title of Arenas's apology, *Before Night Falls* (*Antes que anochezca*), is very significant in this respect. In powerful language, the book illuminates the importance of the writer's Kafkaesque life as a symbol of the lonely struggle of the outcast against a dictatorial government, epitomized by Fidel Castro's administration. In the introductory chapter, the narrator explains how an approaching deadline forced him to work against the clock: "Now darkness was approaching again, only more insidiously. It was the dark night of death. I really had to finish my memoirs before nightfall. I took it as a challenge" ["Ahora la noche avanzaba de nuevo en forma más inminente. Ahora sí tenía que terminar mi autobiografía antes de que anocheciera. Lo tomé como un reto"] (Arenas 1994, xi; 1996, 11). What follows is an uncensored personal self-analysis lacking political hypocrisy or social restrictions on achieving the full expression of desire. Asserting the primacy of affective existence over intellectual life, Arenas refuses categorically to intellectualize sensations: *sentio, ergo sum*. Sensuality, erotic pleasure, and fantasies are an eminent part of the perspicacious and often searing portrayal that both Arenas and Guibert offer of themselves. The effect of AIDS on the narrator becomes more and more devastating since every escape through love or tenderness is a dead end.

When giving a firsthand report of his traumatic confrontations with the mirror, the narrator never seeks to ease the reader's discomfort. Although he cannot sincerely say "I am dead," the enunciative signification of "I am dying" sheds a particular light on Barthes's oft-quoted statement that the death of the author marks the birth of the text (Chambers 1998, 2). *Before Night Falls* even reproduces a "goodbye letter" ("carta de despedida") that Arenas wrote to several of his friends before taking his own life. This letter runs as follows: "Dear friends, Due to my delicate state of health and to the terrible emotional depression that makes me unable to continue writing and struggling for the freedom of Cuba, I end my life" ["Queridos amigos: debido al estado precario de mi salud y a la terrible depresión sentimental que siento al no poder seguir escribiendo y luchando por la libertad de Cuba, pongo fin a mi vida"] (Arenas 1994, 319; 1996, 343; translation adapted). In a sense, his death was his ultimate political statement. The autobiography would be incomplete without this suicide note to which it inexorably leads, although most of it was written not only well before his death, but also before the completion of his fictional work. Like-wise, from the moment that the narrator of Guibert's *To the Friend Who Did Not Save My Life* (*A l'ami qui ne m'a pas sauvé la vie*) stops think-ing of himself as immune, he patiently and meticulously begins planning his suicide. Illustrative in this respect is the ending of Guibert's insight-ful account of how the AIDS pandemic affects friendships: "The infinite regression of my book is closing in on me" ["La mise en abîme [*sic*] de mon livre se referme sur moi"] (1994b, 246; 1990, 284; translation adapted).

The shattering testimonials of Arenas and Guibert not only chronicle with frankness their slow realization that they are infected with an incur-able disease, but can also be considered as a final settlement of accounts with their environment. Because their common aim is to take stock of their lives free of dissimulation, they never seem priggish about present-ing scandalous details to their readers. There is never any question of wal-lowing in self-pity over their own fate in their writings; on the contrary, the two authors admit that they are exhilarated by the close proximity to death. When they begin to write about their innermost thoughts, they find themselves condemned by the inexorable progression of their terminal ill-ness, which acts as a catalyst for the writing process. When Guibert learns he is going to die, he is suddenly seized with the desire to put pen to paper. After his contagion, there is no reason whatsoever to refrain from being entirely sincere: henceforth he is preparing his posthumous publications.

The Guibertian aesthetics of scandal, and the leitmotiv of "the cour-age to be oneself, to say oneself" ("le courage de soi, de se dire") that punctuates his entire oeuvre, seem to reach their climax in this random journal (Guibert 1994a, 77; translation mine). Yet the author repeatedly reminds us that this unflinchingly honest examination of daily life under a death sentence is always a rhetorical construct. Or as he stated once in an interview: "AIDS enabled me to radicalize a little further certain systems of narration, of relationship with truth, of self-involvement even beyond what I thought possible" ["Le sida m'a permis de radicaliser un peu plus encore certains systèmes de narration, de rapport à la vérité, de mise en jeu de moi-même au-delà même de ce que je pensais possible"] (Gaudemar 1990, 21). In a very dramatic way, both autobiographies are dominated by a thematic insistence on Eros and Thanatos, by the obsession to stay alive and to confer a mask or a face—the figure of prosopopeia—upon a voice-less and moribund entity.

The poignant memoirs of Arenas and Guibert lay bare the principle of insincerity upon which friendship and love (in fact, all social interaction patterns in times of oppression) are based. By deliberately breaking the taboos of respectable reticence and permissibility, the two authors shift the limits of the sayable in their fictionalized memoirs. One of the purposes of this self-articulation is doubtless to bring to light what they conceal or ignore in themselves: the claim of literary sincerity is supposed to have left no *terrae incognitae* in the writer's inner labyrinths.

Threatened by a premature death and haunted by the thought of suicide, Arenas and Guibert need a form of dialogue with themselves. But also a dialogue with others: in spite of a pronounced self-centeredness, they are not narcissistic diarists who restrict themselves to confiding their innermost thoughts to paper as the nineteenth-century *intimistes* did. In contrast, they play with the popular genre of the truth-revealing literary memoir. Both Arenas and Guibert devote numerous pages to portraits and stories of intimates. Their project of self-revelation is inextricably bound up with a continuous defacement of the other, with painstaking details and thinly veiled revelations about friend and foe. As I will demonstrate below, this rhetoric of betrayal unmistakably undermines the pursuit of the ideal of sincerity.

Autobiography as Resistance: Removing Castro's Mask

Although the works of Reinaldo Arenas are systematically developed with quasi-autobiographical material, ranging from family oppression in his poverty-stricken early childhood to the repressive intolerance of the Castro regime, he never refrained from blending the fantastic with the real. *Before Night Falls* is an alternately humorous and distraught account of the key episodes of his life from his infancy in Holguín to his last days in his New York apartment four decades later. In between he reports his odyssey as a rebel fighting for the Revolution, his disillusionment with the communist ideals and subsequent expulsion from the UNEAC (Unión de Escritores y Artistas de Cuba), his friendship with colleagues such as Virgilio Piñera and José Lezama Lima, his multiple experiences in several penal institutions and the rehabilitation program in a UMAP camp (Unidad Militar de Ayuda a

la Producción) he was obliged to follow, and—last but not least—his eventual flight from Cuba, which contributed to his self-promoting myth as a
Cuban martyr.

This indictment of the widespread corruption, dishonesty, and sanc-
tioning moral rules that stifle every form of self-realization includes not
only testimonial data about the systematic persecution of dissenters on the
Caribbean island, but also reveals intimate details about his personal life,
such as his homelessness and his all-embracing sexual voracity. The political implications of this confessional narrative that unmasks the Revolution's treatment of critical intellectuals are apparent: by writing this book,
the outlaw Arenas affirms for the very last time his international reputation as a renegade of the Cuban Revolution.

Although the book presents an undeniably reliable documentary of
the literary scene of Havana in the 1960s and 1970s, the extent and scope
of some reactionary events that took place during the high days of the
totalitarian regime are clearly exaggerated by Arenas in his posthumous
memoirs, as a result of which he has been sharply criticized by advocates
of the socialist revolution. Although the mystification takes on the proportions of a real delirium, it is worth considering that *Before Night Falls*
is nevertheless presented as a relentlessly honest, extraordinarily truthful
book, whether it deals with the Padilla case or with confidential avowals.
Obviously, the painful record is also a mode of self-justification, enabling
him to exonerate himself once and for all.

Arenas claims, for instance, that after his first detention the authorities forced him to write insincere letters to foreign editors expressing his
satisfaction with the system: "They wanted me to make a confession stating that I was a counterrevolutionary, that I regretted the ideological weakness I had shown in my published writings. . . . I actually recanted all I had
done in my life" ["Querían que yo hiciera una confesión donde dijera que
era un contrarrevolucionario, que me arrepentía de mi debilidad ideológica
al escribir y publicar los libros que ya había publicado . . . en realidad, rene-
gaba de toda mi vida"] (1994, 204–205; 1996, 229). In order to denounce
the social oppression on the island, he irreverently brings forward his own
inclination and the latent bisexuality of all people, underscoring the liberating dimension of writing as an erotic expression. A true heir to Bataille
and Sade, he describes his sexual indulgence and his erotic encounters with
excellent fathers and exemplary husbands down to the smallest details.

This ferociously greedy novel celebrates sodomy and furtive masturbation as modes not only of escape and solace, but also of protest and redemption. Even the sea reverberates in the young Arenas with erotic resonance.

According to this visionary Cuban post-boom writer, the labor camps for homosexuals and the police officers disguised as willing hustlers actually resulted in the promotion of sexual liberation: "Perhaps as a protest against the regime, homosexuality began to flourish with ever-increasing defiance" ["Quizá como una protesta contra el régimen, las prácticas homosexuales empezaron a proliferar cada vez con mayor desenfado"] (Arenas 1994, 107; 1996, 132–133). Some of his personal adversaries who are in league with the authorities, such as Miguel Barnet (recognizable in the character "Miguel Barniz," whose surname means "varnish") and other agents of the State Security, are systematically labeled "maricón" (faggot), "loca" (queen), and so forth. Partly because of these controversial "outings" of people in positions of power, the book ventures beyond the limits of morality for the majority of the Cuban readership.

As Paul de Man has pointed out, the distinction between fiction and autobiography, which may contain fantasies, dreams, and other deviations from reality, is by definition undecidable. The political agenda that lies half-obscured behind *Before Night Falls* fills the memoir with an array of duplicity. It goes without saying that all autobiographers are to a greater or lesser extent unreliable narrators. Yet what a writer chooses to deform is as revealing as what has really occurred. Arenas's life story is particularly complex because of the apparent lies and misrepresentations—a deliberate, highly strategic decision on the author's part—that permeate the story. When *Before Night Falls* appeared in 1992, some critics adduced that everything it narrated was pure self-invention, that Arenas exaggerated and parodied where he did not fantasize and vice versa; in short, that he had written not a book of reminiscences, but one of shameless vengeance.

In an article published in the Spanish journal *Quimera*, for instance, the Cuban novelist Manuel Pereira asks himself how it is possible to speak of systematic repression in a country where the author claims to have had sexual relations with thousands of men (1992, 57). It is true that hyperbole, a baroque device that frequently appears in erotic memoirs, plays an important part among the rhetorical strategies of the text. The critic Emilio Bejel has argued that Arenas's autobiography, which he characterizes as "an obsession to remain alive, to give a face to someone who is faceless" ["una obsesión por permanecer vivo, por darle un semblante a lo que ya no lo tiene"] (1996, 36; translation mine), should not be taken as "historically accurate" but as "metaphorically authentic" because most of the pages fall short of the truth: "The necessity for the very detailed explanations, the references to known and unknown persons and the large number of examples give the reader food for thought. It is a compulsive confession of a guilty conscience of monumental proportions, of filling an infinite gap. It is that emptiness that governs the textuality of *Before Night Falls*" ["Lo que da qué pensar al leer estas descripciones es la necesidad de tanto detallismo, de tantos nombres de personas conocidas y no conocidas, el voluminoso número de ejemplos. Se trata de la confesión compulsiva de un sentimiento de culpa de proporciones monumentales, de llenar un vacío que parece no tener fin. Este vacío rige la textualidad de *Antes que anochezca*"] (38). According to Severo Sarduy, it is precisely this empty proliferation of signifiers and the whirling movement of artifice and eroticism around a constitutive lack— an absent, mute, deceased entity—that constitutes one of the main characteristics of the so-called neo-baroque aesthetic (1972, 172).

Until the bitter end, Arenas fought with all the weapons he had: an unbridled imagination and a sharp pen. In the case of *Before Night Falls*, the prosopopeic figure is combined with a rhetoric of denunciation that extracts from the figure of death the authority to tell the ultimate truth about Castro's regime. Continually rewriting his own life story and exposing the corruption of the Cuban ruling classes that finally led the nation into the iron grip of "el líder máximo" is all that the author can do to fight against every tendency toward totalitarianism. "All writing is revenge," Arenas once proclaimed in an interview. In order to speak freely, one has to escape from the social confinements of respectability and pre-established roles. But in spite of his peripheral condition and his geographical and mental exile, the narrator does not appear to be honest about his dissembling: his sincerity is indeed far from authentic.

Autobiography Between Betrayal and Anticipation of Death

For Hervé Guibert, writing face-to-face with death almost necessarily implies treason, disloyalty, and estrangement. All his narratives that focus on his HIV ordeals are pervaded by an abhorrence of the hypocritical bourgeois moral codes and by a desire for autobiographical honesty: "It was only natural to betray my secrets, since I'd always done that in all my books, even though this genie could never be stuffed back into its bottle, and I would never again be a part of the human community" ["Il était de l'ordre des choses, moi qui avais toujours procédé ainsi dans tous mes livres, de trahir mes secrets, celui-ci fût-il irréversible, et m'excluant sans retour de la communauté des hommes"] (1994b, 185; 1990, 216). Like his Cuban colleague, who resumed his literary activity in order "to write what I have lived or to live what I have already written" ["escribir sobre lo que he vivido o vivir lo que ya he escrito"] (Béjar 1994, 43), Guibert establishes a paradoxical relationship between his life and its biographical textualization. Ever since he was a child, he had been infatuated with the specter of death and destruction. Indeed, corporal deterioration is a true *leitmotiv* in his work from his youthful writings onwards. With hindsight, the subjects he broached in those early writings on the borderline between autobiography and fiction seem to be amazingly premonitory. For instance, in the stomach-turning novel *Propaganda Death* (*La mort propagande*) (1977), where he takes relish in describing dissections, beatings, torture, excruciations, and the like, Guibert writes prophetically about "a poison that enters with a kiss" ("un poison qui pénètre avec le baiser") (Eribon 1991, 88).

In the 1990 best-seller *To the Friend Who Did Not Save My Life*, an unnervingly intimate novel that was received amid certain controversy, Guibert disclosed the nature of his illness, to which he refers ironically as a "marvelous disease" (1994b, 164) because every step that leads to the end represents for him a unique apprenticeship: "AIDS will have been my paradigm in my project of self-revelation and the expression of the inexpressible" ["le sida . . . aura été pour moi un paradigme dans mon projet du dévoilement de soi et de l'énoncé de l'indicible"] (1994b, 228; 1990, 264). In another passage, he states that AIDS gives death the time to live and enables him to make a huge breakthrough in his life (1994b, 165). Writing of his bodily illness allows Guibert to take himself as the main character and to write in the closest proximity to death. From this perspective, autobiographical writing is a way to postpone mortality: his disease is welcomed almost as a godsend, as the true catalyst that enables him to get closer to this project of self-revelation, whether through writing novels or taking photographs. But by the same token he suffers from writer's block because he is afraid to validate the terrible premonition through writing: "'Disaster had to strike us.' It had to happen—it's awful—for my book to see the light of day" ["'Il fallait que le malheur nous tombe dessus.' Il le fallait, quelle horreur, pour que mon livre voie le jour"] (1994b, 202–203; 1990, 237).

According to Guibert, the French word *journal* is more appropriate to denominate his writerly project than the English term "diary" because it precisely underscores the duality between the public record of factual events (as in a newspaper) and the private space for the daily recounting of personal events. It is most revealing that the last sentence of *L'image fantôme* reads as follows: "Secrets have to circulate" ["Il faut que les secrets circulent"] (Guibert 1981, 170). In *The Compassion Protocol* (*Le protocole compassionnel*), the sequel to *To the Friend Who Did Not Save My Life*, a book that also bears the generic subtitle "novel," the narrator states: "My books are permeated, among other things, with truth and falsehood, with betrayal, with the theme of nastiness" ["[Mes livres] sont traversés, entre autres choses, par la vérité et le mensonge, la trahison, par ce thème de la méchanceté"] (1991, 112–113; translation mine). At the time of publication of *To the Friend Who Did Not Save My Life*, Guibert's meticulous account of Foucault's nightlife and final agony caused an unprecedented outrage in the French republic of letters. A scandal erupted in the press, a sort of trial by the media, because it was found that behind some of the characters real people could be recognized, in particular Isabelle Adjani (whose caprices and marital problems were made public in a way that has close affinities with the sensational press), Patrice Chéreau, Mathieu Lindon, Bernard-Marie Koltès, and, under the guise of "Muzil," Michel Foucault.

In the opinion of many critics, in this book of unbearable realism Guibert had overstepped the limits of propriety by "selling out" his mentor, whose death had not been publicly attributed to an AIDS-related illness in 1984. In view of the poignant description of Foucault's process of dying, it comes as no surprise that Didier Eribon and other biographers have made use of the barely veiled references and the excruciating details in *To the Friend Who Did Not Save My Life* (Sarkonak 1996, 183). The narration of Muzil's death agony poses ethical questions for the narrator since he is perfectly aware that Muzil would have been hurt. Indeed, the philosopher would have been furious if he had known that Guibert was taking notes for his novel all the time he was hospitalized. While telling his own story may have a therapeutic effect, revealing Michel Foucault's is perceived as a violation of the philosopher's privacy. Nonetheless, Guibert feels himself authorized to do this since it is not so much the agony of his friend that he is describing as the suffering that awaits him: "Besides being bound by friendship, we would share the same fate in death" ["En plus de l'amitié, nous étions liés par un sort thanatologique commun"] (1994b, 91; 1990, 107). In his last interview, granted to *Le Nouvel Observateur*, Guibert declares that when he writes staring death in the face, there are no limits, no scruples at all. As a consequence, every book carries with it a crime: "The fact that I display my life does not justify the seizure of biographical elements of others. It's a kind of crime. Always amorous. My characters are always very close friends" ["Le fait que j'étale ma vie ne justifie pas forcément que j'accapare la vie des autres. Je le fais. Voilà tout. C'est une sorte de crime. Toujours amoureux. Mes personnages sont toujours des gens très proches"] (Eribon 1991, 88; translation mine). By means of this literary *ars moriendi*, Guibert tries primarily to exorcize his own impotence and seeks revenge on death. But instead of limiting himself to the practice of intimate self-analysis that is commonly associated with autobiographical narratives, he challenges the conventional understanding of the genre by questioning the private-public dichotomy.

Guibert brings everything under the light of public inquiry and draws the reader-voyeur into an ever closer relationship with the book. By divulging closely guarded secrets of his inner circle to a reading public that is hungry for intimacy and vicarious adventure, the narrator deceives and misleads in an ostentatious way. The sincere autobiographer is assumed to be willing to tell the (subjective) truth about his life, but in the case of *To the Friend Who Did Not Save My Life*, he paradoxically seems to express a desire to be anonymous by repeatedly divulging the confidences of semi-fictitious characters who are well known to the French public.

It is even likely that acquaintances such as Foucault or Bill, the manager of a pharmaceutical laboratory who did not fulfill his promise to vaccinate the narrator, have not only been a gratefully adopted source of inspiration, but even a pretext for writing. As Jean-Pierre Boulé has suggested, the title of the book can be understood perfectly as a sincere dedication (1999, 199). As in "Modesty or Immodesty" (*La pudeur et l'impudeur*), the video diary Guibert made in the months preceding his death, the rhetoric of autobiographical sincerity is not only undercut by the continual play with truth and falsehood that allows the author to write the self, but also by the "role-playing" of the author in television appearances, the repeated betrayal of secrets, and the meticulous *mise-en-scène* or theatricality of the main point of departure of his life-writing, that is to say, his own dying process.

Conclusion

According to Paul de Man, autobiographical writing is an attempt at restoring the author's identity in the face of death. Self-writing resuscitates what will die by endowing it with a textual mask. What is more, the rhetorical figure of prosopopeia confers not only a voice and a face upon the (almost-)dead, but also prefigures the mortality of the reader: the reading process runs parallel to the act of self-restoration in which the author recovers the fragments of his life and turns them into a coherent narrative. Engaged in the writing of their own death, Arenas and Guibert transgress the social conventions concerning self-exhibition in their endeavor to unveil the self and spell out the unsayable.

The project of self-revelation of both authors, who want to express themselves in good faith and offer themselves as "totally naked" to the eyes of the world, rests on a structural denial of privacy. Stricken with the AIDS virus, recognizing the inevitability of their physical death, they are forced to produce fictions and figures in order to arrive at the self-knowledge they seek. Their imminent end gives them a reason to continue writing and prevents them from destroying the directness of genuine thought through patient labor. In their case, sincerity is not to be understood as a peeling away of false masks to reveal an underlying truth, but rather as a rhetoric of exposure that functions as a public performance in the way Paul de Man has described it.

Witnessing the death struggles of the socially excluded people with AIDS, the reader of these books is faced not only with the author's voyeuristic desires, but also—in a cathartic mode—with the shocking spectacle of his own death to come. Like Arenas, Guibert desperately needs the reader in order to write himself. Although the two authors are bent on demonstrating their uprightness and assert the right to say everything in order to fulfill an autobiographical pact with their readership, they probe the limits of sincerity not only by a stylistic extravagance, but also by an excessive disclosure of their personal past, unmasking enemies and betraying the confidences of their bosom friends.

According to Philippe Lejeune, the autobiographical pact implies that writers seek to maintain a sincere relationship to their audiences and to the ethical imperatives of that relation. More specifically, it presupposes a limitation of the writer's self-exposure as a guarantee of the narrator's reliability. The writerly projects of the shameless self-advertisers Arenas and Guibert, however, remain far from this definition. They consist of a courageous act of showing themselves from every possible angle, to own up to all their fears, passions, dreams, and faults, as well as to pour out their own secrets and those of other people, all the while betraying and inventing. By donning a death mask for an extravagant performance, the prosopopeic "voice-from-beyond-the-grave" inevitably falls short of the reader's expectation of sincerity that is considered essential to the autobiographical pact.

REFERENCE MATTER

Notes

1. Bauman has looked at these tall-tale traditions (1986). See also his *Let Your Words Be Few* for an analysis of Puritan pieties and the demeanor of modesty in the seventeenth-century Quaker ideology.

2. Such work recently has been undertaken by Jeff Opland, Liz Gunner, and David Coplan among others.

3. *The Oxford English Dictionary*, s.v. "Sincere," http://www.oed.com/ (accessed December 19, 2005).

4. There is evidence, however, that *Lamentacions* was in part written earlier, during the period of Anne Askew's heresy trial. There is thoughtful discussion of the Edwardian character of the text, with its Lutheran influences, which are suggestive for the dating of the work. See Hiscock (2002).

5. John Foxe's recreation of the scene in his *Book of Martyrs* is ambiguous because it does the work of reconciling his stock misogyny with his sympathy for Parr's Puritanism. His literary strategy is to resolve these through having Parr abuse her own womankind, placing the standard misogynistic rhetoric within her own voice. In Foxe's telling of the scene, it is she who berates herself:

"Your majesty," quoth she, "doth right-well know, neither I myself am ignorant, what great imperfection and weakness by our first creation is allotted unto us women, to be ordained and appointed as inferior and subject unto man as our head; from which head all our direction ought to proceed: and that as God made man to his own shape and likeness, whereby he, being endued with more special gifts of perfection, might rather be stirred to the contemplation of heavenly things." (Quoted in Hiscock 2002, 182.)

Through this act of ostentatious surrender, Parr apparently submits herself to an absolutist patriarchy that must surely be at odds with her own Protestant convictions, as well as with her understanding of her calling.

She is surely moved by a fear for her physical safety when she repeatedly insists on her sincerity. Despite this period of critical threat, Parr managed to outlive her husband, the king. After his death, she had an ally in Henry's son Edward, whom she had raised to Protestant belief. Edward, however, was no more than a boy when he succeeded to the throne and was dead by the age of 15.

6. Francesco Guicciardini, for example, notes in his *Ricordi*: "And yet the position I have filled under several Popes has obliged me for personal reasons to desire their greatness. But for this I should have loved Martin Luther as myself" (cited in Martin 1997, 1321).

7. Up until the thirteenth century, trial by ordeal had provided the common scheme for social justice. Here the accused would be subjected to some kind of test—say, a trial by fire or water—through which the body became the site of proving innocence. There can be little doubt that such findings were essentially arbitrary.

8. This shift that will come, by the seventeenth century, to define the French enemy through antithesis as redolent with "specious tropes." See, for example, Thomas Spratt's *History of the Royal Society* (1667).

9. He effectively suggests that it is upon grounds of habit and convention that "the intelligent Agent" attributes actions to the body associated with itself, whether in the past or in the present.

10. It has been suggested that the first work was a rejected interpretation of the theme by Caravaggio. I became interested in art history's "will to autograph" because of what it suggests about the history of the autonomous subject in relation to knowledge systems, identity, and matters of value. The meaning and value of a work of art have increasingly become assimilated to the named artist, and any such works that have an ambiguous authorship are less desirable and cannot hold their value. I am not suggesting that the identification of evidence (either external or internal to the work of art) is not hermeneutically powerful—and now in ways indispensable—to the practices of art critical writing. Rather, I am curious as to what the stabilizing of that system of knowledge means in relation to poststructuralist enquiry. I see the art historical concern with authentication as instructive about an episteme in which the unconscious imperative is to produce a noncontradictory subject. Various art works are tested against a propositional idea of such a hypothetical subject, and various instruments of testing are brought to bear in order to verify their consistency for a hypothesized continuous identity. The problem of the two "conversion" scenes under discussion constitutes a nice enigma. "Conversion" necessarily invokes the instability of subjectivity. Thus the thematic content of the paintings under discussion (the conversion of St. Paul) is simultaneously staged as an art historical question over authorship and authenticity ("Are they painted by Caravaggio?"), and both paintings foreground early modernity's discourses of selfhood.

11. Much of the substance of this dispute is covered through a set of interactions in the *Burlington Magazine* in which Antonio Morassi asserts that the so-called first version is indeed a Caravaggio and that this was the traditional attribution from as early as 1701 (1952, 118). Denis Mahon uses chronology, and the fact that the work is on cypress wood rather than Caravaggio's favored canvas, in

order to argue that the work must be the work of "an able follower" (Morassi 1952, 119). The argument *for* the use of cypress is that it formed one of the terms of the commission.

12. The celebrated case of Martin Guerre documented by Montaigne and so provocatively analysed by Zemon Davis in recent years provides evidence of this enquiry.

13. Processes may well also have stalled because of the death of its prime mover, the Cardinal, before the chapel was completed.

14. The hugely powerful Catherine de Medici (a relative of Marie's and mother of Henri's previous wife, Marguerite de Valois) had herself played a direct role in the final completion of the basilica through personal donation.

15. Hence the English etymological histories discussed above resonate with Caravaggio's production of images within the Contarelli Chapel. It is significant that Catherine de Medici, who engineered the marriage between France and Rome, was also the mother-in-law of Mary, Queen of Scots, who was the Catholic antagonist ultimately beheaded by the Protestant Queen Elizabeth of England.

16. For those who favour the argument for "version 1" (Figure 1.1) being a Caravaggio, it is identified as the first version of the work commissioned for the Contarelli Chapel, a painting that was rejected by its commissioners. The second version is the work that now hangs *in situ* in the chapel. We see in the lower third of the painting Saul, who lies on the ground, his hands shielding his blinded eyes (Figure 1.2). The groom who accompanies him occupies the attention in the middle ground, and he clasps his spear and shield as if to use them to defend Saul. It has been suggested that the iconographies from the Counter-Reformation often invoked Roman armor in order to establish a visual association linking recent Catholic martyrs with the suffering experienced by the early church. The Council of Trent in the middle of the sixteenth century undertook to engage in a Holy War, establishing seminaries for the training of priests. See Olson 2002.

17. The poem (101 six-line stanzas) is entitled *Sentimenientos a los agravios de Christo nuestro bien por la nación Hebrea*. This episode of flaying the statue is recounted by Daniel L. Heiple.

18. Deleuze suggests that the confounding of inside and outside is inherent in the Baroque project. He discusses the neo-Platonic tradition with its stairway that has at its head a transcendent One, with the ranks of the many in serried rows below (1993, 29–30). This he contrasts with the Baroque paradigm, where there are only two floors, with a split between upper and lower along the seam of a fold that turns back upon itself, like a prototypical Möbius strip. Deleuze cites Tintoretto and El Greco in making his case, but I would suggest that Caravaggio's *Conversion of St. Paul* (version 2) follows this pattern through his metaphorics of surface and interiority.

19. Sharon Achinstein traces the hardening of attitudes toward Jews in John

Foxe's writings, which manifest an increasingly racialized characterization of Jewishness. Foxe interprets Luther's attitude to the Jewish question as changing ground, with a considerable shift from his early, relatively sympathetic inclusionism, to the later vitriol of his "On the Jews and Their Lies," a tract that calls for the burning of synagogues, the razing of Jewish homes, and the destruction of sacred texts. Achinstein, "John Foxe and the Jews."

20. A related argument has been made by Julia Reinhard Lupton (1997, 73–89).

CHAPTER 2

1. "At that time, Jesus, alone with Peter, was roaming / Along the bank of the lake, near Nazareth, / In the burning, flat sun of midday . . ."

2. Adorno, cited in Nicholson (1999, 62). The passage comes from Adorno's essay "Charmed Language," concerning the poetry of Rudolf Borchardt.

3. Journal entry for 19 December 1906, in Renard (1960, 1096).

4. Freud, letter to Martha Bernays, 8 November 1885, cited in Shattuck (1991, 39).

5. Including foreigners: the Cours de gramophonie got its start a few years earlier, in 1905, in a "live" course sponsored by the Alliance Française.

6. Mockel's review functioned as a kind of advertisement for the book of poems, which had been published by the press of the *Mercure de France* in 1904. I suspect that this detailed reading of Van Lerberghe played a role in Fauré's conception of the songs, because it was Mockel himself who apparently introduced Fauré to the poetic cycle when Fauré traveled to Brussels in 1906.

CHAPTER 3

1. Vondel lived from 1587 to 1679. On the situation in the Dutch Republic and on sixteenth- and seventeenth-century theory about the political system, see van Gelderen (1992, 2001, 2002, 2003). On the issue of sovereignty in relation to Vondel's plays, see Korsten (2006).

2. See Douglas (1986); Ann Swidler, "Culture in Action: Symbols and Strategies," *American Sociological Review* 51, no. 2 (April 1986): 273–286; and Brunsson (1989), who are at the basis of Krasner's study on the nature and types of sovereignty in the modern world. The latter considers hypocrisy the result of the conflict between two kinds of logic: "Logics of consequences see political actions and outcomes, including institutions, as the product of rational calculating behaviour designed to maximize a given set of unexplained preference. . . . Logics of appropriateness understand political action as a product of rules, roles, identities that stipulate appropriate behaviour in given situations" (Krasner 1999, 5). As a result, Krasner sees hypocrisy as a deviation from a basis of appropriateness.

3. On the historical development of the *hypocrita* into a dissembler and actor, see Wikander (2002).

4. See, for instance, Smit (1956–1962, 205).

5. On *Lucifer* as a dramatical failure, see King (1979). On the fact that heaven is a state in *Lucifer*, see Osterkamp (1979).

6. On this, see Ankersmit (1996, 21–63) and Hoogers (1999).

7. Some commentators see the play as an allegorical reflection on political problems in the Netherlands in the last half of the 1640s. Stern (1999) sees in Phaiton the over-ambitious stadtholder William II.

8. Despotism does not represent the absolute opposite of democracy in this context. Plato accused democracy of being the despotism of the street, which of course is also a form of what Ankersmit (1996) would call mimetic representation.

9. On checking political responsibility by asking for an account of what rulers have done, not what they plan to do, see van Gunsteren (1999).

10. Foucault (1997). See also Tina Besley, "Foucault, Truth Telling and Technologies of the Self in Schools," *Journal of Educational Enquiry* 6, no. 1 (2005): 76–89.

11. On the first performance of the play, see Smit (1956–1962). On its historical importance and reception, see Vondel (1994b) and Porteman (1988).

12. See especially Koppenol (1999). All translations from the play are mine.

13. See especially van Stipriaan (1996).

14. Of major importance are Heidegger (2004) and Schmitt (2004). Heidegger discussed the passage in his early Freiburg lectures of 1920–1921, and Schmitt implicitly took issue with these already in his book *Politische Theologie* of 1922. On this, see Grossheutschi (1996). On the way in which Heidegger deals with the notion in his *Der Nomos der Erde im Völkerrecht des Jus Publicum Europaeum* (1950), see Versluis (2006).

15. On the importance of Badeloch, see Prandoni (2005).

16. See Lefort, *Essais sur le politique* and *L'invention démocratique* (1986, 1995).

17. The process of mediatization took place especially in Napoleonic Germany. See, for example, Velde (2006).

CHAPTER 4

1. For external and internal points of view, see Hart (1994, 89–91).

2. Explicitly Dworkin (1977), and, less explicitly (among others), MacCormick (1978) and Peczenick (1990).

CHAPTER 5

1. Interestingly, George Pichter, in his recollections of Austin's seminars at Harvard, also uses the term "conversion" to evoke the impression and effect made

by the "new philosophy." What to think of a philosophy whose mode of reception seems to be—or cannot but be—"conversion"?

2. The second chapter of Cavell's *A Pitch of Philosophy*, entitled "Counter-Philosophy and the Pawn of Voice" (1994, 53–127), appeared in a shorter version in his *Philosophical Passages* (1995, 42–65). The latter book also contains the transcription of a discussion devoted to the same theme (1995, 66–90).

3. Cavell, *The Claim of Reason: Wittgenstein, Skepticism, Morality, and Tragedy* (Oxford: Oxford University Press, 1979, reprint 1999), 310, 362, 373, 391.

4. That is to say, both the "illocutionary force" and the "perlocutionary effect" of its "locution" must have seriousness—and sincerity—as their element or target for the utterance to be felicitous in this respect. Does the "so as to be taken seriously" imply that seriousness and sincerity are up to me, up to the "I" of the performative after all, even where the effect on others—the perlocution—is at issue? Is the "effect" not up to the others, to the "you" whose call it is to decide on the effect that "my" words take? If so, there would be no distinction between the performative and passionate utterance, that is to say, between the illocutionary force and perlocutionary effect, as Cavell seems to suggest. We will come to that.

5. Here is the dialogue in which the line appears:

Hippolytus. O mother earth, O open sunlight, what unspeakable words I have heard uttered!
Nurse. Silence, my son, before someone hears you shout!
Hippolytus. I have heard dread things: I cannot now be silent.

. . .

Nurse. My child, I beg you, do not break your oath!
Hippolytus. My tongue swore, but my mind is not on oath.

6. In addition to the types of infelicities Austin has introduced in passing, he mentions "certain other kinds of ill which infect *all* utterances." And these "likewise," he continues, "though again they might be brought into a more general account, we are deliberately at present excluding. I mean, for example, the following: a performative utterance will, for example, be *in a peculiar way* hollow or void if said by an actor on the stage, or if introduced in a poem, or spoken in soliloquy. This applies in a similar manner to any and every utterance—a sea-change is special circumstances. Language in such circumstances is in special ways—intelligibly—used not seriously, but in ways *parasitic* upon its normal use—ways which fall under the doctrine of the *etiolations* of language. All this we are *excluding* from consideration. Our performative utterances, felicitous or not, are to be understood as issued in ordinary circumstances" (1975, 21–22).

7. Hammer (2002, 161), quoting Cavell (1994, 75).

8. Again: "Our performative utterances, felicitous or not, are to be understood as issued in ordinary circumstances" (Austin 1975, 22).

9. In response to the questions "To what variety of 'act' does the notion of

infelicity apply?" and "How widespread is infelicity?" Austin writes the following: "infelicity is an ill to which *all* acts are heir which have the general character of ritual or ceremonial, all *conventional* acts: not indeed that *every* ritual is liable to every form of infelicity (but then nor is every performative utterance)" (1962, 18–19). Austin refers to the domains of law and ethics to substantiate this point, but he also leaves no doubt that infelicities apply to "*all* ceremonial acts, not merely verbal ones" (25).

10. More specifically, while Cavell deems the "comparison" between Austin and Freud on these matters "uncontroversially welcome," he criticizes their interpretation in light of what he calls "controversial theories of reference." Lacan's "differential referential" would be a case in point, but so is Emile Benveniste's "linguistic [re]interpretation" of Austin's performative (Cavell 2003, xv).

11. But a critical aside might be in order here: could one not be serious and sincere, without *prima facie* being (or having) a body, say, while on the phone, on line, or represented by "writing" (in the most general sense Derrida gives to the term)? Are technological media, as Mark Hansen suggests in his *New Philosophy for New Media*, just tied to different forms of embodiment? Or are things more complicated, more novel? And are these serious, not to mention sincere, questions?

CHAPTER 6

I would like to thank Ernst van Alphen, Mieke Bal, Kiarina Kordela, and Bhaskar Sarkar for their generous, critical, and altogether invaluable comments on this essay, as well as Matthew Hadley for his research assistance. I would like also to acknowledge the obvious: Gayatri Chakravorty Spivak's influential essay "Can the Subaltern Speak?" inspired the title of my own essay. Whereas in the end the answer I give to the titular question of my essay is the very same answer she gives to the titular question of her essay, I do not share her assessments of Gilles Deleuze, Michel Foucault, and Jacques Derrida in that essay. See Spivak, "Can the Subaltern Speak?" in *Marxism and the Interpretation of Culture*, eds. C. Nelson and L. Grossberg (Basingstoke: Macmillan, 1988), 271–313.

1. Spinoza 2000, 150; translation modified.

2. This preface and its formulations regarding sincerity are indebted to Kiarina Kordela's work, and, in particular, to her understanding of the momentous implications of Spinoza's definition of truth (as the standard both of itself and of the false) for any theory of power and of ideology. For a compelling account of Spinoza's definition of truth as the "primary psychoanalytic principle," see her brilliant study *$urplus. Lacan, Spinoza* and especially the second section of the introduction, "Scientific 'Neo-Spinozism' and Hegel" (Kordela 2007).

3. For a relevant discussion of Pasolini's documentary and of Foucault's review, see Schérer (2004) 177–185, and, in particular, 183–184.

4. In Gramsci, not only are the concept of subalternity and the Southern Question intricately related to one another, but also the latter constitutes the crucial condition of possibility for the former, to the extent to which it was precisely the confrontation with the Italian South that made it necessary for Gramsci to produce a concept expressive of power relations that would include yet not be limited to class relations. A similar point has been made recently by Spivak when she writes that the "starting point for a singular itinerary of the word 'subaltern' can be Antonio Gramsci's 'Southern Question' rather than his more general discussions of the subaltern" (Spivak 1988, 475). I understand Spivak to be suggesting that it is in his discussion of the Southern Question that one is to look for more substantive elaborations of the concept of subalternity. In another and complementary essay ("The Southern Answer: Pasolini, Gramsci, Decolonization"), I discuss more extensively the relation between subalternity and the Southern Question by focusing on Pasolini's poetry of the 1950s and 1960s, as well as by discussing relevant moments in the writings of Frantz Fanon, Sékou Touré, Edward Said, and Gramsci himself. In this essay, I argue that Pasolini needs to be considered the most important and most original inheritor of the Gramscian project inasmuch as (a) he was the first to understand that Gramsci's engagement with the Southern Question had to be rethought in global terms, and (b) he catapulted the concept of subalternity at once into the planetary as well as the sexual arena.

5. For a thoughtful discussion of Pasolini's idiosyncratic and sustained engagement with the genre of the documentary, see Vighi (2002, 491–510). Although Vighi does not discuss *Love Meetings*, one of the main arguments of his essay is fully consonant with my own arguments regarding this documentary. Vighi writes, for example, that "Pasolini's use of the nonfictional camera seems to be underpinned by the ideological attempt to preserve a specifically chosen dimension of the historical real; and, what is more significant, to record a dimension of the real that by its own nature defies discursive appropriation" (493). This is an assessment that I will corroborate below.

6. Viano notes astutely that this passage ought to be related to Pasolini's obsessive use of frontal close-ups in this documentary. Such use of the close-up, Viano suggests, indexes Pasolini's attempt to wring psychological truth from those interviewed (1993, 124).

7. Foucault seems to have caught a glimpse of precisely such an eroticism when he writes of some of the interviewees that "they gather round, approve or grumble, arms on shoulders, face against face. Laughter, affection, a bit of fever quickly circulate among these bodies that bunch together or lightly touch each other. And they speak of themselves with all the more restraint and distance as their contact is livelier and warmer" (1998b, 230). In an interview on Sade—two years before writing his review of *Love Meetings*—Foucault credits Sade with having "formulated an eroticism proper to a disciplinary society" and concludes by stating: "It's

time to leave all that behind, and Sade's eroticism with it. We must invent with the body, with its elements, surfaces, volumes, and thicknesses, a nondisciplinary eroticism—that of a body in a volatile and diffused state, with its chance encounters and unplanned pleasures" (1998a, 226–227). Undoubtedly, one of the reasons why Foucault found himself so drawn to Pasolini's documentary is that he sensed the palpable presence of such a nondisciplinary eroticism in it.

8. See Deleuze (1988, 70–93), as well as Foucault (1990b, 9–58). On these and related matters, see also my "Philopoesis: A Theoretico-Methodological Preface" (Casarino 2002, xiii–xli and especially xix–xxii). The confines of this essay do not allow me to explicate fully a claim that is nonetheless implied throughout, namely, a claim regarding the close proximity between the Deleuzian-Foucaultian concept of the outside and the Lacanian concept of the real. Here, I will limit myself to pointing out that these concepts are at the very least analogous to one another, in the strict sense of being similar in function yet not in structure.

9. As they famously argue in the *Manifesto of the Communist Party*, the bourgeoisie "compels all nations, on pain of extinction, to adopt the bourgeois mode of production; it compels them to introduce what it calls civilization in their midst, *i.e.* to become bourgeois themselves. In one word, it creates a world after its own image" (Marx and Engels 1978, 477).

10. I have written elsewhere about the crucial role that this image plays in Pasolini's cinematic iconography. See especially my "Pasolini in the Desert" (Casarino 2004, 97–102), but see also my "Oedipus Exploded: Pasolini and the Myth of Modernization" (Casarino 1992, 27–47).

11. The crucial importance of this opening sequence, and in particular the role played by the Sicilian children in it, are also noted and discussed by Angelo Restivo in his excellent study *The Cinema of Economic Miracles: Visuality and Modernization in the Italian Art Film* (2002, 78).

12. In this sense, I could not disagree more with Viano's assessment of the roles played by Moravia and Musatti here as well as of Pasolini's understanding of his own project in *Love Meetings*. In brief, Viano takes the conversation among Moravia, Musatti, and Pasolini completely at face value, and concludes that Pasolini not only shares their views on the importance of the documentary but also "sees himself as a crusader, a soldier of God fighting to liberate the Holy Land (the body and society) from the infidels (ignorance and fear)" (Viano 1993, 122–123). Although spoken in a different context—an interview regarding the film he made immediately after *Love Meetings*, namely, *The Gospel According to St. Matthew*—Pasolini's following comment is nonetheless relevant here: "It is against my nature . . . to desacralize things and people." When Pasolini suggests during the conversation with Moravia and Musatti that they understand his documentary as a crusade against ignorance and fear and as a desacralization of sex, thus, he is indicating implicitly that his own understanding of this project

is indeed quite different from theirs. The excerpt from the interview is cited in Naomi Greene (1990, 72).

13. Cited in "Pegasos: a literature-related site in Finland," http://www.kirjasto .sci.fi/moravia.htm.

14. See Fredric Jameson's famous dictum: "History is what hurts" (1981, 102). If earlier I stated that "the real" and "the outside" are analogous concepts (see note 8 above), here I am suggesting that "history" in the Jamesonian sense is analogous to both those concepts. This triangulation too needs to be elaborated further at a later time.

15. Here is the original version: "Dove si vede una specie di commesso viaggiatore che gira l'Italia a sondare gli Italiani sui loro gusti sessuali: e ciò non per lanciare un prodotto, ma nel più sincero proposito di capire e di riferire fedelmente."

CHAPTER 7

1. See, for example, Attwell: "The TRC [is] an obvious reference point of the hearings in part one" (2001, 866); Gorra argues that the book is not an allegory of the TRC, yet the connection can be "no accident" (1999); Kossew writes that "Coetzee's novel also resonates with the national public spectacle of shame, confession and forgiveness that was the Truth and Reconciliation Commission" (2003, 155).

2. The fact that the conventional nature of speech acts can always potentially undermine their seriousness was first demonstrated by Derrida, "Signature Event Context," in a response to Austin (1975). For an overview of this discussion see Culler (1981). Felman (2003) investigates the implications of this insight for an understanding of literature.

3. It is important to note that the actual TRC did not make atonement a condition of amnesty. As Attwell points out, in this "Coetzee seems to be in agreement with it, not in opposition to it" (2001, 866).

4. "[T]he self cannot tell the truth of itself to itself and come to rest without the possibility of self-deception. True confession does not come from the sterile monologue of the self or from the dialogue with its own self-doubt but . . . from faith and grace" (Coetzee 1999a, 291).

5. See, for example, Gordimer (1984). Gordimer, in "Living in the Interregnum," relates realism to *integrity* when she states that the task of the South African writer "can be fulfilled only in the integrity Chekhov demanded: 'to describe so truthfully . . . that the reader can no longer evade it'" (1988, 250). Coetzee, in turn, criticizes the view that novels like his own, which were not "investigations of real historical forces," were somehow "lacking in *seriousness*," defending the view that a novel should not necessarily "depend on the model of history" for "its principal structuration," but "operate in terms of its own procedures and issues" (1988, 2, 3). Attwell offers a subtle defense of Coetzee's mode of writing as an intervention

into the political situation of South Africa, coining the term "situational metafiction" (2001).

6. Coetzee's contributions to *The Lives of Animals* were later included in *Elizabeth Costello: Eight Lessons*. All references will be to this edition.

7. For example, Boehmer concludes: "The surrender of self through empathy is a state which Lurie in time does come to achieve" (2002, 346). Kossew states that Lurie finds "a kind of 'grace' at the novel's end" (2003, 156).

8. Compare Costello's remark on the Holocaust: "The horror is that the killers refused to think themselves into the place of their victims, as did everyone else" (Coetzee 2003, 79).

9. Earlier, during a dinner following her first lecture, Costello states, "I don't know what I think. . . . I often wonder what thinking is, what understanding is. . . . Understanding a thing often looks to me like playing with one of those Rubik cubes. Once you have made all the little bricks snap into place, hey presto, you understand" (Coetzee 2003, 90).

10. Indeed, Costello opens her lecture by pointing out that we rely on metaphors of slaughter when we try to make sense of the Holocaust: "'They went like sheep to the slaughter.' 'They died like animals.' 'The Nazi butchers killed them.' Denunciation of the camps reverberates so fully with the language of the stockyard and the slaughterhouse that it is barely necessary for me to prepare the ground for the comparison I am about to make" (Coetzee 2003, 64–65). By preparing the *ground* of her comparison in this way, she destabilizes the relation between the *comparant* and the *comparé*. It is unclear which of the two is "literal" and which one is "figural."

CHAPTER 8

1. See, for example, Maurizio Lazzarato, "Immaterial Labour" (Hardt and Virno 1996, 133–146); Paolo Virno, "Virtuosity and Revolution" (Hardt and Virno 1996, 189–209); and Brian Holmes (2005).

2. "Post-Fordism is the empirical realisation of the 'Fragment on Machines' by Marx" (Virno 2004, 100). The "Fragment on Machines" passage can be found in Marx (1973, 699–743). For reservations concerning the separation of labor power and value, see Wright (2005, 34–45), Caffentzis (2005), and Dyer-Witheford (2005).

3. My use of the term "tactics" here is derived from Michel de Certeau, who distinguishes a tactic from a strategy and defines it as "a calculus which cannot count on a 'proper' (a spatial or institutional localization), nor thus on a borderline distinguishing the other as a visible totality" (1984, xix).

4. I would argue that Ranciere's deployment of what he calls *dissensus*, Bruno Latour's characterisation of *imbroglios*, and Michel Foucault's *dispositif* all in their different ways point to the merits of an ontology embedded, in a strong sense, in

relational terms. In this regard it might also be timely to recall (as does Bourriaud) Marx's famous "Sixth Thesis on Feuerbach," in which he claims that "the essence of man is no abstraction inherent in each single individual. In reality, it is the ensemble of the social relations" (1976, 122). Marx accuses Feuerbach of abstracting the "religious sentiment" from the "historical process." If we mischievously replace "religious sentiment" with "aesthetic taste" here, we may have the seeds of a salutary warning against the activities of the contemporary art world's border police.

5. The term "*la Perruque*" is used by de Certeau to describe a form of micro-subversion in which "the worker's own work (is) disguised as work for his employer" (1984, 25).

6. At the time of writing, Jens Haaning, the Russian collective "What Is to Be Done?" Aleksandra Mir, Multiplicity, Bureau d'Etude, Critical Art Ensemble, Raqs Media Collective, and the Yes Men comprise the core of my personal canon, but the examples are legion and growing rapidly.

7. For further discussion of the unequal distribution of cultural capital in the contemporary art sector, see McNeill (2002).

CHAPTER 9

This chapter has been excerpted from Adelson (2005, 123–126, 133–149). This material is reprinted here with permission of Palgrave Macmillan and the author, who retains the copyright. For complete original notes, see Adelson (202–210).

1. Sassen, "Spatialities and Temporalities," 216.

2. Sassen similarly approaches gender in a global economy as "a strategic nexus" of structural developments rather than a predominantly experiential category (1998, 85).

3. Appadurai takes the extreme position that "*the imagination as a social practice*" becomes "the key component of the new global order" (1996, 31).

4. Ha underscores dehumanization by likening the experience of migrant laborers in Germany to both Nazi mechanisms of genocidal "selection" and "a modern 'slave market'" (1999, 20). Only the initial emphasis on dehumanization is characteristic of citations of Frisch generally. (Unless otherwise indicated, translations of work cited are by Adelson.)

5. National narratives of the two postwar German states are shaped by similar regimes of rhetorical incorporation. The Basic Law of the Federal Republic asserts the inviolability of human dignity for individuals, and the German Democratic Republic was formally conceived as a state of workers and farmers.

6. As the anthropologist Levent Soysal observes, "The migration story differentiates its subject, the migrant, along gender and ethnic lines" (2003, 496).

7. Y. Soysal, *Limits of Citizenship*, 135; L. Soysal, "Labor to Culture," 500.

8. Occasionally Chow uses gender and sexuality interchangeably in reference to minority subjects, but her overarching arguments focus on gender and ethnic-

ity. Contrast this with Judith Butler's account of sociolinguistic interpellation, which stresses the production of abjection that minority subjects struggle to counter, while Chow foregrounds the production of ethnicity as a commodity. For Chow, "feminism in the West" is complicit with liberalism, her primary target (Butler 1997; Chow 2002, 154).

9. For Chow, "*to be ethnic is to protest*—but perhaps less for actual emancipation of any kind than for the benefits of worldwide visibility, currency, and circulation" (2002, 48).

10. Other aspects of Chow's project and mine are incompatible or simply different. For example, Chow faults liberal tolerance for "recurrent antagonisms, atrocities, and genocides that take place every day around the world" (2002, 26). I am not persuaded that liberal forms of violence are the root cause of "racial and ethnic unrest in the contemporary world today" (15). This is in any event not the subject of my investigation.

11. Citing Azade Seyhan on the "almost exclusively autobiographical" form of migrant writing today (Seyhan 1996, 180), Chow illuminates the problematic relationship between celebrations of hybridity and the genre of autobiography (Chow 2002, 138–146).

12. Like Chow, Seyhan speaks of a "confessional idiom," especially for women writers of Turkish migration (Seyhan 2001, 136).

13. For Chow, "the ethnic community" seems to refer to a second-order source of pressure on individuals to perform as protestant ethnics (2002, 190–191). It is not clear how Chow understands the relationship between community and capitalism.

14. One looks in vain, however, for a definition of cultural capital in Guillory's book, for Guillory claims to follow "Bourdieu's own practice in constructing the concept through the contexts of its deployment" (Guillory 1993, 341).

15. The Turkish version was subsequently published in 1985 by a German press. Adapted from the Turkish, the English translation differs greatly from the German, on which my analysis is based. To avoid confusion I will therefore use the German-language title here. I provide my own translations for passages cited where such details matter, but page references are to the German and English publications.

16. See Gil Gott (1994), who favors the kind of "protestant" claim that Chow disparages.

17. B. Venkat Mani discusses *Bitte nix Polizei* and other work by Ören against the foil of another writer's "death knell" for guest worker literature and the victim narratives of cultural difference it ostensibly represented (Mani 2002, 113). According to Mani, Ören's novella revolves around "financial troubles" experienced by German and Turkish characters in an earlier phase of West German history, while a later novel is "symptomatic" of changed material circumstances in the 1990s (117, 125). To the degree that Ören's evolving depiction of Ali Itir

challenges cultural and economic stereotypes, then and now, Mani argues, the specter of guest workers "will continue to haunt the house of German literature for years to come" (129). Mani and I agree that the figure of the guest worker is spectral but not peripheral to contemporary German culture. Yet Mani's largely thematic discussion of economy and ethnicity cannot explain how the narrative embrace of these motifs comes to matter (in both senses of the term) in Ören's work. The discussion here thus articulates the materiality of the text in terms of literary labors of imagination and the cultural capital of migration.

18. Rosa Luxemburg's body was found in this canal in 1919 after she and Karl Liebknecht, another founding member of the German Communist Party, had been murdered by members of a right-wing militia.

19. In the German, police are convinced that a rape occurred despite "a few things that don't match up in the depiction of the event" (Ören 1983, 79). In the more tenuous English version, police "sensed that an assault might have taken place" but doubt "the credibility" of certain details in the woman's report (1992, 118). Ören may have taken some cues for this story from a rape trial resulting from events in 1978 involving a German woman and Turkish youths. The trial became ensconced in public lore when Werner Schiffauer, a social scientist, used it to situate sexuality at the center of cultural conflict. Heidi Rösch explicitly compares Schiffauer and Ören in intercultural terms (1992, 101–108).

20. Suggesting that only the manner of death is uncertain, Mani assumes that the corpse fished from the canal is Ali Itir's (2002, 117). The English translation explicitly lists suicide, accident, and murder as possible causes of death; the German indicates only that the deceased may have been the "victim of a crime" (Ören 1981, 87).

21. Ören, *Please, No Police*, 25.

22. The case is never investigated as murder. Only the rumor mill produces the image of the brutal foreigner, which is missing in the English translation.

23. See, for example, Susan Anderson (2002).

24. In German this is rendered "Unperson" (Ören 1981, 20). The English translation weakens this: "not even a 'person'" (1992, 25). A passing reference to ritual ablutions identifies Ali Itir as a Muslim, but this attribution never becomes a narrative motif.

25. Bruno Gramke, the German *pater familias* in the story, articulates a parallel between this situation and his own in the early 1950s, when Germans who came west from the "Soviet Zone" were treated "like illegals" (Ören 1983, 59; 1992, 87).

26. According to Sassen, citizenship was also "of minor importance in the 1970s and 1980s" where social services for migrant laborers were concerned. "What mattered above all was residence and legal alien status" (1998, 23).

27. The German text uses two different words for contraband, one denoting goods that are smuggled and one for goods traded on the black market.

28. See Adelson (2005) for extended reflections on "touching tales" as an analytic.

29. In linguistic terms Emile Benveniste considers "the 'third person' . . . literally a 'non-person'" (1971, 221). Bianca Theisen makes a similar observation in her study of "indexical realism" in postwar Austrian literature (2003, 109).

30. This last example conjoins heterosexual normativity, economic solvency, and symbolic personhood.

31. Susan C. Anderson rightly registers the importance of snow and ice in Ören's narrative, but our assessments of these motifs diverge. For Anderson, the snow dangerously obscures "distinctions between Turks and Germans" (2002, 150). I emphasize an indexical economy of representation that cannot be grasped in terms of personal or collective identities.

32. The German words *Tathergang* and *Täter* derive from the verb *tun*, "to do." The standard translation of *Täter* is "perpetrator," but literally it means "one who commits an act." *Tathergang* literally means "the course of an action." Ali's surname derives from the transitive Turkish verb *itmek*, to "push" or "compel," which connotes an effect exerted by action.

CHAPTER 11

1. Derrida, "Le cinéma et ses fantômes," 82; translation mine. I have supplied my own translation in cases where no English translation has been published.

2. Considering Derrida's mode of writing, Hobson insists on the importance of what she refers to as syntax. Concepts, that is, do not exist independently of the context in which they appear. Thus, she rejects a "lexematic" reading of Derrida organized around individual terms—like *différance* or "dissemination," for instance—that does not take into account their functionality within larger "circuits of argument" (1998, 3).

3. The notion of iterability makes concepts—like any sign—ghostly and unstable, since they become haunted by the structural possibility of transformation through repetition. As Derrida puts it in *Limited Inc.*, his famous response to John Searle, "Once it is iterable, to be sure, a mark marked with a supposedly 'positive' value . . . can be made to carry its other, its negative double. But iterability is also, by the same token, the condition of the values said to be positive. The simple fact is that this condition of possibility is structurally divided or 'differing-deferring' (*différante*)" (Derrida 1988, 70).

4. Authorization, as I understand it in this context, refers to a pair of distinct yet related concepts. First, it refers to the act of confirming something on the basis of one's authority, an authority that is itself constituted through authorizing strategies. In Western legal practice, for instance, witnesses may authorize themselves, and their testimonies, by swearing to "tell the truth and nothing but the truth." Second, authorization alludes to what Michel Foucault, in his semi-

nal essay "What Is an Author?" has termed the "author-function." As a discursive function, the entity called author—and its position toward the text—changes according to time, culture, and type of discourse (1980, 130, 137–138).

5. I take the notion of *performing truth* from Derrida's discussion of St. Augustine's *Confessions*: "When he asks in truth of God and already of his readers why he confesses himself to God when God knows everything, the response makes it appear that what is essential to the avowal or the testimony does not consist in an experience of knowledge. Its act is not reduced to informing, teaching, making known." Rather, it is a performative act "in order to 'stir up love' by 'doing the truth (*veritatem facere*)'" (Derrida 1992, 286).

6. In "History of the Lie," Derrida relates his "conceded confession," that it is impossible to know whether he is sincere or not, explicitly to the spectral (2001b, 65).

7. *Ghost Dance* moves between two languages (English and French) as well as between two cities (London and Paris). Often, it is not even clear where a particular scene takes place, or why the actors speak which language, since the transitions are neither marked nor motivated by the narrative. When quoting French dialogue, I give my translation first, and add the original in brackets.

8. In the writings and films that I consider, Derrida describes the "beings" (or "non-beings") associated with haunting as *revenants, spectres*, and *fantômes*. The latter terms are etymologically grounded in the visual: their roots are the Latin word *spectrum*, "image, apparition," and the Greek word *phantazein*, "make visible." The *revenant*—the one supposedly returning from the dead—is not necessarily connected to that kind of visibility (Derrida and Stiegler 2002, 116). However, the Derrida of *Ghost Dance* claims that all ghosts (*fantômes*) are also *revenants*: "Les fantômes reviennent . . . , ils sont des revenants."

9. It is right at the beginning of the Luton interview that Derrida mentions his meeting with the filmmaker (1996, 213). Regarding the improvisation he talks about, it seems as if neither McMullen's question nor Derrida's answer has been included (in the precise form cited by Derrida) in the released version of *Ghost Dance*. In the completed film, the philosopher does not say that "an improvisation is absolutely impossible." Thus, the subject of improvisation comes up only once throughout *Ghost Dance*, namely in the short remark that I am considering (*un scénario filmique plus ou moins improvisée*).

10. The screenplay of *Derrida* attributes this voiceover narration to an unpublished interview from 1982 (Dick and Kofman 2005, 93). Could this be the "missing scene" from *Ghost Dance*, returning to haunt another film?

11. Talking to Bernard Stiegler, Derrida regrets his use of the term "science" in the office scene from *Ghost Dance*: "it came to me while improvising" (Derrida and Stiegler 2002, 117). This remark could be related to the complicity between spectral ventriloquy (i.e., something coming to the speaker) and improvisation.

12. These allusions point to the film's international title, which is "Derrida's Elsewhere," while the German title reads "Apropos Jacques Derrida."

CHAPTER 12

For their insightful comments on various versions of this essay, I'm grateful to Ernst van Alphen, Mieke Bal, Peter Rush, Carel Smith, and an anonymous reviewer.

1. See, for example, responses to the revelations that Binjamin Wilkomirski wrote a "memoir" of a Holocaust childhood he did not experience (1997), for example, Maechler (2001) and Vice (2000); see also the imaginary (to some degree) memoir of a mother-daughter relationship by Drusilla Modjeska (1989).

2. See, for example, the criticisms directed at Damien Hirst and Karlheinz Stockhausen, who both made comparisons between the attacks and works of art. On Hirst, see Matthews (2003); on Stockhausen, see Lentricchia and McAuliffe (2003, 6–7).

3. These and other examples can be seen in photographs taken on and after September 11 by hundreds of individuals, exhibited in a storefront in SoHo and later published as *Here Is New York: A Democracy of Photographs* (George et al. 2002). See also Feldschuh (2002).

4. Edkins notes that President Bush was in such haste to commemorate the event that he called for a minute's silence in remembrance of the victims during a press conference at approximately 9:30 a.m., before the third plane had hit the Pentagon and before the towers had collapsed—that is, in the very midst of the attack (2003, 102–103). The will to memorialize thus started even before the event was over, and has included the Tribute in Light (the two blue beams of light projected upwards from Ground Zero, first switched on at the sixth-month anniversary of the attacks); the ceremonies held on September 11 in each subsequent year; and the massive public consultation process regarding the redevelopment of Ground Zero and the need to commemorate the attacks (on the latter, see the discussion in Young [2005, 131–140]).

5. For an interesting account of the limit-case of trauma in the context of autobiography, see Gilmore (2001).

6. A comic book version of the *9/11 Report* has been produced (Jacobson and Colon 2006). No doubt anticipating the possible aspersions that could be cast upon the very idea of a comic book about an event few would associate with comedy, its authors have sought to emphasize the sincerity of their enterprise vis-à-vis the *9/11 Report*, stating that their intention has not been to mock the Commission but to produce an easy-to-read version. Many mainstream American magazines and newspapers refused to publish an earlier comic strip, *In The Shadow of No Towers* (Spiegelman 2004).

7. The Commission presages this at the outset, stating, "our aim has not been to assign individual blame" (National Commission 2004, xvi).

8. Direct criticism is made of the Federal Aviation Authority (FAA), whose staff had told the Commission that it was not seen as their responsibility to tell airlines what to tell pilots regarding security crises on the planes: to that, the *Report* retorts, "We believe such statements do not reflect an adequate appreciation of the FAA's responsibility for the safety and security of civil aviation" (National Commission 2004, 11)—but this is a comment that still fails to *directly* castigate any party for its actions during the attacks.

9. The day of the attacks made literal the cliché that disaster can strike "out of the blue." A frequent theme in survivors' accounts in the aftermath, and in media reports on the day, was that September 11 had begun as a beautiful day with a clear blue sky.

10. In beginning its account of the events in New York, the *Report* states, "we are mindful of the unfair perspective afforded by hindsight. *Nevertheless, we will try to describe what happened* in the following 102 minutes" (National Commission 2004, 285; emphasis added).

11. For a reading of the *Report* that analyzes it less as a government report and more as an example of "the tradition of reconstructed nonfiction narrative," emphasizing its "allegiance to the truth" and "its literary style," see Yagoda (2004).

12. See, for example, the excerpts of calls made by flight attendants Amy Sweeney and Betty Ong on American 11 (National Commission 2004, 6–7). Here is an excerpt of a call from Peter Hanson on United 175 to his father, Lee: "It's getting bad, Dad—A stewardess was stabbed—They seem to have knives and Mace—They said they have a bomb—It's getting very bad on the plane—Passengers are throwing up and getting sick—The plane is making jerky movements— I don't think the pilot is flying the plane—I think we are going down—I think they intend to go to Chicago or someplace and fly into a building—Don't worry, Dad—If it happens, it'll be very fast—My God, my God" (National Commission 2004, 8).

13. See, for example, on United 175: "The hijackers attacked sometime between 8:42 and 8:46. . . . The first operational evidence that something was abnormal on United 175 came at 8:47 when the aircraft changed beacon codes twice within a minute. At 8:51, the flight deviated from its assigned altitude, and a minute later New York air traffic controllers began repeatedly and unsuccessfully trying to contact it. At 8:52, in Easton, Connecticut, a man named Lee Hanson received a phone call from his son, Peter, a passenger on United 175" (National Commission 2004, 7).

14. The hijacking of United 93 and the attempt by passengers to regain control of the plane have been the subject of a number of popular cultural representations. See, for example, the made-for-television movies *Let's Roll: The Story of Flight 93* (2002, dir. Chris Oxley); *Portrait of Courage: The Untold Story of Flight 93* (2006,

dir. David Priest); *Flight 93* (2006, dir. Peter Markle); and the Hollywood release *United 93* (2006, dir. Paul Greengrass). Memoirs written by relatives about various passengers on the flight include Barrett, *Hero of Flight 93* (2002); Beamer and Abraham, *Let's Roll* (2006); and Glick and Zegart, *Your Father's Voice* (2004).

15. A dread suspense arises in this chapter regarding the fate of those within the Towers. For example, "Most civilians . . . began evacuating without waiting for instructions over the intercom system. Some remained to wait for help, as advised by 911 operators. Others simply continued to work" (National Commission 2004, 287). As the chapter progresses, individuals' stories separate themselves into accounts of escape or implicitly death-bound narratives—for example, "By 9:59, at least one person had descended from as high as the 91st floor of [the South] tower, and stairwell A was reported to have been almost empty. Stairwell B was also reported to have contained only a handful of descending civilians at an earlier point in the morning. But just before the tower collapsed, a team of NYPD [Emergency Service Unit] officers encountered a stream of civilians descending an unidentified stairwell" (296).

16. At numerous points, the *9/11 Report* insists that the attacks were "unimaginable" (National Commission 2004, 289). Indeed, a whole section of chapter 11 ("Foresight—and Hindsight") is devoted to what the Commission identifies as one of four key failures in relation to the attacks: a failure in "imagination" (339–348). In this section, the *Report* sketches governmental security policy that might have approached—but did not—awareness of the type of eventual attack. In one example, Richard Clarke, of the National Security Council, gave testimony to the Commission that he had been concerned about the danger posed by aircraft in the context of the Olympic Games in Atlanta in 1996; however, he "attributed this awareness more to Tom Clancy novels than to warnings from the intelligence community" (347). And it is notable that, consistent with the Commission's refusal to assign blame, it holds no agency responsible for the listed failures ["we believe the 9/11 attacks revealed four kinds of failure: in imagination, policy, capabilities, and management" (339)]: that is, they are failures *that simply exist*; they are not failures *by* any particular individual, agency, or government.

17. The event's unimaginability is the fatal flaw that stymied many institutional responses to the attacks. For example, when American Flight 11 transmitted the message that was mistakenly relayed to other aircraft and to air traffic controllers, "We have some planes. Just stay quiet and you'll be okay. We are returning to the airport," the air traffic controller could not understand the message, hearing only "something unintelligible" that was relayed to his manager for deciphering (National Commission 2004, 19). Although the controller understood the second and third messages broadcast in error from American 11, the meaning of this first key statement remained unknown for over half an hour. Further, despite American 11, United 175, and American 77 all being much hijacked earlier than United 93,

officials had been unable to connect reports of one hijacking with another in order to construct a picture of multiple events. On United 93, the hijackers attacked at 9:28; awareness of the earlier hijackings had occurred as early as 8:19 with phone calls from American 11 to the aviation authorities. The *Report* states that, for the authorities concerned, acceptance of the multiple hijackings was a "staggering realization," too staggering as it turned out, since, as the *Report* goes on to state, "it does not seem to have occurred to [the airlines' and FAA] leadership that they needed to alert other aircraft in the air that they too might be at risk" (10).

18. Joshua Foer comments that "for the sake of bipartisan unity the panel ducked some tough questions, like whether the Bush or Clinton Administration was more blameworthy and whether the war in Iraq has made the US safer" (2004).

19. David Ray Griffin states that "the 9/11 Commission for the most part simply omits evidence that would cast doubt on the official account of 9/11" (2005, 19).

20. Iñárritu says that these photographs were "banned by an American magazine because they were too politically incorrect for that moment. I felt angry, frustrated, disappointed. I was only trying to point out the dangers, injustices and tragic consequences of what was going on in Afghanistan because of the strange nationalism that has been reborn in this country" (2002).

21. The directors are Samira Makhmalbaf (Iran), Ken Loach (Great Britain), Alejandro González Iñárritu (Mexico), Youssef Chahine (Egypt), Claude Lelouch (France), Sean Penn (United States), Idrissa Ouedraogo (Burkina Faso), Shohei Imamura (Japan), Danis Tanovic (Bosnia), Amos Gitai (Israel), and Mira Nair (India).

22. Brigand's enterprise has clear parallels with the French collective film entitled *Loin de Vietnam* (1967), made as "an act of conscience against the war in Vietnam" (Dixon 2004, 117). The filmmakers involved were Jean-Luc Godard, Chris Marker, Alain Resnais, Joris Ivens, William Klein, Agnès Varda, and Claude Lelouch. Note that Lelouch is also one of the eleven directors featured in *11′09″01*.

23. *Variety*, for instance, called it "stridently anti-American" (Dixon 2004, 118).

24. Note that over the four years since the film's release, audience reactions to Iñárritu's contribution have become more positive. A survey of "user comments" on the Internet Movie Database (www.imdb.com) shows that Iñárritu's film is frequently mentioned by these non-professional reviewers as the most powerful and affecting segment. One online reviewer, on a different Web site, categorized Iñárritu's film as one of his favorites and describes its impact on him: "[It] hit me like a ton of bricks; I was hardly able to breathe by the end of the segment." See http://www.moviepie.com/filmfests/11_09_01.htm.

25. The news excerpts are taken from broadcasts in Vietnam, South Africa, Poland, Portugal, Italy, France, Germany, and Canada.

26. The question recalls the title of the series of photographs taken by Iñárritu and refused publication, "Blinded by the Light."

27. On spectatorial responsiveness that goes beyond the sense of sight, see Sobchack (1995). Others have had similar experiences: note again the comments of the anonymous reviewer mentioned above ("Split-second images of people hurling themselves from the towers hit me like a ton of bricks; I was hardly able to breathe by the end of the segment").

28. Iñárritu described the film in these terms: dedicated "in memory of [3 names], who taught a lesson of love and hope through their messages, of the 2,823 victims who died that day, and of all the innocent people around the world who have died before and after the event as a consequence of the blinded reasons of an official or unofficial terrorism" (2002).

29. A number of these images exist, some initially shown on television, although broadcasting of such shots was halted early in the television coverage of the event. One of the best-known still photographs is "A Person Falls Head-first from the North Tower of the New York World Trade Center, Sept. 11th 2001" (2001) by Richard Drew (Associated Press). This image was published in a number of newspapers, all of which were criticized for its publication. He describes his motivation in taking the picture and in submitting it for publication: "This was a very important part of the story. It wasn't just a building falling down, there were people involved in this. This is how it affected people's lives at that time, and I think that is why it's an important picture. I didn't capture this person's death. I captured part of his life. This is what he decided to do, and I think I preserved that. . . . I like to say, I didn't capture his death, I captured part of his life. That has been very important to me" (Howe 2001). This photograph has also been the subject of a documentary film, *9/11: The Falling Man* (2006, dir. Henry Singer). Less known in mainstream culture but popular on the fringes of the Internet are Web sites such as www.nasty.com, which made available images of people falling or jumping from the towers set to music: see the critical discussions of such Web sites and users' reactions to the images in Brottman (2004). On the relation of the spectator to news media images of September 11, see Chouliaraki (2006).

CHAPTER 13

1. For an extensive historical overview of such anti-theatrical tendencies, see Barish (1981).

2. The Bin Laden family were allowed to fly out of the country at a moment when no other airplanes were, and allowed to leave without being questioned by the CIA, whereas hundreds of other people were arrested just because they were from the Middle East or fitted a very general description.

3. This paradox is what Stanislavski's so-called method acting (based on a

selection of Stanislavski's ideas) is about. Method acting has been and still is the cornerstone of Hollywood acting.

4. Fried refers to Diderot's *Salons* and *Oeuvres esthétiques*. My text is based on Fried's reading of these texts in Chapter 3 of his book (1980, 107–160).

5. This notion of a "critical vision machine" is a core concept in a larger project on theatricality, visuality, and politics of which this essay presents one part. See also Bleeker (2005; 2006a; 2006b).

CHAPTER 14

1. Initially proposed by Rousseau and Sade, this right to "say everything" (*tout dire*) was later promoted by psychoanalysis.

Bibliography

Abraham, Nicholas, and Maria Torok. 2001. "Deuil ou Mélancolie, Introjecter-Incorporer." In *L'écorcé et le noyau*, 259–275. Paris: Flammarion. (Orig. pub. 1972.)

Achinstein, Sharon. 2001. "John Foxe and the Jews." *Renaissance Quarterly* 54:86–120.

Ackermann, Irmgard. 1997. "Ali Itirs Wandlungen: Aras Örens Romanheld zwischen Wirklichkeit und Phantasie." In *Interkulturelle Konfigurationen: Zur deutschsprachigen Erzählliteratur von Autoren nichtdeutscher Herkunft*, edited by Mary Howard, 17–30. Munich: Iudicium.

Adelson, Leslie A. 2005. *The Turkish Turn in Contemporary German Literature: Toward a New Critical Grammar of Migration*. New York: Palgrave Macmillan.

Adorno, Theodor W. 1970. *Negative Dialektik*. Frankfurt: Suhrkamp.

Agamben, Georgio. 1999a. "Aby Warburg and the Nameless Science." In *Potentialities: Collected Essays in Philosophy*, translated by Daniel Heller-Roazen, 89–103. Stanford: Stanford University Press.

———. 1999b. "Kommerell, or On Gesture." In *Potentialities: Collected Essays in Philosophy*, translated by Daniel Heller-Roazen, 77–85. Stanford: Stanford University Press.

———. 2000. "Notes on Gesture." In *Means Without End: Notes on Politics*, translated by Vincenzo Binetti and Cesare Casarino, 49–60. Minneapolis: University of Minnesota Press.

Anderson, Susan C. 2002. "Outsiders, Foreigners, and Aliens in Cinematic or Literary Narratives by Bohm, Dische, Dörrie, and Ören." *German Quarterly* 75, no. 2:144–159.

Ankersmit, Frank. 1996. *Aesthetic Politics: Political Philosophy Beyond Fact and Value*. Stanford: Stanford University Press.

Appadurai, Arjun. 1996. *Modernity at Large: Cultural Dimensions of Globalization*. Minneapolis: University of Minnesota Press.

Arenas, Reinaldo. 1994. *Before Night Falls*. London and New York: Penguin Books.

———. 1996. *Antes que anochezca*. Barcelona: Tusquets.

Arendt, Hannah. 1989. *The Human Condition*. Chicago: University of Chicago Press.

———. 1990. *On Revolution*. London: Penguin Books.

Attwell, David. 1993. *J. M. Coetzee: South Africa and the Politics of Writing*. Berkeley: University of California Press.

———. 2001. "Coetzee and Post-Apartheid South Africa." *Journal of Southern Africa Studies* 27, no. 4:865–867.

Austin, J. L. 1975. *How to Do Things with Words*. Edited by J. O. Urmson and Marina Sbisà. Cambridge, MA: Harvard University Press. (Orig. pub. 1962.)

———. 1979. "Pretending." In *Philosophical Papers*, 253–271. Oxford: Oxford University Press.

Avery, Harry C. 1968. "My Tongue Swore, but My Mind Is Unsworn." *Transactions and Proceedings of the American Philosophical Association* 99:19–35.

Barish, Jonas. 1981. *The Antitheatrical Prejudice*. Berkeley: University of California Press.

Barrett, Jon. 2002. *Hero of Flight 93: Mark Bingham*. New York: Advocate Books.

Bauman, Richard. 1983. *Let Your Words Be Few*. Prospect Heights: Waveland Press.

———. 1986. *Story, Performance, and Event: Contextual Studies of Oral Narrative*. Cambridge: Cambridge University Press.

Bazin, André. 2005. "Theater and Cinema." In *What Is Cinema?* translated by Hugh Grey, 76–124. Berkeley: University of California Press. (Orig. pub. 1951.)

Beamer, Lisa, and Ken Abraham. 2006. *Let's Roll: Ordinary People, Extraordinary Courage*. New York: Tyndale House Press.

Beccaria, Marcella. 2005. "Process and Meaning in the Art of Candice Breitz." In *Candice Breitz*, edited by Marcella Beccaria, 19–81. Milan: Skira. (An exhibition catalog.)

Being John Malkovich. 1999. DVD. Directed by Spike Jonze, written by Charlie Kaufman. Hollywood, CA: Universal Studios.

Béjar, Eduardo. 1994. "Reinaldo Arenas." In *Modern Latin-American Fiction Writers, Second Series* (*Dictionary of Literary Biography*, vol. 145), edited by W. Luis and A. Gonzalez, 42–49. Detroit: Gale.

Bejel, Emilio. 1996. "*Antes que anochezca*: autobiografía de un disidente cubano homosexual." *Hispamérica* 74:29–46.

Benjamin, Walter. 1969. "The Work of Art in the Age of Mechanical Reproduction." In *Illuminations: Essays and Reflections*, translated by Harry Zohn, edited by Hannah Arendt, 217–252. New York: Schocken. (Orig. pub. 1936.)

Bennington, Geoffrey, and Jacques Derrida. 1993. *Jacques Derrida*. Translated by Geoffrey Bennington. Chicago: University of Chicago Press. (Orig. pub. 1991.)

Benveniste, Emile. 1971. *Problems in General Linguistics*. Translated by Mary Elizabeth Meek. Coral Gables, FL: University of Miami Press.

Berlin, Isaiah. 1973. "Austin and the Early Beginnings of Oxford Philosophy." In *Essays on J. L. Austin*, edited by Isaiah Berlin, 1–16. Oxford: Clarendon Press.

Bernard, Tristan. 1926. *Ce que l'on dit aux femmes*. In *Théâtre de Tristan Bernard IV*, 83–168. Paris: Calmann-Lévy.

Bernhardt, Sarah. 1969. *The Art of the Theatre*. New York: Benjamin Blom.

Bishop, Claire. 2004. "Antagonism and Relational Aesthetics." *October* 110:51–79.

Blair, Tony. 2003. "Transcript of Tony Blair's Iraq Interview." Interview by Jeremy Paxman. *Newsnight*, BBC News (February 6).

Bleeker, Maaike. 2005. "Stories for a New World II: Whose Story Is This, Actually? Peter Sellars' *The Children of Heracles* vs. Gerardjan Rijnders' *Antigona*." In *Multicultureel Drama?* edited by Maaike Bleeker, Lucia van Hetern, Chiel Kattenbelt, and Kees Vuyk, 58–68. Amsterdam: Amsterdam University Press, 2005.

———. 2006a. "Innerlijke transformaties als gevolg van feitelijke gebeurtenissen: Over het theaterwerk van Carina Molier." In *Theater en Openbaarheid*, edited by Chiel Kattenbelt and Frank Mineur, 108–131. Amsterdam: Theater Instituut Nederland.

———. 2006b. "Theatricality and the Search for an Ethics of Vision." *Performing Arts Journal: MASKA* 21:41–45.

Bodin, Jean. 1977. *Les six livres de la république—avec l'apologie de René Herpin*. Aalen, Germany: Scientia Verlag. (Orig. pub. 1576.)

Boehmer, Elleke. 2002. "Not Saying Sorry, Not Speaking Pain: Gender Implications in *Disgrace*." *Interventions* 4, no. 3:342–351.

Bogad, L. M. 2005. *Electoral Guerrilla Theatre: Radical Ridicule and Social Movements*. New York: Routledge.

Boulé, Jean-Pierre. 1999. *Hervé Guibert: Voices of the Self*. Liverpool: Liverpool University Press.

Bourriaud, Nicolas. 1998. *Esthétique relationnelle*. Paris: Les Presses du Réel.

Brecht, Stefan. 1978. *The Theatre of Visions: Robert Wilson*. Frankfurt: Suhrkamp.

Brémont, Léon. 1903. *L'art de dire les vers, suivi d'une étude et d'une conférence sur l'adaptation musicale*. Paris: Charpentier et Fasquelle.

Brigand, Alain. 2002. "Interview with Artistic Producer." *11'09"01*. DVD. Directed by Alejandro González Iñárritu. London: Artificial Eye Film Company.

Brooks, Peter. 2000. *Troubling Confessions*. Chicago: University of Chicago Press.

Brottman, Mikita. 2004. "The Fascination of the Abomination: The Censored Images of 9/11." In *Film and Television After 9/11*, edited by Winston Wheeler Dixon, 163–177. Carbondale: Southern Illinois University Press.

Brunsson, Nils. 1989. *The Organization of Hypocrisy: Talk, Decisions and Action in Organizations*. Chichester, UK: John Wiley and Sons.

Butler, Judith. 1997. *Excitable Speech: A Politics of the Performative*. New York: Routledge.

Caffentzis, George. 2005. "Immeasurable Value?: An Essay on Marx's Legacy." *The Commoner* 10:87–114.

Caruth, Cathy, ed. 1995. *Trauma: Explorations in Memory*. Baltimore: Johns Hopkins University Press.

Casarino, Cesare. 1992. "Oedipus Exploded: Pasolini and the Myth of Modernization." *October* 59:27–47.

———. 2002. "Philopoesis: A Theoretico-Methodological Preface." In *Modernity at Sea: Melville, Marx, Conrad in Crisis*, xiii–xli. Minneapolis: University of Minnesota Press.

———. 2004. "Pasolini in the Desert." *Angelaki* 9, no. 1:97–102.

Castells, Manuel. 1996. *The Information Age: Economy, Society and Culture*. 3 vols. Malden, MA: Blackwell.

Cavell, Stanley. 1995. *Philosophical Passages: Wittgenstein, Emerson, Austin, Derrida*. Oxford: Blackwell

———. 1996. *A Pitch of Philosophy: Autobiographical Exercises*. Cambridge, MA, and London: Harvard University Press.

———. 2003. "Foreword." In Shoshana Felman, *The Scandal of the Speaking Body: Don Juan with J. L. Austin, or Seduction in Two Languages*, translated by Catherine Porter, xi–xii. Stanford: Stanford University Press.

Certeau, Michel de. 1984. *The Practice of Everyday Life*. Translated by Steven Rendall. Berkeley: University of California Press.

Chafets, Zev. 2002. "It's the War, Stupid." *Jewish World Review*, November 18. http://jewishworldreview.com/1102/chafets11802.asp (accessed July 1, 2008).

Chakrabarty, Dipesh. 2000. "Universalism and Belonging in the Logic of Capital." *Public Culture* 12, no. 3:653–678.

Chambers, Ross. 1998. *Facing It: AIDS Diaries and the Death of the Author*. Ann Arbor: University of Michigan Press.

Chiellino, Carmine, ed. 2000. *Interkulturelle Literatur in Deutschland: Ein Handbuch*. Stuttgart: Metzler.

Chin, Rita C. K. 2002. "Imagining a German Multiculturalism: Aras Ören and the Contested Meanings of the 'Guest Worker', 1955–1980." *Radical History Review* 83:44–72.

Chouliaraki, Lilie. 2006. *The Spectatorship of Suffering*. London: Sage.

Chow, Rey. 2002. *The Protestant Ethnic and the Spirit of Capitalism*. New York: Columbia University Press.

Coetzee, J. M. 1988. "The Novel Today." *Upstream* 6, no. 1:2–5.

———. 1992. "Confession and Double Thoughts." In *Doubling the Point: Essays and Interviews*, edited by David Attwell. Cambridge, MA: Harvard University Press.

———. 1999a. *Disgrace*. London: Penguin.

————. 1999b. *The Lives of Animals.* Edited by Amy Gutmann. Princeton, NJ: Princeton University Press.

————. 2003. *Elizabeth Costello: Eight Lessons.* London: Random House.

Croce, Benedetto. 1919. "Shakespeare e la critica shakespeariana." *La Critica. Rivista di letteratura, storia e filosofia* 17:129–138.

Cuddon, J. A., ed. 1991. *A Dictionary of Literary Terms and Literary Theory.* 3rd ed. Oxford: Blackwell.

Culler, Jonathan. 1981. "Convention and Meaning: Derrida and Austin." *New Literary History* 13, no.1:15–30.

D'ailleurs Derrida [film]. 1999. Directed by Safaa Fathy. Paris: Gloria Films/ La Sept Arte.

Davis, Natalie Zemon. 1983. *The Return of Martin Guerre.* Cambridge, MA: Harvard University Press.

Davis, Tracy. 2003. "Theatricality and Civil Society." In *Theatricality,* edited by Tracy Davis and Thomas Postlewait, 127–155. Cambridge: Cambridge University Press.

Deleuze, Gilles. 1953. *Empirisme et subjectivité.* Paris: Minuit.

————. 1988. *Foucault.* Translated by Séan Hand. Minneapolis: University of Minnesota Press.

————. 1993. *The Fold: Leibniz and the Baroque.* Translated by Tom Conley. Minneapolis: University of Minnesota Press.

————. 2003. *Francis Bacon: The Logic of Sensation.* Translated by Daniel W. Smith. London and New York: Continuum.

Deleuze, Gilles, and Félix Guattari. 1996. *A Thousand Plateaus: Capitalism and Schizophrenia.* London: The Athlone Press.

de Man, Paul. 1971. "The Rhetoric of Temporality." In *Blindness and Insight: Essays in the Rhetoric of Contemporary Criticism,* 187–228. Minneapolis: University of Minnesota Press.

————. 1979. "Autobiography as De-Facement." *Modern Language Notes* 94: 919–930.

————. 1986. *The Resistance to Theory.* Minneapolis: University of Minnesota Press.

Derrida. 2002. DVD. Directed by Kirby Dick and Amy Ziering Kofman. New York: Zeitgeist Films.

Derrida, Jacques. 1972. "Signature Event Context." In *Margins of Philosophy,* translated by Alan Bass, 307–330. Brighton, UK: Harvester Press.

————. 1988. *Archive Fever: A Freudian Impression.* Translated by Eric Prenowitz. Chicago: University of Chicago Press.

————. 1988. *Limited Inc.* Translated by Samuel Weber and Jeffrey Mehlman, edited by Gerald Graff. Evanston, IL: Northwestern University Press.

———. 1992. "Post-scriptum: Aporias, Ways and Voices." In *Derrida and Negative Theology*, edited by Harold Coward and Toby Foshay, translated by John Leavy Jr., 283–323. Albany: SUNY Press.

———. 1994. *Specters of Marx: The State of Debt, the Work of Mourning and the New International.* Translated by Peggy Kamuf. London: Routledge.

———. 1996. "'As If I Were Dead': An Interview with Jacques Derrida." In *Applying: to Derrida*, edited by John Brannigan, Ruth Robbins, and Julian Wolfreys, 212–226. London: Macmillan.

———. 2000. "Lettres sur un aveugle: Punctum caecum." In *Tourner les mots: Au bord d'un film*, edited by Jacques Derrida and Safaa Fathy, 71–126. Paris: Galilée/Arte Editions.

———. 2001a. "Le cinéma et ses fantômes." *Cahiers du Cinéma* no. 556, 75–85.

———. 2001b. "History of the Lie. Prolegomena." In *Futures: Of Jacques Derrida*, translated by Peggy Kamuf, edited by Richard Rand, 65–98. Stanford: Stanford University Press.

Derrida, Jacques, and Bernard Stiegler. 2002. *Echographies of Television: Filmed Interviews.* Translated by Jennifer Bajorek. Cambridge: Polity Press. (Orig. pub. 1996.)

Dick, Kirby, and Amy Ziering Kofman. 2005. "Derrida" [Screenplay]. In *Derrida: Screenplay and Essays on the Film*, edited by Kirby Dick and Amy Ziering Kofman, 51–109. Manchester, UK: Manchester University Press.

Didi-Huberman, Georges. 2001. "Dialektik des Monstrums: Aby Warburg and the Symptom Paradigm." *Art History* 24, no. 5:621–645.

Dixon, Winston Wheeler. 2004. "Teaching Film After 9/11." *Cinema Journal* 43.2:115–118.

Douglas, Mary. 1986. *How Institutions Think.* Syracuse, NY: Syracuse University Press.

Dworkin, Ronald. 1977. *Taking Rights Seriously.* London: Duckworth.

———. 1986. *Law's Empire.* London: Fontana Press.

Dyer-Witheford, Nick. 2005. "Cyber-Negri: General Intellect and Immaterial Labour." In *The Philosophy of Antonio Negri*, edited by Timothy Murphy and Abdul-Karim Mustapha, 151–155. London: Pluto Press.

Edbauer, Jenny. 2004. "Executive Overspill: Affective Bodies, Intensity, and Bush-in-Relation." *Postmodern Culture* 15, no. 1:1–25.

Edkins, Jenny. 2003. *Trauma and the Memory of Politics.* Cambridge: Cambridge University Press.

———. 2004. "Ground Zero: Reflections on Trauma, In/distinction and Response." *Journal for Cultural Research* 8, no. 3:247–270.

Ekman, Paul. 2003. "Darwin, Deception, and Facial Expression." In *Emotions Inside Out: 130 Years After Darwin's* The Expression of the Emotions in Man and Animals. *Annals of the New York Acadamy of Sciences* 1000:205–221.

Ekman, Paul, and Wallace V. Friesen. 1969. "Nonverbal Leakage and Clues to Deception." *Psychiatry* 32, no. 1:88–106.

Eribon, Didier. 1991. "Hervé Guibert et son double." *Le Nouvel Observateur* (July 18):87–89.

Estévez, Abilio. 1994. "Between Nightfall and Vengeance: Remembering Reinaldo Arenas." *Michigan Quarterly Review* 33, no. 4:859–867.

Euripides. 1995. *Children of Heracles. Hippolytus. Andromache. Hecuba.* Edited and translated by David Kovacs. Loeb Classical Library. Boston, MA: Harvard University Press.

———. 2003. *Tragédies.* Vol. 2, edited and translated by Louis Méridier. Paris: Les Belles Lettres.

Fahrenheit 9/11. 2004. DVD. Directed by Michael Moore. New York: Sony Pictures.

Feldschuh, Michael, ed. 2002. *The September 11 Photo Project.* New York: Regan.

Fellot, Henri. 1904. "Lieder Français." *Revue musicale de Lyon*, March 23, 265–269.

Felman, Shoshana. 2002. *The Juridical Unconscious: Trials and Traumas in the Twentieth Century.* Cambridge, MA: Harvard University Press.

———. 2003. *The Scandal of the Speaking Body: Don Juan with J. L. Austin, or Seduction in Two Languages.* Stanford: Stanford University Press. (Orig. pub. 1983.)

Fischer-Lichte, Erika. 2005. *Theatre, Sacrifice, Ritual: Exploring Forms of Political Theatre.* New York: Routledge.

Fish, Stanley. 1982. "Working on the Chain Gang: Interpretation in Law and Literature." *Texas Law Review* 60:551–567.

Foer, Joshua. 2004. "Commission: Failure." *Slate*, July 23. http://www.slate.com/id/2104253/ (accessed May 10, 2008).

Foucault, Michel. 1980. "What Is an Author?" In *Language, Counter-Memory, Practice: Selected Essays and Interviews*, edited by Donald F. Bouchard, translated by Donald F. Bouchard and Sherry Simon, 113–138. Ithaca, NY: Cornell University Press. (Orig. pub. 1969.)

———. 1990a. *The History of Sexuality.* Vol. I, *An Introduction*, translated by Robert Hurley. New York: Vintage Books.

———. 1990b. "Maurice Blanchot: The Thought from Outside." In *Foucault/Blanchot*, translated by Jeffrey Mehlman and Brian Massumi, 9–58. New York: Zone Books.

———. 1997. "Writing the Self." In *Foucault and His Interlocutors*, edited by A. Davidson, 234–247. Chicago: University of Chicago Press.

———. 1998a. "Sade: Sargeant of Sex." In *Aesthetics, Method, and Epistemology*, edited by James D. Faubion, translated by Robert Hurley, 226–227. New York: The New Press.

———. 1998b. "The Gray Mornings of Tolerance.," In *Aesthetics, Method, and*

Epistemology, edited by James D. Faubion, translated by Robert Hurley, 229–231. New York: The New Press.

———. 2001. *Fearless Speech*. Edited by J. Pearson. Los Angeles: Semiotext(e).

Franklin, Benjamin. 1986. *The Autobiography and Other Writings*. Harmondsworth, UK: Penguin.

Fried, Michael. 1980. *Absorption and Theatricality: Painting and Beholder in the Age of Diderot*. Berkeley and London: University of California Press.

Frisch, Max. 1976. *Gesammelte Werke in zeitlicher Folge,* Vol. 2, edited by Hans Mayer and Walter Schmitz. Frankfurt am Main: Suhrkamp.

Garber, Marjorie. 1999. "Reflection." In *The Lives of Animals*, by J. M. Coetzee, 73–84. Princeton, NJ: Princeton University Press.

Gaudemar, Antoine de. 1990. "La vie sida: Interview with Hervé Guibert." *Libération* (March 1), 21.

Gelderen, Martin van. 1992. *The Political Thought of the Dutch Revolt, 1555–1590*. Cambridge: Cambridge University Press.

———. 2001. "From Domingo de Soto to Hugo Grotius: Theories of Monarchy and Civil Power in Spanish and Dutch Political Thought, 1555–1609." In *The Origins and Development of the Dutch Revolt*, edited by Graham Darby, 151–170. London and New York: Routledge.

———. 2002. "Aristotelians, Monarchomachs and Republicans: Sovereignty and *Respublica mixta* in Dutch and German Political Thought, 1580–1650." In *Republicanism: A Shared European Heritage*. Vol. I, *Republicanism and Constitutionalism in Early Modern Europe*, edited by Martin van Gelderen and Quentin Skinner, 195–217. Cambridge: Cambridge University Press.

———. 2003. "The State and Its Rivals in Early-Modern Europe." In *States and Citizens: History, Theory, Prospects*, edited by Quentin Skinner and Bo Strath, 79–97. Cambridge: Cambridge University Press.

George, Alice Rose, Gilles Peress, Michael Shulan, and Charles Traub, eds. 2002. *Here Is New York: A Democracy of Photographs*. New York and Zurich: Scalo.

Ghost Dance [film]. 1983. Directed by Ken McMullen. UK and Germany: Channel 4/ZDF.

Gibbs, Anna. 2001. "Contagious Feelings: Pauline Hanson and the Epidemiology of Affect." *Australian Humanities Review*. http://www.lib.latrobe.edu.au/AHR/archive/Issue-December-2001/gibbs.html (accessed May 10, 2008).

Gibbs, Anna, and Maria Angel. 2006. "Media, Affect and the Face: Biomediation and the Political Scene." *Southern Review* 38, no. 2:24–39.

Gilmore, Leigh. 2001. "Limit-Cases: Trauma, Self-Representation and the Jurisdictions of Identity." *Biography* 24.1:128–139.

Glick, Lyz, and Dan Zegart. 2004. *Your Father's Voice: Letters for Emmy About Life with Jeremy—and Without Him After 9/11*. New York: St. Martin's Press.

Gordimer, Nadine. 1984. "The Idea of Gardening." *New York Review of Books*, February 2, 3–6.

———. 1988. "Living in the Interregnum." In *The Essential Gesture: Writing, Politics and Places*, edited by Stephen Clingman, 219–250. Cape Town: David Philop.

Gorra, Michael. 1999. "After the Fall." *New York Times*, November 28. http://www .nytimes.com/books/99/11/28/reviews/991128.28gorrat.html (accessed May 10, 2008).

Gott, Gil Michael. 1994. "Migration, Ethnicization and Germany's New Ethnic Minority Literature." Ph.D. diss., University of California–Berkeley.

Gramsci, Antonio. 1959. "The Southern Question." In *The Modern Prince and Other Writings*. New York: International Publishers.

Greenblatt, Stephen. 1980. *Renaissance Self-Fashioning*. Chicago: University of Chicago Press.

———. 1988. *Shakespearean Negotiations: The Circulation of Social Energy in Renaissance England*. Oxford: Clarendon Press.

Greene, Naomi. 1990. *Pier Paolo Pasolini: Cinema as Heresy*. Princeton, NJ: Princeton University Press.

Griffin, David Ray. 2005. *The 9/11 Report: Omissions and Distortions*. Northampton, MA: Olive Branch Press.

Grossheutschi, Felix. 1996. *Carl Schmitt und die Lehre vom Katechon*. Berlin: Duncker und Humblot.

Guibert, Hervé. 1981. *L'image fantôme*. Paris: Minuit.

———. 1990. *A l'ami qui ne m'a pas sauvé la vie*. Paris: Gallimard.

———. 1991. *Le protocole compassionnel*. Paris: Gallimard.

———. 1994a. *La piqûre d'amour et autres textes*. Paris: Gallimard.

———. 1994b. *To the Friend Who Did Not Save My Life*. London and New York: High Risk Books.

Guillory, John. 1993. *Cultural Capital: The Problem of Literary Canon Formation*. Chicago: University of Chicago Press.

Gunsteren, Herman R. van. 1999. *Verantwoording: Regeren door terugzien*. Amsterdam: KNAW.

Gusdorf, Georges. 1991. *Auto-bio-graphie*. Paris: Odile Jacob.

Ha, Kien Nghi. 1999. *Ethnizität und Migration*. Münster, Germany: Westfälisches Dampfboot.

Hammer, Espen. 2002. *Stanley Cavell: Skepticism, Subjectivity, and the Ordinary*. Cambridge: Polity Press.

Hardt, Michael, and Antonio Negri. 2000. *Empire*. Cambridge, MA: Harvard University Press.

Hardt, Michael, and Paolo Virno, eds. 1996. *Radical Thought in Italy: A Potential Politics*. Minneapolis: University of Minnesota Press.

Hart, H. L. A. 1994. *The Concept of Law*. Oxford: Oxford University Press. (Orig. pub. 1961.)

Head, Dominic. 2006. "A Belief in Frogs: J. M. Coetzee's Enduring Faith in Fiction." In *J. M. Coetzee and the Idea of the Public Intellectual*, edited by Jane Poyner, 100–117. Athens: Ohio University Press.

Heidegger, Martin. 2004. "Phenomenological Explication of Concrete Religious Phenomena in Connection with the Letters of Paul." In *The Phenomenology of Religious Life*, translated by Matthias Fritsch and Jennifer Anna Gosetti-Ferencei, 47–89. Bloomington: Indiana University Press.

Heine, Matthias. 2002. "Die Rückkehr des Bundestags Weltstadt Bonn." *Die Welt*, June 29.

Heinze, Hartmut. 1986. *Migrantenliteratur in der Bundesrepublik Deutschland: Bestandsaufnahme und Entwicklungstendenzen zu einer multikulturellen Literatursynthese*. Berlin: Express Edition.

Heiple, Daniel L. 1994. "Political Posturing on the Jewish Question by Lope and Faria e Sousa." *Hispanic Review* 62, no. 2:217–234.

Heywood, Thomas. 1999. *An Apology for Actors*. London: Scholars' Facsimiles & Reprints. (Orig. pub. 1612.)

Hiscock, Andrew. 2002. "'A supernal liuely faith': Katherine Parr and the Authoring of Devotion." *Women's Writing* 9, no. 2:177–197.

Hobson, Marian. 1998. *Jacques Derrida: Opening Lines*. London: Routledge.

Hohoff, Ulrich, and Irmgard Ackermann. 1999. "Aras Ören." In *Kritisches Lexikon zur deutschsprachigen Gegenwartsliteratur*, edited by Heinz Ludwig Arnold. Munich: Richard Boorberg Verlag.

Holmes, Brian. 2005. "Transparency and Exodus: On Political Process in the Mediated Democracies." *Open* 4, no. 8:48–60.

Hoogers, Gerard. 1999. *De verbeelding van het souvereine: Een onderzoek naar de theoretische grondslagen van politieke representatie*. Deventer, Netherlands: Kluwer.

Howe, Peter. 2001. "Richard Drew." *The Digital Journalist*. http://digitaljournalist.org/issue0110/drew.htm (accessed May 10, 2008).

Hunt, Simon. 1998. "Send in the Clown: The Pauline Pantsdown Story" (unpublished documentary narration).

Huyssen, Andreas. 2003. *Present Pasts: Urban Palimpsests and the Politics of Memory*. Stanford: Stanford University Press.

Iñárritu, Alejandro González. 2002. "Interview with Director." *11'09"01*. DVD. Directed by Alejandro González Iñárritu. London: Artificial Eye Film Company.

Jacobson, Sid, and Ernie Colon. 2006. *The 9/11 Report: A Graphic Adaptation*. New York: Hill & Wang.

James, Susan. 1997. *Passion and Action: The Emotions in Seventeenth-Century Philosophy.* Oxford: Oxford University Press.

Jameson, Fredric. 1981. *The Political Unconscious: Narrative as a Socially Symbolic Act.* Ithaca, NY: Cornell University Press.

Jauss, Hans Robert. 1982. *Toward an Aesthetic of Reception.* Translated by Timothy Bahti. Minneapolis: University of Minnesota Press.

Jean-Aubry, Georges. 1916. "Paul Verlaine et les musicians." In *La musique française d'aujourd'hui.* Paris: Perrin.

Jolivet, Régis. 1950. *Essai sur le problème et les conditions de la sincérité.* Paris: E. Vitte.

Jones, Tobias. 2003. *The Dark Heart of Italy: Travels Through Time and Space Across Italy.* London: Faber and Faber.

King, Peter. 1979. "Vondels Lucifer. Een mislukt theologisch toneelstuk." In *Visies op Vondel na 300 jaar: een bundel artikelen ter gelegenheid van de driehonderdste sterfdag van Joost van den Vondel,* edited by Sonja Witstein and E. K. Grootes, 218–235. Den Haag, Netherlands: Nijhoff.

Kommerell, Max. 1933. *Jean Paul.* Frankfurt: Klostermann.

———. 1956. *Gedanken über Gedichte.* Frankfurt: Klostermann.

Koppenol, Johan. 1999. "Nodeloze onrust: Het 'roomse karakter' van Vondels *Gysbreght van Aemstel.*" *Nederlandse letterkunde* 4, no. 4:313–329.

Kordela, Kiarina. 2007. *$urplus. Lacan, Spinoza.* Albany: SUNY Press.

Korsten, Frans-Willem. 2006. *Vondel belicht: Voorstellingen van soevereiniteit.* Hilversum, Netherlands: Verloren.

Kossew, Sue. 2003. "The Politics of Shame and Redemption in J.M. Coetzee's *Disgrace.*" *Research in African Literatures* 34.2:155–162.

Krasner, Stephen D. 1999. *Sovereignty: Organized Hypocrisy.* Princeton, NJ: Princeton University Press.

Lang, Candace. 1982. "Autobiography in the Aftermath of Romanticism." *Diacritics* 12:2–16.

Lefort, Claude. 1986. *Essais sur le politique. XIXe–XXe siècles.* Paris: Seuil.

———. 1995. *L'invention démocratique.* Paris: Fayard. (Orig. pub. 1981.)

Legouvé, Ernest. 1878. *Les pères et les enfants au XIXe siècle.* Paris: Bibliothèque d'Education.

Lejeune, Philippe. 1989. *On Autobiography.* Minneapolis: University of Minnesota Press.

Lentricchia, Frank, and Jody McAuliffe. 2003. *Crimes of Art + Terror.* Chicago: University of Chicago Press.

Locke, John. 1990. *An Essay Concerning Human Understanding.* Oxford: Clarendon Press. (Orig. pub. 1690.)

Lupton, Julia Reinhard. 1997. "Othello Circumcised: Shakespeare and the Pauline Discourse of Nations." *Representations* 57:73–89.

MacCormick, Neil. 1978. *Legal Reasoning and Legal Theory.* Oxford: Clarendon Press.

Maechler, Stefan. 2001. *The Wilkomirski Affair: A Study in Biographical Truth.* New York: Schocken.

Mahon, Denis. 1951. "Caravaggio's Chronology Again." *Burlington Magazine* 93, no. 582:286–292.

———. 1952. "Addenda to Caravaggio." *Burlington Magazine* 94, no. 586:2–23.

Malzacher, Florian. 2002. "Die Vertreter der Vertreter." *Die Tageszeitung,* March 16.

Mani, Bala Venkat. 2002. "Phantom of the 'Gastarbeiterliteratur': Aras Ören's Berlin Savignyplatz." In *Migration und Interkulturalität in neueren literarischen Texten,* edited by Aglaia Blioumi, 112–129. Munich: Iudicium.

Marion, Jean-Luc. 2005. "Ce qui ne se dit pas—l'apophase du discours amoureux." In *Le visible et le révélé,* 119–142. Paris: Les Editions du Cerf.

Markell, Patchen. 2006. "The Rule of the People: Arendt, *Archê,* and Democracy." *American Political Science Review* 100:1–14.

Martin, John. 1997. "Inventing Sincerity, Refashioning Prudence: The Discovery of the Individual in Renaissance Europe." *The American Historical Review* 102, no. 5:1309–1342.

Marx, Karl. 1973. *Grundrisse.* Harmondsworth, UK: Penguin. (Orig. pub. 1858.)

———. 1976. *The German Ideology.* New York: International Publishers.

———. 1977a. *Capital: A Critique of Political Economy.* Vol. 1, translated by Ben Fowkes. New York: Vintage.

———. 1977b. "Preface." In *A Contribution to the Critique of Political Economy.* Moscow: Progress Publishers.

Marx, Karl, and Friedrich Engels. 1978. "Manifesto of the Communist Party." In *The Marx-Engels Reader,* edited by Robert C. Tucker. New York: Norton & Company.

Massumi, Brian. 1996. "The Autonomy of Affect." In *Deleuze: A Critical Reader,* edited by Paul Patton, 217–239. Oxford and Cambridge, MA: Blackwell.

———. 2002. *Parables for the Virtual: Movement, Affect, Sensation.* Durham, NC, and London: Duke University Press.

———. 2005. "Fear (The Spectrum Said)." *Positions: East Asia Critique* 13, no. 1: 31–48.

Matthews, Peter. 2003. "One Day in September." *Sight & Sound,* January. http://www.bfi.org.uk/sightandsound/review/1493 (accessed May 10, 2008).

McGowan, Moray. 2000. "Aras Ören." In *Encyclopedia of German Literature,* edited by Matthias Konzett, 780. Chicago: Fitzroy Dearborn.

———. 2001. "Multiple Masculinities in Turkish-German Men's Writing." In *Conceptions of Postwar German Masculinity,* edited by Roy Jerome, 289–312. Albany: SUNY Press.

McIntyre, Ian. 1999. *Garrick*. London: Penguin.

McNeill, David. 2002. "Planet Art: Resistance and Affirmation in the Wake of 9/11." *Australian and New Zealand Journal of Art* 3, no. 2:11–32.

———. 2005. "Review of Nicolas Bourriaud 'Postproduction.'" *Australian and New Zealand Journal of Art* 6, no. 1:124–128.

Michaud, Philippe-Alain. 2004. *Aby Warburg and the Image in Motion*. Translated by Sophie Hawkes. New York: Zone Books.

Miller, D. A. 1981. *Narrative and Its Discontents: Problems of Closure in the Traditional Novel*. Princeton, NJ: Princeton University Press.

Miller, Mark Crispin. 2001. *The Bush Dyslexicon: Observations on a National Disorder*. New York: Norton.

Mitchell, W. J. T. 1995. "Representation." In *Critical Terms for Literary Study*, edited by Frank Lentricchia and Thomas McLaughlin, 11–22. Chicago and London: University of Chicago Press.

Mockel, Albert. 1904. "Charles Van Lerberghe." *Mercure de France* 4, no. 50.

Modjeska, Drusilla. 1989. *Poppy*. New York: McPhee Gribble.

Montaigne, Michel de. 2007. *Les Essais*. Edited by J. Balsamo, M. Magnien, and C. Magnien-Simonin. Paris: Gallimard.

Montesquieu, Charles-Louis, baron de. 1949. *The Spirit of the Laws*. Translated by F. Neumann. New York and London: Hafner Press.

Morassi, Antonio. 1952. "The Odescalchi-Balbi 'Conversion of St Paul.'" *Burlington Magazine* 94, no. 589:118–119.

Morrison, Toni. 1993. "Nobel Lecture," December 7. http://nobelprize.org/nobel_prizes/literature/laureates/1993/morrison-lecture.html (accessed May 10, 2008).

National Commission on Terrorist Attacks upon the United States. 2004. *The 9/11 Commission Report*. New York: Norton.

Nicholson, Shierry Weber. 1999. *Exact Imagination, Late Work: On Adorno's Aesthetics*. Cambridge, MA: MIT Press.

Nord, Philip. 1995. *The Republican Moment*. Cambridge, MA: Harvard University Press.

Olson, Ted P. 2002. "Pitiful Relics: Caravaggio's 'Martyrdom of St. Matthew.'" *Representations* 77:107–142.

Ong, Walter J. 1982. *Orality and Literacy*. London and New York: Routledge.

Ören, Aras. 1981. *Bitte nix Polizei: Kriminalerzählung*. Translated by Cornelius Bischoff. Düsseldorf: Claassen.

———. 1985. *Bütün Eserleri I: Manej, Bitte nix Polizei*. Frankfurt am Main: Dağyeli.

———. 1992. *Please, No Police*. Translated by Teoman Sipahigil. Austin: Center for Middle Eastern Studies, University of Texas at Austin.

———. 1999. *Privatexil: Ein Programm? Tübinger Poetik-Vorlesungen*. Translated by Cem Dalaman. Tübingen: Konkursbuchverlag.

Osterkamp, Ernst. 1979. *Lucifer: Stationen eines Motivs*. Berlin and New York: De Gruyter.

Pasolini, Pier Paolo. 1987. "*Trilogy of Life* Rejected." In *Lutheran Letters*, translated by Stuart Hood, 49–52. New York: Carcanet Press.

Pazarkaya, Yüksel. 1986. "Über Aras Ören." In *Chamissos Enkel: Zur Literatur von Ausländern in Deutschland*, edited by Heinz Friedrich, 15–21. Munich: Deutscher Taschenbuch Verlag.

Peczenik, Aleksander. 1990. "Coherence, Truth and Rightness in the Law." In *Law, Interpretation and Reality: Essays in Epistemology, Hermeneutics, and Jurisprudence*, edited by Patrick Nerhot, 275–309. Dordrecht, Holland, and Boston, MA: Kluwer Academic Publishers.

Pereira, Manuel. 1992. "Reinaldo antes del alba." *Quimera* 111:54–58.

Pitcher, George. 1973. "Austin: A Personal Memoir." In *Essays on J. L. Austin*, edited by Isaiah Berlin, L. W. Forguson, D. F. Pears, G. Pitcher, J. R. Searle, P. F. Strawson, and G. J. Warnock, 17–30. Oxford: Clarendon Press.

Plato. 2004. *Theatetus*. Translated by Robin A. H. Waterfield. London: Penguin Books.

Pomerantsev, Vladimir. 2004. "On Sincerity in Literature." *SovLit.com*. http://www.sovlit.com/sincerity/ (accessed May 10, 2008). (Orig. pub. 1953.)

Porteman, Karel. 1988. "De receptie van 'Gysbreght van Aemstel' in de Zuidelijke Nederlanden." *Spektator* 17.5:404–414.

Prandoni, Marco. 2005. "Badeloch: de constructie van een tragisch vrouwenpersonage." *TNTL* 121, no. 2:97–116.

Presser, Jacques. 1969. "Memoires als geschiedbron." In *Uit het werk van J. Presser*, 277–282. Amsterdam: Athenaeum, Polak en Van Gennep.

Psycho. 1998. DVD. Directed by Alfred Hitchcock. Hollywood, CA: Paramount.

Rancière, Jacques. 2004. *The Politics of Aesthetics*. Bodmin, UK: Gabriel Rockill.

Renard, Jules. 1960. *Journal 1887–1910*. Edited by Léon Guichard. Paris: Gallimard.

Restivo, Angelo. 2002. *The Cinema of Economic Miracles: Visuality and Modernization in the Italian Art Film*. Durham, NC: Duke University Press.

Riley, Denise. 2005. *Impersonal Passion: Language as Affect*. Durham, NC, and London: Duke University Press.

Rösch, Heidi. 1992. *Migrationsliteratur im interkulturellen Kontext: Eine didaktische Studie zur Literatur von Aras Ören, Aysel Özakin, Franco Biondi und Rafik Schami*. Frankfurt: Verlag für Interkulturelle Kommunikation.

Sarduy, Severo. 1972. "El barroco y el neobarroco." In *América Latina en su literatura*, edited by César Fernández Moreno, 167–184. Mexico: Siglo XXI Editores.

Sarkonak, Ralph. 1996. "Traces and Shadows: Fragments of Hervé Guibert." *Yale French Studies* 90:172–202.

Sassen, Saskia. 1998. *Globalization and Its Discontents: Essays on the New Mobility of People and Money.* New York: The New Press.

———. 2000. "Spatialities and Temporalities of the Global: Elements for a Theorization." *Public Culture* 12, no. 1:215–232.

Schérer, Réne. 2004. "L'enfer de l'hedonisme." *Multitudes* 18:177–185.

Schiffauer, Werner. 1983. *Die Gewalt der Ehre: Erklärungen zu einem deutsch-türkischen Sexualkonflikt.* Frankfurt am Main: Suhrkamp.

Schmitt, Carl. 2003. *Nomos of the Earth in the International Law of Jus Publicum Europaeum.* Translated by G. L. Ulmen. New York: Telos. (Orig. pub. 1950.)

———. 2004. *Politische Theologie: Vier Kapitel zur Lehre von der Souveränität.* Berlin: Duncker & Humblot. (Orig. pub. 1922.)

Seyhan, Azade. 1996. "Ethnic Selves/Ethnic Signs: Invention of Self, Space, and Genealogy in Immigrant Writing." In *Culture/Contexture: Explorations in Anthropology and Literary Studies,* edited by E. Valentine Daniel and Jeffrey M. Peck, 175–194. Berkeley: University of California Press.

———. 2001. *Writing Outside the Nation.* Princeton, NJ: Princeton University Press.

Shakespeare, William. 1997. "Titus Andronicus." In *The Norton Shakespeare,* edited by Stephen Greenblatt, Walter Cohen, Jean E. Howard, Katharine Eisaman Maus, and Andrew Gurr. New York and London: Norton.

Shattuck, Roger. 1991. "Review of Arthur Gold and Robert Fizdale, *The Divine Sarah: A Life of Sarah Bernhardt,*" *The New Republic* 205.16 (14 October).

Singer, Peter. 1999. "Reflection." *Coetzee* 2:85–92.

Smit, W. A. P. 1956–1962. *Van Pascha tot Noah: een verkenning van Vondels drama's naar continuiteit en ontwikkeling in hun grondmotief en structuur.* Vols. I, II, III. Zwolle, Netherlands: Tjeenk-Willink.

Smits-Veldt, Mieke B. 1994. "Inleiding." In *Gysbreght van Aemstel,* edited by Joost van den Vondel, 1–21. Amsterdam: AmsterdamUniversity Press.

———. 1996. "3 januari 1638: Opening van de Amsterdamse schouwburg met Vondels *Gysbreght van Aemstel*—begin van een traditie en het beheer van de schouwburg." In *Een theatergeschiedenis der Nederlanden: Tien eeuwen drama en theater in Nederland en Vlaanderen,* edited by R. L. Erenstein, 204–211. Amsterdam: Amsterdam University Press.

Sobchack, Vivian. 1995. "Phenomenology and the Film Experience." In *Viewing Positions: Ways of Seeing Film,* edited by Linda Williams, 36–58. Rutgers, NJ: Rutgers University Press.

Şölçün, Sargut. 1992. *Sein und Nichtsein: Zur Literatur in der multikulturellen Gesellschaft.* Bielefeld, Germany: Aisthesis.

Soysal, Levent. 2003. "Labor to Culture: Writing Turkish Migration to Europe." In *Relocating the Fault Lines: Turkey Beyond the East-West Divide,* edited by Sibel Irzak and Güven Güzeldere, 491–508. Durham, NC: Duke University Press.

Soysal, Yasemin Nuhoğlu. 1994. *Limits of Citizenship: Migrants and Postnational Membership in Europe.* Chicago: University of Chicago Press.

———. 2002. "Citizenship and Identity: Living in Diasporas in Postwar Europe?" In *The Postnational Self: Belonging and Identity,* edited by Ulf Hedetoft and Mette Hjort, 137–151. Minneapolis: University of Minnesota Press.

Spiegelman, Art. 2004. *In The Shadow of No Towers.* New York: Pantheon.

Spinoza, Baruch. 2000. *Ethics.* Translated by G. H. R. Parkinson. Oxford: Oxford University Press.

Spivak, Gayatri Chakravorty. 1988. "Can the Subaltern Speak?" In *Marxism and the Interpretation of Culture,* edited by C. Nelson and L. Grossberg, 271–313. Basingstoke, UK: Macmillan.

Starobinski, Jean. 1988. *Jean-Jacques Rousseau: Transparency and Obstruction.* Chicago: University of Chicago Press.

Stern, Jill D. 1999. "A Playwright in His Time: Vondel's Drama *Faeton* of 1663." *Dutch Crossing* 23, no.1:22–57.

Stipriaan, René van. 1996. "Gysbreght van Aemstel als tragische held." *De zeventiende eeuw* 12:359–377.

Stratton, Jon. 1999. "'I Don't Like It': Pauline Pantsdown and the Politics of Inauthenticity." *Perfect Beat: The Pacific Journal of Research into Contemporary Music and Popular Culture* 4, no. 4:3–29.

Suhr, Heidrun. 1990. "*Fremde* in Berlin: The Outsiders' View from the Inside." In *Berlin: Culture and Metropolis,* edited by Charles W. Haxthausen and Heidrun Suhr, 219–242. Minneapolis: University of Minnesota Press.

Targoff, Ramie. 1997. "The Performance of Prayer." *Representations* 60:49–69.

Taylor, Jane. 1999. "The Impossibility of Ethical Action." *Mail & Guardian,* July 9, 25.

Theisen, Bianca. 2003. *Silenced Facts: Media Montages in Contemporary Austrian Literature.* Amsterdam: Rodopi.

Tocqueville, Alexis de. 2004. "Some Reflections on American Manners." In *Democracy in America.* Charlottesville, VA: American Studies at the University of Virginia. http://xroads.virginia.edu/~HYPER/DETOC/ch3_14.htm (accessed May 10, 2008). (Orig. pub. 1835.)

Tomkins, Silvan. 1962. *Affect Imagery Consciousness.* Vol. 1, *The Positive Affects.* New York: Springer.

———. 1991. *Affect Imagery Consciousness.* Vol. 3, *The Negative Affects.* New York: Springer.

Tomkins, Silvan, and Elaine Virginia Demos. 1995. *Exploring Affect: The Selected Writings of Silvan S. Tomkins.* Cambridge and New York: Cambridge University Press.

Trilling, Lionel. 1972. *Sincerity and Authenticity.* Cambridge, MA: Harvard University Press.

Velde, François. 2006. "Mediatization in Germany (1803–15)." In *Heraldica*, edited by François R. Velde. http://www.heraldica.org/topics/royalty/mediatization .htm (accessed May 10, 2008).

Versluis, Arthur. 2006. "Carl Schmitt, the Inquisition, and Totalitarianism." In *The New Inquisitions: Heretic Hunting and the Intellectual Origins of Modern Totalitarianism*, 40–51. Oxford: Oxford University Press.

Viano, Maurizio. 1993. *A Certain Realism: Making Use of Pasolini's Film Theory and Practice*. Berkeley: University of California Press.

Vice, Sue. 2000. *Holocaust Fiction: From William Styron to Binjamin Wilkomirski*. London and New York: Routledge.

Vighi, Fabio. 2002. "Beyond Objectivity: The Utopian in Pasolini's Documentaries." *Textual Practice* 16, no. 3:491–510.

Virno, Paolo. 1996. "Virtuosity and Revolution: The Political Theory of Exodus." In *Radical Thought in Italy: A Potential Politics*, edited by Michael Hardt and Paolo Virno, 188–209. Minneapolis: University of Minnesota Press.

———. 2004. *A Grammar of the Multitude*. Los Angeles: Semiotext(e).

Vondel, Joost van den. 1927. *De werken van Vondel: Volledige en geïllustreerde tekstuitgave in tien delen*. Edited by J. F. M. Sterck, H.W. E. Moller, C. G. N. de Vooys, C. R. De Klerk, C. C. van der Graft, L. C. Michels, B. H. Molkenboer, J. Prinsen, L. Simons, and A. A. Verdenius. Amsterdam: Mij.

———. 1994a. *Gysbreght van Aemstel*. Edited by Mieke B. Smits-Veldt. Amsterdam: Amsterdam University Press.

———. 1994b. "Inleiding." In *Gysbreght van Aemstel*, edited by Mieke B. Smits-Veldt, 1–21. Amsterdam: Amsterdam University Press.

Whaler, Marc-Olivier. 2006. "Interview." *Flash Art* 39, no. 246:41.

Wikander, Matthew H. 2002. *Fangs of Malice: Hypocrisy, Sincerity and Acting*. Iowa City: University of Iowa Press.

Wilde, Oscar. 1998. *The Picture of Dorian Gray*. Oxford: Oxford University Press.

Wilkomirski, Binjamin. 1997. *Fragments: Memories of a Wartime Childhood*. New York: Schocken.

Wind, Edgar. 1968. *Pagan Mysteries of the Renaissance*. New York: Norton. (Orig. pub. 1958.)

Wittgenstein, Ludwig. 1953. *Philosophical Investigations*. Translated by G. E. M. Anscombe. Malden, MA, and Oxford: Blackwell.

———. 1972. *On Certainty*. Translated by D. Paul & G. E. M. Anscombe, edited by G. E. M. Anscombe and G. H. von Wright. New York: Harper Torchbooks.

Wood, James. 2003. "A Frog's Life." Review of *Elizabeth Costello: Eight Lessons*, by J. M. Coetzee. *London Review of Books*, October 23. http://www.lrb.co.uk/v25/ n20/wood02_.html (accessed May 10, 2008).

Wright, Steve. 2005. "Reality Check: Are We Living in an Immaterial World?" *Mute* 2, no. 1:34–45.

Yagoda, Ben. 2004. "The 9/11 Commission Report: How a Government Committee Made a Piece of Literature." *Slate*, November 8. http//www.slate.com/id/2109277/ (accessed May 10, 2008).

Young, Alison. 2005. *Judging the Image: Art, Value, Law.* London and New York: Routledge.

Zeldin, Theodore. 1977. *France, 1848–1945.* Vol. 2, *Intellect, Taste and Anxiety.* Oxford: Clarendon Press.

Žižek, Slavoj. 1993. "From Courtly Love to *The Crying Game*." *New Left Review* 202:98–128.

———. 2005. "The Subject Supposed to Loot and Rape: Reality and Fantasy in New Orleans." *In These Times*, October 20. http://www.inthesetimes.com/site/main/article/2361/ (accessed May 10, 2008).

Index

Abraham, Ken: *Let's Roll*, 301*n*14
Abraham, Nicholas, 222, 223
Achinstein, Sharon, 285*n*19
Ackermann, Irmgard, 183–84
Adjani, Isabelle, 276
Adorno, Theodor, 45, 57; "Charmed Language," 286*n*2; on the moral imperative, 107
affect: amplifiers of, 207–13; vs. emotion, 199, 200, 205–6, 211; Massumi on, 208, 213; as media-effect, 13, 206–13; and repetition, 209, 210, 211; Tomkins on, 199, 213
Afghanistan, 261–62, 302*n*20
Agamben, Giorgio, 196, 209; on comedy of gesture, 211; on the gag, 201; on gesture and language, 198–99, 207; "Kommerell, or On Gesture," 198–200, 206–7
allegory vs. realism, 153–54, 155–56
Al-Qaeda, 253, 256
Amis, Martin, 167
Anderson, Susan C., 297*n*31
Angel, Maria, 211
Ankersmit, Frank: *Aesthetic Politics*, 64, 287*n*6, 287*n*8
Appadurai, Arjun: on the ethnoscape, 180; on imagination, 175–76, 294*n*3
Appiah, K. Anthony, 175
Aquinas, Thomas: on animals, 151
The Arabian Nights, 133
Arenas, Reinaldo: *Before Night Falls*, 15–16, 269–74, 278–79; and Castro government, 266, 269, 271–74; death of, 266, 268–70, 278, 279

Arendt, Hannah: *The Human Condition*, 68; on hypocrisy, 61–63, 67–68; *On Revolution*, 61–63, 67–68; on political action, 70, 72
Aristophanes: *The Frogs*, 100
Aristotle: on imitation, 155; on man as *zoon politikon*, 130; *Rhetoric*, 100
arts, the: aesthetic creativity in, 161–62; art galleries, 165, 166, 170–71, 172; a-sincerity among artists, 172–73; Baroque art, 35, 285*n*18; Bishop on, 161–63; conceptual and installation art, 170; expansion of contemporary art, 170–71; and online share trading, 166–70; opera, 30; plastic arts, 30; vs. productive labor, 159–61; relational/immersive art, 161–62; relationship to politics, 158–59, 161; relationship to urban development, 165–66; representations of sincerity, 27–28, 30–31, 57–58, 247. *See also* Caravaggio; drama; literature; music
a-sincerity, 12, 172–73
Askew, Anne, 24, 283*n*4
Atta, Mohammed, 235
Attwell, David, 292*nn*1,3,5
Augustine, Saint: *Confessions*, 298*n*5
Austin, J. L.: Berlin on, 116–18; Cavell on, 9, 90–97, 99, 101, 108, 109–10, 111, 114–15; Derrida on, 9, 92–94, 95, 96, 103, 109, 111, 115, 292*n*2; on descriptivism/constative fallacy, 93, 98, 99, 102, 113, 114–15; Felman on, 9, 95, 96, 103–4, 109; and Frege, 93;